AF905153

Status of Forces: Criminal Jurisdiction over Military Personnel Abroad

Joop Voetelink

Status of Forces: Criminal Jurisdiction over Military Personnel Abroad

ASSER PRESS

Springer

Joop Voetelink
Faculty of Military Science
Netherlands Defence Academy
Breda
The Netherlands

Translated by Marielle Matthee

ISBN 978-94-6265-056-5 ISBN 978-94-6265-057-2 (eBook)
DOI 10.1007/978-94-6265-057-2

Library of Congress Control Number: 2015931533

Published by T.M.C. ASSER PRESS, The Hague, The Netherlands www.asserpress.nl
Produced and distributed for T.M.C. ASSER PRESS by Springer-Verlag Berlin Heidelberg

© T.M.C. ASSER PRESS and the author 2015
No part of this work may be reproduced, stored in a retrieval system, or transmitted in any form or by any means, electronic, mechanical, photocopying, microfilming, recording or otherwise, without written permission from the Publisher, with the exception of any material supplied specifically for the purpose of being entered and executed on a computer system, for exclusive use by the purchaser of the work.
The use of general descriptive names, registered names, trademarks, service marks, etc. in this publication does not imply, even in the absence of a specific statement, that such names are exempt from the relevant protective laws and regulations and therefore free for general use.

Printed on acid-free paper

Springer Science+Business Media B.V. Dordrecht is part of Springer Science+Business Media
(www.springer.com)

Contents

Part II The International Law Perspective

Abbreviations

AAP	Allied Administrative Publication
ACT	Allied Command Transformation
ADCON	Administrative Control
ADMCON	Administrative Control
AJIL	American Journal of International Law
AMIB	Inter-African Mission to Monitor the Bangui Agreements
AMIS	African Mission in Sudan
AMISOM	African Union Mission to Somalia
ATS	Australian Treaty Series
AU	African Union
BGBl	Bundesgesetzblatt
CAEMC	Central African Economic and Monetary Community
CAR	Central African Republic
CFSP	Common Foreign and Security Policy
CIS	Commonwealth of Independent States
CMF	Commonwealth Monitoring Force
CPA	Coalition Provisional Authority
CSDP	Common Security and Defence Policy
CSTO	Collective Security Treaty Organization
DRC	Democratic Republic of the Congo
EADRU	Euro-Atlantic Disaster Response Unit
EAG	European Air Group
EAS	Executive Agreements Series
EASBRICOM	Eastern Africa Standby Brigade Coordination Mechanism
EC	European Community
ECCAS	Economic Community of Central African States
ECOWAS	Economic Community of West African States
ECtHR	European Court of Human Rights
EDC	European Defense Community
EEAW	European Participating Air Forces' Expeditionary Air Wing
EGF	European Gendarmerie Force

EJIL	European Journal of International Law
EU	European Union
EUF	European Union Force
EUFOR	European Union Force
EUMM	European Union Monitoring Mission
FOMUC	Multinational Force Central African Republic
FRG	Republic of Germany
FRONTEX	European Agency for the Management of Operational Cooperation at the External Borders of the Member States of the European Union
FSIA	Foreign Sovereign Immunities Act
FULLCOM	Full Command
GDR	German Democratic Republic
HQ	Headquarters
HQ ACT	Headquarters Allied Command Transformation
ICJ	International Court of Justice
ICTY	International Criminal Tribunal for the former Yugoslavia
IFOR	Implementation Force
IGO	International Governmental Organisations
ILC	International Law Commission
ILDC	International Law in Domestic Courts
ILR	International Law Reports
INTERFET	International Force in East Timor
IPKF	Indian Peacekeeping Force
IPMT	International Peace Monitoring Team
ISAF	International Security Assistance Force
ISF	International Stabilization Force
JFC	Joint Force Command
JMBl	Justizministerialblatt
KAV	Kavass Series
KFOR	Kosovo Force
LNOJ	League of Nations Official Journal
LNTS	League of Nations Treaty Series
MAAG	Military Assistance Advisory Group
MCDA	Military and Civil Defence Assets
MFO	Multinational Force and Observers
MICOPAX	Mission for the Consolidation of Peace
MIF	Multinational Interim Force
MinBl	Ministerialblatt
MINURCA	UN Mission in the Central African Republic
MINURCAT	UN Mission in the Central African Republic and Chad
MINUSMA	UN Multidimensional Integrated Stabilization Mission in Mali
MINUSTAH	UN Stabilization Mission in Haiti
MNF	Multinational Force
MNF-I	Multinational Force Iraq

MONUC	Mission de l'Organisation des Nations Unies en République Démocratique du Congo
MOPEP	Military Observer Mission Ecuador-Peru
MOU	Memorandum of Understanding
MStGB	Militärstrafgesetzbuch
MTA	Military Technical Agreement
NA5CRO	Non-Article 5 Crisis Response Operations
NATO	North Atlantic Treaty Organization
NC3A	NATO Consultation, Command and Control Agency
NGO	Non-governmental Organisation
NTM-I	NATO Training Mission Iraq
OAS	Organization of American States
OAU	Organisation of African Unity
OCHA	Office for the Coordination of Humanitarian Affairs
OECS	Organization of Eastern Caribbean States
OEF	Operation Enduring Freedom
OJ	Official Journal of the European Union
OLA	Office of Legal Affairs
ONUC	UN Mission in the Congo
OPCOM	Operational Command
OPCON	Operational Control
OSCE	Organisation for Security and Cooperation in Europe
PCA	Permanent Court of Arbitration
PCIJ	Permanent Court of International Justice
PfP	Partnership for Peace
PITSE	Pacific Islands Treaty Series
PSC	Peace and Security Council
RAMSI	Regional Assistance Mission to Solomon Islands
ROE	Rules of Engagement
RSS	Regional Security System
SADC	Southern African Development Community
SBA	Sovereign Base Areas
SCO	Shanghai Cooperation Organisation
SFOR	Stabilization Force
SHAPE	Supreme Headquarters Allied Powers in Europe
Shirbrig	Stand-By Forces High Readiness Brigade
SIA	State Immunity Act
SOFA	Status of Forces Agreement
SOMA	Status of Mission Agreement
SPPKF	South Pacific Peacekeeping Force
SSD	Security Sector Development
SSR	Security Sector Reform
SU	Soviet Union
TACOM	Tactical Command
TACON	Tactical Control

TEU	Treaty on European Union
TIAS	Treaties and other International Acts Series
TMG	Truce Monitoring Group for Bougainville
TOA	Transfer of Authority
TTP	Tactics, Techniques and Procedures
UAE	United Arab Emirates
UK	United Kingdom
UKTS	United Kingdom Treaty Series
UNAMSIL	UN Assistance Mission in Sierra Leone
UNCLOS	UN Convention on the Law of the Sea
UNDOF	UN Disengagement Observer Force
UNEF	UN Emergency Force
UNIFIL	UN Interim Force in Lebanon
UNIIMOG	United Nations Iran–Iraq Military Observer Group
UNITAF	United Task Force
UNMEE	UN Mission in Ethiopia and Eritrea
UNMIL	UN Mission in Liberia
UNMIS	UN Mission in the Sudan
UNMIT	UN Integrated Mission in Timor-Leste
UNOSOM	UN Operation in Somalia
UNPROFOR	UN Protection Force
UNSC	United Nations Security Council
UNSCOB	UN Special Committee on the Balkans
UNTAET	UN Transitional Administration in East Timor
UNTAG	UN Transition Assistance Group
UNTS	UN Treaty Series
UNTSO	UN Truce Supervision Organization
US	United States

Chapter 1
Introduction

Abstract The legal status of armed forces stationed abroad is an important issue to all States and international organisations involved. Today the status of forces is often set out in Status of Forces Agreements (SOFAs) defining the rights and obligations of the deployed forces. Key in these agreements is immunity of military personnel from criminal jurisdiction of host State courts, as follows from the doctrine of immunity of States. Moreover, international military operational practice shows that the exercise of criminal jurisdiction over deployed military personnel is even more important to States deploying their troops.

Contents

© T.M.C. ASSER PRESS and the author 2015

J. Voetelink, *Status of Forces: Criminal Jurisdiction over Military Personnel Abroad*,
DOI 10.1007/978-94-6265-057-2_1

1.1 An Example: Afghanistan, 2001–2014

The 2001 attacks on the Twin Towers in New York and the Pentagon in Washington D.C. gave rise to Operation Enduring Freedom (OEF) within the framework of the global War on Terror of the United States (US) against terrorism.[1] The first military operations against Al-Qaeda and the Taliban regime in Afghanistan started on 7 October 2001. Within a short period of time an international coalition of states under US command and with support of local armed militias united in the North Alliance gained control over a large part of the country.

On 5 December 2001 the *Bonn-Agreement* was signed establishing the Interim Administration for Afghanistan,[2] which formally ended the regime of the Taliban. In Annex I to the *Bonn-Agreement*, the United Nations Security Council (UNSC) was requested to consider sending an international security force. The UNSC followed up on this request by authorising the establishment of the International Security Assistance Force (ISAF) for Afghanistan.[3]

Although operating simultaneously in the same geographic area, OEF and ISAF have different legal bases, which entails differences in their tasks. Also, the legal status of the forces participating in OEF and ISAF differs. After the Interim Administration had come into being and had formally taken over authority in Afghanistan, the US and the new Afghan government concluded an international agreement on the status of the US armed forces.[4] Some States, such as Canada and the United Kingdom, followed this procedure,[5] while other States that had deployed armed forces to Afghanistan in support of OEF in any period of time refrained from doing so. In view of the particular circumstances under which their forces operated the latter group of States probably considered the law of armed conflict to be sufficient to cover the status of their forces.

The status of members of ISAF is covered by the *Military Technical Agreement* (MTA), concluded by the ISAF Commander and the Interim Administration on 4 January 2002.[6] In Annex A of the MTA, *Arrangements regarding the status of the*

---

[1] As from 2009 the term 'War on Terror' is officially not in use any more, as the preferred term is now the more neutral wording 'overseas contingency operations'; Wilson and Kamen 2009.

[2] *Agreement on Provisional Arrangements in Afghanistan Pending the Re-establishment of Permanent Government Institutions*; Bonn, 5 December 2001. www.un.org/news/dh/latest/afghan/afghan-agree.htm. Accessed November 2014.

[3] *UN Doc* S/RES/1386 (2001) of 20 December 2001, establishing ISAF.

[4] *Agreement regarding the status of United States military and civilian personnel of the U.S. Department of Defense present in Afghanistan in connection with cooperative efforts in response to terrorism, humanitarian and civic assistance, military training and exercises, and other activities*; 26 September and 12 December 2002 and 28 May 2003; 28 May 2003 (6192 *KAV* i).

[5] These agreements have not been published.

[6] *Military Technical Agreement between the International Security Assistance Force* (ISAF) *and the Interim Administration of Afghanistan*; 4 January 2002. www.operations.mod.uk/isafmta.pdf. Accessed 13 November 2014.

International Security Assistance Force, both parties agreed that ISAF personnel remained subject to the exclusive criminal jurisdiction of the sending States.[7]

Several States support both OEF and ISAF directly or indirectly by granting foreign forces basing rights and overflight and landing rights. Agreements on the status of military units were also concluded with these States.[8] For reasons of national security many of these agreements are classified as secret and, consequently, have not been published.

1.2 Status of Forces

1.2.1 Status of Forces vis-à-vis Military Operations and International Military Cooperation

The agreements mentioned above, related to the operations in and around Afghanistan, are indicative of the importance that States and international organisations attach to the legal position, or status, of military personnel stationed on the territory of other States.[9] For States deploying armed forces abroad (sending States), as well as States receiving those forces on their territory (host States), status of forces is a continuous point of attention.[10] Sending States often cooperate in multinational forces under the authority of international organisations, such as the United Nations (UN) or NATO, or are part of a coalition of States.[11] For the most part they operate in one State, while using facilities in other States to make the operations possible. In the framework of this book, those third countries giving, for instance, logistic and operational support, are also regarded as host States.

[7] When NATO assumed leadership of ISAF operations in August 2003, it concluded a supplementary agreement with Afghanistan on the status of NATO forces; *Exchange of letters between NATO and Afghanistan regarding the status of NATO and its personnel when present on the territory of Afghanistan in the execution of ISAF*; 5 September 2004 and 22 November 2004 (this classified agreement has not been published).

[8] An example is the basing in Qatar of Dutch military personnel and an aircraft in support of the operations in Afghanistan, for which the Netherlands and Qatar concluded a special agreement on the status of the Dutch forces: *Status of forces Agreement for military personnel and equipment for the forces between the Kingdom of the Netherlands and the State of Qatar*; Doha, 11 March 2002 (Vol. 2204 *UNTS* 2004, No. 39128).

[9] The Dutch government, for instance, has repeatedly underlined the importance of SOFAs, which are one of the key topics of the memorandum on legal aspects of deployment of armed forces; *Dutch Parliamentary Papers I* 2003/04, 29 200 X, C, pp. 3–4 and *Dutch Parliamentary Papers I* 2005/2006, 30 300 X, A, p. 5.

[10] In the literature and international practice, terms like 'receiving States', 'host Nations' or 'receiving Member States' are also used.

[11] The term 'coalition' denotes an ad hoc arrangement of two or more States conducting combined military action, sometimes described as coalition of the willing; see Cathcart 2010, p. 236.

The interest of States in status of forces issues is not limited to situations of armed conflict or crisis-management operations. Also within the framework of peacetime international military cooperation, the status of forces is part of legal considerations. Defining that status is of increasing importance in a period of time when worldwide contacts are growing continuously and international relations have become more intense and complex over the past decades. This development also applies to the military, as States have committed themselves to cooperating in military matters based on a wide range of defence and security agreements, and support arrangements. As a consequence, visiting forces agreements have been concluded facilitating the entry and stay of significant numbers of military personnel, sometimes accompanied by their families, on the territory of other States for an extended period of time.

1.2.2 Criminal Jurisdiction and Immunity

The importance of the status of forces stems from the special position of the armed forces as an inherent part of sovereign States even when deployed abroad. This means that military personnel are not present in another State in a personal capacity, but in their capacity as servicemen acting under the military command and political authority of the sending States' authorities. Often, they are allowed to wear their national uniform and to carry arms. Consequently, their position is quite different from, for instance, international businessmen or tourists. Therefore, military personnel enjoy immunity in host States; moreover, sending States need to exercise jurisdiction over them (see for an explanation of the concepts of immunity and jurisdiction Sect. 1.4.4). Immunity and jurisdiction are key issues for the States involved and are generally laid down in so-called Status of Forces Agreements (SOFAs) that define the rights and obligations of the sending States' armed forces while present on the territory of host States.

The focal point of SOFAs is the exercise of criminal jurisdiction over visiting foreign forces.[12] In other words, SOFAs answer the question which State has jurisdiction to actually prosecute a serviceman of the sending State who has committed a criminal offence in the host State. Generally, sending States prefer to be able to exercise criminal jurisdiction over their forces deployed abroad at all times. However, years of international practice made it clear that in specific situations host States have their own interests in exercising criminal jurisdiction over visiting

[12] Moreover, criminal jurisdiction is often a controversial topic in SOFA negotiations, leading to lengthy discussions and often claiming most of the attention; e.g., Rouse and Baldwin 1957; Snee 1961, pp. 3 and 29; Conderman 2013, para 15; Liivoja 2011, p. 132. Furthermore, in cases where parties do not reach agreement on the exercise of criminal jurisdiction, this could lead to cancellation of planned foreign deployment of armed forces; Munoz-Mosquera 2011, pp. 2–3.

forces[13] based on legal considerations, also taking into account the circumstances under which the foreign forces are present in their countries and their relationship with the sending States. Notwithstanding the focus on criminal jurisdiction, contemporary SOFAs cover a wide range of other topics as well. What issues are dealt with exactly and the level of detail depend on the situation at hand.

1.3 Structure

1.3.1 General

In the course of time, criminal jurisdiction over armed forces stationed in other States has been the subject of many studies. In the literature about military operational law researchers have often put much emphasis on particular SOFA issues, like, of course, criminal jurisdiction, but also on matters like claims-procedures and tax issues, or have focused on analysing specific agreements, like the *NAVO-SOFA*.[14] The position of SOFAs in the broader context of international law has not yet received much attention, however, neither has the relationship between SOFAs and military operational practice.

Conversely, international law has not revealed much interest in criminal jurisdiction over deployed armed forces,[15] mostly briefly referring to the current international practice to deal with the matter by international agreements based on international law. Although within specific fields of international law, such as international criminal law,[16] the position of visiting forces on occasion receives more attention, in general it seems to be a somewhat neglected or, perhaps, forgotten issue in international law.[17]

Neither of these two approaches does justice to the issue. As relations between the legal arguments and other relevant factors remain obscure, a patchy picture emerges that does not really cover the full scope of the criminal jurisdiction issue and cannot explain

---

[13] The final evaluation of the Dutch contribution to Operation Enduring Freedom (*Dutch Parliamentary Papers II* 2003/04, 27 925, nr. 135) is a good example. It mentions that during the negotiations on the status of Dutch armed forces especially States from the Gulf region held on to their sovereignty, resulting in SOFAs that limited criminal jurisdiction of Dutch authorities over their forces deployed to these states, p. 33.

[14] *Agreement between the parties to the North Atlantic Treaty regarding the status of their forces*; London, 19 June 1951 (Vol. 199 *UNTS* 1954, No. 2678); see Chap. 5, Sect. 5.2.2 of this book.

[15] E.g., the Dutch advisory report to the government on immunity of foreign State officials ignores the issue completely; Advisory Committee on Issues of Public International Law 2001.

[16] E.g., see van Sliedregt et al. 2008, paras 2.12.4, 6.1.4 and 7.1.5.

[17] E.g., Brownlie, in Principles of Public International Law, discusses status of forces in a brief section, Brownlie 2008, pp. 372–375 and Fox defines in a concise manner the special position of foreign visiting forces, Fox 2008, pp. 717–724. However, often the position of the forces is not taken into consideration; e.g., Horbach and Lefeber 2007.

current practice nor does it offer any guidance for future developments. This book brings together the international law and military operational law perspectives contributing to the theory on which criminal jurisdiction over armed forces stationed abroad builds and, in the final chapter, will propose to develop a Status-of-Forces Compendium as a practical tool for drafting and using SOFAs.

Since the beginning of the nineteenth century the armed forces can be considered an instrument and organ of the State.[18] At the same time, the position of the armed forces in their extraterritorial execution of sovereign tasks also started to find a place in case law and the literature. Therefore, this book takes the beginning of the nineteenth century as point of departure.

As extraterritorial operations are intertwined with the vital interests and security of the States involved, information can be classified and, therefore, is not always in the public domain.[19] Moreover, some agreements on the status of forces have been concluded as arrangements that are not considered as treaties under international law and, subsequently, do not have to be published.[20] In addition, many agreements on the status of forces are indeed freely accessible, but the parties involved are less open about the drafting process.[21] Consequently, the background of some agreements sometimes remains obscure.

Part I of this book provides a historical overview of the development of the sending States' exercise of criminal jurisdiction, taking three frameworks for stationing forces abroad as point of departure: the consensual stationing of allied forces on co-belligerent territory during armed conflict, participation in crisis management operations, and participation in international military cooperation. Part II concentrates on SOFAs from the perspective of international law, establishing the relation between the State and its armed forces and analysing State immunity and immunities of State officials. Furthermore, it briefly touches upon the functions of international organisations. Part III, finally, elaborates on criminal jurisdiction as part of the law of visiting forces, from the perspective of military operational law. After detailing some specific military terms, this Part analyses criminal jurisdiction from the legal bases that are related to the three frameworks for stationing forces abroad as described in Part I.

1.3.2 Part I: Historical Analysis

The Afghanistan example illustrates that States take different approaches when it comes to the status of their forces stationed abroad. Interest in the subject has a long history and came to a climax in 1812, when the American Supreme Court

---

[18] This development varies from State to State.

[19] E.g., the US are party to more than 100 SOFAs, at least ten of which are classified due to security reasons; Mason 2011.

[20] E.g., Aust 2007, p. 43. These documents do not have to be registered with the UN in accordance with Article 102 *UN Charter*.

[21] Engdahl 2007, p. 152.

touched upon the matter for the first time in the *The Schooner Exchange v. McFaddon*-case,[22] considering that when a State approves the transit of foreign military forces, it has implicitly waived its jurisdiction over these forces.

In the following period, a modest number of court cases building on *The Schooner Exchange v. McFaddon*-case were published and, also, experts in the field of international law started to address the status of forces issue. Since the beginning of the twentieth century it has become part of specific international agreements.[23] Between both World Wars, the League of Nations adopted a resolution on the status of forces participating in the organisation's international force, as the first of its kind.[24] Since World War II, the issue developed rapidly and the content and form of the agreements changed during that post-war period.

At first sight, it might be hard to detect a clear line in the development of SOFAs over the past two centuries. Many researchers concentrate on the period as a whole or focus on certain elements of the development often as part of a broader discussion. As a result, several aspects relating to the status of forces, such as the interests of the States involved, remain largely unexplored. This book is based on the belief that analysing criminal jurisdiction over visiting foreign forces within a specific framework will give insight in the background of the development of SOFAs and will help explaining current practice. In this regard, aspects of international law and military operational law are of particular interest and will be discussed in the following two sections.

1.3.3 Part II: International Law Perspective

The literature and case law frequently refer to existing practices and customs with respect to the status of forces suggesting that the law relating to visiting foreign forces is a specific part of international law: the law of visiting forces.[25] However, this does not mean that the status of military forces is a self-contained regime. It cannot be separated from some of the basic tenets of international law, such as the jurisdiction of States and State immunity. In 1648, the Peace of Westphalia formally introduced the principle of sovereignty of States as the modern foundation of the political order between States. To defend their sovereignty, States disposed of armed forces to protect their vital interests. Since the nineteenth century, the

---

[22] U.S. Supreme Court 24 February 1812, *The Schooner Exchange v McFaddon* 11 U.S. 116 (1812). supreme.justia.com/us/11/116/case.html. Accessed November 2014.

[23] The first agreements were concluded at the beginning of the First World War; e.g. *Agreement between Belgium and France relative for the better prosecution of acts prejudicial to the armed forces;* Brussels, 14 August 1914 (*The Consolidated Treaty Series,* edited and annotated by Clive Parry, Vol. 220, 1914–1915, p. 274).

[24] Resolution of the Council of 11 December 1934, *League of Nations Official Journal*, December 1934, pp. 1762–1763.

[25] Fleck 2003, p. 12.

existence and actions of armed forces became inextricably linked to the State,[26] explaining the States' interest in exercising jurisdiction over their armed forces.

The possibility to exercise criminal jurisdiction over armed forces stationed on foreign territory implies the servicemen's immunity from the criminal jurisdiction of local courts. Immunity can be based on customary law and international agreements and is closely connected to the sovereign position of the State. Therefore, any analysis of the status of visiting forces requires an understanding of the position of the State and its organs in their relations with other States under international law.

In those relations, sovereign States are equal and independent from other States and have the exclusive power to execute the functions of the State within their territory[27]: to prescribe and enforce the rules and administer justice. From this principle of sovereignty the status of armed forces on foreign territory has been derived. Viewed from an international law perspective, warships and their crews even have a special position for which specific rules and practices have developed that today are partly laid down in treaties and general arrangements.

The sovereignty of States has been a key concept in the development of international law. Initially, international law regulated the co-existence of States and delimited their competences. As States started to cooperate to jointly address cross-border problems they delegated part of their powers to institutions they had established together and which, as international organisations, acquired a place of their own under international law. Important international organisations, in particular the UN, play their own unique role in the development with respect to status of forces.

1.3.4 Part III: Military Operational Law Perspective

SOFAs are one of the main topics of military operational law, which itself is a sub discipline of military law. The latter is a hybrid discipline of law, which is difficult to define, and is sometimes described as: "all parts of law related to military personnel and the military".[28] In contrast to military law, which has a really broad scope, addressing the relation between law and military personnel, military operational law concentrates on the actual deployment of armed forces in military operations and can be described as:

> the various bodies of national and international law which are applicable to and regulate the planning and conduct of military operations.[29]

Military operational law has its origin in the aftermath of the Vietnam War. In response to serious crimes committed by US servicemen during the conflict, the US

---

26 Ducheine 2008, p. 12.

27 PCA 4 April 1928, *The Island of Palmas case (or Miangas), United States v the Netherlands*, Award of the Tribunal, p. 8. www.pca-cpa.org. Accessed November 2014.

28 Gill 2006, p. 184.

29 Gill and Fleck 2010, p. 3.

armed forces improved education and training in the law of armed conflict.[30] More important with respect to operational law, legal review of the operational plans was introduced, which integrated law in the preparation and the execution of military operations. This interrelation became known as military operational law.

From a military operational law perspective, SOFAs are to be considered in the larger context of the law of visiting forces. Within this context, SOFAs do not stand alone, but build on the legal bases for the foreign stationing of forces. From those bases follow the operational objectives of the forces' foreign presence which, to a large extent, determine the status of the forces, in particular, the exercise of criminal jurisdiction over the forces.

Today, SOFAs not only deal with criminal jurisdiction, but can cover a wide range of subjects, such as immunities from civil jurisdiction, procedures for entering the host States, freedom of movement in the host States and the right to carry arms. The contents of SOFAs affect the commander's ability to execute his mission. For instance, in practice during the deployment of sizeable military units, damage, for example, because of traffic accidents is unfortunately unavoidable. SOFAs that allow for a flexible and expedient process to solve these matters contribute to the local population's acceptance of the visiting forces.[31] Furthermore, during crisis management operations, that today also aim to restore the rule of law in the aftermath of an armed conflict, this type of process helps to restore confidence in the local legal order.[32] A SOFA tailor-made for a specific mission contributes to the successful accomplishment of the mission.

1.4 Terminology

1.4.1 Consent

This book deals with the consensual stationing of armed forces abroad only. Therefore, situations where host States have refrained from giving their consent to the foreign military's presence have not been taken into consideration. Armed conflict, especially the hostile occupation of a State,[33] is clearly a situation in which

---

[30] Id., pp. 26 et seq.

[31] E.g., Borch 2001, pp. 25 and 73.

[32] ECHR 31 May 2007, *Behrami v France and Saramati v France and others*, Application no. 71412/01, para 48.

[33] In a situation of occupation, parts of the territory of a State fall de facto under the authority of the hostile army (Article 42 *Regulations Respecting the Laws and Customs of war on Land*, Annex to the *Hague Convention IV Respecting the Laws and Customs of War on Land*; The Hague, 18 October 1907; see also ICJ 19 December 2005, *Case concerning Armed Activities on the Territory of the Congo* (Democratic Republic of the Congo v. Uganda), Judgment, I.C.J. Reports 2005, p. 168, paras 173–178). This rule also applies if the occupation did not meet armed resistance (Common Article 2 to the Geneva Conventions of 1949) and to the extent that no valid agreement had been concluded with the occupied State (Roberts 2009, para 4).

consent is lacking. In that particular situation, the status of forces follows from the law of armed conflict. Consequently, local courts in occupied territory do not have criminal jurisdiction over the occupying hostile armed forces,[34] which remain subject to the exclusive criminal jurisdiction of the authorities of the sending State. To this end, the occupying powers can establish military tribunals on the basis of Article 66 of the *Fourth Geneva Convention*.[35]

There are other situations in which military personnel is deployed abroad without host State consent. In principle, operations in the context of Chapter VII of the Charter of the United Nations[36] do not require host States' approval, but the UN will attempt to obtain their consent.[37] In peacetime host States will have jurisdiction over illegal military activities conducted on their territory by foreign State officials present without their consent.[38] An example is the 1985 attack on the Greenpeace vessel 'Rainbow Warrior'. Agents of the French intelligence service sank the 'Rainbow Warrior' when it was berthed in the port town of Auckland, New Zealand, killing a Dutch photographer. Two French servicemen involved in the action, and operating without the consent of the government of New Zealand, were arrested and convicted by the local court.[39]

---

[34] This aspect is not explicitly mentioned in treaties such as the *Hague IV Convention relating to the Laws and Customs of War on Land* and the *Geneva Conventions*. However, this situation is in accordance with the actual balance of power; Schneider 1964, p. 1. In general, see: JAGS Text No. 11 1944, p. 238; von Glahn 1957, p. 340; Dinstein 2009, p. 136. According to Robin, this results from Article 43 of the *Hague IV Convention relating to the Laws and Customs of War on Land*; Robin 1913, p. 141.

[35] Pictet 1958, p. 340. In 1947, on the question whether Dutch courts had jurisdiction over hostile forces, the court in the *Ahlbrecht* case considered that an army occupying foreign territory brings its own criminal codes, courts martial and criminal proceeding; Special Council of Cassation, 17 February 1947, *Ahlbrecht*, NJ 1947, 87. In the case *In re Verhulsdonck* the Belgian judge concluded that Belgian criminal law was not applicable to the German occupation forces during the Second World War; Court of Cassation 12 February 1951, *In re Verhulsdonck*, ILR 18, p. 532. Prisoners of war are an exception. They are subject to the law of the State that has imprisoned them (e.g., Article 82 *Third Convention relative to the Treatment of Prisoners of War;* Geneva, 12 August 1949). Another exception are the war crime trials after the armed conflict has ended; see Liivoja 2011, p. 146. In these cases, the homes States of the prosecuted officials had never invoked immunity; see *UN Doc* A/CN.4/631 (2010), ILC Second report on immunity of State officials from foreign criminal jurisdiction, 10 June 2010, para 69.

[36] *Charter of the United Nations*; San Francisco, 26 June 1945 (*S.* 1945, F 253).

[37] *United Nations Peacekeeping Operations. Principles and guidelines*, New York: United Nations, 18 January 2008, p. 31. In case of so called 'enforcement operation' consent may be lacking and the law of armed conflict will apply.

[38] See *UN Doc* A/CN.4/631 (2010), ILC Second report on immunity of State officials from foreign criminal jurisdiction, 10 June 2010, para 85.

[39] For more details on this topic, see Ruling by the Secretary-General of the United Nations, 6 July 1986, *Case concerning the differences between New Zealand and France arising from the Rainbow Warrior affair*, United Nations Reports of International Arbitral Awards, Vol. XIX, pp. 199–221.

1.4.2 Internal Order and Discipline

The armed forces are a hierarchal organisation, in which the command structure is clearly defined. With a view to the sometimes exceptional circumstances under which the servicemen must operate, military criminal, disciplinary and administrative law emphasise the military command relationships, authorising the commander to issue orders and service regulations, which all servicemen under his command are obliged to follow.[40] The commander can enforce his orders and regulations, if necessary, by taking disciplinary or administrative action.

Military criminal, disciplinary and administrative law are an inherent part of an effective force and must, therefore, continue to apply when the forces are deployed abroad.[41] This cannot be regarded as a serious obstacle by the host State as long as the rules concern the internal order of the visiting forces and do not affect host State public order. In general, it is accepted that sending States have the exclusive authority over the internal order of their forces. However, legal systems of states vary and the question of whether the public order of the host State is concerned will have to be answered on a case-to-case basis. Unless indicated otherwise, this book does not address internal disciplinary and administrative law.

1.4.3 Crisis Management Operations

The terminology related to military operations does not have a legal basis and is quite ambiguous. The UN include in the description of peace operations several related and partly overlapping activities, such as conflict prevention, peacemaking, peace enforcement, peacekeeping and post-conflict peacebuilding.[42] Peacekeeping operations are an important tool for the UN with a highly diverse character, varying from traditional observation missions to the modern multi-dimensional peacekeeping operations that include military, police and civilian elements.[43]

NATO distinguishes between collective self-defence operations on the basis of Article 5 of the *NATO-Treaty*,[44] on the one hand, and operations that are not based on this article (the Non-Article 5 Crisis Response Operations, NA5CRO), on the other. This term has a rather broad scope and includes a wide variety of military

---

40 Ducheine 2010, pp. 145–154.

41 In this context, reference has been made to the concept of organic jurisdiction, Sari 2008, pp. 77 et seq; Liivoja 2011, p. 239, in which the specific relation between the State and its organs is solely subject to national law; Seyersted 2008, p. 84.

42 *United Nations Peacekeeping Operations. Principles and Guidelines*, New York: United Nations, 18 January 2008, pp. 18–19 and Fig. 1.

43 Ibid, p. 22.

44 *North Atlantic Treaty*; Washington, 4 April 1949 (Vol. 34 *UNTS* 1949, No. 541).

activities, such as peacekeeping activities, humanitarian assistance and evacuation of non-combatants. Since 2003, the EU has undertaken military operations and civilian missions in the context of the Common Security and Defence Policy (CSDP).[45] The organisation uses the term crisis management to include all activities undertaken in this context.[46] This book follows the latter terminology using crisis management operation as a generic term for any military operation taking place with host State consent.

1.4.4 Jurisdiction and Immunity

Although distinct concepts, jurisdiction and immunity are closely related[47] and are central in the discussion on the status of forces. When addressing the status of State officials abroad international law generally focuses on the concept of immunity, while from the military operational law perspective jurisdiction is equally, if not more, important. Therefore, in anticipation of a more detailed analysis in Part II, Chaps. 6 and 7, it is useful to briefly discuss both concepts.

Jurisdiction refers to the powers of sovereign States to prescribe, adjudicate and enforce their national laws.[48] In principle, jurisdiction and the State's exercise thereof is territorial by nature (see Fig. 1.1).

On the basis of generally accepted principles of jurisdiction under international law, a State can extend its law to apply to persons or activities outside its own territory. In this way, the State extends its legislative jurisdiction beyond its borders. As a consequence, that State can prosecute acts committed by its nationals abroad, or which have an effect on its territory or legal order within certain generally accepted parameters. In that case, State A can prosecute a suspect when he is within its territory or when a court of State A renders a decision *in absentia*.

State A can lay down by law the authority of its courts to sit outside its own territory. However, this authority does not imply that those courts have the right to actually operate in State B and can, for example, conduct a criminal investigation. The extraterritorial exercise of the powers to adjudicate and enforce requires either the consent of the States involved, or a legal basis under international law.

---

45 Before the *Treaty of Lisbon* came into effect, CSDP was called the European Security and Defence Policy; *Treaty of Lisbon amending the Treaty on European Union and the Treaty establishing the European Community*; Lisbon, 13 December 2007 (*OJ* 2007, C 306).

46 Naert 2010, p. 204, footnote 1025.

47 The concepts of jurisdiction and immunity are inextricably linked: "If there is no jurisdiction *en principe*, then the question of an immunity from a jurisdiction which would otherwise exist simply does not arise"; ICJ 14 February 2002, *Arrest warrant of 11 April 2000* (*Democratic Republic of the Congo v. Belgium*), Judgment, I.C.J. Reports 2002, p. 3, separate opinion of Judges Higgins, Kooijmans and Buergenthal para 3. As a result, immunity is the exception to jurisdiction and can only be invoked if there is jurisdiction. (ibid, para 70).

48 Restatement of the Law (1987) pp. 230 et seq.

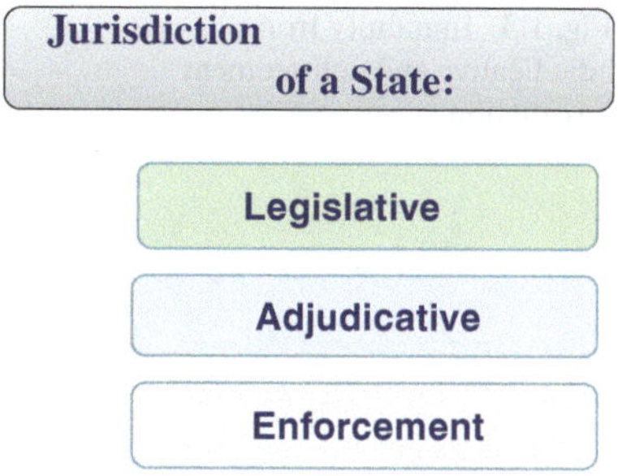

Fig. 1.1 State jurisdiction

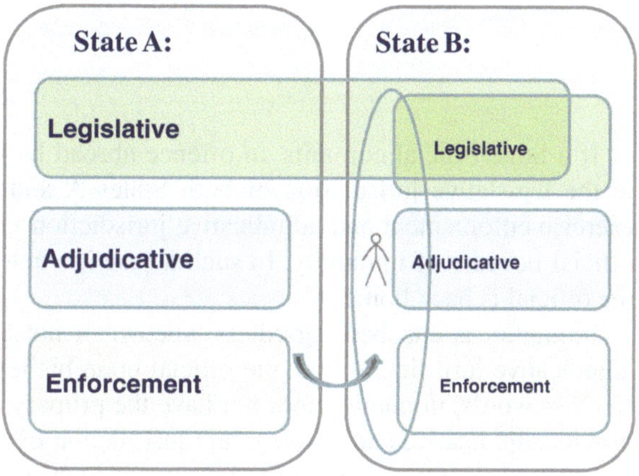

Fig. 1.2 State jurisdiction; State A's national abroad

In case a national of State A visits State B, he falls under the legislative, adjudicative, and enforcement jurisdiction of the latter State notwithstanding any possible extraterritorial legislative jurisdiction of his home State. If State A made use of its power to exercise extraterritorial legislative jurisdiction, this would result in the possibility that a particular act could constitute an offence under the laws of both States A and B, implying a degree of concurrent jurisdiction (see Fig. 1.2). No specific rules of precedence apply in situations like these and normally the State that is in the best position to act, for example the State, where the offence was committed and the perpetrator apprehended, will initiate criminal proceedings.

State B has, *inter alia*, adjudicative and enforcement jurisdiction over the visiting national from State A, except when that person is a foreign State official, like a diplomat or serviceman, present on State B's territory with its consent (see Fig. 1.3), who enjoys immunity from the adjudicative and enforcement jurisdiction of State B.[49] Officials enjoying immunity remain, however, subject to the legislative jurisdiction of both State B and State A, if the latter has extended its legislative jurisdiction beyond its borders. In cases of State officials this will virtually always be the case.

[49] Staff members of international organisations can also enjoy immunity (see Chap. 9).

Fig. 1.3 Immunity from adjudicative and enforcement jurisdiction

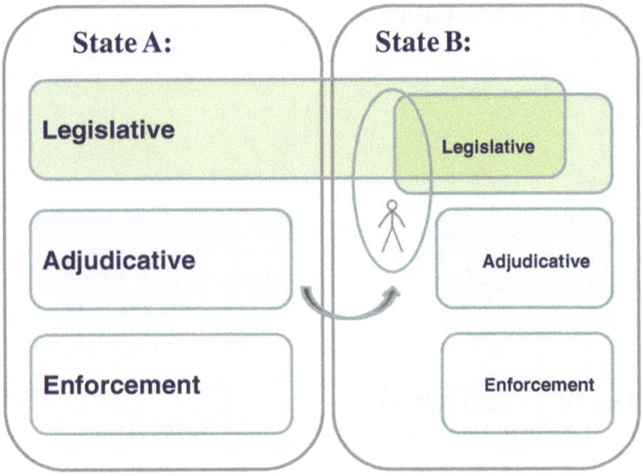

If a State official commits an offence abroad he will almost always be subject to the legislative jurisdiction of both States A and B. State B, however, cannot exercise enforcement and adjudicative jurisdiction vis-à-vis the official acts of the official because of immunity. In such a case it would fall to State A to do so once the official is back home.

Immunity is attached regardless whether or not State A decides to exercise its adjudicative jurisdiction over the official upon his return to State A or *in absentia*. In other words, immunity does not have the primary aim to enable State A to exercise its adjudicative and enforcement jurisdiction extraterritorially vis-à-vis its official abroad. However, its aim is to prevent State B from exercising those powers over the foreign official.

With regard to visiting forces present on another State's territory the situation is different. Many SOFAs put more emphasis on the sending States' possibility to exercise their criminal jurisdiction than on immunities granted by host States. For instance, several SOFAs state that members of the armed forces deployed abroad are subject to the exclusive jurisdiction of their respective sending States,[50] thereby expressing the parties' understanding that State A, as sending State, to the exclusion of State B, as host State, may exercise its adjudicative and enforcement jurisdiction over the servicemen. State B, therefore, refrains from exercising its adjudicative and enforcement jurisdiction over the servicemen, who thus enjoys immunity in State B (see Fig. 1.4).

In this context, jurisdiction and immunity are closely interlinked as the report resulting from the experiences of the United Nations Emergency Force (UNEF) in Egypt shows (see Sect. 4.3.2). In the report, the Secretary-General of the UN stated that the members of the force "should be immune from the criminal jurisdiction of the host State" and that the SOFA "accordingly provided that members of the Force should be under the exclusive jurisdiction of their respective national.

[50] A well-known example is para 47 (b) *Model Status-of-Forces Agreement for Peace-Keeping Operations*, Report of the Secretary-General, *UN Doc* A/45/594 of 9 October 1990.

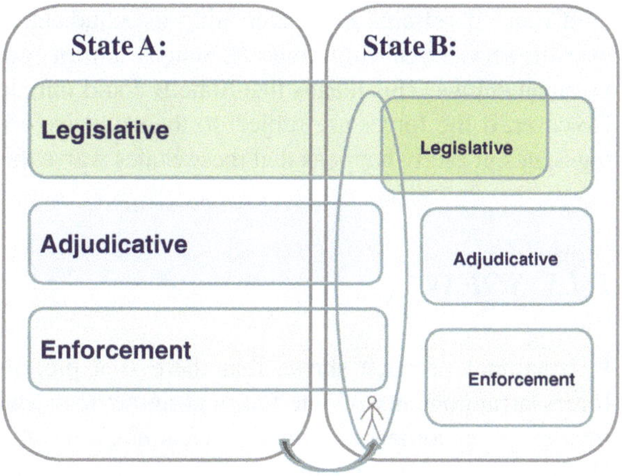

Fig. 1.4 Exclusive jurisdiction in relation to immunity

States with regard to any criminal offences committed by them in Egypt".[51] In 2004 the Office of Legal Affairs stated that forces participating in UN operations:

> are … subject to the exclusive criminal jurisdiction of their respective national authorities, and so enjoy absolute and complete immunity from legal criminal process in States hosting peacekeeping operations.[52]

In the literature the relation between jurisdiction and immunity vis-à-vis military forces is not subject to debate and often the exclusive criminal jurisdiction of the sending States over their armed forces is almost naturally equated with the criminal immunity of these forces.[53]

In my opinion, emphasising the sending States' jurisdiction rather than the immunity granted by host States highlights the special relation between sending States, on the one hand, and their armed forces in the execution of their mission abroad, on the other. The military force functioning as an organised entity under single military command is a necessity for mission accomplishment. This means that sending States must be able to exert their authority and command over the forces without host State interference, which requires the forces' immunity from the jurisdiction of the host States and, above all, that sending States can exercise their jurisdiction over servicemen who have violated sending State and host State law. In other words, the military function requires that forces deployed abroad remain to a certain extent subject to the jurisdiction of the sending States and that the host States partly refrain from the exercise of these powers.

---

[51] See *UN Doc* A/3943 (1958), Summary study of the experiences derived from the establishment and operation of the Force, Report of the Secretary General, 9 October 1958, para 136.

[52] Office of Legal Affairs, 'Letter to the Acting Chair of the Special Committee on Peacekeeping Operations, United Nations, regarding immunities of civilian police and military personnel', 14 April 2004, *United Nations Juridical Yearbook 2004*, New-York: United Nations, Office of Legal Affairs 2004, p. 325.

[53] See for example Siekman 1988, p. 170; Bothe and Dörschel 2003, p. 505; Liivoja 2011, p. 250.

If State B refrains from exercising its adjudicative and enforcement jurisdiction over the serviceman from State A, State A in turn could waive the immunity the serviceman enjoys. This means that State B could initiate criminal proceedings instead. However, if the forces are subject to the exclusive criminal jurisdiction of the sending States, it rarely happens that these States waive their forces' immunity.[54]

1.4.5 SOFAs

International practice shows that there is a preference for setting out status of forces arrangements in international agreements, which mostly take the form of treaties in accordance with the *Vienna Convention on the Law of Treaties*.[55] However, other instruments are also used. For instance, in 2003 during the occupation of Iraq by US and British forces, the Coalition Provisional Authority of Iraq unilaterally adopted an order that regulated the conditions for the presence of foreign forces.[56] With the consent of the Iraqi authorities this order continued to be in force long after the period of occupation had ended. Furthermore, States sometimes lay down the status of forces in other instruments than legally binding international agreements that are often referred to as Memoranda of Understanding (MOU).[57] In addition, in several cases the UN Security Council (provisionally) dealt with the status of forces by resolution.[58] This book will refer to all these instruments with the generic term SOFA. Besides, rules on the status of forces are also partly of a customary nature, as will be discussed below.

---

[54] Forces participating in the Multinational Force and Observers (MFO) in the Sinai were subject to the sending States' exclusive criminal jurisdiction on the basis of para 11(a) Appendix of the Annex to the *Protocol relating to the establishment and maintenance of a Multinational Force and Observers (with annex)*; Washington, 3 August 1981 (Vol. 1335 UNTS 1983 No. 22403). In supplementary agreements with Israel MFO member States waived the immunity of MFO-members on leave in Israel with respect to certain crimes; e.g., *Exchange of notes constituting an agreement relating to privileges and immunities for United States military members and civilian observers of the Multinational Force and Observers on leave in Israel*; Jerusalem, 28 September 1982, and Tel Aviv, 1 October 1982 (Vol. 1871 *UNTS* 1995, No. 31960). For an opposite opinion, see Engdahl 2007, p. 183.

[55] *Vienna Convention on the Law of Treaties*; Vienna, 23 May 1969 (Vol. 1155 *UNTS* 1980, No. 18232).

[56] *CPA Order 17 (rev.)*: *Coalition Provisional Authority Order Number 17 (revised)*: *Status of the Coalition Provisional Authority, MNF-Iraq, Certain missions and Personnel in Iraq*; 27 June 2004. http://www.iraqcoalition.org/regulations/20040627_CPAORD_17_Status_of_Coalition__Rev__with_Annex_A.pdf. Accessed November 2014.

[57] In contrast to treaties MOUs are not subject to international law and, as a result, they are not legally binding; see Aust 2007, pp. 20–21.

[58] See for example, the United Nations Mission in the Central African Republic (MINURCA), *UN Doc* S/RES/1158 van 27 March 1998, para 19. This practice is frequently adopted, see, e.g. UNMEE (*UN Doc* S/RES/1320 (2000), para 6); MINUSTAH (*UN Doc* S/RES/1542 (2004), para 11); MINURCAT (*UN Doc* S/RES/1778 (2007), para 4).

SOFAs are to be distinguished from agreements that lay down the legal basis for the visits of foreign forces. In Part III of this book these latter agreements will be referred to as visiting forces agreements.

1.4.6 Definition

In the literature SOFAs are discussed in rather general terms avoiding the need to define them.[59] For the purpose of this book I propose the following definition:

> A SOFA is an arrangement, no matter in what form, delineating the legal status of servicemen from a sending State who stay with the consent of the host State on its territory, and that at least includes rules on the exercise of criminal jurisdiction over the sending State's servicemen.

The definition includes some specific elements. First, host States have to consent to the presence of the foreign military forces. Consent does not necessarily have to be part of the SOFA itself, but can precede it, for example, in a visiting forces agreement. Second, key to SOFAs is the provision on the exercise of criminal jurisdiction over the servicemen deployed abroad. Third, SOFAs normally do not deal with military personnel exclusively, but address the status of other categories as well, for example civilian personnel employed by the armed forces, and family members or civilian contractors working for the armed forces. As this book focuses on the military, other categories are left out of the proposed definition. Finally, the form of the SOFA is of less importance and the arrangement could be laid down in a treaty, MOU, or other international, multilateral or unilateral, instrument.

References

Advisory Committee on Issues of Public International Law (2001) Advisory report on immunity of foreign State officials. Advisory Report no. 20, The Hague. cms.webbeat.net/ContentSuite/upload/cav/doc/cavv-report-nr-20-immunity_foreign_officials.pdf. Accessed Nov 2014

Aust A (2007) Modern treaty law and practice. Cambridge University Press, Cambridge

Borch FL (2001) Judge advocates in combat: army lawyers in military operations from Vietnam to Haiti. Office of the Judge Advocate General and Center of Military History United States Army, Washington

Bothe M, Dörschel T (2003) The UN peacekeeping experience. In: Fleck D (ed) The handbook of the law of visiting forces. Oxford University Press, Oxford, pp 487–506

Brownlie I (2008) Principles of public international law. Oxford University Press, Oxford

[59] Other documents most often do not include a definition of a SOFA either. For example, NATO keeps an extensive overview of the terminology used within the organisation (Allied Administrative Publication, AAP-06, 2013, NATO Glossary of Terms and Definitions). However, this document does not include a definition of a SOFA.

Cathcart B (2010) Command and control in military operations. In: Gill TD, Fleck D (eds) The handbook of international law of military operations. Oxford University Press, New York, pp 235–244

Conderman PJ (2013) Status of armed forces on foreign territory agreements (SOFA). In: Max Planck encyclopedia of public international law. www.mpepil.com. Accessed Nov 2014

Dinstein Y (2009) The international law of belligerent occupation. Cambridge University Press, Cambridge

Ducheine PAL (2008) Krijgsmacht, geweldgebruik & terrorismebestrijding. Een onderzoek naar juridische aspecten van de rol van strijdkrachten bij de bestrijding van terrorisme. Wolf Legal Publishers, Nijmegen

Ducheine PAL (2010) De status van aanwijzingen van buitenlandse commandanten bij de beoordeling van functioneel militair geweldgebruik, Een reactie op de bijdrage van mr. A.F. Vink over de Tactical Directive. Militair Rechtelijk Tijdschrift 103:86–91

Engdahl O (2007) Protection of personnel in peace operations: the role of the safety convention against the background of general international law. Martinus Nijhoff Publishers, Leiden

Fleck D (2003) (ed) The handbook of the law of visiting forces. Oxford University Press, Oxford

Fox H (2008) The law of state immunity. Oxford University Press, Oxford

Gill TD (2006) Voordracht ter gelegenheid van de oprichting van de Gezamenlijke Militaire Juridische Dienst. Militair Rechtelijk Tijdschrift 99:184–189

Gill TD, Fleck D (2010) The handbook of international law of military operations. Oxford University Press, New York

Horbach N, Lefeber R (2007) Staatsaansprakelijkheid. In: Horbach N, Lefeber R, Ribbelink O (eds) Handboek internationaal recht. T.M.C. Asser Press, The Hague, pp 309–345

JAGS Text No. 11 (1944) Law of belligerent occupation. Judge Advocate General's School, Ann Arbor

Liivoja R (2011) An axiom of military law: Applicability of national criminal law to military personnel and associated civilians abroad. Centre of Excellence in Global Governance Research, Helsinki

Munoz-Mosquera A (2011) Host nation support arrangements: the NAC-approved military-to-military tools. NATO Legal Gaz 24:2–8

Naert F (2010) International law aspects of the EU's security and defence policy with a particular focus on the law of armed conflict and human rights. Intersentia, Antwerpen-Oxford-Leuven

Pictet JS (1958) Commentary IV Geneva convention relative to the protection of civilian persons in times of war. ICRC, Genève ICRC

Roberts A (2009) Termination of military occupation. In: Max Planck encyclopedia of public international law. www.mpepil.com. Accessed Nov 2014

Robin R (1913) Des occupations militaires en dehors des occupations de guerre. Division of International Law of the Carnegie Endowment for International Peace, Washington (Translated and reproduced, 1942)

Rouse JH, Baldwin GB (1957) The exercise of criminal jurisdiction under the NATO status of forces agreement. AJIL 51(1):29–62

Sari A (2008) The jurisdictional immunities of visiting forces under public international law. a case study of the European security and defence policy. Thesis, University College London (not published; on file with author)

Schneider G (1964) Die Exterritorialität der Truppen in strafrechtlicher Hinsicht, unter besonderer Berücksichtigung der das deutsche Territorium betreffenden Truppenverträge. Albert-Ludwig Universität, Saarbrücken

Seyersted F (2008) Jurisdiction over organs and officials. In: Seyersted F (ed) Common law of international organizations. Brill, Leiden, pp 81–105

Siekmann RCR (1988) Juridische aspecten van de deelname met nationale contingenten aan VN-vredesmachten (Nederland en UNIFIL). Amsterdam University, Amsterdam

Snee JM (1961) NATO agreements on status: traveaux préparatoires. In: International law studies, vol 54. Naval War College, Newport

Restatement of the Law (1987) Third, foreign relations law of the United States. American Law Institute, Washington

van Sliedregt E, Sjöcrona JM, Orie AMM (red) (2008) Handboek internationaal strafrecht. Schets van het Europese en internationale strafrecht. Kluwer, Deventer

von Glahn G (1957) The occupation of enemy territory: a commentary on the law and practice of belligerent occupation. The University of Minnesota Press, Minneapolis

Wilson S, Kamen A (2009) Global war on terror is given new name. Washington Post, 25 March 2009

Part I
Historical Analysis

In the past two centuries the scope of criminal jurisdiction over military forces stationed on the territory of other States with their consent has not always been defined in a uniform way. For this reason the first part of this book has a historical bias and concentrates on the development of criminal jurisdiction over visiting forces in the past few centuries and the particular circumstances explaining this development. Part I also briefly deals with aspects of an international and military operational nature. Based on the *Historical Analysis* provided in Part I, these aspects will be further analysed in Parts II and III.

Part I describes the development of the arrangements and practice relating to the status of forces in two ways, one of which is chronological by nature and starts at the beginning of the nineteenth century. Towards the end of the nineteenth century the chronological method modifies into a thematic method dealing with specific frameworks relating to the various circumstances in which the visiting forces find themselves: stationed on co-belligerent territory during an armed conflict, participating in crisis management operations and partaking in international military cooperation activities abroad. The thematic method also takes into account the circumstances under which the forces are based abroad, the interests of the States involved, and their mutual relations. The three frameworks will be further discussed in the following chapters; they will also be the basis for analysis from a military operational law perspective in Part III.

Chapter 2 aims to define the ground rule relating to criminal jurisdiction over visiting forces in the extraterritorial execution of their tasks through a historical analysis. Findings in this chapter are in the first place based on the literature and case law. However, as States have concluded formal SOFAs ever since World War I, these agreements will play an increasingly important role in the following chapters. Furthermore, these chapters examine to what extent State practice corresponds with the ground rule and identifies the limits of the ground rule. Chapter 3 focuses on the status of allied forces stationed on co-belligerent territory during armed conflict. Chapter 4 addresses the status of the armed forces participating in crisis management operations. Part I ends with Chap. 5 on the status of forces in the context of international military cooperation.

Chapter 2
The Ground Rule

Abstract In 1812 the US Supreme court addressed the status of armed forces passing through the territory of a foreign friendly State and concluded that consent of that State implied its waiver of all jurisdiction over the visiting forces. Based on this court case and subsequent case law a general ground rule on the exercise of jurisdiction can be framed: A host State refrains from exercising criminal jurisdiction over armed forces of a sending State, in case it has given consent to their entry and presence on its territory, thus allowing the sending State to exercise criminal jurisdiction over its forces abroad. Case law and the literature limit the scope of the ground rule somewhat, indicating that it applies to visiting forces as an organised military unit and while the members of the forces are present at the designated military bases and installations or are on duty outside the bases and installations.

Contents

2.1 Introduction

Throughout the centuries States have deployed their armed forces abroad in order to protect or further their national interests, which could generally be defined in terms of the law of armed conflict as international armed conflicts and occupation. In the past, armed forces largely consisted of soldiers recruited by private entrepreneurs that later in history were partly replaced by regiments hired from other States. During the first part of the nineteenth century, the introduction

© T.M.C. ASSER PRESS and the author 2015

J. Voetelink, *Status of Forces: Criminal Jurisdiction over Military Personnel Abroad*,
DOI 10.1007/978-94-6265-057-2_2

of, *inter alia*, mandatory military service put an end to this practice in Continental Europe and the armed forces developed into an instrument of the sovereign State in its relations with other States. In the same period the legal status of armed forces stationed in other States started to find a place in both case law and the literature.

This chapter examines in what ways ideas on criminal jurisdiction over military forces based abroad took shape during the nineteenth century and have further evolved since then. It starts with a discussion of the first court case in which the status of visiting forces was addressed: *The Exchange v. McFaddon*-case (Sect. 2.2).[1] Considerations of the decision are confirmed by later American court decisions (Sect. 2.3). In this chapter, these decisions serve as a reference for the formulation of the ground rule on criminal jurisdiction over armed forces of sending States on foreign territory (Sect. 2.4). This rule appears to be absolute in nature. However, case law and the literature will clarify that the status of armed forces can be interpreted in a more balanced way (Sect. 2.5). In this approach the application of the ground rule is subject to specific conditions that affect the scope of the exercise of criminal jurisdiction (Sect. 2.6).

2.2 The Exchange v. McFaddon

In 1812, a case concerning a vessel called *The Exchange* was brought before the US Supreme Court. The vessel, property of two American citizens, was seized on the high seas in 1810 on orders of the French Emperor Napoleon who had commissioned it under the name of *Balaou* as a French naval vessel. During a voyage to the Caribbean *The Exchange* sustained damage forcing its crew to dock at the port of Philadelphia for repairs. When the US owners, including McFaddon, learned about this, they had the vessel put under embargo on 24 August 1811 and claimed its restitution to them. In 1812, the case was brought before the US Supreme Court, which rejected the claim.

The key question of the case was whether an American citizen could claim ownership of another State's warship that was within the US territorial waters. Although this was a civil court case, the considerations of Chief Justice Marshall had broader implications. He noted that the jurisdiction of a State within its own territory is exclusive and absolute. Any external restrictions upon it would result in an abatement of sovereignty. Therefore, all exceptions to the jurisdiction must be traced to the express or implied consent of the State itself, which had already become customary practice between equal States.

According to Marshall, this full and absolute territorial jurisdiction did not confer any extraterritorial power. A sovereign can enter foreign territory only under the express license, or in the confidence that the immunities belonging to his

[1] U.S. Supreme Court 24 February 1812, *The Schooner Exchange v. McFaddon* 11 U.S. 116 (1812). supreme.justia.com/us/11/116/case.html. Accessed November 2014.

independent sovereign position implicitly extend to him. In State practice, this led to situations in which a State was supposed to have partly refrained from its full territorial jurisdiction.

One of the situations to which Marshall refers was the presence of foreign armed forces. When the sovereign explicitly allowed foreign forces free passage through his territory, his action implied a waiver of all jurisdiction over the forces and the recognition that they were subject to the criminal jurisdiction of their commander:

> The grant of a free passage therefore implies a waiver of all jurisdiction over the troops during their passage, and permits the foreign general to use that discipline and to inflict those punishments which the government of his army may require.

Marshall reasoned that if the host State were to exercise its jurisdiction over the foreign armed forces:

> …the purpose for which the free passage was granted would be defeated and a portion of the military force of a foreign independent nation would be diverted from those national objects and duties to which it was applicable, and would be withdrawn from the control of the sovereign whose power and whose safety might greatly depend on retaining the exclusive command and disposition of this force.

In this consideration, Marshall emphasises that by allowing the passage of foreign forces, the host State acknowledges the purpose for which the foreign forces are present on its territory. He also confirms the nexus of a State and its armed forces, even in case the forces are deployed abroad for the protection of the State's interests.

Host State consent to the free passage of foreign armed forces was considered by Marshall to be a key element. If forces of one State entered the territory of another State without its consent, the latter could consider this act as hostile and the 'visiting' armed forces would by no means be entitled to any privileges.

Admitting warships into its ports was less dangerous and problematic for a State than granting a foreign army free passage through its territory. If a State had not closed its ports for warships, they were considered to be open to the public ships of other States. Marshall reasoned that warships were part of the military force of a State under direct command of the sovereign, who commissioned the vessels for national tasks. If other States prevented warships from executing their tasks, it would prejudice the State's dignity. On these grounds, Marshall considered that visiting warships were implicitly exempted from foreign jurisdiction. In applying the above-mentioned principles to the *Balaou*, Marshall concluded that at the time the ship docked at the port of Philadelphia, it was exempted from the jurisdiction of the US, as it was classified as a French warship.

2.3 Coleman v. Tennessee and Dow v. Johnson

The US Supreme Court built on *The Exchange v. McFaddon* in two later cases relating to the American Civil War. Although this book does not address the status of armed forces under the law of armed conflict, both judgments contain relevant considerations that refer back to *The Exchange v. McFaddon*. In both cases, the judge decided in general terms on the jurisdiction of a host State over foreign military forces. Consequently, the validity of the decisions extends to situations beyond those of armed conflicts.

The case of *Coleman v. Tennessee*[2] concerned an American soldier who murdered a woman in Tennessee. A court martial had sentenced the soldier to death for this offence, but for reasons unknown, the sentence had not been carried out. After the war had come to an end, a local court in the state of Tennessee convicted the soldier once more for the same offence. The Supreme Court considered that at the time of the offence, the Southern Confederate States were regarded as hostile territory. This also applied to the part of Tennessee where the murder had taken place and which was occupied by the US Army. On the basis of the rules of war, courts-martial of the US had the exclusive jurisdiction to prosecute their own servicemen for crimes committed. Consequently, members of the armed forces were only accountable to their own government and were not subject to the jurisdiction of local laws and courts.

In his considerations the judge referred to the Supreme Court's decision in *The Exchange v. McFaddon*. He noted that it was generally accepted that an army having the approval to enter, or be stationed on, the territory of a friendly State would be exempted from the State's civil and criminal jurisdiction. Consequently, if this were the case, it would be evident that an army having invaded an enemy State would not fall under the State's jurisdiction.

One year later, the case *Dow v. Johnson* was brought before the Supreme Court.[3] In 1863, Bradish Johnson had taken his case against US Army General Neil Dow before the court of New Orleans. Johnson claimed that on General Dow's orders US forces had confiscated sugar from his plantation and plundered the Johnson residence. The Supreme Court had to decide whether a local court in an enemy State had civil jurisdiction over an officer of the US Army. The judge referred to the above mentioned consideration in the *Coleman v. Tennessee* case and its reference to *Exchange v. McFaddon*, concluding that servicemen in times of war were only accountable to their own government and were not subject to the criminal jurisdiction of local laws and courts. The judge concluded that the same reasoning would apply here with respect to civil jurisdiction.[4]

---

[2] U.S. Supreme Court October 1878, *Coleman v. Tennessee*, 97 U.S. 509 (1878). supreme.justia.com/us/97/509/case.html. Accessed November 2014.

[3] U.S. Supreme Court October 1879, *Dow v. Johnson*, 100 U.S. 158 (1879). supreme.justia.com/us/100/158/case.html. Accessed November 2014.

[4] Ibid.

2.4 The Ground Rule

Case law, as in *Coleman v. Tennessee* and *Dow v. Johnson,*[5] confirms what had already been decided in *The Exchange v. McFaddon* on the jurisdiction over armed forces abroad and even widens the scope of that case from the free passage of forces to the stationing of forces. The judge noted that this practice was "well-settled". So, in his opinion it was a generally accepted practice that host State consent to the entry and presence of foreign armed forces implied its waiver of jurisdiction over the sending States' forces.

It is hard to establish to what extent this practice reflects international customary law. In *The Exchange v. McFaddon* the judge interpreted the facts on the basis of general principles and indicated that he was not led by precedents or by *lex scripta*. The fundamental nature of his interpretation, based on the absolute jurisdiction of a State, indicates that he was led by what he presumed to be the law. The judge thus referred to a rule that applied to armies present on the territory of friendly States and not just to practice or custom. Likewise, the judge classified the right of warships to visit a port as a principle of public law. Furthermore, it has to be taken into account that the considerations in *The Exchange v. McFaddon* were accepted by other judges as a matter of course for more than a century.

On the basis of the considerations outlined above, it can be concluded that, according to the US Supreme Court, the waiver of criminal jurisdiction over visiting armed forces was based on a general rule of law. In summary, this rule, which will be referred to as the ground rule in this, reads:

> A host State refrains from exercising criminal jurisdiction over visiting armed forces of a sending State, in case it has given its consent to their entry into and presence on its territory, thus allowing the sending State to exercise criminal jurisdiction over its forces abroad.

The ground rule consists of three elements. First, the host State must have given its consent to the entry and presence of the foreign armed forces. This is obviously not the case in a situation of armed conflict or enemy occupation, which is therefore beyond the scope of the ground rule. Sometimes a State's decision on the entry and stationing of foreign armed forces on its territory has not been made in complete freedom, but under some pressure. The continued presence of occupying forces on the basis of a Peace Agreement is an example of such a situation. As these situations formally fulfil the requirement of a given consent, they will be considered in the context of the ground rule.

Second, the ground rule includes a waiver from the host State: it refrains from exercising its criminal jurisdiction over the armed forces of a sending State from the moment the forces have received consent to be present on its territory. In practice, the waiver implies immunity of the visiting forces from the criminal

[5] See also a later decision from the beginning of the twentieth century: U.S. Supreme Court 6 January 1902, *Tucker v. Alexandroff*, 183 U.S. 424 (1902). supreme.justia.com/us/183/424/case.html. Accessed November 2014. Other decisions are mentioned in: Re 1956, p. 369.

jurisdiction of the host State. This immunity is not necessarily absolute, and may depend upon the context within which the forces operate on foreign territory (see Chaps. 3, 4 and 5).

Finally, in military practice it is not sufficient that servicemen committing crimes are not subject to the criminal jurisdiction of the host State. In order to operate efficiently, sending States must be able to freely exert their authority and power, including the exercise of criminal jurisdiction, over its deployed armed forces. The third component of the ground rule is closely related to the waiver and can be considered the flipside of the same coin. It concerns the power of sending States to exercise their criminal jurisdiction over their forces abroad. As the next chapters show, many SOFAs emphasise this component in particular and hardly address the armed forces' immunity.

Jurisdiction over own armed forces abroad is sometimes referred to as the law of the flag.[6] This terminology follows from Napoleon Bonaparte's statement that the French army is never abroad, because it always operates under the national flag: "Il faut regarder le drapeau comme le domicile. Partout où est le drapeau, là est la France".[7] The flag symbolises the State represented by its forces. In this approach the armed forces can be considered as an extension of the State with which the State and its forces are inextricably linked. Formerly, this was discussed as part of the concept of extraterritoriality.[8] This concept was based on the notion that State officials working abroad, such as diplomats, were assumed to be still within the territory of the sending State. As they were assumed to be on home territory, they would logically not fall under the jurisdiction of the host State. In this way, they would enjoy the same rights and privileges as if they were in their home State.

2.5 Nineteenth Century Practice

In the beginning of the nineteenth century passage of armed forces through the territory of friendly States (as Marshall had in mind in *The Exchange v. McFaddon*) occurred frequently. Many treaties mainly focused on the political and operational aspects of the passage,[9] while the exercise of jurisdiction over the armed forces was

---

6 Lazareff 1971, p. 11. 'Ubi signa et jurisdictio' in Court of Cassation 24 July 2008, *Lozano v. Italy*, Case No 31171/2008; ILDC 1085 (IT 2008), para 3. German: 'Recht der Fahne', Scheider 1964, p. 2.

7 Fenet 1827, pp. 46–48, *addition* p. 32; Thibaudeau 1827, pp. 427–428.

8 The word extra-territoriality is also used; these concepts have, however, lost their significance; see Liivoja 2011, p. 105.

9 E.g., the military agreement relating to the free passage of Dutch forces to the fortress of Maastricht, concluded by Belgium and the Netherlands on the occasion of the independence of Belgium: *Convention entre les Pays-Bas et la Belgique, conclue a Zonhoven, relativement aux communications militaires de la forteresse de* Maastricht; z.p. 18 November 1833 (*Recueil des Traités et conventions conclus par le Royaume des Pay-Bas, E.G. Lagemans,* The Hague 1859, No 136).

rarely part of the agreements.[10] Sometimes an agreement would mention the disciplinary powers of the commander to maintain the order and discipline of his armed forces during the free passage: "ils [the commanders] veilleront en général au maintien d'une discipline rigoureuse et du bon ordre".[11] Because of these often detailed agreements the burden to the host States of the passage of the foreign forces was considerably minimised. So, although they would lose jurisdiction over the foreign forces due to the application of the ground rule, the situation could not be perceived as seriously affecting host State sovereignty.

The consensual presence of significant numbers of foreign forces on host State territory was not a frequent event.[12] For instance, Moore only mentions a handful of situations in which foreign forces had been allowed to enter or to stay on the territory of the US during a period of more than a 100 years.[13] Moreover, the armed forces would mainly consist of small units that would stay for a short period of time at previously determined locations, which also applied to visiting warships. The temporary presence of the crews would generally be restricted to the ports. As a result, the application of the ground rule to these situations was clearly restricted in time and place and to a limited number of people and as such it would not seriously affect the host State's legal order.

A completely different matter was territorial rights. States concluded treaties for the military use of areas and facilities in other States from the end of the nineteenth century onwards. An example is the establishment of logistic bases to supply warships, such as the 1903 *Agreement between the US and Cuba relating to Guantanamo Bay*.[14] In contrast to the agreements mentioned above, these particular treaties contain provisions that grant rights to the visiting State over certain territories that are almost comparable to sovereign rights. For instance, Article III of the agreement between Cuba and the US states that the US "...shall exercise complete jurisdiction and control over and within said areas...". As such

---

[10] E.g., one of the exceptions is Article VI *Agreement Providing for the Reciprocal Crossing of the International Boundary Line by the Troops of their Respective Governments, in Pursuit of Savage Hostile Indians, under the Conditions hereafter Stated*; Washington, 29 July 1882 (9 *Bevans* 847 1968).

[11] Article VI *Convention between Austria and Saxony respecting the passage of troops;* Vienna, 8 April 1813 (*The Consolidated Treaty Series*, edited and annotated by Clive Parry, Vol. 62, 1812–1818, pp. 213 et seq.).

[12] In the nineteenth century conquest and colonisation were the primary reasons for stationing forces abroad; see Harkavy 2007, pp. 72 and 73.

[13] Moore's description covers the period 1790–1906; Moore 1906, Sect. 213.

[14] *Agreement between the United States and Cuba for the lease of lands for coaling and naval stations*; 23 February 1903 (avalon.law.yale.edu/20th_century/dip_cuba002.asp). The agreement is further developed: *Lease to the United States by the Government of Cuba of certain areas of land and water for naval or coaling stations in Guantanamo and Bahia Honda*; Havana, 2 July 1903. (avalon.law.yale.edu/20th_century/dip_cuba003.asp). In 1912 Cuba and the US agreed that the use of Bahia Honda would end in exchange for the extension of the area around Guantanamo Bay. This Agreement was never ratified, but overall, it was implemented. Strauss 2009, pp. 53–59.

provisions made explicit arrangements on criminal jurisdiction over foreign military personnel redundant, the ground rule does not apply here.

This approach can be regarded as indicative of the subordinate position of the host State. In the literature this form of foreign presence was sometimes referred to as occupation, which reflected the unequal relationship between the host State and the sending State.[15] This approach became obsolete after World War II and, over time, most of the arrangements establishing territorial rights were amended or came to an end. Nevertheless, there are still military forces based in areas where sending States enjoy territorial rights.[16]

2.6 The Scope of Criminal Jurisdiction

Nineteenth century practice seems to have been that the exercise of criminal jurisdiction over foreign armed forces was in the hands of the sending States as a matter of course. Furthermore, the exercise of that jurisdiction appears to be absolute in nature in the sense that the sending States' forces would be in all circumstances exempted from the criminal jurisdiction of the host States' courts. A sequence of agreements between Mexico and the US that mutually granted both States the right to pursue rebellious Indians on each other's territory illustrates this point. The agreements mention that crimes committed by the pursuing forces would be punished by the sending State.[17]

The nineteenth century's literature and case law of courts other than the US Supreme Court give a more balanced view. Various court cases make clear that host States did not fully waive their criminal jurisdiction over sailors while ashore in foreign ports. An example is the *Affaire Der*-case of 1868.[18] Machel Der, sailor on a British warship, got involved in a scuffle in Saigon, at that time part of the French colony Indo-China, in which he attacked a local police officer. The French Cour de Cassation decided that, as the crime had not taken place on board a warship but ashore, the principle of territoriality would prevail and the host State could exercise its jurisdiction.[19] This view is reflected in Article 18 of the *Règlement sur le régime légal des navires et de leurs équipages dans les ports étrangers* of 1898 of the 'Institut de Droit International':

[15] This inequity is regularly associated with imperialism and colonialism, emphasizing the unequal position of the relevant states; see Stambuk 1963, p. 155.

[16] E.g., the American use of Guantanamo Bay in Cuba and the British use of the Sovereign Base Areas in Cyprus; Article 1 *Treaty Concerning the Establishment of the Republic of Cyprus*; Nicosia, 16 August 1960 (Vol. 382 *UNTS* 1960, No. 5476).

[17] E.g., Article VI *Agreement Providing for the Reciprocal Crossing of the International Boundary Line by the Troops of their Respective Governments, in Pursuit of Savage Hostile Indians, under the Conditions hereafter Stated*; Washington, 29 July 1882 (9 *Bevans* 847 1968).

[18] Barton 1950, p. 80.

[19] Schneider 1964, p. 80.

> Si des gens du bord se trouvant à terre commettent des infractions aux lois du pays, ils peuvent être arrêtés par les agents de l'autorité territoriale et déférés à la justice locale. [20]

Nineteenth-century authors, although using the considerations in *The Exchange v. McFaddon* as a starting point, did not consider the ground rule to be absolute in character either. For instance, Lawrence indicates that armed forces "...are exempt in a greater or less degree from local jurisdiction", without further clarifying this statement, by the way.[21] Hall restricted the immunity only to those servicemen that were under the direct command of the commander of the unit:

> ...it is believed that the commanders, not only of forces in transit, through a friendly country with which no convention exists, but also of forces stationed there, assert exclusive jurisdiction in principle in respect of offences committed by persons under their command.[22]

Moore added that this case concerned organised armed forces that were exercising their right of free passage and not "...individuals merely possessing a military character".[23] What Moore, in my view, wanted to make clear was that an individual soldier may formally be under military command, but the commander may in reality not be able to exercise his power over the soldier in case the latter is located in another State.[24] Practically the commander may not be able to prosecute and punish him, in which case only the host State can exercise its jurisdiction over the soldier.

Oppenheim thought that the possibilities for sending States to assert jurisdiction were even more restricted and emphasised the position of the armed forces as organs of the sending States when in foreign territory.[25] In his opinion, the sending States could only exercise jurisdiction in case a crime had been committed at the location where the forces were based. Examples he used show that he interpreted location narrowly. He described crimes committed in the garrison of a fort and referring in particular to places where the commander had direct control over his forces.[26] According to Oppenheim, immunity applied outside the military camp only if the soldier was on duty.

---

[20] *Règlement sur le régime légal des navires et de leurs équipages dans les ports étrangers*; The Hague, 23 August 1898. In Article 20 of the 1928 Resolution of the 'Institut de Droit International', this aspect reappears.

[21] Lawrence 1885, p. 47. See Sari 2008, p. 115.

[22] Hall 1895, p. 206.

[23] J.B. Moore 1906, p. 560.

[24] E.g., Hyde 1922, pp. 432 and 434.

[25] Oppenheim 1905, p. 483.

[26] The same approach can be found in the draft regulation adopted in Latin America in 1912. Article 96 of this predecessor of the *Bustamante code* (see next chapter) regulated immunity for "crimes committed within the precincts of the camp"; mentioned in: Barton 1954, p. 344.

The previous sections show that case law and the literature give a more balanced view of the scope of the ground rule indicating that the rule applies to military personnel who are stationed on the territory of the host State as an organised military unit. The rule applies to members of the visiting armed forces on duty or while at a military camp. When a member of the forces is not on duty and outside the camp, for example in case of leave, and he commits a crime, the host State can exercise its jurisdiction.

2.7 Conclusion

This chapter has analysed the development of ideas on criminal jurisdiction over armed forces abroad during the nineteenth century. The starting point was *The Exchange v. McFaddon*-case of 1812, which is doubtlessly the most cited and discussed court decision on jurisdiction over armed forces stationed abroad. This decision has helped to define a general ground rule on the exercise of jurisdiction: A host State refrains from exercising criminal jurisdiction over armed forces of a sending State, in case it has given consent to their entry and presence on its territory, thus allowing the sending State to exercise criminal jurisdiction over its forces abroad.

The consent of the host State is a pre-condition for the ground rule to apply. Armed forces of the sending State enjoy immunity from the host State's criminal jurisdiction allowing the sending State to exercise its jurisdiction instead. In the nineteenth century the nature and scope of the extraterritorial deployment of armed forces with the consent of the host State was still rather limited in time and place. This meant that the application of the ground rule did not seriously affect the national legal order of the host State.

In my opinion it is an established rule that the consent of the host State for the entry and presence of foreign armed forces entails the waiver of its jurisdiction. State practice, case law and the literature all confirm this rule. However, the waiver of the host State does not always imply full immunity of the forces. The only situation in which host States fully refrain from exercising their jurisdiction is when the sending State is granted territorial rights over an area in another State. This implies that the scope of the ground rule must be further refined. The ground rule does not seem to apply when the link between the visiting military force and its actions as an organ of the Sending State becomes less strong. The literature suggests that the scope of the ground rule is delineated by armed forces abroad as an official organ of the sending State. Host States only waive their jurisdiction over members of visiting armed forces belonging to a military unit and under the direct command of their commander. This is the case when, for example, the forces are located at a military camp or are on duty outside that camp.

The next chapters analyse the application of the ground rule to visiting armed forces in the following situations: when allied forces are stationed on co-belligerent territory during an armed conflict, when forces participate in crisis management operations and when they are abroad partaking in international military cooperation activities.

References

Barton GP (1950) Foreign armed forces: immunity from criminal jurisdiction. Br Yearb Int Law 27:186–235
Barton GP (1954) Foreign armed forces: qualified jurisdictional immunity. Br Yearb Int Law 31:341–370
Fenet PA (1827) Recuil complet des travaux prèparatoires du Code Civil. Tome huitième, Paris
Hall WE (1895) A Treatise on international law. Stevens & Sons, Oxford
Harkavy RE (2007) Strategic basing and the great powers, 1200–2000. Routledge, Oxon
Hyde CC (1922) International law. Chiefly as interpreted and applied by the United States, vol I. Little, Brown, and company, Boston
Lawrence TJ (1885) A handbook of public international law. Deighton, Bell and Co., Cambridge
Lazareff S (1971) Status of military forces under current international law. Sijthoff, Leiden
Liivoja R (2011) An axiom of military law. Applicability of national criminal law to military personnel and associated civilians abroad. Centre of Excellence in Global Governance Research, Helsinki
Moore JB (1906) A digest of international law as embodied in diplomatic discussions, treaties and other international agreements, international awards, the decision of municipal courts, and the writings of jurists, vol II. Washington
Oppenheim L (1905) International law, a treatise, vol I, peace. Longmans, Green and Co, London
Re ED (1956) The NATO status of forces agreement and international law. Northwest Univ Law Rev 53(8):349–394
Sari A (2008) The jurisdictional immunities of visiting forces under public international law. A case study of the European security and defence policy. Not published; on file with author
Schneider G (1964) Die Exterritorialität der Truppen in strafrechtlicher Hinsicht, unter besonderer Berücksichtigung der das deutsche Territorium betreffenden Truppenverträge. Albert-Ludwig Universität, Saarbrücken
Stambuk G (1963) American military forces abroad: their impact on the western state system. Ohio State University Press, Columbus
Strauß J (1957) Strafrechtliche Probleme bei der Stationierung von Truppen auf fremdem Hoheitsgebiet Albert-Ludwigs-Universität
Strauss MJ (2009) The Leasing of Guantanamo Bay. Praeger Security International, Westport
Thibaudeau AC (1827) Mémoires sur le consulat. 1799 à 1804. Ponthieu et Cie, Paris

Chapter 3
Foreign Armed Forces on Allied Territory During Armed Conflict

Abstract The status of visiting armed forces and especially criminal jurisdiction over those forces depends, inter alia, on the framework within they operate on foreign territory. When stationed on allied territory during armed conflict the status of forces is generally set out in formal agreements with the host States from World War I on. These agreements show that the ground rule is generally applied in full, subjecting the visiting forces to the exclusive criminal jurisdiction of their respective sending States. Only insofar operational conditions allow host States can exercise their jurisdiction over the visiting forces to a certain extent.

Contents

3.1 Introduction

In the previous chapter the ground rule was formulated as: A host State refrains from exercising criminal jurisdiction over visiting armed forces of a sending State, in case it has given its consent to their entry into and presence on its territory, thus allowing the sending State to exercise criminal jurisdiction over its forces abroad. This chapter analyses the application of this rule within the framework of armed forces stationed on the territory of allied States during armed conflict.

International armed conflicts are rarely limited to the territory of just two States. Often, belligerents are directly supported by armed forces from allied States.

© T.M.C. ASSER PRESS and the author 2015
J. Voetelink, *Status of Forces: Criminal Jurisdiction over Military Personnel Abroad*,
DOI 10.1007/978-94-6265-057-2_3

Consequently, the stationing of allied forces on co-belligerent territory during armed conflict is an accepted practice. World War I was different from previous conflicts because of the duration and scale. Huge military forces amassed on the territory of allied states to fight a common enemy. This practice was repeated during World War II and other large-scale armed conflicts, such as the Korean War in the early 1950s.

In the nineteenth century the exercise of jurisdiction over foreign forces had not given rise to much discussion. The fact that the scope of the ground rule had not been exactly delineated did not encourage States to formally negotiate the status of armed forces deployed abroad. At the beginning of World War I all this changed, when States started to make explicit arrangements on the status of forces in formal agreements. For this reason, World War I is the starting point for the analysis of the ground rule in cases where allied forces are based on the territory of allied States during armed conflict. This chapter focuses both on World War I (Sect. 3.2) and World War II (Sect. 3.3), as it was during these wars that the first SOFAs were adopted and then further developed. These agreements and those adopted after World War II (Sect. 3.4), as well as case law and the literature interpreting the agreements, serve as a basis for analysing the ground rule in today's armed conflicts (Sect. 3.5). As stated before, the status of forces on enemy territory has a completely different legal basis, i.e. the law of armed conflict, and will therefore not be discussed in this chapter.

3.2 World War I Practice

During World War I military cooperation led to the large-scale and long-term stationing of armed forces on allied territory for the first time in history. These forces were deployed as national contingents that remained under the command of the sending States. The Allied Powers set out the status of the forces in a number of almost identical bilateral international agreements. The Central Powers (Germany and Austria-Hungary and their allies), on the other hand, adopted military agreements at executive level.

3.2.1 Allied Powers

Within 2 weeks after the outbreak of World War I, on 14 August 1914, Belgium and France concluded the first agreement.[1] The core provision reads:

> chaque armée garde sa juridiction quant aux faits susceptibles de lui nuire, quels que soient les territoires où elle se trouve et la nationalité de l'inculpé[2]

---

[1] *Agreement between Belgium and France relative for the better prosecution of acts prejudicial to the armed forces;* Brussels, 14 August 1914 (*The Consolidated Treaty Series,* edited and annotated by Clive Parry, Vol. 220, 1914–1915, p. 274).

[2] Chalufour 1927, p. 47. Translated as "each army retains its jurisdiction with respect to acts capable of prejudicing it, whatever territory where it is found or the nationality of the culprit" in: Stanger 1957/1958, pp. 116–117.

Table 3.1 Overview of status agreements between the allied powers during World War I

14 Aug 1914	Belgium–France	Bilateral	All forces maintain jurisdiction over crimes committed against them
Nov 1914	Belgium–France	Bilateral	Supplementary agreement to the agreement of 1914
15 Dec 1915	France–UK	Bilateral	Exclusive jurisdiction of tribunal over their own staff (armées d'opérations)
29 Jan 1916	Belgium–France	Bilateral	Similar to agreement FRA—UK
15 Apr 1916	Belgium–UK	Bilateral	Similar to agreement FRA—UK
14 Dec 1916	France–Serbia	Bilateral	Similar to agreement FRA—UK
4 Jul/13 Aug 1917	France–Italy	Bilateral	Similar to agreement FRA—UK
15 Oct 1917	France–Portugal	Bilateral	Similar to agreement FRA—UK
3/14 Jan 1918	France–US	Bilateral	Similar to agreement FRA—UK
24 May 1918	France–Siam	Unilateral	FRA recognises the exclusive jurisdiction of Siam tribunals over their staff
5 Jul/6 Sep 1918	Belgium–US	Bilateral	Similar to agreement FRA—UK

This provision, however, did not yet focus on the criminal jurisdiction over the visiting forces. Allied agreements of a later date were fundamentally different and recognised the exclusive jurisdiction of sending States over their own armed forces. The first provision of this type was included in the agreement between France and the UK of 15 December 1915[3] (for the complete agreement, see Annex A), in which both States declare:

> …to recognize during the present war the exclusive competence of the tribunals of their respective Armies with regard to persons belonging to these Armies, in whatever territory and whatever nationality the accused may be.

Similar provisions were central to subsequent allied agreements (see Table 3.1).[4] Reference in the agreement to armed forces as 'Armies' warrants special attention. The French version of the agreement uses the more specific term 'armées

[3] *Declaration between France and Great Britain respecting military penal jurisdiction*; London, 15 December 1915 (*The Consolidated Treaty Series,* edited and annotated by Clive Parry, Vol. 221, 1915–1916, p. 227; *The London Gazette*, 31 December 1915).

[4] The agreements sometimes regulated specific aspects in different ways. For instance, in the American military legal system personnel of organisations such as the Red Cross or the Salvation Army could be subject to US military law. As a result, the agreements in which the US was a party also contained provisions regulating the criminal jurisdiction of the US over members of these organisations: e.g., *Exchange of notes between France and the United States respecting the jurisdiction of courts martial*; Washington, 3 and 4 January 1918 (*The Consolidated Treaty Series,* edited and annotated by Clive Parry, Vol. 223, 1917–1918, pp. 39 et seq.; *Foreign Relations of the United States, Papers relating to the foreign relations of the United States*, 1918, Supplement 2, pp. 735–737).

d'opérations'. In the Belgian-UK agreement, which was concluded a month later, the wording 'armies in the field' appeared, which has, as will be discussed later, a more restricted meaning.

3.2.2 Central Powers

According to Mettgenberg, Germany considered extraterritoriality of foreign forces as a rule of international law[5] with the restriction that it applied to "geschlossener Truppenverbände". Viewed from this angle, individual foreign servicemen in Germany were only subject to their home States' criminal jurisdiction while on duty. Servicemen on leave and servicemen that had left their garrison without permission were subject to German jurisdiction.[6] This is exemplified in the criminal case against a Greek soldier belonging to the Greek Fourth Army Corps who fled to Germany.[7] The German judge concluded he had jurisdiction over the soldier, as the Greek Army Corps was not in Germany in *dienstlicher Eigenschaft* and their presence on German territory was not on orders from the competent Greek authorities. In fact, they had sought refuge in Germany against their orders.

Agreements between the Central Powers with respect to the stationing of forces on each other's territory were mainly adopted at the executive level, for instance, as military agreements concluded by the general staffs.[8] They were not all formally published, obscuring details on the practice of the parties. However, various sources indicate that, generally, sending States had exclusive jurisdiction over their forces. A joint decision (*Erlaß*) of the German Ministers of Justice, the Interior and War of 27 May 1916 stated the following with regard to Austrian-Hungarian forces on German territory:

> Strafanzeigen gegen Angehörige von österreichisch-ungarischen auf deutsches Gebiet Eingerückten Truppenteilen sind, soweit nicht eine unmittelbare Abgabe an die ortsanwesende österreichisch-ungarische Militärbehörde einfacher ist, der nächsten deutschen Militär-(Kommando-) Behörde zu übergeben; im Falle der Festnahme ist ihr der Beschuldigte unverzüglich zuzuführen. Dieser Behörde liegt die Weiterleitung an die nächste österreichisch-ungarische Militärbehörde zur Veranlassung des weiteren an zuständiger Stelle ab.[9]

---

[5] Mettgenberg 1929, p. 25.

[6] Id., p. 26.

[7] Ibid. On 26 September 1916 this unit sought German protection to maintain its neutral position and subsequentely enjoyed, fully armed and equipped, 'Gastrecht' in Görlitz, Germany.

[8] Mettgenberg mentioned the stationing of Austrian units in Germany and the corresponding '*besonderen Vereinbarungen*'; ibid.

[9] *Strafanzeigen gegen österreichisch-ungarische Militärpersonen*; Berlin, 27 May 1916, Justiz-Ministerialblatt für die preußische Gesetzgebung und Rechtspflege (Preuß. JMBl), Berlin, 1916, Band 135; Ministerialblatt für die preußische Innere Verwaltung (MinBl f. D. Innere Verwaltung), 1916, Band 156 and Armee-Verordnungsblatt 1916, Band 237.

This regulation suggests that criminal offences committed by members of the Austrian-Hungarian armed forces in Germany were judicially reviewed as soon as possible by the Austrian-Hungarian military authorities, or if necessary, through German military authorities. The explanatory notes to the publication of the joint decision in the German *Armee-Verordnungsblatt* stated that similar measures were adopted for German forces on the territory of Austria-Hungary. In Turkey, the legal status of the German military mission and the combined German-Turkish unit *Heersegruppe Yildirim* (*Falke*) was laid down in the military agreement of 18 November 1916.[10] The literature suggests that both States applied the 'Recht der Fahne', which meant that the German forces fell under exclusive German criminal jurisdiction.[11]

3.3 World War II Practice

In comparison to World War I, the Allied Powers' practice[12] during World War II gives a more mixed impression. Status arrangement continued to be set out in treaties; however, these agreements were more elaborate documents than during World War I and comprised provisions on other subjects than criminal jurisdiction only. Although in most cases sending States had exclusive criminal jurisdiction over their forces, host States did not always waive their jurisdiction over foreign forces to the full extent.

The agreements concluded by the UK and the US in their capacity as sending States contain, without exception, a host State's waiver of their rights to exercise criminal jurisdiction over visiting US and UK forces.[13] In cases where no agreements were adopted, practice shows that the host States did not exercise jurisdiction over UK and US forces. For instance, the Netherlands never prosecuted UK or US forces on the territory of the Netherlands Antilles or US forces on the territory

[10] Schneider 1964, p. 69 and Wunderlich 1932 pp. 86, 89.

[11] Its legal basis was § 7 of the MStGB (Militärstrafgesetzbuch): "*der deutsche Soldat wird nach deutschem Rechte bestraft, wo er sich auch befindet*", Strauß 1957, p. 15. A similar provision existed for Turkish soldiers Wunderlich 1932, p. 89.

[12] There is no information available on SOFAs between Germany, Italy, Japan, and their allies.

[13] E.g., agreement between UK and Ethiopia: para 5(a), Annex to Article VI *Agreement for the regulation of mutual relations*; Addis Ababa, 19 December 1944 (*UNTS* 1951, No. 272): "…no member of the mission shall be subject to the criminal jurisdiction of the courts Ethiopia" and the agreement between Egypt and the US: *Jurisdiction over criminal offenses committed by the armed forces of the United States in Egypt*: *agreement between the United States of America and Egypt*; Cairo, 2 March 1943 (*EAS* 1944, No. 356): "…the Egyptian Government has decided to accord… immunity from jurisdiction in criminal matters to members of the United States Forces in Egypt".

of Surinam during World War II.[14] In the court case of *In re Gilbert* a Brazilian judge concluded that the Brazilian courts did not have jurisdiction over a soldier who had killed a Brazilian citizen while on guard duty, and that the US judiciary bodies could exercise jurisdiction instead. Apparently, the fact that the US forces assisted Brazil in the "…emergency situation arising out of the need for the defence of the nation…" was decisive for this conclusion.[15]

One of the few exceptions to the exclusive jurisdiction of the US over their forces can be found in the *Leased Bases Agreement*[16] between the US and the UK, which built on the *Destroyers for Bases Agreement.*[17] Article IV of the *Leased Bases Agreement* restricted US criminal jurisdiction over its forces as the UK did not waive its jurisdiction with regard to offences that were not of a military nature and committed outside the leased areas.[18] With regard to all other offences, the US had "the absolute right in first instance to assume and exercise jurisdiction".

To the US it was self-evident that the allied forces temporarily in the US to participate in courses and training enjoyed immunity from criminal jurisdiction. According to the US, international law recognises:

> …the immunity from local jurisdiction in criminal matters of members of the armed forces of a foreign sovereign on the territory by permission or with the consent of the local sovereign.[19]

---

[14] Dutch National Archive, The Hague, Archief Ministerie van Marine: (Militaire) instanties en onderdelen in de gebiedsdelen Curaçao en Suriname, 1934–1947, nummer toegang 2.12.33, inventarisnummer 247, Letter of the Secretary of the Navy to the Secretary for Foreing Affairs, Exercise of jurisdiction by Dutch courts martial on US Territory, London 30 April 1945, nr. A 18/9/4/45. No SOFA was concluded between the Netherlands, the UK and the US for these overseas territories.

[15] Supreme Federal Court 22 November 1944, *In Re Gilbert* (*Admiral Ingram Camp Case*), ILR 13, p. 86.

[16] *Agreement for use and operation of naval and airbases*; London, 27 March 1941 (*AJIL* Vol. 35, No. 3, Supplement: Official Documents (July 1941), pp. 134–159). This agreement was adopted prior to the US's entry into war.

[17] *Destroyers for Bases Agreement, Exchange of notes*; London and Washington, 2 September 1940 (www.history.navy.mil/faqs/faq59-24.htm. Accessed November 2014). This agreement served as the basis for the transfer of 50 old American destroyers to the UK. In exchange the UK leased its naval and air bases in Bermuda, the Bahamas, Jamaica, Saint Lucia, Trinidad, Antigua and British Guiana; King 1942, p. 533.

[18] King 1942, p. 555. *Note* The US had not yet declared war.

[19] Memorandum of the US to the Canadian government in this case: The Supreme Court of Canada 3 August 1942, *Reference re Exemption of United States Forces from Proceedings in Canadian Criminal Courts*, ILR 12, pp. 124–133. Mention of this is made in: Stanger 1957/1958, p. 79.

This interpretation is clearly reflected in subsequent US legislation[20] and, for instance, the draft agreements of 1941 and 1942 proposed by the US to the Netherlands to regulate the stationing of US forces in Surinam. Article 1(1) reads:

> United States military authorities shall have exclusive jurisdiction as provided by international law over their own forces in all respect...[21]

There were certain circumstances under which foreign armed forces would not always enjoy full immunity from the criminal jurisdiction of the host States' courts. These cases particularly concerned European forces that sought refuge abroad after the German invasion of their countries. In France, the newly established Czechoslovakian armed forces were even fully subject to the French military criminal law and courts martial.[22]

Most agreements, however, did not completely deny States jurisdiction over their armed forces that had sought refuge on the territory of another State.[23] In the UK, the *Allied Forces Act* and some bilateral agreements, concluded between the UK as host State and sending States, contained a provision on the status of the forces that had fled their countries.[24] These agreements restricted the sending

---

[20] The Act of 30 June 1944, *Act to implement the jurisdiction of service courts of friendly foreign forces within the United States, and for other purposes* (58 Stat. 643; 22 U.S.C. 701–702) implicitly assumed the existence of the foreign courts' jurisdiction in the US and allowed for American assistance in procedures conducted by foreign courts in the US, such as arresting suspects. After the US President's promulgation, the Act became applicable to foreign forces; Bathurst 1946, p. 341 and Barton 1949, p. 407.

[21] Dutch National Archive, The Hague, Archief Gouverneur van Suriname; Geheim archief 1887–1951, Nummer toegang 2.10.18, inventarisnummer 370, Concept Agreement covering the maintenance of the Armed Forces of the United States of America cooperating with the forces of the Netherlands in the Netherlands colony of Surinam, April 1942. The provision can be interpreted in various ways. The Attorney General at the Court of Justice in Surinam seems to have opted for the interpretation allowing the US to exercise jurisdiction to the extent allowed under international law; Dutch National Archive, The Hague, Archief Gouverneur van Suriname; Geheim archief 1887–1951, nummer toegang 2.10.18, inventarisnummer 370, Letter of the Attorney General to the Court of Justice in Surinam to the Governor of Surinam; Paramaribo 28 January 1942.

[22] Article IV(b) *Military Agreement Regarding the Reconstruction of the Czechoslovak Army in France*; Paris, 2 October 1939 (published in: 1942 *Czechoslovak Yearbook of International Law*, pp. 232–234).

[23] However, Poland did have jurisdiction over the forces it was to establish in France. Article 1 *Protocol relating to the organisation of Polish Military Tribunal in France*, to the *Agreement between France and Poland concerning the Reconstitution of the Polish Army in France*; Paris, 4 January 1940 (British and Foreign State Papers, Vol. 144, London 1952, pp. 407–412). The agreement shows that France waived the exercise of its criminal jurisdiction over Polish soldiers.

[24] On 25 October 1940, the UK concluded the first of these agreements with Czechoslovakia. Subsequent agreements, including the ones with the Norway and the Netherlands, were similar to that agreement.

States' criminal jurisdiction over their forces as the agreement with Norway illustrates[25]:

> the offences of murder, manslaughter and rape shall be tried only by the Civil Courts of the United Kingdom. (Article 3)
>
> Acts or omissions constituting offences against the law of the United Kingdom other than murder, manslaughter and rape will be liable to be tried by the Civil Courts of the United Kingdom. (Article 4)[26]

British rules had a direct effect on legislation in the British colonies and dominions of the Commonwealth of Nations (hereafter: the Commonwealth). Their legislation had been based on the *Allied Forces Act* and provided the visiting allied forces with rights similar to the ones applicable in the UK.[27]

The Soviet Union also restricted the criminal jurisdiction of sending States over their forces that had sought refuge within Soviet territory. The status of Polish forces was regulated in a military agreement of 14 August 1941.[28] Article 8 states that Polish soldiers on Russian territory:

> ...will be subject to Polish military laws and decrees. Polish military courts will be established in the units for dealing with military offences and crimes against the establishment, the safety, the routine or the discipline of the Polish Army.

However:

> For crimes against the State soldiers of the Polish Army on the territory of the U.S.S.R. will be answerable to the military courts of the U.S.S.R.

---

[25] *Appendix IV (Relating to jurisdiction over Members of the Norwegian Armed Forces) to the Armed Forces Agreement between His Majesty's Government in the United Kingdom and the Royal Norwegian Government in Respect of the Norwegian Armed Forces in the United Kingdom*; 28 May 1941. home.online.no/~gestrom/history/treaties.htm. Accessed November 2014.

[26] A provision similar to Article 4 is included in the *Allied Forces Act*. The Polish Court Martial used this provision as the legal basis for concluding that the UK did not have jurisdiction over a Polish reservist accused of stealing (Polish Court Martial in Great Britain 6 June 1941, *Allied Forces (Polish Court of Honour) case*, ILR 10). Likewise, the British judge used it to exercise jurisdiction in the case of a shooting incident in which a Czechoslovakian soldier had killed a colleague (High Court, Warwick Assizes 11 March 1942, *Rex v. Navratil*, ILR 11).

[27] In the Colonies on the basis of the *Allied Forces (Application of Acts to Colonies, &c) (No. 1)* Order of 1941 and in the Dominions on the basis of national legislation that used the *Allied Forces Act* as a model from which it only deviated in the regulation of some details; Barton 1949, p. 406. For instance, jurisdiction over Dutch forces based in, inter alia, Australia and Canada was regulated in this way: Australia: *National Security (Allied Forces) Regulations*, December 1941 and Canada: *Foreign Forces Order*, April 1941. Mentioned in: Barton 1949, p. 406.

[28] *Polish-Soviet Military Agreement*; Moscow, 14 August 1941 (Polish-Soviet Relations 1918–1943, Official Documents, p. 126). The agreement is an annex to the *Agreement between the USSR and the Polish Government-in-exile concerning resumption of diplomatic relations and mutual aid in the war against Germany*; London, 30 July 1941 (mentioned in: Slusser and Triska 1959).

As a result, Polish servicemen were subject to Soviet criminal jurisdiction in case of crimes committed against the Soviet Union. A similar agreement with Czechoslovakia was adopted on 27 September 1941.[29]

It is not entirely clear to what extent these agreements allowed Poland and Czechoslovakia to exercise jurisdiction over their own forces. The Soviet Union applied the concept of 'crimes against the State' in a broad sense covering counter-revolutionary crimes and especially dangerous crimes against the Soviet State.[30] The repressive nature of the Soviet regime at the time leads to the presumption that under Soviet law a crime would easily be interpreted as a crime against the State, limiting the possibility for sending States to exercise criminal jurisdiction over their forces.[31]

As World War II entered its final stage, the Soviet Union, the UK and the US and several other States adopted the so-called Civil Affairs Agreements. These treaties addressed the administration of occupied territories in Europe and Asia during and directly after the liberation. One of the first agreements was concluded with Norway on 16 May 1944, which served as an example agreement for a number of States.[32] On the basis of these Civil Affairs Agreements allied forces exercised exclusive criminal jurisdiction over their forces on the territories of the occupied States during the liberation.[33] Although not mentioned in the agreements adopted by the Soviet Union, the wording of the documents leads to the conclusion that the exercise of the jurisdiction over Soviet forces by the host State was excluded.[34]

---

[29] *Military Aagreement between the Soviet High Command and the High Command of Czechoslovakia*; Moscow, 27 September 1941 (mentioned in: Robert M. Slusser, Jan F. Triska, *A Calendar of Soviet Treaties* 1917–1957, Stanford 1959).

[30] Ginsburgs 1966, pp. 378–379.

[31] There is no knowledge of case law in which these agreements are addressed.

[32] Donnison 1961, p. 40. Civil Affairs Agreements were concluded with Belgium, China, France, Greece, Italy, Luxembourg, the Netherlands (referring to both the Netherlands and the Dutch East Indies), Norway, Poland and Czechoslovakia (see Table 3.2).

[33] E.g., Para 8 of the Civil Affairs Agreement concluded between the US and the Netherlands *Agreement between the United States of America and the Netherlands respecting the arrangements for civil administration and jurisdiction in Netherlands territory liberated by an Allied Expeditionary Force*; London, 16 May 1944 (Vol. 132 *UNTS* 1952, No. 440; *TIAS 2212*). This agreement and the identical agreement between the UK and the Netherlands were together referred to as the 'Legal Agreement'.

[34] E.g., Para 6 *Agreement Regarding Relations between the Chinese Administration and the Soviet Commander-in-Chief of the Soviet Forces after Entry of Soviet Troops into the "Three Eastern Provinces" of China during the Present Joint Military Operations against Japan*; Moscow, 14 August 1945 (The China White Paper 1949, pp. 592–593).

Table 3.2 Overview of civil affairs agreements

8 May 1944	SU	Czechoslovakia	Agreement concerning the relationship between the Czechoslovak administration and the soviet commander-in-chief on the entry of Soviet troops into Czechoslovak territory[a]
16 May 1944	US	Norway	Memorandum of agreement between Norway and the United States of America respecting the arrangements for civil administration and jurisdiction in Norwegian territory liberated by an allied expeditionary force[b]
16 May 1944	US	Netherlands	Agreement between the United States of America and the Netherlands respecting the arrangements for civil administration and jurisdiction in Netherlands territory liberated by an allied expeditionary force[c]
16 May 1944	UK	Netherlands	Memorandum of agreement regarding civil administration and jurisdiction in Netherlands territory liberated by an allied expeditionary force[d]
16 May 1944	UK	Belgium	Exchange of notes (with annexed memorandum of agreement) constituting an agreement concerning civil administration and jurisdiction in Belgian territory liberated by an allied expeditionary force[e]
16 May 1944	US	Id.	Agreement between the United States of America and Belgium respecting the arrangements for civil administration and jurisdiction in Belgian territory liberated by an allied expeditionary force[f]
26 July 1944	SU	Poland	Agreement on relations between the Soviet commander-in-chief and the Polish administration after entry of Soviet troops into the territory of Poland[g]
27 July 1944	US	Luxembourg	Memorandum of Agreement between the United States of America and luxembourg respecting the arrangements for civil administration and jurisdiction in Norwegian territory liberated by an allied expeditionary force[h]
25 Aug 1944	US	France	Exchange of notes constituting an agreement between the United States of America and France relating to civil administration and jurisdiction in liberated French territory[i]
24 Nov 1944	UK	Greece	Exchange of notes constituting an agreement between the United States of America and Greece[j]
10 Dec 1944	US	Netherlands	Principles governing arrangements for civil administration and jurisdiction in Netherlands territory in the southwest Pacific area[k]
31 Jan 1945	US	Greece	Memorandum of agreement between Greece and the United States of America regarding questions concerning civil administration, jurisdiction and relief arising out of military operations in Greek territory[l]

(continued)

Table 3.2 (continued)

14 Aug 1945	SU	China	Agreement regarding relations between the chinese administration and the Soviet commander-in-chief of the Soviet forces after entry of soviet troops into the "three eastern provinces" of China during the present joint military operations against Japan
24 Aug 1945	UK	Netherlands	Principles governing arrangements for civil administration and jurisdiction in Netherlands Indies territory in the South East Asia command[m]
28 Sept 1945	US	Italy	No information available
3 Sept 1947	US	Italy	Exchange of Notes (with annex) constituting an agreement relating to military and civil affairs with respect to (1) rights and privileges of United States forces in Italy, and (2) the transfer of responsibility from the allied military government to the Italian Government[n]

[a] archive.org/details/Czechoslovak-russianTreatyMay81944. Accessed November 2014
[b] Vol. 67 *UNTS* 1950, No. 223; *TIAS* 1514
[c] Vol. 132 *UNTS* 1952, No. 440
[d] On file with author
[e] Vol. 90 *UNTS* 1951, No. 266; TS No. 19 (1947)
[f] *FRUS* 1944, Vol. III, pp. 296/299
[g] In: Rothstein, p. 94
[h] 9 *Bevans* 714
[i] Vol. 138 *UNTS* 1952, No. 449; *TIAS* 2313
[j] 8 *Bevans* 385
[k] *FRUS* 1944, Vol V
[l] Ibid
[m] On file with author
[n] Vol. 67 *UNTS* No. 863

3.4 Post World War II Practice

Although there have not been armed conflicts comparable to either of the World Wars since 1945, many other armed conflicts were fought in which States have supported their allies by sending armed forces. This section discusses some examples.

In 1950, after the armed attack on the Republic of Korea (South Korea) by forces of North Korea, the UN Security Council recommended UN Member States to render assistance to South Korea.[35] The armed forces provided by States responding to the request were placed under "a unified command under the United States of America".[36] The US and South Korea agreed on the exclusive jurisdiction of the US

[35] *UN Doc* S/RES/83 (1950).

[36] *UN Doc* S/RES/84 (1950).

over its forces in South Korea.[37] However, the agreement did not apply to servicemen from other States that were under the direct command of an American commander and neither these States nor the United Nations concluded such an agreement with South Korea.[38] Practically speaking, war-torn South Korea was not capable of exercising its criminal jurisdiction over the foreign forces on its territory. So, sending States exercised jurisdiction over their forces without objections of South Korea.[39]

During that period of time, the conflict in Vietnam was building up. Initially, the US only sent a Military Assistance Advisory Group (MAAG), whose status was based on the annex to the *Agreement for Mutual Defense Assistance in Indochina*.[40] The treaty included the provision that members of the MAAG would be attached to the Embassy and would enjoy the same status as diplomats resulting in full immunity from criminal jurisdiction for US military personnel in Vietnam. Later, when the US got actively engaged in the conflict, this provision also applied to the hundreds of thousands of American armed forces.[41]

On 2 August 1990, 5 days after the annexation of Kuwait by neighbouring Iraq, the US initiated operation Desert Shield to prevent a possible Iraqi invasion of Saudi Arabia. Six months later, on 16 January 1991, operation Desert Storm was launched against the Iraqi armed forces in Kuwait and Iraq. No agreement on the status of the forces participating in the operation had been concluded with Saudi Arabia, as this country seemed to prefer not to conclude any formal agreements at all.[42] As the US prosecuted criminal offences committed by its servicemen in Saudi Arabia, it seems likely that Saudi Arabia had agreed not to exercise any jurisdiction over the American forces.[43]

After Iraqi forces had been expelled from its territory, Kuwait fully supported subsequent military operations in Iraq, such as the 2003 invasion of Iraq by a US-led military coalition (Operation Iraqi Freedom). The agreement on the status

---

[37] *Exchange of notes constituting an agreement between the United States of America and the Republic of Korea relating to jurisdiction over offenses by United States forces in Korea*; Taejun, 12 July 1950 (Vol. 222 *UNTS* 1955, No. 3029).

[38] Bowett 1964, p. 57. The only agreement between Korea and the UN concerned two specialised bodies operational in Korea: *Exchange of letters constituting an agreement between the United Nations and Korea regarding privileges and immunities to be enjoyed by the United Nations in the Republic of Korea*; Pusan, 21 September 1951 (Vol. 104 *UNTS* 1951, No. 322).

[39] E.g., The Netherlands established a special court martial for the Netherlands Detachment United Nations (NDVN) that exercised its powers with the implicit consent of South Korea; Buurman van Vreeden 1953, pp. 354–355.

[40] *Agreement between the United States of America and Cambodja, France, Laos and Viet-Nam for mutual defence assistance in Indochina*; Saigon, 23 December 1950 (Vol. 185 *UNTS* 1954, No. 2456).

[41] Prugh 1975, p. 88. As Vietnam and the US had decided not to conclude a new SOFA, the SOFA of 1950 was the only agreement that applied to all US forces; Borch 2001, p. 6, fn. 7.

[42] As can be deduced from the negotiations on Saudi support to the US forces; Borch 2001, p. 135.

[43] Id, pp. 187–191.

of US forces in Kuwait is classified. Allegedly, the US exercised exclusive criminal jurisdiction over its armed forces.[44] During the period following the invasion, the Coalition forces in Iraq were considered to be an occupying power in the context of the law of armed conflict. Consequently, no specific regulations were adopted.

After the US-led attack on the Taliban regime in Afghanistan, the US negotiated a SOFA with the newly established Afghan authorities (see Chap. 1), which allowed the US to exercise exclusive criminal jurisdiction over its forces. Other States, such as the Netherlands, did not follow suit and refrained from entering into a SOFA applying to their forces in Afghanistan participating in Operation Enduring Freedom. In view of the wartime conditions under which their forces operated it is reasonable to assume they considered the law of armed conflict to be a sufficient legal basis for the status of their forces.

3.5 Analysing International Practice

The issue of the status of armed forces active on or passing through the territory of an allied State, particularly the issue of the exercise of criminal jurisdiction over these forces continues to be a focal point for States cooperating in times of armed conflict. In the analysis of the international practice during both world wars, the Allied Forces' use of formal international agreements with respect to the status of forces stands out.

It is not fully clear why States took recourse to these instruments to deal with the status of their forces at that time in particular. A number of arguments can be put forward. First, some authors regard the stationing of forces on allied territory as a qualified form of occupation.[45] Defining the situation as such means, however, that there is no general legal regime that applies to the 'occupation with consent', contrary to situations of hostile occupation during armed conflicts to which the law of armed conflict applies. Therefore, this type of occupation could only be governed by formal international agreements providing the legal basis and delineating the conditions for the 'occupation'.[46]

Second, the use of agreements makes it possible to settle other aspects with respect to the temporary basing of forces as well. Initially, many SOFAs only addressed the issue of criminal jurisdiction over visiting forces.[47] Over the years

---

[44] Katzman 2008, p. 2.

[45] 'Conventional occupation', Robin 1913. p. 1; 'Pacific occupation', JAGS Text No. 11 1944, p. 13, Dinstein 2009, p. 35; 'Non-belligerent occupation', Arai-Takahashi 2009, p. 41; Occupation consentie', Clunet 1918, p. 516.

[46] Robin 1913, pp. 14–15.

[47] Additional matters were often included in separate agreements. For instance, in 1944 the UK and the US adopted an agreement relating to damages. Nowadays, this topic is almost always automatically incorporated in SOFAs: *Exchange of notes constituting an agreement between the United States of America and the United Kingdom relating to claims for damages resulting from acts of armed forces personnel*; London 29 February and 28 March 1944 (Vol. 15 *UNTS* 1948, No. 104).

that aspect has remained a key part of SOFAs, but a wide range of other topics were also included in agreements concluded after World War II.

Third, the literature reveals an ambiguity about the scope of the ground rule, mentioned in Chap. 2.[48] In this context, Baty noted that the rights of visiting forces were "exceedingly obscure" and suggested it would be better to set out these rights in formal agreements.[49] The fact that the first agreements merely focused on criminal jurisdiction and were sometimes subject to long negotiations[50] may be an indication of the divergent opinions on this matter. Be that as it may, States were conscious of the complexity of the issue and the opposing interests of the parties involved.[51]

Fourth, the unprecedented large scale and long-lasting presence of armed forces on the territory of other allied States may also have contributed to the conclusion of formal agreements.[52] These conditions put a heavy burden on the host States, for example by the increasing chance of criminal offences. This could have been the reason for both host States and sending States to further delineate the scope of the ground rule by international agreement.

A final argument for concluding formal agreements can be that sending States wanted to have exclusive jurisdiction over their forces during wartime. Under the more balanced approach to the ground rule, as could be found in the literature and case law, sending States could not always exercise jurisdiction over their servicemen, for example if a crime was committed off duty and outside military premises. Formal international agreements would be a way to secure the sending States' jurisdiction under all circumstances.

It can be concluded that States generally prefer the widest application of the ground rule within the framework of armed conflict. In the majority of the wartime SOFAs, the allied States agree to the exclusive criminal jurisdiction of the sending States over their forces. Only when hostilities do not take place in the host States or the threat of war is less strong, may host States exercise jurisdiction over visiting forces to some extent. This situation occurs when visiting forces are not based in or close to the area of operations or when they are not directly involved in the hostilities. The use of the wording 'armies in the field' or 'armées d'opérations' in World War I agreements denotes that SOFAs may not have been intended to apply outside the area of actual conflict, as was concluded in the *Aughet v. The King* case.[53]

When a Belgian soldier was indicted by a British court for injuring a Belgian colleague in London, the Belgian authorities referred to the agreement of 1916 in which Belgium and the UK agreed on the exclusive jurisdiction of the national

48 Supervielle 1994, p. 7.

49 Mentioned in: Re 1956, p. 379.

50 The negotiations between the US and the UK during World War I even lasted until the end of the war and the withdrawal of the forces, which made a final agreement unnecessary.

51 Stanger 1957/1958, p. 139.

52 Kuratowski 1942, p. 3.

53 Mentioned in Barton 1950, pp. 189 et seq.

courts over their forces. However, the British government informed the court that the agreement was not applicable in the UK, because neither of the Belgian servicemen was part of the Army of Operations at the moment the offence was committed. Thus being far away from the 'zone of operations', the Belgian court did not have jurisdiction in the UK. Other examples of host States exercising jurisdiction over visiting forces were the agreements concluded by the Soviet Union and the UK during World War II with respect to foreign armed forces personnel that had found refuge in these States.

However, practice shows that the examples described above are rather exceptions to the rule. During armed conflict, allied forces generally fall under the exclusive jurisdiction of the sending States. The purpose of sending States' forces and the circumstances under which they operate contribute to this practice, as shall be discussed in Part III. The final part of this chapter will briefly address the circumstances under which forces are stationed abroad, the interests of the States involved and their mutual relations.

During wartime, massive armed forces stay on foreign territory for a considerable period of time. Their long-lasting and intensive contacts with the local population may entail violations of local law and the host State would logically prefer to retain jurisdiction. However, if the basing takes place on a large scale and is concentrated in specific areas, it may be a significant burden to the local judicial authorities whose resources may already be strained because of the wartime conditions. In that case the sending States' exercise of their jurisdiction would also benefit the host State.

The balance of power between host States and sending States is particularly important.[54] States may find themselves in a dependent position due to the fact that their forces needed to seek refuge in another State or because their territorial integrity is being threatened. Under these circumstances, their bargaining position is not particularly strong and they will be more inclined to accept the conditions put forward by the supporting States. In contrast, States that are strong in military terms and can make a decisive contribution to the conflict will have more negotiating power and will more likely be able to persuade host States to accept their ideas and demands concerning jurisdiction over their forces.[55] For instance, because of its military power the US was the only State during World War II to obtain exclusive jurisdiction over its forces on UK territory.[56]

---

[54] See the consideration "Law cannot be divorced from politics or power"; ICJ 20 February 1969, *North Sea Continental Shelf*, Judgement, I.C.J. Reports 1969, p. 3, pp. 42–43.

[55] See Priest-Hamilton 2000, p. 612.

[56] *Agreement between the United States of America and the United Kingdom of Great Britain and Northern Ireland, Jurisdiction over criminal offences committed by armed forces*; London, 27 July 1942 and 6 August 1942 (*EAS* 1944, No. 355; Vol. 117 *UNTS* 1951, No. 378. This agreement deviated strongly from the agreements previously adopted by the UK. The British commentary therefore mentioned in para 3: "...the very considerable departure which the above arrangements will involve from the traditional system and practice of the United Kingdom...".

Other interests of host States and sending States come into play as well. Receiving foreign military aid is fully in the interest of the host State that sees its existence threatened by military actions of its enemies. Under these circumstances host States will not consider the presence of allied forces and the subsequent waiver of exercising criminal jurisdiction as disproportionately affecting their sovereignty. Besides, the SOFAs are, in principle, intended to last only as long as the military threat itself.[57] Furthermore, the fight against the common enemy does not only serve the interests of individual States, but may also largely serve those of the coalition as a whole. By waiving jurisdiction over the visiting forces host States recognise and respect the larger perspective of common interests.

3.6 Conclusion

This chapter has analysed the application of the ground rule within the framework of armed conflict during which allied forces are based on co-belligerent territory. It focussed on the mutual assistance between States in the fight against their common enemies during both world wars and some of the subsequent international armed conflicts. In these situations, vast military units were based on the territory of other States in order to protect threatened areas and to prepare for and execute military operations. Sometimes they stayed for a longer period of time. Their status was regulated through the conclusion of formal SOFAs, which provided a formal basis for the status of visiting allied forces, while at the same time clearly defining the scope of the ground rule in these critical situations.

The full application of the ground rule was key to the majority of the agreements. Only insofar as operational circumstances allowed, could host States sometimes to a limited extent exercise their jurisdiction over the visiting forces. Important factors that contribute to the full application of the ground rule are the purpose of the allied forces' presence and the operational circumstances related to the allied support. These aspects will be further discussed in Part III. Besides these aspects, other factors play a role as well. The dependent position of the host State threatened by the hostilities and the vital role of the States rallying in support of their allies are of particular importance. This explains the often dominant position of the sending States in the negotiations about the terms of the SOFAs.

[57] Several SOFAs contain the explicit provision stating that the agreement would be applicable until the end of the armed conflict; e.g., consideration 10, *Agreement between the United States of America and the United Kingdom of Great Britain and Northern Ireland, Jurisdiction over criminal offences committed by armed forces*; London, 27 July 1942 and 6 August 1942 (*EAS* 1944. No. 355; Vol. 117 *UNTS* 1951, No. 378 and *Jurisdiction over criminal offenses committed by armed forces of the United States in the Belgian Congo*: *Agreement between the United States of America and Belgium*; Washington, 31 March, 27 May, 23 June and 4 August 1943 (*EAS* 1944, No. 395).

Annex A Anglo-French Declaration, 15 December 1915

Numb. 29421. 13019

The London Gazette.

Published by Authority.

The Gazette is registered at the General Post Office for transmission by Inland Post as a newspaper. The postage rate to places within the United Kingdom, for each copy, is one halfpenny for the first 6 ozs., and an additional halfpenny for each subsequent 6 ozs. or part thereof. For places abroad the rate is a halfpenny for every 2 ounces, except in the case of Canada, to which the Canadian Magazine Postage rate applies.

**** For Table of Contents, see last page.*

FRIDAY, 31 DECEMBER, 1915.

War Office,

15th *December,* 1915.

His Britannic Majesty's Government and the Government of the French Republic agree to recognize during the present war the exclusive competence of the tribunals of their respective Armies with regard to persons belonging to these Armies, in whatever territory and of whatever nationality the accused may be.

In the case of infringements committed jointly or in complicity by individuals belonging to these two Armies, the French authors or accomplices shall be handed over to the French military jurisdiction and the British authors or accomplices shall be handed over to the British military jurisdiction.

The two Governments further agree to recognize during the present war the exclusive competence in French territory of French justice: with regard to foreign persons in the British Army who may commit acts prejudicial to that Army, and the exclusive competence in British territory of British justice with regard to foreign persons in the French Army who may commit acts prejudicial to the said Army.

References

Arai-Takahashi Y (2009) The law of occupation. Continuity and change of international humanitarian law, and its interaction with international human rights law. Martinus Nijhoff Publisher, Leiden

Barton GP (1949) Foreign armed forces: immunity from supervisory jurisdiction. Br Yearb Int Law 26:380–413

Barton GP (1950) Foreign armed forces: immunity from criminal jurisdiction. Br Yearb Int Law 27:186–235

Bathurst ME (1946) Jurisdiction over friendly foreign armed forces: the American law. Br Yearb Int Law 23:338–341

Borch FL (2001) Judge advocates in combat. Army lawyers in military operations from Vietnam to Haiti. Office of the Judge Advocate General and Center of Military History United States Army, Washington

Bowett DW (1964) United Nations forces. A legal study. Stevens & Sons, London

Buurman van Vreeden JTh (1953) De militaire strafrechter te velde (inleiding tijdens bijeenkomst Militair Rechtelijke Vereniging). Militair Rechtelijk Tijdschrift 46:350–357

Chalufour A (1927) Le statut juridique des troupes alliées pendant la guerre 1914–1918. Paris

Clunet E (1918) La présence des Allies en France et l'exterritorialité. Journal du droit international 1918:514–517

Dinstein Y (2009) The international law of belligerent occupation. Cambridge University Press, Cambridge

Donnison FSV (1961) Civil affairs and military government North-West Europe 1944–1946. London

Ginsburgs G (1966) Soviet status-of-forces agreements: pre-war and wartime experience. Univ Toronto Law J 16(2):368–395

JAGS Text No. 11 (1944) Law of belligerent occupation. Judge Advocate General's School, Ann Arbor

Katzman K (2008) Kuwait: Post-Saddam issues and US policy. CRS Report for Congress, Congressional Research Service

King A (1942) Jurisdiction over friendly foreign armed forces. AJIL 36(4):539–567

Kuratowski R (1942) International law and the naval, military and air force courts of foreign governments in the United Kingdom. Trans Grotius Soc 28:1–25

Mettgenberg W (1929) Freies Geleit und Exterritorialität. Dümmlers Verlagsbuchhandlung, Berlin, Ferd

Priest-Hamilton KC (2000) Who really should have exercised jurisdiction over the military pilots implicated in the 1998 Italy gondola accident. J Air Law Commer 65(3):605–638

Prugh GS (1975) Law at war: Vietnam 1964–1973. Vietnam studies. Department of the Army, Washington

Re ED (1956) The NATO status of forces agreement and international law. Northwest Univ Law Rev 53(8):349–394

Robin R (1913) Des occupations militaires en dehors des occupations de guerre. (Translated and reproduced by the Division of International Law of the Carnegie Endowment for International Peace, Washington, 1942)

Rothstein A (1946) Soviet foreign policy during the patriotic war: documents and materials, vol II. Hutchinson & Co, London

Schneider G (1964) Die Exterritorialität der Truppen in strafrechtlicher Hinsicht, unter besonderer Berücksichtigung der das deutsche Territorium betreffenden Truppenverträge. Albert-Ludwig Universität, Saarbrücken

Slusser RM, Triska JF (1959) A calendar of Soviet treaties: 1917–1957. Stanford University, Stanford

Stanger RJ (1957/1958) Criminal jurisdiction over visiting armed forces. International law studies, vol LII. Naval War College, Newport

Supervielle MEF (1994) The legal status of foreign military personnel in the United States. The Army Lawyer, pp 3–25

The China White Paper (1949) Vol II. Stanford University Press, Stanford

Wunderlich G (1932) Die Gerichtsbarkeit der Heeresgruppe Yildirim (F). Mitteilungen der Deutschen Gesellschaft für Völkerrecht, Heft 11:79–108

Chapter 4
Armed Forces Participating in Crisis Management Operations

Abstract The status of visiting armed forces and especially criminal jurisdiction over those forces depends, inter alia, on the framework within they operate on foreign territory. When participating in crisis management operations the status of forces is generally set out in bilateral SOFAs or in SOFAs concluded by the international organisations leading the operations. Because of the international function of the international forces the members of these forces enjoy full immunity from the exercise of criminal jurisdiction by the local courts and are subject to the exclusive jurisdiction of their respective sending States.

Contents

4.1 Introduction

The armed conflicts between States discussed in the previous chapter, their termination and settlement may pose a threat to regional and international peace and security and harm the interests of other States. That threat can lead to the establishment

© T.M.C. ASSER PRESS and the author 2015
J. Voetelink, *Status of Forces: Criminal Jurisdiction over Military Personnel Abroad*,
DOI 10.1007/978-94-6265-057-2_4

of crisis management operations. These types of operations have a long tradition, starting in the middle of the nineteenth century.[1]

Crisis management operations are often associated with the UN. Since its establishment the UN has indeed initiated many crisis management operations[2] due to its key role in keeping and restoring international peace and security.[3] Today, many other international organisations, such as NATO and the EU, and coalitions of States, play a crucial role in this field as well. Crisis management operations sometimes consist of small military units, while on occasions more significant peacekeeping forces are involved. The tasks of the forces are diverse and based on an international mandate or the consent of the States involved. The operations may vary from supervising a ceasefire or a peace agreement concluded by the parties to an armed conflict to the execution of complex military operations in cooperation with other non-military entities, such as other governmental agencies, police forces and non-governmental organisations.

The previous chapter analysed the application of the ground rule within the framework of armed forces stationed in allied States during armed conflict. This chapter focuses on the scope of the ground rule within the framework of forces deployed abroad to participate in crisis management operations. It begins with the status of forces that participated or were intended to participate in the international military forces established by the League of Nations (Sect. 4.2). The next sections will give an overview of the status of forces participating in crisis management operations led by the UN (Sect. 4.3), NATO or the EU, or in multilateral operations of a coalition of States (Sect. 4.4). Building on the results of these paragraphs the application and scope of the ground rule within the framework of crisis management operations is analysed (Sect. 4.5).

4.2 League of Nations

In 1920 the League of Nations took the first step in establishing an International Force. Eventually the force that was meant to assist in the plebiscite in Vilna (being part of a territory disputed by Poland and Lithuania),[4] was not deployed.

---

1 Oswald et al. 2010, p. 3. An early example is the 1913 international peacekeeping force sent to assist the newly independent State of Albania in order to maintain order and security. In the period 1913–1914, the Netherlands contributed a small military unit that was tasked to organise the Albanian gendarmerie corps. The soldiers entered into the service of the Albanian gendarmerie corps. On the basis of Article 20 *Règlement relatif à position des officiers (sous-officiers) néerlandais qui prennant du service dans la Gendarmerie albanaise* they were not subject to Albanian jurisdiction. The agreement can be found in: De Veer and Thomson 1914, pp. 127–131.

2 Many recent operations are based on Chap. VII *UN Charter*. However, most operations, especially traditional peacekeeping operations, are not explicitly based on the UN *Charter*. In practice, they are generally accepted, though.

3 See Article 1(1) UN *Charter*.

4 Resolutions of the League of Nations of 28 October and 21 and 25 November 1920.

Fifteen years later the international force tasked to maintain public security during the 1935 plebiscite in the Saar was actually deployed to that region.[5]

According to the League of Nations, sending States would retain full jurisdiction over their participating forces. During the preparations for the mission to Vilnius, the Secretary-General of the League of Nations, in answer to questions from the Dutch government, stated: "…chacune des Puissances ayant fourni un contingent conserve une jurisdiction complète sur ses troupes".[6] This point of view was reflected in the decision relating to the establishment of the Saar force. Consideration 4 of the decision reads[7]:

> The command of the international force, its organs and services and the members of the said force shall be exempt from the jurisdiction of the courts of the Territory.

4.3 UN

When the UN was founded in 1945, it obtained, inter alia, the leading role to maintain international peace and security.[8] On the basis of this mandate, the UN continued the practice of establishing international forces as initiated by the League of Nations. As early as the 1940s, the UN formed unarmed observer missions. Later, it also established armed peacekeeping forces, which today may be supported by police forces and civilian elements in so-called multidimensional operations. Even though the *UN Charter* does not explicitly provide a legal basis for these missions and forces, this power is undisputed because of the organisation's tasks.[9]

---

[5] Wainhouse 1966, p. 25. Vilna: Resolution of the Council of 21 November 1920, *League of Nations Official Journal*, December 1920. The Saar: *League of Nations Official Journal*, December 1934, p. 1730.

[6] The Dutch question concerned the forces that were intended to go to Vilna; Dutch National Archive, The Hague, Archief Ministerie van Buitenlandse Zaken: A-dossiers 1919–1940, nummer toegang 2.05.21, inventarisnummer 1795, Letter of the Secretary of the League of Nations to the Minister of Foreign Affairs dated 30 November 1920. In the *Militair Rechtelijk Tijdschrift* it was noted that the participating States had full power and jurisdiction over their forces: Nederlandsche militairen naar Wilna, p. 386. E.g., *In re Polimeni-case* in which the Italian court martial considered that it had jurisdiction over an Italian member of the force who had killed a British colleague. Barton 1950, p. 220.

[7] Resolution of the Council of 11 December 1934, *League of Nations Official Journal*, December 1934, pp. 1762–1763. International railway troops commissioned in the Saar from 1927 to 1930 also enjoyed immunity. However, it was based on a regulation of the governmental commission responsible for the administration of the territory; Schmalenbach 2004, pp. 138–139.

[8] Article 24 UN *Charter*.

[9] Oswald et al. 2010, p. 3.

4.3.1 Experts on Mission

In 1947 the UN General Assembly decided to send military observers to Greece as part of the UN Special Committee on the Balkans (UNSCOB),[10] being the first operation under the auspices of the UN. Other observer missions quickly followed, such as the United Nations Truce Supervision Organization (UNTSO), which is still active today.[11] The status of the UN observers is based on Article 105(2) of the *UN Charter* and Article VI of the *Convention on the Privileges and Immunities of the United Nations*. Article 105(2) of the *UN Charter* states that representatives of UN Member States and UN officials enjoy privileges and immunities necessary to fulfil the independent execution of their functions in connexion with the UN. The *Convention on the Privileges and Immunities of the United Nations* elaborates on this article[12] and distinguishes various categories of UN officials. Military observers are included in the category mentioned in Article VI: Experts on missions for the United Nations. These external experts are not part of the UN, but use their expertise for different tasks as requested by the organisation.[13]

The *Convention on the Privileges and Immunities of the United Nations* does not provide a definition of expert on mission, which is difficult to formulate. In *Mazilu*, the ICJ circumvented the challenge by stating that it was the nature of the mission that determined whether a person was to be considered an expert on mission. The ICJ continued with enumerating tasks entrusted to experts on mission by the UN in the past,[14] which also mentions persons who "...*have participated in certain peacekeeping forces* ...". Military observers are to be considered as such.[15]

When States contribute military observers to the UN, they will work as international officials under the responsibility of the UN[16] and serve the UN "in a per-

---

[10] *UN Doc* A/RES/109(II) (1947), UNSCOB, 21 October 1947.

[11] *UN Doc* S/RES/50 (1948).

[12] *Convention on the Privileges and Immunities of the United Nations*; 13 February 1946 (*UNTS* 1946–1947, No. 4).

[13] This practice can be traced back to the time of the League of Nations, when the problem of the lack of these persons' legal protection had arisen, Miller 2007, p. 18.

[14] ICJ 15 December 1989, *Applicability of Article* VI, *Section* 22 *of the Convention on the privileges and immunities of the United Nations* (*Mazilu case*), Advisory Opinion, I.C.J. Reports 1989, p. 177, paras 47–48; see also: ICJ 29 April 1999, *Difference Relating to Immunity from Legal Process of a Special Rapporteur of the Commission on Human Rights* (*Cumaraswamy case*), Advisory Opinion, I.C.J. Reports 1999, p. 62.

[15] Other servicemen the UN considered experts on mission are the personnel on the Force Commander's staff. E.g., the UNPROFOR-mission included the crews of airplanes that supported the mission (Miller 2007, pp. 28 and 3) and technicians providing logistic assistance to the Rapid Reaction Force of UNPROFOR (Sharp 1996, p. 129). Both categories were considered experts on mission. Staff members of the German battalion were appointed experts on mission for the United Nations Operation in Somalia UNOSOM II; Fleck and Saalfeld 1994, p. 83.

[16] Oswald et al. 2010, p. 6.

sonal capacity and not as representatives of their State".[17] As experts on mission they enjoy immunities necessary to fulfill their function independently. These immunities include immunity from criminal jurisdiction:

> in respect of words spoken or written and acts done by them in the course of the performance of their mission...[18]

As a result, they can exercise their function without intimidation or interference from the host State.[19] Immunities serve the interests of the UN and are not for the benefit of the individual observers themselves. Therefore, the Secretary-General can waive the immunities granted to an expert on mission when he is of the opinion that the immunity may impede the course of justice and when it will be without prejudice to the interest of the UN.[20]

At the start of the first mission the legal position of observers was not specifically taken into account.[21] Later, the practice developed that in the SOFAs concluded between the UN and the host States military observers were designated as experts on mission as meant in Article VI of the *UN Charter*.[22]

The highest officials of a UN observer mission, for example the Chief Military Observer, are accorded the same immunities as diplomatic agents under international law. As a result, they enjoy full criminal immunity (on the status of diplomatic agents, see Sect. 7.3.3.4). Sometimes also the other members of a mission, including military observers, may be granted the same immunities as diplomatic agents, if the mission circumstances require so.[23]

---

17 *UN Doc* A/62/329 (2007) Criminal accountability of United Nations officials and experts on mission, Note by the Secretariat, 11 September 2007, para 55.

18 Section 22(b) *Convention on the Privileges and Immunities of the United Nations*. Section 22 provides experts on mission with the so-called functional immunity; see 'Letter to the Acting Chair of the Special Committee on Peacekeeping Operations, United Nations, regarding immunities of civilian police and military personnel', 14 April 2004, p. 324.

19 Oswald and Bates 2011, p. 377.

20 Section 23 *Convention on the Privileges and Immunities of the United Nations*.

21 Bowett 1964, p. 83.

22 Miller 2007, p. 21; e.g., *Exchange of letters constituting an agreement establishing the United Nations Iran-Iraq Military Observer Group* (*UNIIMOG*); New York, 19 August 1988 and Teheran, 28 March 1989 (Vol. 1512 *UNTS* 1988, No. 26126). When no SOFA is concluded the *Convention on the Privileges and Immunities of the United Nations* applies to the status of the experts on mission; 'Letter to the Acting Chair of the Special Committee on Peacekeeping Operations, United Nations, regarding immunities of civilian police and military personnel', 14 April 2004.

23 E.g., *Exchange of letters constituting an agreement between the United Nations and Lebanon concerning the status of the United Nations Observation Group in Lebanon*; New York, 13 June 1958 (Vol. 303 *UNTS* 1958, No. 4386) and *Exchange of letters constituting an agreement relating to the privileges, immunities and facilities for the Observation Operation along the Saudi Arabia-Yemen border established pursuant to the Security Council resolution of 11 June 1963*; New York, 23 August 1963 (Vol. 474 *UNTS* 1963, No. 6879).

4.3.2 Troops

In contrast with the large-scale peacekeeping forces established by the UN since the middle of the 1950s, observer missions are relatively small in size. The first UN operation of this kind was started after the Suez crisis in 1956. After British and French interference in the conflict between Israel and Egypt, the Secretary-General of the UN presented a report in which he introduced his plans for an "emergency force for the United Nations".[24] In November 1956 this resulted in the creation of the United Nations Emergency Force (UNEF), responsible for the supervision of the cessation of hostilities and the withdrawal of foreign forces from Egypt.[25]

Unlike the military observers who are sent on an individual basis, the forces that participate in peacekeeping operations constitute national contingents under the command of their national commander.[26] At the time of the Suez crisis it was not entirely clear whether they would fall under the scope of the *Convention on the Privileges and Immunities of the United Nations*,[27] as the Convention was adopted in view of protecting the execution of diplomatic functions by UN officials.[28] For this reason the UN and Egypt concluded a mission-specific SOFA to settle the status of UNEF and the participating troops (referred to as the *UNEF-SOFA*).[29] Within the context of the agreement UNEF was considered a body of the General Assembly. Paragraph 11 the *UNEF-SOFA* contained the provision on the jurisdiction over the participating forces:

> Members of the Force shall be subject to the exclusive jurisdiction of their respective national States in respect of any criminal offences which may be committed by them in Egypt.

The Secretary-General had also adopted internal rules for UNEF (referred to as the *UNEF-regulation*).[30] These rules reiterated that the members of UNEF forces were subject to the exclusive criminal jurisdiction of their own State and that the

---

[24] *UN Doc* A/3302 (1956), Second and final report of the Secretary-General on the plan for an emergency international United Nations Force, requested in the resolution adopted by the General Assembly on 4 November 1956 (A/3276), 6 November 1956, pp. 1–8.

[25] *UN Doc* A/3354, Resolutions adopted by the General Assembly during its first emergency special session from 1 to 10 November 1956; Resolution 1,000 (ES-1) of the General Assembly of the UN.

[26] Unlike observers, they are "...provided by a sending State as representatives of that State", *UN Doc* A/62/329 (2007) Criminal accountability of United Nations officials and experts on mission, Note by the Secretariat, 11 September 2007, para 56.

[27] Higgins 1969, p. 382. Today it is generally assumed that members of the forces do not fall under the scope of the Convention; Bourloyannis-Vrailas 1995, p. 570.

[28] Fleck 2006, p. 146.

[29] As Israel did not give its consent to the stationing of UN forces on its territory, only a SOFA with Egypt was needed: *Exchange of letters constituting an agreement between the United Nations and the Government of Egypt concerning the status of the United Nations Emergency Force in Egypt*; New York, 8 February 1957 (Vol. 260 *UNTS* 1957, No. 3704).

[30] *UN Doc* ST/SGB/UNEF/1, *Regulations for the United Nations Emergency Force*, 20 February 1975.

sending States were responsible for actually exercising their jurisdiction when their troops were involved in criminal offences.

The sending States that contributed troops to UNEF were not party to the *UNEF-SOFA*. However, through bilateral agreements with the UN on the conditions under which they would contribute forces, they had given their consent. In the agreements they explicitly agreed with the provisions on the exercise of jurisdiction as laid down in the *UNEF-SOFA* as well as the *UNEF-regulation*:

> This immunity from the jurisdiction of Egypt is based on the understanding that the authorities of the participating states would exercise such jurisdiction as might be necessary with respect to crimes or offences committed in Egypt by any members of the Force provided from their own military service.[31]

During subsequent peacekeeping operations the UN consistently held on to the practice of subjecting troops to the exclusive criminal jurisdiction of the sending States.[32]

UN experiences gained in the course of time were used by the Secretary-General to adopt a Model Status-of-Forces Agreement for UN peacekeeping operations (hereinafter: *Model UN-SOFA*).[33] Ever since then this model has been the basis and framework used during negotiations between the UN and a host State for the adoption of a formal mission-specific SOFA.[34] Evidently, the mission-specific SOFA can deviate from the Model, if circumstances in the host State or special conditions for the relevant mission require so and if the host State agrees with it.[35]

Section 46 of the *Model UN-SOFA* contains a clause on the immunity of all members of a UN operation[36]:

---

[31] E.g., Section 5 *Exchange of letters (with annexes) constituting an agreement concerning the service with the United Nations Emergency Force of national contingent provided by the Government of Canada*; New York, 21 June and 29 July 1957 (Vol. 274 *UNTS* 1957, No. 3957). Similar provisions are included in the agreements with other States that contributed troops.

[32] For several operations no SOFAs have been adopted (e.g., UNEF II, United Nations Disengagement Observer Force, UNDOF and United Nations Transition Assistance Group, UNTAG). The reports of the UN Secretary-General refer to the provisions on immunity included in the *Convention on the Privileges and Immunities of the United Nations* (*UN Doc* S/11052/Rev. 1 (1973), 27 October 1973, para 4b; *UN Doc* S/12611 (1978), 19 March 1978, para 4b and *UN Doc* S/12827 (1978) 29 August 1978, para 19). Because the reports express that they were adopted "having in mind past experience", it is most likely that in practice the agreement of UNEF 1 was used as a basis. Siekmann 1988, p. 173. At a certain moment the Operation Plan and the Rules of Engagement replaced the Force Regulations; Bothe and Dörschel 2003, p. 494.

[33] *Model Status of Forces Agreement for Peace-Keeping Operations*, Report of the Secretary-General, *UN Doc* A/45/594 van 9 October 1990.

[34] *UN Doc* A/54/670 (2002), Implementation of the recommendations of the Special Committee on Peacekeeping Operations, Report of the Secretary-General, para 50.

[35] For amendments and supplements to the *Model Status-of-Forces Agreement* that can be found back in recent UN SOFAs, see Oswald et al. 2010, pp. 39 et seq. For an inventory of such deviations, see Background Paper on UN Peacekeeping and The Model Status of Forces Agreement 2010, Annex 1.

[36] This provision is similar to Article 22(b) *Convention on the Privileges and Immunities of the United Nations.*

> All members of the United Nations peace-keeping operation including locally recruited personnel shall be immune from legal process in respect of words spoken or written and all acts performed by them in their official capacity.

Next to the provision on functional immunity for all members of the operation, Section 47 of the *Model UN-SOFA* includes a provision specifically pertaining to the participating troops. As mentioned above, in military practice when host States waive their right to exercise criminal jurisdiction over foreign visiting armed forces, it is necessary that the sending States can exercise jurisdiction over their own forces. For this reason, Section 47(b) states:

> Military members of the military component of the United Nations peace-keeping operation shall be subject to the exclusive jurisdiction of their respective participating States in respect of any criminal offence which may be committed by them in [host country/territory].

Almost identical provisions to the ones contained in Sections 46 and 47 of the *Model UN-SOFA* can be found in other mission-specific SOFAs the UN concluded with host States. They follow the example of UNEF. In line with these provisions, Section 48 of the *Model UN-SOFA* states that the Secretary-General is to assure the participating States' willingness to actually exercise criminal jurisdiction over their forces.[37]

In practice, the realisation of a mission-specific SOFA can be a cumbersome and lengthy affair. Sometimes no SOFA is concluded[38] or a SOFA is agreed upon long after the operation has started.[39] In order to fill the gap, the UN Security Council, when planning a new UN mission, sets a time frame to adopt the mission-specific SOFA[40] and decides that pending the conclusion of the SOFA the *Model UN-SOFA* will apply provisionally.[41] Furthermore, the Security Council has

[37] See Article 7 quinquiens, Model *Memorandum of understanding between the United Nations and [participating State] contributing resources to [the United Nations Peacekeeping Operation]*, *UN Doc A/C.5/63/18* of 29 January 2009, pp. 161 et seq.

[38] E.g., Because there was no time, there was no operational government in the area of the operation (UNOSOM II), or it was unclear whether the territory was occupied (UNDOF); Bothe and Dörschel 2003, p. 493. During UNEF II and UNDOF applicability and incompatibility of Israeli law also played a role; Siekmann 1988, p. 159, fn 11.

[39] Murphy 2008a, p. 110. In the case of the United Nations Interim Force in Lebanon (UNIFIL), for unclear reasons, it took even 20 years before a SOFA was concluded. In addition, Croatia signed the SOFA for UNPROFOR as late as 1995. As a result, since 1993 the UK had exercised its jurisdiction over its forces on the basis of informal arrangements; Rubin 2004, p. 30.

[40] *UN Doc* A/RES/52/12 B (1997), Renewing the United Nations: a programme for reform, para 7.

[41] The first time the Security Council followed this approach was in the Central African Republic (CAR) for the United Nations Mission in the Central African Republic (MINURCA), *UN Doc* S/RES/1158 27 March 1998, para 19. Nowadays, this approach is regularly followed; e.g., UNMEE (*UN Doc* S/RES/1320 (2000), sect. 6); MINUSTAH (*UN Doc* S/RES/1542 (2004), para 11); MINURCAT (*UN Doc* S/RES/1778 (2007), para 4) and MINISMA (*UN Doc* S/RES/2100 (2013), para 33).

on several occasions decided that a current SOFA would continue to apply to subsequent operations under the authority of another international organisation, for instance, when the EU took over the SFOR mission in Bosnia-Herzegovina from NATO.[42] Occasionally, the UN has elaborated on SOFAs by adopting supplementary SOFAs.[43]

In the course of time the nature of UN operations changed and operations were increasingly conducted in areas where a conflict was still ongoing. In 1994, as a result of the increasing violence against UN staff, the *Convention on the Safety of United Nations and Associated Personnel* was signed.[44] The Convention and *Optional Protocol* aim to secure the protection of UN and associated personnel necessary to execute their tasks during a UN operation.[45] Although the Convention does not regulate the status of forces, Article 4 instructs host States to conclude an agreement on the status of the UN operation and all personnel involved as soon as possible.

Occasionally, the UN concludes SOFAs with third States that support the operation or consent to the transit of UN forces through their territory.[46] For example, with respect to UNEF, the UN concluded an agreement with Lebanon on a UNEF-Leave Centre in Lebanon[47] and on a transit unit at the international airport of Beirut.[48] In these agreements the UN also laid down that troops were subject to the exclusive jurisdiction of the sending States.

---

[42] The Council decided that the SOFAs included in Appendix B, Annex 1-A the *Dayton Agreement: General Framework Agreement for peace in Bosnia and Herzegovina*; Paris, 14 December 1995 (www.ohr.int/dpa/. Accessed November 2014) provisionally applied to the EU mission and its participating forces; sect. 20, *UN Doc* S/RES/1551 (2004) of 9 July 2004.

[43] Oswald and Bates 2010, p. 384 mention in this context the *Supplemental Arrangements between the United Nations Mission in Sudan and the Government of National Unity of Sudan*; Khartoem, 28 December 2005 (Annex to the *Agreement between the Government of Sudan and the United Nations concerning the status of the United Nations Mission In Sudan*, Khartoum 28 December 2005. unmis.unmissions.org/Portals/UNMIS/Documents/General/sofa.pdf. Accessed November 2014.

[44] *Convention on the Safety of the United Nations and Associated Personnel*; New York, 9 December 1994 (Vol. 2051 *UNTS* 1999, No. 35457).

[45] Article 1(c) of the Convention defines the concept of UN operation. The *Optional Protocol* grants States the possibility to enlarge the scope of protection under the Convention to other categories of operations: *Optional Protocol to the Convention on the Safety of United Nations and Associated Personnel*; New York, 8 December 2005 (Vol. 2698 *UNTS* 2010, No. 35457).

[46] Bourloyannis-Vrailas 1995, p. 573.

[47] *Exchange of letters constituting a provisional arrangement concerning the United Nations Emergency Force Leave Centre in Lebanon*; Beirut, 20 and 29 April and 1 May 1957 (Vol. 226 *UNTS* 1957, No. 3827).

[48] *Exchange of letters (with aide-mémoire) constituting an agreement concerning the establishment and operation by the United Nations Emergency Force of a transit unit at the Beirut International Airport*; Gaza, 21 December 1957 and Beirut, 20 January 1958 (Vol. 286 *UNTS* 1958, No. 4166).

4.4 Other Organisations and Coalitions

The UN traditionally plays a key role when it comes to crisis management operations because of its functions with respect to maintaining international peace and security. However, this position does not exclude other institutions, such as regional organisations under Chap. VIII of the *UN Charter*, international organisations and coalitions of States, from playing an important role as well.[49]

4.4.1 General

Until 1989 the role of other organisations and coalitions was still limited to a small number of operations. The scarce sources on the status of forces in these operations indicate that sending States had exclusive criminal jurisdiction over their forces (see Table 4.1).[50]

For example, the status of members of the Multinational Force and Observers (MFO) in Egypt was set out in the Appendix to the *MFO-Protocol*.[51] Section 11 states that members of the MFO are subject to the exclusive criminal jurisdiction of the respective sending States. Section 11(d) of the Appendix allows participating States to make supplementary arrangements with the host State on the status of MFO members. Several States used the option to conclude agreements with Israel on military personnel on leave on its territory.[52] In these agreements sending States have waived their right to exercise criminal jurisdiction, as accorded by the *MFO-Protocol,* in the case of certain weapons and drugs-related crimes.[53]

---

[49] Heldt 2008, p. 9.

[50] *Status of forces agreement of the Arab League Force in Kuwait*; Kuwait, 12 August 1961 (published in: Terry M. Mays, Historical Dictionary of Multinational Peacekeeping, Lanham, 1996, Appendix II); *Agreement between the Transitional National Union Government of the Republic of Chad and the Organization of African Unity (OAU) regarding the status of a Pan-African peacekeeping force in Chad*; Nairobi, 28 November 1981 (Annex in: Terry M. Mays, *Africa's First Peacekeeping Operation, the OAU in Chad 1981–1982*, Westport 2003); *Exchange of notes constituting an agreement on United States participation in a multinational force in Beirut*; Beirut, 18 and 20 August 1982 (Vol. 1751 *UNTS* 1993, No. 30567) and *Exchange of notes constituting an agreement on United States participation in a Multinational Force in Beirut*; Beirut, 25 September 1982 (Vol. 1777 *UNTS* 1994, No. 31022). The agreements with France and Italy are not published in the UNTS.

[51] *Protocol relating to the establishment and maintenance of a Multinational Force and Observers (with annex)*; Washington, 3 August 1981 (Vol. 1335 *UNTS* 1983, No. 22403).

[52] E.g., Australia, the Netherlands, the UK and the US.

[53] E.g., *Exchange of notes constituting an arrangement in respect of the immunities of British military members of the Multinational Force and Observers (MFO) while on leave in Israel*; Jerusalem, 28 September 1982, and Tel Aviv, 30 September 1982 (Vol. 1335 *UNTS* 1983, No. 22398).

Table 4.1 Criminal jurisdiction and crisis management operations; until 1989

Criminal jurisdiction and crisis management operations international organisations until 1989 (non-UN)		
Operation	**Jurisdiction of sending state**	**Remarks**
Arab League		
• Kuwait (1961)	Exclusive[a]	–
• Jordan (1970)	Unknown	Unknown whether SOFA was concluded
• Lebanon (1976)	Unknown	No SOFA concluded[b]
Organization of American States, OAS		
• Observers (various)	Unknown	Unknown whether SOFA was concluded
• Dominican Rep. (1965)	Unknown	Unknown whether SOFA was concluded
Organisation of Eastern Caribbean States, OECS		
• Grenada (1983)	Unknown	Unknown whether SOFA was concluded
Organisation of African Unity, OAU		
• Chad (1979–1982)	Exclusive[c]	–
Criminal jurisdiction and crisis management operations coalitions of states until 1989		
Multinational Force and Observers, MFO		
Egypt (1981–…)	Exclusive[d]	–
Multinational Force, MNF		
Lebanon (1982–1984)	Status cf. diplomatic relations treaty[e]	
Inter-African Force, IAF		
Zaïre (1978–1979)	Unknown	Unknown whether SOFA was concluded
Commonwealth Monitoring Force, CMF		
Rhodesia/Zimbabwe (1979–1980)	Unknown	Unknown whether SOFA was concluded
Indian Peacekeeping Force, IPKF		
Sri Lanka (1987–1990)	Unknown	Unknown whether SOFA was concluded
Maledives (1988)	Unknown	Unknown whether SOFA was concluded

[a] Paragraph 11 *Exchange of Letters between His Highness the Prince of the State of Kuwait and the Secretary General of the League of Arab States*; Kuwait, 12 August 1961 (*UN Doc* S/5007, 30 November 1961)
[b] Schmalenbach 2004, p. 518
[c] Paragraph 5(9) *Agreement between the Transitional National Union Government of the Republic of Chad and the Organization of African Unity (OAU) regarding the status of a Pan-African peacekeeping force in Chad*; Nairobi, 28 November 1981 (in Mays 2003, Annex)
[d] Paragraph 11(a) Appendix to Annex, of the *Protocol relating to the establishment and maintenance of a Multinational Force and Observers (with annex)*; Washington, 3 Augustus 1981 (Vol. 1335 *UNTS* 1983, No. 22403)
[e] *Exchange of notes constituting an agreement on United States participation in a multinational force in Beirut*; Beirut, 18 and 20 August 1982 (Vol. 1751 *UNTS* 1993, No. 30567) and para viii, *Exchange of notes constituting an agreement on United States participation in a Multinational Force in Beirut*; Beirut, 25 September 1982 (Vol. 1777 *UNTS* 1994, No. 31022). Agreements concluded by France and Italy have not been published in the UNTS

The changing international political relations in the post Cold War era initially gave new élan to crisis management operations. The Russian Federation made less frequent use of its power of veto in the Security Council, which subsequently could operate more effectively and in general States were more inclined to contribute troops to these operations. After 1989, both the number of UN operations and the role of (sub) regional organisations,[54] military alliances and coalitions of States increased.

Table 4.2 shows to what extent sending States could exercise criminal jurisdiction over their forces participating in various crisis management operations led by international organisations (excluding UN, NATO and EU) since the end of the Cold War. Although a great number of the SOFAs have been not published, it can be derived from other agreements that sending States in general had exclusive criminal jurisdiction over their armed forces.

The following sections will address the well-documented practice of NATO and the EU, which play an increasingly important role in the crisis management operations.

4.4.2 NATO

Similar to the UN, NATO does not possess its own armed forces, so operations under NATO command are conducted by forces provided by NATO Member States. In the early 1990s the organisation made its first steps in the field of crisis management conducting naval and air operations in and around the Balkans.[55] In 1995, after parties to the conflict in the former Yugoslavia had signed the *Peace Agreement of Dayton*,[56] NATO answered to the UN Security Council's call to establish a multinational military Implementation Force (IFOR).[57] Later, NATO extended its activities in the Balkans to, inter alia, Kosovo and Macedonia. Afterwards, the organisation led various operations outside European territory, such as the ISAF operation in Afghanistan,

---

[54] Regional organisations play an important role in the area of international peace and security within the UN system. See Article 53 *UN Charter*. The report of the Secretary-General 'Agenda for Peace' and a subsequent addition emphasised the need for an active role for regional organisations in this field. (*UN Doc* A/47/277-S/24111 (1992), An Agenda for Peace, 17 June 1992 and *UN Doc* S/1995/1 - A/50/60 (1995), Supplement to An Agenda for Peace, 25 January 1995).

[55] Since 1992 the organisation executed operations to follow up on the arms embargo and the economic sanctions imposed by the UN. Later, NATO monitored violations of the no-fly zone and could launch air strikes (Operation Sky Monitor and Operation Deny Flight).

[56] *General Framework Agreement for peace in Bosnia and Herzegovina*; Paris, 14 December 1995 (www.ohr.int/dpa/. Accessed November 2014).

[57] In Article I(1) Annex 1-A to the *Peace agreement of Dayton* (*Agreement on the military aspects of the peace settlement*) the parties invited the UN Security Council to establish a peacekeeping force. The Security Council responded to this request by adopting Resolution 1031: *UN Doc* S/RES/1031 (1995) of 15 December 1995. After 1 year IFOR became the Stabilization Force (SFOR), also led by NATO, *UN Doc* S/RES/1088 (1996) of 12 December 1996.

Table 4.2 Criminal jurisdiction and crisis management operations international organisations (excl. UN, NATO and EU); post 1989

Commonwealth of Independent States, CIS		
• Moldova (1992–…)	Status cfm. UN treaty; expert on mission[a]	–
• S-Ossetia (1992–2008)	Idem	–
• Abkhazia (1993–2008)	Idem	–
• Tajikistan (1993–2000)	Idem	–
Organisation for Security and Cooperation in Europe, OSCE		
• Various missions	Unknown	Unpublished MOUs
• Uganda (1993)	Unknown	Unknown whether SOFA was concluded
• Burundi (1994–1996)	Unknown	Unknown whether SOFA was concluded
African Union, AU		
• Burundi (2003–2004)	Unknown	Unknown whether SOFA was concluded
• Sudan (2004–2007)	Exclusive[b]	–
• Somalia (2007–…)	Exclusive[c]	–
• Comoros (2006)	Unknown	Contents of SOFA are unknown
• Comoros (2007–2008)	Unknown	contents of SOFA is unknown
Economic Community of West African States, ECOWAS		
• Liberia (1990–1999)	Unknown[d]	Contents of SOFA are unknown
• Sierra Leone (1997–1999)	Unknown	Unknown whether SOFA was concluded
• Guinea-Bissau (1998–1999)	Exclusive[e]	–
• Ivory Coast (2002–2004)	Unknown	Unknown whether SOFA was concluded
• Liberia (2003)	Unknown	Unknown whether SOFA was concluded
Central African Economic and Monetary Community, CAEMC		
• CAR (2002–2008)	Exclusive[f]	–
Economic Community of Central African States, ECCAS		
• CAR (2008–…)	Unknown[g]	Contents of SOFA are unknown

(continued)

Table 4.2 (continued)

Southern African Development Community, SADC		
• Congo (1998)	Unknown	Unknown whether SOFA was concluded
• Lesotho (1998–1999)[h]	Unknown	Contents of SOFA is unknown

[a]Paragraph 39 *Statute on Collective Peace-keeping Forces in the Commonwealth of Independent States*; Moskow, 19 January 1996 (*UN Doc* A/51/62; S/1996/74)
[b]Paragraph 62(b) *Status of mission agreement on the establishment and management of the ceasefire commission in the Darfur area of Sudan*; Khartoum, 4 June 2004 (www.issafrica.org/AF/profiles/sudan/darfur/soma.pdf. Accessed November 2014)
[c]Article XII (55)(b) *Status of Mission Agreement (SOMA) between the Transitional Federal Government of the Somali Republic and the African Union on the African Union Mission in Somalia (AMISOM)*; Addis Ababa, 6 March 2007 (storage.globalcitizen.net/data/topic/knowledge/uploads/20100505103429290.pdf. Accessed November 2014)
[d]Allegedly, 8 years after the start of the mission a secret SOFA was concluded; Schmalenbach 2004, p. 521
[e]Article VII (24) *Agreement defining the operations, composition and status of ECOMOG on the territory of the Republic of Guinea-Bissau*; Bissau, 22 March 1999 (*UN Doc* S/1999/445 (1999) 20 April 1999)
[f]Multinational Force Central African Republic (FOMUC); Article 11 *Protocole Relatif au mandat et au statut de la force multinationale de la CEMAC en République Centrafricaine*; 3 June 2003 (www.juriafrica.com. Accessed November 2014)
[g]In 2008 ECCAS took over command of the operation in CAR from CAEMC, called Mission for the Consolidation of Peace (MICOPAX)
[h]Operation Boleas

Operation Unified Protector in Libya and a number of naval operations,[58] as well as giving support to the African Union (AU) and its operations.

For NATO the status of the participating forces has always been a focal point, exclusive jurisdiction of the sending States over their forces being paramount (see Table 4.3). For instance, the SOFA annexed to the *Peace Agreement of Dayton* determines[59]:

> NATO military personnel under all circumstances and at all times shall be subject to the exclusive jurisdiction of their respective national elements in respect of any criminal or disciplinary offenses which may be committed by them…[60]

[58] Combating terrorism (Operation Active Endeavour in the Mediterranean (6 October 2001–today)), protection of food supply transportation (Operation Allied Provider (October–December 2008)) and the prevention of piracy, Operation Allied Protector (March 2009–17 August 2009) and Operation Ocean Shield (17 August 2009–today).

[59] *Agreement between the Republic of Bosnia and Herzegovina and the North Atlantic Treaty Organisation (NATO) concerning the status of NATO and its personnel; Agreement between the Republic of Croatia and the North Atlantic Treaty Organisation (NATO) concerning the status of NATO and its personnel and Agreement between the Federal Republic of Yugoslavia and the North Atlantic Treaty Organisation (NATO) concerning transit arrangements for peace plan operations*; Wright-Patterson Air Force Base, Ohio, 21 November 1995 and Paris 14 December; Appendix B to Annex 1-A to the *Peace agreement of Dayton* (www.ohr.int/dpa/. Accessed November 2014).

[60] In December 2004 the EU took over the operation from NATO. On the basis of Security Council Resolution 1575 (*UN Doc* S/RES/1575 (2004) of 22 November 2004) the status of EU forces is the same as that of the NATO forces.

Table 4.3 Criminal jurisdiction and crisis management operations NATO; post 1989

Operation	Jurisdiction sending State	Remarks
• IFOR/SFOR (1994–2004)	Exclusive[a]	–
• Kosovo (1999–…)	Exclusive[b]	–
• Albania (1999–2010)	Exclusive[c]	–
• Macedonia (2001–2003)	Unknown	Classified; not published
• Afghanistan (2003–…)	Exclusive[d]	–

[a]Article 7 *Agreement between the Republic of Bosnia and Herzegovina and the North Atlantic Treaty Organisation (NATO) concerning the status of NATO and its personnel*; Article 7 *Agreement between the Republic of Croatia and the North Atlantic Treaty Organisation (NATO) concerning the status of NATO and its personnel* en Article 10 *Agreement between the Federal Republic of Yugoslavia and the North Atlantic Treaty Organisation (NATO) concerning transit arrangements for peace plan operations*; Wright-Patterson Air Force Base, Ohio, 21 November 1995 and Paris 14 December; Appendix B to Annex 1-A to the *Dayton Peace Agreement* (www.ohr.int/dpa/. Accessed November 2014)

[b]Section 2(2.4) *Regulation No. 2000/47 on the status, privileges and immunities of KFOR and UNMIK and their personnel in Kosovo*; 18 August 2000

[c]*Agreement between the government of the Republic of Albania and NATO concerning the status of NATO and its personnel present on the territory of the Republic of Albania*; Brussels, 24 June 1999 (NAVO Document SG(99)1003, 25 June 1999)

[d]Section 1(3) Annex A, *Military Technical Agreement between the International Security Assistance Force* (ISAF) and the Interim Administration of Afghanistan; 4 January 2002

Similar provisions formulated somewhat differently were also used in other SOFAs.[61] Several agreements are classified and have, therefore, not been published.

Decades of NATO practice show that host States never exercised criminal jurisdiction over the foreign forces. Unlike the UN and the EU (see below), NATO has not adopted a model SOFA that could clarify the organisation's position on this point. As far as can be established, NATO has not concluded any mission-specific SOFA for its naval operations or for its assistance to the AU.

NATO member States participating in an operation are not party to the mission-specific SOFAs signed by NATO's Secretary-General. Pursuant to Article 36 of the *Vienna Convention on the Law of Treaties*, consent of third States for whom rights arise out of treaty provisions, are to be presumed as long as the contrary is not indicated.[62] Unlike UN practice, NATO member States do not conclude agreements on their contribution of forces to a NATO mission, in which they accept the SOFA provisions. However, the applicability of the SOFAs can be deduced from the decision-making procedure of NATO (see also Sect. 9.4.2), which is based on consensus. This means that the decision of the North Atlantic Council approving

[61] E.g., *Agreement between the government of the Republic of Albania and NATO concerning the status of NATO and its personnel present on the territory of the Republic of Albania*; Brussels, 24 June 1999 (NATO Document SG(99)1003, 25 June 1999) and *Regulation No. 2000/47 on the status, privileges and immunities of KFOR and UNMIK and their personnel in Kosovo*; 18 August 2000 (www.unmikonline.org/regulations/2000/reg47-00.htm. Accessed November 2014).

[62] *Vienna Convention on the Law of Treaties*; Vienna, 23 May 1969 (Vol. 1155 *UNTS* 1980, No. 18232).

the final text of a SOFA implies acceptance by its members. It can also be argued that the sending State's transfer of command over its military units to a NATO commander (see Sect. 11.3) results in the sending State's implicit acceptance of the provisions made by NATO.

4.4.3 EU

In 1992, with the signing of the *EU Treaty,* the Common Foreign and Security Policy (CFSP) of the EU was established.[63] In 1999, the European Council meeting in Cologne defined the European (since the *Treaty of Lisbon*[64] formulated as Common) Security and Defence Policy as part of the CFSP.[65] This meant that the EU could deploy armed forces to execute the so-called Petersberg tasks: humanitarian and rescue tasks, peacekeeping tasks and tasks of combat forces in crisis management operations.[66]

The implementation of the *Lisbon Treaty* has led to reformulating the tasks as missions "…for peace-keeping, conflict prevention and strengthening international security …" (Article 42(1), *EU Treaty*). The *Lisbon Treaty* provides the EU with the possibility to entrust execution of tasks to a group of Member States (Article 42(5) *EU Treaty*).

Since 31 March 2003 the EU has undertaken crisis management operations,[67] for which member States and third countries provide armed forces. On 2 December 2004, after the successful execution of several smaller missions,[68] the EU took over from SFOR in Bosnia-Herzegovina, from then on called EUFOR Althea/BiH. Later, the EU also mounted operations in Africa.[69] On 31 December 2008 the EU launched Operation Atalanta, its first naval mission, to protect the vessels of the World Food Programme and to combat piracy off the coast of Somalia.

---

63 *Treaty on European Union*; Maastricht, 7 February 1992 (*OJ* 1992, C 191).

64 *Treaty of Lisbon amending the Treaty of European Union and the Treaty establishing the European Community*; Lisbon, 13 December 2007 (*OJ* 2007, C 306).

65 Murphy 2008b, p. 67.

66 Article 17(old) *EU Treaty*.

67 Besides other mainly civilian missions, such as police, rule of law and observer missions, the European Community, succeeded by the EU, also executed an observer mission in the former Yugoslavia; see, Naert 2010, p. 98. As these missions are of a non-military nature, they will not be discussed here.

68 Operation Concordia in Macedonia (31 March 2003–15 December 2003) and Operation Artemis under French command (or in EU terminology: framework nation) in Bunia, East of the Democratic Republic of the Congo (12 June–1 September 2003).

69 From April to November 2006 the EUFOR DRC assisted the United Nations Organisation Mission in the Democratic Republic of the Congo (MONUC). From 28 January 2008 to 14 March 2009 the EU executed an operation in Chad and the Central African Republic (CAR) (EUFOR Chad/RCA). From 18 July 2005 to 31 December 2007 the EU assisted in the mission of the African Union Mission in Sudan (AMIS).

The EU has almost always concluded SOFAs with the host States, the first of which with Macedonia.[70] Article 6 of the SOFA read:

> EUF personnel shall be granted treatment, including immunities and privileges, equivalent to that of diplomatic agents granted under the Vienna Convention on Diplomatic relations dated 18 April 1961.

On the basis of this provision military personnel enjoyed full criminal immunity. Third States participating in the mission concluded agreements with the EU on the participation of their forces,[71] in which applicability of the SOFA to the participating forces was confirmed.[72]

Subsequent SOFAs show that absolute criminal immunity of the sending States' forces was paramount to the EU, although no longer was referred to the *Vienna Convention on Diplomatic relations*. Article 6 of the SOFA concluded with Gabon, where EU forces were based to support EUFOR in de Democratic Republic of the Congo, read[73]:

> EUFOR-personnel shall enjoy immunity from the criminal jurisdiction of the Host State under all circumstances.

Furthermore, besides immunity of their forces, the SOFA allowed sending States to exercise criminal jurisdiction in the host State (Article 8):

> The competent authorities of a Sending State shall have the right to exercise on the territory of the Host State all the criminal jurisdiction and disciplinary powers conferred on them by the law of the Sending State with regard to all EUFOR personnel subject to the relevant law of the Sending State.

Such provisions were also included in later EU agreements,[74] for instance, concerning the EU Naval Force Somalia and the operation in Chad[75] and the Central

---

[70] *Agreement between the European Union and the former Yugoslav Republic of Macedonia on the status of the European Union-led forces in the former Yugoslav Republic of Macedonia*; Skopje, 21 March 2003 (*OJ* 2003, L 82/46).

[71] Many of these agreements have been concluded. For this particular operation there were twelve such agreements; see, Naert 2007, p. 71.

[72] E.g., Article 3 *Agreement between the European Union and the Slovak Republic on the participation of the armed forces of the Slovak Republic in the European Union-led Forces (EUF) in the Former Yugoslav Republic of Macedonia*; Brussels, 9 December 2003 (*OJ* 2004, L 12/54).

[73] Article 6(3) *Agreement between the European Union and the Gabonese Republic on the status of the European Union-led forces in the Gabonese Republic*; Libreville, 16 July 2006 (*OJ* 2006, L 187/43).

[74] E.g., The EU has concluded agreements with Djibouti, Somalia and the Seychelles. E.g., *Agreement between the European Union and the Republic of Djibouti on the status of the European Union-led forces in the Republic of Djibouti in the framework of the EU military operation Atalanta*; Djibouti, 5 January 2009 (*OJ* 2009, L 33/43). The agreement with the Seychelles contains the additional provision: "The Host State shall endeavour to facilitate the exercise of jurisdiction by the competent authorities of the Sending State"; Article 8, last sentence, *Agreement between the European Union and the Republic of Seychelles on the status of the European Union-led forces in the Republic of Seychelles in the framework of the EU military operation Atalanta of the EU*; Victoria, 10 November 2010 (*OJ* 2009, L 323/19).

[75] *Agreement between the European Union and the Republic of Chad on the status of the European Union-led forces in the Republic of Chad*, N'Djamena, 6 March 2008 (*OJ* 2008, L 83/40).

Table 4.4 Criminal jurisdiction and crisis management operations EU; post 1989

Operation	Jurisdiction sending State	Remarks
• Macedonia (2003)	Status cfm. Diplomatic Relations Treaty[a]	
• Congo DRC (2003 en 2006)	–	No SOFA concluded
• Bosnia (2004–...)	Exclusive[b]	–
• Chad (2008–2009)	Exclusive[c]	–
• CAR (2008–2009)	Exclusive[d]	–

[a]Article 6(1) *Agreement between the European Union and the Former Yugoslav Republic of Macedonia on the status of the European Union-led Forces (EUF) in the Former Yugoslav Republic of Macedonia*; Skopje, 21 March 2003 (*OJ 2003*, L 82/46)
[b]Paragraph 12 *UN Doc* S/RES/1575 (2004), 22 November 2004 in which the UN Security Council stated that SOFAs to the *Dayton Peace Agreement* are applicable to NATO and EU forces
[c]Article 6(3) *Agreement between the European Union and the Republic of Chad on the status of the European Union-led forces in the Republic of Chad*; N'Djaména, 6 March 2008 (*OJ* 2008, L 83/40)
[d]Article 6(3) *Agreement between the European Union and the Central African Republic on the status of the European Union-led forces in the Central African Republic*; Bangui, 16 April 2008 (*OJ* 2008, L 136/46)

African Republic (CAR) (see Table 4.4).[76] Today, the provisions mentioned above are part of the *Model Agreement on the status of the European Union-led forces* (the *Model EU-SOFA*).[77] These provisions are more specific about criminal immunity than the provisions included in the SOFAs adopted by the UN and NATO. However, they have similar consequences for the exercise of criminal jurisdiction over the participating forces.

The applicability of the SOFAs to the armed forces of participating States is undisputed. On the basis of Article 216(2) of the *Treaty on the Functioning of the European Union*, all agreements concluded by the Union are binding for the institutions of the Union and the Member States.[78] With other participating States the EU concludes Participation Agreements. These agreements include a provision declaring the SOFAs EU is a party to as applicable to the participating non-member States.[79] Furthermore, the Participation Agreements explicitly state that third States can participate in the EU-led forces.

---

[76] *Agreement between the European Union and the Central African Republic on the status of the European Union-led forces in Central African*; Bangui, 16 April 2008 (*OJ* 2008, L 136/46).

[77] Adopted by the Council on 13 June 2005; Note of the Council to the European Council dated on the same day, nr. 10032/05. In a revised draft of the *Model EU-SOFA*, the provision on criminal jurisdiction remained unmodified; see *EU Doc* (11894/07), corrigendum of 5 September 2007 (*EU Doc* 11894/07 COR 1). Both documents can be classified as the basis for negotiations on future SOFAs; *EU Doc* 12616/07 of 6 September 2007.

[78] *Treaty on the Functioning of the European Union*; Rome, 25 March 1957 (Consolidated version: *OJ* 2012, 326/47); until 1 December 2009, this Treaty was referred to as the *Treaty establishing the European Economic Community*.

[79] E.g., Naert 2011, p. 232.

4.4.4 Coalitions of States

After the Cold War the number of operations led by international organisations increased, as did the number of coalition operations. The operations in East Timor are an example of the latter. In August 1999, after the population of this region had voted by referendum in favour of independence from Indonesia, serious disturbances occured. The deployment of multinational forces authorised by the UN had to restore peace and security and to facilitate humanitarian assistance operations.[80] Australia led the International Force in East Timor (INTERFET). On 24 September 1999, through an exchange of notes, it concluded an agreement with Indonesia on the status of the INTERFET-forces.[81] The treaty is classified and for that reason unpublished. Apparently, the sending States retained full criminal jurisdiction over their forces.[82]

On 28 February 2000 the United Nations Transitional Administration in East Timor (UNTAET) succeeded INTERFET. Until the independence of East Timor (Timor Leste) on 20 May 2002 UNTAET administered the territory. In 2006 the security situation worsened and subsequently the government of Timor Leste requested international assistance to restore peace and security. In June 2006, in response to the request, Australia and New Zealand sent the International Stabilization Force (ISF).[83] The status of the forces was regulated in two SOFAs concluded by East Timor with Australia and New Zealand, respectively.[84] They included a provision stating that the personnel would be granted the status:

> …equivalent to that accorded administrative and technical staff of the Contributing Governments under the Vienna Convention on Diplomatic Relations of April 18, 1961.

This reference to the *Vienna Convention on Diplomatic Relations* is exceptional in the area of crisis management operations. In general the SOFAs concluded for other coalition operations show that, as far as the information is available, also in the context of coalition operations, the forces are subject to the exclusive criminal jurisdiction of the sending States (see Table 4.5).

---

[80] *UN Doc* S/RES/1264 (1999) of 15 September 1999.

[81] Rogers 2005, pp. 570–571.

[82] See Riordan 2001, p. 22.

[83] The ISF and the United Nations Integrated Mission in Timor-Leste (UNMIT), established by the UN in August 2006, operated side by side.

[84] *Exchange of notes between the government of New Zealand and the government of the Democratic Republic of Timor-Leste concerning the restoration and maintenance of security in Timor-Leste and the status of visiting personnel in Timor-Leste*; Dili, 26 May 2006 (www.laohamutuk.org/reports/UN/06SOFAs.html#Australia. Accessed November 2014).

Table 4.5 Criminal jurisdiction and crisis management operations coalitions of States; post 1989

Operation	Jurisdiction sending State	Remarks
United Task Force, UNITAF		
Somalia (1992–1993)	–	No SOFA concluded
Operatie Turquoise		
Rwanda (1994)	Unknown	Unknown whether SOFA was concluded
Multinational Force, MNF		
Haiti (1994–1995)	Exclusive[a]	–
South Pacific Peacekeeping Force, SPPKF		
Papua New Guinea (1994)	Exclusive[b]	
Military Observer Mission Ecuador-Peru, MOPEP		
Ecuador/Peru (1995–1999)	Unknown	Unknown whether SOFA was concluded
Multinational Protection Force, MPF		
Albania(1997)	Exclusive[c]	
Inter-African Mission to Monito the Bangui Agreements, AMIB		
CAR (1997–1998)	Status cfm. Diplomatic Relations Treaty[d]	
Truce Monitoring Group for Bouganville, TMG		
Papua New Guinea (1997–1998)	Exclusive[e]	–
International Force in East Timor, INTERFET		
East-Timor (1999–2000)	Full immunity	Classified; precise contents SOFA unknown
International Peace Monitoring Team, IPMT		
Solomon Islands (2000–2002)	Full immunity	(*except when the sending States "expressly consent otherwise"*)[f]
International Security Force, ISAF		
Afghanistan (2001–2003)	Exclusive[g]	
Opérátion Licorne		
Ivory Coast (2002–…)	Functional[h] immunity	*Also: immunity on base*
Regional Assistance Mission to Salomon Islands, RAMSI		
Solomon Islands (2003–…)	Functional[i] immunity	*however, host State cannot exercise jurisdiction when sending State exercises that right*[j]
Multinational Force Iraq, MNF-I		
Iraq (2003–2009)	Exclusive[k]	–
Multinational Interim Force, MIF		
Haiti (2004)	Unknown	Unknown whether SOFA was concluded

(continued)

Table 4.5 (continued)

Operation	Jurisdiction sending State	Remarks
International Stabilization Force, ISF		
Timor Leste (2006–…)	Status cfm. Diplomatic Relations Treaty[l]	

[a]Paragraph 43(b) *Agreement between the governments participating in the multinational force ("MNF") authorized persuant to Security Council Resolution 940 and the Republic of Haiti on the status of MNF in Haiti*; Miami, 8 December 1994 and Washington, 22 December 1994 (Law and Military Operations in Haiti 1994–1995, Lessons Learned for Judges Advocates)
[b]Article 9(2) *Agreement between Papua New Guinea and Fiji, Tonga, Solomon Islands, Vanuata, Australia and New Zealand, concerning the status of elements of the defence forces of those countries deployed in North Solomon's province of Papua New Guinea as part of the South Pacific Peackeeping Force*; Suva, 28 September 1994 (1994 *PITSE* 20)
[c]Article III(3) *Agreement between the government of the Republic of Albania and the governments of the nations contributing to the multi-national protection force bearing on the status of the said force*; Rome, 21 April 1997 (nomoi.info/%CE%A6%CE%95%CE%9A-%CE%91-9-1998-%CF%83%CE%B5%CE%BB-2.html. Accessed November 2014)
[d]Article 2 *Agreement between the Government of the Central African Republic and the Governments of Burkina Faso, the Republic of Chad, the Gabonese Republic, the Republic of Mali, the Republic of Senegal, and the Tongolese Republic on the status of the forces of the Inter-African Mission to monitor the Bangui Agreements*; Bangui, 25 January 1997 (*UN Doc* S/1997/561 (1997), 22 July 1997)
[e]Article 10(2) *Agreement between Australia, Papua New Guinea, New Zealand, Fiji and Vanuatu concerning the Neutral Truce Monitoring Group for Bougainville*; Port Moresby, 5 December 1997 (1997 *ATS* 30)
[f]*Exchange of letters between the government of New Zealand and the government of the Solomon islands constituting an agreement on the deployment of New Zealand personnel to the Solomon islands as members of the International Peace Monitoring Team (with accompanying statutory Declaration*; Honiara, 9–10 November 2000 (2000 *Pacific Islands Treaty Series* 7)
[g]Section 1(3) Annex A, *Military Technical Agreement between the International Security Assistance Force (ISAF) and the Interim Administration of Afghanistan*; 4 January 2002 (www.operations.mod.uk/isafmta.pdf. Accessed November 2014)
[h]Article 1 Annex to the *Accord d'assistance militaire technique entre la République Française et la République de Côte -d' Ivoire*; Paris 5 February 1962 (*Journal Officiel de la République Française*, 5 februari 1962). The SOFA is based on the two States' previous military cooperation. As France is of the opinion that troops during military operations are continuously on duty, in practice France has always full jurisdiction over its forces
[i]Article 10(2) Agreement between Solomon Islands, Australia, New Zealand, Fiji, Papua New Guinea, Samoa and Tonga concerning the operations and status of the police and armed forces and other personnel deployed to Solomon Islands to assist in the restoration of law and order and security; Townsville, 24 July 2003 (2003 ATS 17; 2003 PITSE 12)
[j]Idem Article 10(3)
[k]Section 2(3) *CPA Order 17 (rev.)*: *Coalition Provisional Authority Order Number 17 (revised): Status of the Coalition Provisional Authority, MNF-Iraq, Certain missions and Personnel in Iraq*; 27 June 2004 (www.iraqcoalition.org/regulations/20040627_CPAORD_17_Status_of_Coalition__Rev__with_Annex_A.pdf. Accessed November)
[l]Paragraph 2 Annex A, *Exchange of notes between the government of New Zealand and the government of the Democratic Republic of Timor-Leste concerning the restoration and maintenance of security in Timor-Leste and the status of visiting personnel in Timor-Leste*; Dili 26 May 2006 (www.laohamutuk.org/reports/UN/06SOFAs.html#Australia. Accessed November 2014)

4.5 Stationing in and Transit Through Third States

Weapon systems are sometimes based on the territory of States other than those where crisis management operations take place. Support from these third States may also involve the transfer or storage of equipment and supplies, or the passage of forces on their territory. Furthermore, support may entail facilitation of, for example logistic and medical services, which also requires further arrangements with these third States on the status of the visiting soldiers.

International organisations and coalitions sometimes conclude the necessary SOFAs. Some examples taken from UN practice have already been mentioned in the last paragraph of Sect. 4.3.2. NATO concluded several transit agreements in the context of its operations in the Balkans and Afghanistan. Furthermore, NATO assisted the EU by providing air-transport capacity for the AMIS operation in Sudan, during which Aerial Ports of Embarkation and Debarkation had to be used in various States. Besides some exceptions, arrangements with these third States have not been published and, therefore, it is not known in what way jurisdiction over NATO forces had been agreed on.[85]

The EU concluded several SOFAs with third States with respect to operations in and around Africa; for example, one with Uganda with respect to the support to the EU-led operation Artemis in the Democratic Republic of Congo (DRC).[86] In this agreement the status of participating force was based on the 1946 *UN Treaty on privileges and immunities*. Pursuant to this UN treaty the forces enjoyed a similar status as experts on mission, meaning that they enjoyed immunity from criminal prosecution for acts conducted during the exercise of their duty. When assisting subsequent operations in Africa and naval operations off the coast of Somalia, the EU has concluded several SOFAs that allowed sending States to exercise exclusive criminal jurisdiction.[87]

---

[85] The transit of NATO forces through Austria fell under the criminal jurisdiction of the relevant sending States: *Exchange of letters constituting an agreement between Austria and the North Atlantic Treaty Organization on Privileges and immunities*; Brussels, 15 and 16 December 1995 (Vol. 1912 *UNTS* 1996, No. 32623).

[86] *Agreement between the government of the Republic of Uganda and the Government of the French Republic concerning the status of the French armed forces participating in the deployment of the interim emergency multinational force and other provisions relating to their presence in the Republic of Uganda*; Kampala, 18 June 2003 (Vol. 2227 *UNTS* 2004, No. 39494; *EU Doc* 10773/03 j° 12225/03 (Brussels, 4 September 2003)) was extended to include participating forces from the EU and third States; Note Verbal Ministry of Foreign Affairs of Uganda, 20 Augustus 2003 (*EU Doc* 12225/03); also see Naert 2010, p. 115, n. 461.

[87] E.g., Article 6(3) *Agreement between the European Union and the Gabonese Republic on the status of the European Union-led forces in the Gabonese Republic*; Libreville, 16 July 2006 (*OJ* 2004, L 187). The EU concluded similar agreements to regulate the transit of EU-led forces on the territory of Cameroon in support of the EU operation in CAR and Chad. For the naval operation Atalanta, see: Article 6(3) *Agreement between the European Union and the Republic of Djibouti on the status of the European Union-led forces in the Republic of Djibouti in the framework of the EU military operation Atalanta*; Djibouti, 5 January 2009 (*OJ* 2009, L 33/43);

In many cases organisations leave it to sending States to make arrangements with third States resulting in divergent agreements. In most cases States have the right to exercise exclusive criminal jurisdiction over their servicemen, but in some cases host States restrict the jurisdiction over the visiting forces. For instance, in Qatar, the Netherlands could only exercise criminal jurisdiction related to criminal offences committed by Dutch soldiers "...against their property, safety, fellow personnel or equipment".[88] However, the Netherlands had the possibility to request Qatar to waive its criminal jurisdiction.

4.6 Disaster Relief

Disaster relief provided in emergency situations constitutes a special category of operations whose aim is to give relief to the population that has been affected by disasters. The military contribution to disaster relief abroad is of great importance, as military forces dispose of directly deployable means that are urgently required to provide aid, such as advanced communication equipment, specialised engineers units and air, road and sea transportation.[89]

The status of foreign military personnel participating in disaster relief operations is partly set out in existing treaties. Some of these follow the same line as is the case in other types of operations, in which sending States retain exclusive criminal jurisdiction over their forces.[90] Occasionally agreements restrict the exercise of jurisdiction to on duty offences.[91]

Footnote 87 (continued)

Agreement between the European Union and the Somali Republic on the status of the European Union-led naval force in the Somali Republic in the framework of the EU military operation Atalanta; Nairobi, 31 December 2008 (*OJ* 2009, L 10/29). The EU concluded similar agreements with the Seychelles and Somalia.

88 Article 12(3) *Status of forces Agreement for military personnel and equipment for the forces between the Kingdom of the Netherlands and the State of Qatar*; Doha, 11 March 2002 (Vol. 2204 *UNTS* 2004, No. 39128).

89 *UN Doc* A/54/670 (2002), Implementation of the recommendations of the Special Committee on Peacekeeping Operations, Report of the Secretary-General; also see Fisher 2007, p. 154.

90 E.g., Article 10 *Convention on the prediction and prevention of major hazards and mutual assistance in the event of natural or man-made disasters*; Paris, 16 September 1992 (Vol. 1962 *UNTS* 1997, No. 33532) and Article 9(3) *Agreement among the Governments of the Participating States of the Black Sea Economic Cooperation (BSEC) on collaboration in Emergency Assistance and Emergency Response to natural and man- made disasters*; Sochi, 15 April 1998 www.bsec-organization.org/documents/LegalDocuments/agreementmous/agr4/Documents/Emergencyagreement%20071116.pdf. Accessed November 2014.

91 Article 21(2)(a) *Agreement establishing the Caribbean Disaster Emergency Response Agency (CDERA)*; 1991, www.caricom.org/jsp/secretariat/legal_instruments/agreement_cdera.jsp. Accessed November 2014.

The *Oslo Guidelines,* the primary contemporary source of reference concerning military and civil defence assets in disaster relief,[92] take functional immunity as the base line. In Annex I, the document contains a *Model agreement covering the status of Military and Civil Defence Assets (Model-MCDA agreement).* Article 21 of the *Model-MCDA agreement* considers personnel mobilised and deployed at the request of the UN Office for the Coordination of Humanitarian Affairs (OCHA) as experts on mission. Personnel not mobilised and deployed at the request of the OCHA enjoy:

> ...immunity from legal process in respect of words spoken or written and all acts performed by them in their official capacity (Article 41).

This provision is similar to the *Model UN-SOFA*. The latter also contains, as mentioned above, the provision that the forces are subject to the exclusive criminal jurisdiction of sending States. This provision, however, is not part of the *Model-MCDA agreement.*

The preference for this functional approach is not entirely clear. To the drafters of the *Oslo Guidelines* rendering military support to disaster relief is a sensitive matter, as it is considered to be a non-military activity. This background may explain their intention to level the status of all categories of personnel involved in disaster relief, regardless of their position and to consider an exceptional position of military forces unnecessary.

NATO chooses a similar approach to regulate the status of personnel of the civil and military elements of the Euro-Atlantic Disaster Response Unit (EADRU). In Annex 4 of the Standing Operating Procedures for this unit, a *Model agreement covering the status of national elements of the EADRU on mission in the territory of a stricken nation* is included.[93] Consideration 6.2.1. determines that the immunities consist of, inter alia:

> immunity from legal process, arrest and detention, in respect of words spoken or written acts or omissions done by them in their official capacity and within the limits of their authority; ...

The NATO agreement with Pakistan concluded after the heavy earthquakes in 2005 illustrate that practice sometimes deviates from this functional approach. Both civilian and military personnel NATO deployed for this disaster relief operation was "under all circumstances and at all times" subject to the exclusive jurisdiction of the sending States.[94]

---

[92] *UN Doc* A/CN.4/590 (2007), Protection of persons in disasters. Memorandum by the Secretariat, para 190. E.g., the US has included the Guidelines in their military doctrine (Joint Publication 3–29, Foreign Humanitarian Assistance; Ohlweiler 2011, p. 14.

[93] *Standing operating procedures for the Euro-Atlantic Disaster Response Unit* (*EADRU*), 1998 www.nato.int/eadrcc/sop/sop.htm. Accessed November 2014.

[94] Article 7 *Exchange of letters between NATO and the Islamic Republic of Pakistan*; November 2005 (NATO DOC SG(2005)0798 of 4 November 2005). On the occasion of the assistance provided by NATO after the 2010 floods in Pakistan the agreement took effect again.

There is not much information available on SOFAs pertaining to disaster relief operations, which generally are undertaken in emergency situations in the host State and often last only for a short period of time. Therefore, formal agreements are sometimes not concluded, while other less formal arrangements are seldom made public.

4.7 Analysis of Crisis Management Practice

The status of forces participating in crisis management operations, particularly the exercise of criminal jurisdiction over these forces, is a continuous focal point for the participating States and the international organisations involved. Its importance is reflected by the practice to set out the status of forces in formal legal instruments and, in most cases, by the absolute application of the ground rule.

The League of Nations settled the status of forces participating in the International Force in a decision of its Council. The UN followed this approach in cases where it could not conclude an agreement in time. In general, the UN chooses to set out the status of the UN forces in treaties. By signing the treaty host States formalise their consent with the mission.[95] Furthermore, the mostly large-scale crisis management operations require the regulation of various aspects other than the exercise of criminal jurisdiction. Thus, the conclusion of a legally binding international agreement is a logical step.

Furthermore, the operations entail the long-lasting presence of a significant number of foreign forces from different States. Similar to the wartime cooperation between allied States, crisis management operations involve a high risk of incidents, which makes an unambiguous application of the ground rule highly desirable. In the years after World War II States cooperated more intensively in the area of defence. The resulting agreements reveal that exercising criminal jurisdiction by sending States was not a matter of course, as will be demonstrated in the next chapter. Under these circumstances it is important to rule out any ambiguity over the scope of the ground rule. An agreement that takes away the ambiguity responds to the States' search for "a greater degree of precision and predictability than may be available under customary international law".[96]

States and international organisations have followed UN practice. Tables 4.2, 4.3, 4.4 and 4.5. show that many mission-specific SOFAs have been concluded, though from a number of operations information about the status of the participating forces is not available.[97] Besides the practice to set out the status of forces by

[95] Besides impartiality and limited use of force, the involved States' approval of the operations is one of the principles of UN operations, e.g., Oswald et al. 2010, p. 7.

[96] Oxman 2007, para 33.

[97] It is possible that States or organisations have simply omitted to comply with Article 102 *UN Charter* to register the adopted agreements and accorded a less formal status to the agreement or arrangements for reasons of confidentiality. It may also be possible that for some missions, no agreements have been concluded at all.

treaty, today some form of standardisation is discernible, as the use of model SOFAs and reference to existing treaties testify.[98]

This chapter has demonstrated that the forces participating in crisis management operations on the territory of other States enjoy full immunity from the exercise of criminal jurisdiction by the judicial authorities of the host States. Often SOFAs determine that the forces are subject to the exclusive criminal jurisdiction of the sending States. The allocation of exclusive criminal jurisdiction to sending States can partly be based on the same reasons as has been described in the previous chapter. Also, in the context of crisis management operations both the purpose of the forces' deployment and the operational circumstances under which the operations take place are important. Part III further elaborates on these fundamental aspects. The next part of this section focuses on the interests of the States involved and their mutual relationships.

An important aspect to note is the fact that participation in crisis management operations does not solely serve the sending States' own interests. For instance, the Council of the League of Nations already considered the problem of the Saar as an international matter,[99] in which the international forces were considered to be above other parties.[100] Likewise, in an evaluation of UNEF, the Secretary-General of the UN emphasised the exclusive international nature of the UN operations.[101] To continue guaranteeing its international nature, he declared that it was crucial that UN forces could operate independently from the host State, for which criminal immunity was considered to be essential.[102] So, as regards the allocation of criminal jurisdiction over foreign forces, the common interests of the international community at large prevails over the interests of an individual host State.[103] As practical point the Secretary-General also pointed out that granting immunities would be an incentive for States to continue contributing forces to an operation.[104]

The balance of power also plays a role in the context of crisis management operations. In general, the international organisation involved, or a State on behalf of a coalition of States, will conclude the SOFA. This multinational

---

[98] Especially reference to the *Vienna Convention on Diplomatic Relations* or the UN *Convention on the Privileges and Immunities*.

[99] Dutch Parliamentary Papers 1935, Overzicht betreffende de door Nederland verleende medewerking bij de voorbereiding van de volksstemming in het Saargebied, 13 januari 1935, p. 3.

[100] Article 2 of the instruction to the commander of the Dutch contingent for the International Force explicitly mentioned that the international forces are no occupation army but a force that is neutral and impartial; National Archive, The Hague, Nederlands Detachement Saargebied, 1934–1935, nummer toegang 2.13.01.05 and Militair Rechtelijk Tijdschrift 1934/1935, p. 457.

[101] *UN Doc* A/3943, Summary study of the experiences derived from the establishment and operation of the Force, report of the Secretary-General, 9 October 1958, para 14.

[102] Id., para 136.

[103] Servicemen participating in the operations were also considered as international staff; for instance: Superior Provincial Court (Oberlandesgericht) of Vienna, 26 February 1979, *N.K. v. Austria*, ILR 77, p. 473.

[104] *UN Doc* A/3943, Summary study of the experiences derived from the establishment and operation of the Force, report of the Secretary-General, 9 October 1958, para 136.

commitment gives them more leverage to put pressure on the host State to meet the international aspirations.[105] Furthermore, the circumstances under which the forces operate are equally important. Operations take place in States that have been involved in armed conflicts, where local judicial institutions may not be equipped to exercise criminal jurisdiction over large international military forces.

Nonetheless, on occasion military personnel do not enjoy full immunity, such as military observers provided by States to the UN as expert on mission and forces participating in operations of the Commonwealth of Independent States, which only enjoy functional immunity.[106]

When forces participating in crisis management operations are based in, or transit, third States, exclusive jurisdiction may not always be acceptable to the host State. It can be argued that activities not directly supporting the operation and taking place outside the area of operations do not necessarily require the exercise of criminal jurisdiction by the sending State. Besides, as the operation does not take place in the third State itself that State's interests may not be at stake. Most of the time sending States will have to conclude the SOFAs with third States themselves and consequently may have less leverage, while their supporting activities may also be considered of less international importance.

4.8 Conclusion

This chapter has analysed the scope of the ground rule applied in the context of crisis management operations. The available SOFAs lead to the conclusion that forces executing the operations almost without exception enjoy full criminal immunity from the exercise of criminal jurisdiction by the judicial institutions of the host State and are for the most part fully subject to the criminal jurisdiction of the sending States. Only in the context of some specific operations, or when soldiers are provided as experts on mission to the UN, may immunity of the forces be restricted to functional immunity.

The international function of the forces participating in crisis management operations may explain the preference to grant them full immunity. Furthermore, the involved international organisations and coalitions of States that lead the operations have more influence on the negotiations of a SOFA and are, therefore, better able to ensure that the aspirations of the sending States are included in the final document. A final reason for opting for full immunity is that local judicial institutions may not be sufficiently equipped to exercise jurisdiction over the large military forces.

---

[105] Cathcart 2010, p. 236.

[106] See Table 4.2. The reason may be that CIS operations do not take place in third States, but in the member States of the CIS.

The territorial scope of the SOFAs is limited to the territory of the States in which the operation takes place. Members of the forces who during the mission travel to other States, for instance, to spend their leave there, do not enjoy criminal immunity as members of the peacekeeping force.[107] If forces are based in third States in support of crisis management operations elsewhere, the conclusion of SOFAs is equally important. Practice shows that the contents of SOFAs may differ. Occasionally, supporting personnel can be subject to the criminal jurisdiction of the sending States, while in other cases criminal jurisdiction remains partly in the hands of the host State.

The status of forces participating in disaster relief operations is less clear. Some model provisions restrict the scope of the criminal jurisdiction to acts necessary for the execution of certain tasks of the forces. However, practice reveals a possible preference for full criminal jurisdiction for sending States over the forces.

References

Bothe M, Dörschel T (2003) The UN Peacekeeping experience. In: Fleck D (ed) The handbook of the law of visiting forces. Oxford University Press, Oxford, pp 487–506

Bourloyannis-Vrailas MC (1995) The Convention on the Safety of United Nations and Associated Personnel. 44 Int Comp Law Q 44(3):560–590

Bowett DW (1964) United Nations forces. A legal study. Stevens & Sons, London

Cathcart B (2010) Command and control in military operations. In: Gill TD, Fleck D (eds) The handbook of international law of military operations. Oxford University Press, New York, pp 235–244

Fisher D (2007) Law and legal issues in international disaster response: a desk study, International Federation of Red Cross and Red Cross Crescent Societies

Fleck D (2006) Securing status and protection of peacekeepers. Practice and policies of modern peace support operations under international law. Transnational Publishers, Ardsley, pp 141–156

Fleck D, Saalfeld M (1994) Combining efforts to improve the legal status of UN peacekeeping forces and their effective protection. Int Peacekeep 1(3):82–84

Heldt B (2008) Trends from 1948–2005: how to view the relation between the United Nations and non-UN entities. In: Peace operations. Trends, progress and prospects. Georgetown University Press, Washington

Higgins R (1969) United Nations peacekeeping 1946–1967, documents and commentary, I The Middle East. Oxford University Press, Oxford

Jansen FNJ (2007) Militaire juristen op oefening in een joint en combined scenario: een analyse van de oefening Joint Caribbean Lion 06 vanuit een juridisch oogpunt. Militair Rechtelijk Tijdschrift 100:358–363

[107] E.g., an Israeli court considered a Senegalese UNIFIL soldier stationed in Lebanon to fall under Israeli criminal jurisdiction during his visit to Israel; District Court of Haifa 10 May 1979, *Israel v. Papa Ben Coli Dista Saar*, UN Juridical Yearbook 1979. The court held that the soldier had permission to enter Israel as a tourist or a visitor and that his acts were not considered as executed in the "framework of his job". This may lead to the conclusion that the court would have come to a different conclusion if the soldier had acted while on duty and had stayed in Israel with that State's permission.

Mays TM (2003) Africa's first peacekeeping operation, the OAU in Chad 1981–1982, Westport 2003

Miller AJ (2007) United Nations experts on mission and their privileges and immunities. Int Organ Law Rev 4(1):11–56

Murphy R (2008a) UN peacekeeping in Lebanon, Somalia and Kosovo. Operational and legal issues in practice. Cambridge University Press, Cambridge

Murphy R (2008b) The European Union and developments in crisis management operations and peacekeeping. Connect Q J 8(1):58–91

Naert F (2007) ESDP in practice: increasingly varied and ambitious EU security and defence operations. In: Trybus M, White ND (eds) European security law. Oxford University Press, Oxford

Naert F (2010) International law aspects of the EU's security and defence policy with a particular focus on the law of armed conflict and human rights. Intersentia, Antwerpen-Oxford-Leuven

Naert F (2011) Legal aspects of EU military operations. J Int Peacekeep 15(1):218–242

Oswald B, Bates A (2011) Privileges and immunities of United Nations police. J Int Peacekeep 14(3):375–402

Oswald B, Durham H, Bates A (2010) Documents on the law of peace operations. Oxford University Press, Oxford

Oxman BH (2007) Jurisdiction of states. Max Planck Encyclopedia of Public International Law. www.mpepil.com. Accessed Nov 2014

Riordan K (2001) Operations law—peacekeeping operations in East Timor: a New Zealand military perspective. N Z Armed Forces Law Rev 2001:19–24

Rogers F (2005) The international force in East Timor. Legal aspects of maritime operations. Univ NSW Law J 28(2):566–580

Rubin GR (2004) United Kingdom SOFAs and rules of engagement in Yugoslavia: some further reflections. In: Pritchard J, Carey J, Dunlap J (eds) International humanitarian law challenges. Transnational Publishers, Ardsley, pp 175–199

Sharp WG (1996) Protecting the avatars of international peace and security. Duke J Comp Int Law 7(1):93–183

Schmalenbach K (2004) Die Haftung Internationaler Organisationen im Rahmen von Militäreinsätzen und Territorialverwaltungens. Frankfurt am Main

Siekmann RCR (1988) Juridische aspecten van de deelname met nationale contingenten aan VN-vredesmachten (Nederland en UNIFIL). Amsterdam University, Amsterdam

Wainhouse DW (1966) International peace observation. A history and forecast. The John Hopkins Press, Baltimore

Chapter 5
Military Cooperation

Abstract The status of visiting armed forces and especially criminal jurisdiction over those forces depends, inter alia, on the framework within they operate on foreign territory. When stationed abroad in the framework of international peacetime military cooperation, the status of forces is generally set out in bilateral and multilateral agreements. In general, interests of the sending States and host States are more balanced than during armed conflict or crisis management operations, allowing the interests of the host States to have more impact on the arrangements often resulting in a balanced allocation of criminal jurisdiction to the host States and sending States.

Contents

5.1 Introduction

The previous chapters have analysed the ground rule (a host State refrains from exercising criminal jurisdiction over visiting forces, thus allowing the sending State to do so) within the framework of armed conflict and crisis management operations. This chapter examines the scope of the ground rule within the framework of international military cooperation.

© T.M.C. ASSER PRESS and the author 2015
J. Voetelink, *Status of Forces: Criminal Jurisdiction over Military Personnel Abroad*,
DOI 10.1007/978-94-6265-057-2_5

In the nineteenth century and the first half of the twentieth century, the basing of foreign military forces within this framework of military cooperation was still rather rare. Reference is often made to the British forces based in Iraq and Egypt during the 1920s and 1930s,[1] or to the American military advisory missions in South and Central America in the 1930s.[2] Other activities mostly concerned small detachments for which no specific formal arrangements were adopted.[3]

After World War II this practice changed considerably. The ideological divide between the US and the Soviet Union (SU) and their allies widened, developing into the Cold War, which brought along a division on the international political scene that would affect international relations for decades to come. It led to intensive military cooperation on either side, at times reflected in the large-scaled stationing of foreign forces (Sect. 5.2).

After the Cold War military cooperation continued, adapted to the conditions current at the time. The reduction of the tension between East and West resulted in the decreasing necessity of large-scale forces stationed on foreign territory. However, as new threats to international peace and security were emerging, stationing of forces in friendly States remained necessary. For this reason, the US in particular has kept a large military presence in countries like Germany, Japan and South Korea. At the same time States intensified cooperation, for example, by establishing multinational units (Sect. 5.3).

Also within the framework of military cooperation the status of forces is an important issue and for this purpose numerous SOFAs have been adopted, mostly by European and North American States. Naturally, SOFAs have also been concluded in other regions of the world, but not many details of these agreements are available.[4] As a result this chapter will focus on the application of the ground rule by European and North American States.

---

[1] *Treaty of Alliance*; Bagdad, 10 October 1922 (*LNTS*, 1925, No. 892) and *Treaty of Alliance Between His Majesty in Respect of the United Kingdom and His Majesty The King of Egypt*; 26 August 1936 (*AJIL*, Vol. 31, No. 2, Supplement: Official Documents (April 1937), pp. 77–90).

[2] These missions, generally consisting of a small number of military personnel, were meant to improve the efficiency of the military forces of the host States. They often enjoyed the same rights as diplomatic agents; e.g., Article 21 *Agreement between the United States of America and the United States of Brazil, concerning a military mission of the United States of America to Brazil*; Washington, 10 May 1934 (150 *LNTS* 1934, No. 445).

[3] Dutch servicemen, for instance, frequently paid official visits abroad. Archives reveal that relevant agreements did not address their status. Likewise, the legal position of foreign military personnel in the Netherlands was not a topic of negotiations either. E.g., when the UK requested the Netherlands to allow the transit of British forces stationed in the Rhineland after World War I across the Rhine, a number of issues were discussed, like the carrying of weapons, the number of soldiers and logistic matters, but the status of British soldiers was not mentioned in the correspondence. Harkavy mentions the interbellum examples of Soviet airbases in Czechoslovakia and Japanese airbases in Siam; see Harkavy 2007, pp. 72 en 73. It is unknown whether in these cases SOFAs were adopted.

[4] States will most likely have published a number of the SOFAs in their native language. However, international literature contains little information on their contents. Besides, many SOFAs remain classified for reasons of State security.

This chapter divides the relevant timeframe into the period prior to 1989 (the end of the Cold War) and the period from 1989 onwards and examines the SOFAs concluded within the framework of international military cooperation with a special focus on the *NATO-SOFA* and related arrangements.

5.2 The Cold War

After World War II the differences in ideological and political views between the US and the SU raised the tension between the two powers, bringing about a division in international relations. For Germany and Korea, the changing international relations even led to a physical division of the countries; the newly drawn borders symbolising the separation between East and West. On either side of the borders, the SU and the US maintained an unprecedented level of armed forces with the aim to restrict the influence of the other side: an effort that could only be sustained with the assistance of their allies.

5.2.1 The Aftermath of World War II

At the end of World War II allied forces held large parts of their former opponents' territory. The occupation came officially to an end when the forces withdrew from the occupied territories,[5] or when the States continued the stationing of the forces on other terms.[6] In some cases foreign forces stayed longer to monitor compliance with the peace agreement.[7] States like West-Germany and Japan considered the continued stationing of foreign forces on their territory after World War II necessary mainly because of the changing security situation, which led to military cooperation between former opponents. They settled the status of forces through agreements that initially offered the sending States extensive rights to exercise

---

[5] The allied forces withdrew from, for example, Bulgaria and Italy on the basis of the *Peace agreements of Paris* of 10 February 1947 (Article 73 *Treaty of peace with Italy*; Paris, 10 February 1947 (Vol. 49 *UNTS* 1950, No. 747) and Article 20 *Treaty of peace with Bulgaria*; Paris, 10 February 1947 (Vol. 41 *UNTS* 1949, No. 643)).

[6] The (peace) agreement ended the occupation and delineated the purpose for which the former occupying forces would continue their stay in the host State; see A. Roberts 2009, Sect. 17.

[7] During the Peace Conference in April 1919, for example, it was decided that the Rhineland would remain occupied for a period of 15 years to guarantee the implementation of the Peace Treaty of Versailles; see Article 428 *Treaty of Versailles*; 29 June 1919 (avalon.law.yale.edu/subject_menus/versailles_menu.asp. Accessed November 2014).

criminal jurisdiction over their own forces[8]; in that respect SOFAs resembled a continuation of the occupying regime. Over time, as States renewed the agreements, Germany and Japan, as host States, obtained broader jurisdiction over visiting foreign forces.[9] Consequently, these SOFAs closely resembled the practice of other cooperating States following the *NATO-SOFA* approach to criminal jurisdiction (discussed in the next section below).

After the end of World War II allied forces sometimes stayed in the liberated West European States, initially as occupying forces, later pursuant to bilateral and multilateral defence agreements. Initially, the way the status of forces was regulated varied widely. In several States the Civil Affairs Agreements,[10] which were only intended to remain in force during the war, stayed in force longer than planned.[11] On the basis of these agreements, sending States had exclusive criminal jurisdiction over their forces. Sometimes new agreements were concluded that built on the Civil Affairs Agreements.[12]

Other agreements provided the host States with more extensive rights to exercise criminal jurisdiction over the visiting forces. France, being a strategically important country for the supply of the British and American occupying forces

[8] On the basis of the *Forces Convention* authorities of former Western occupying forces in their capacity of sending State could exercise criminal jurisdiction over the members of their forces, to the exclusion of the Federal Republic of Germany (Article 6(1)). Only in case the sending State had no jurisdiction according to its own laws (Article 6(2)) or in case the sending State had granted jurisdiction over specific types of incidents to German courts (Article 6(4)), the Federal Republic of Germany could exercise jurisdiction (under conditions); *Convention (with annexes) on the rights and obligations of foreign forces and their members in the Federal Republic of Germany*; Bonn, 26 May 1952 (as modified by *Schedule II to the Protocol on the termination of the occupation régime in the Federal Republic of Germany*; Paris 23 October 1954 (Vol. 332 *UNTS* 1959, No. 4760). In Japan, American forces enjoyed full immunity on the basis of Article XVII *Administrative Agreement under article III of the Security Treaty between the United States of America and Japan*; Tokyo, 28 February 1952 (Vol. 208 *UNTS* 1955, No. 2817).

[9] Germany became party to the *NATO-SOFA* and the *Administrative Agreement* with Japan was adjusted to be in conformity with *NAVO-SOFA* with regard to the issue of criminal jurisdiction. In additional arrangements both Germany and Japan partly refrained from exercising jurisdiction.

[10] See Sect. 3.3.

[11] See Lazareff 1971, p. 274, who stated that France continued to apply the procedures of the agreements concluded during the war, including the claims provisions of the Civil Affairs Agreement.

[12] An example is the *Treaty relating to the status and facilities to be accorded in Belgium to the forces under the British High Command taking part in the occupation of Germany and Austria*; Brussels, 11 March 1946 (Vol. 26 *UNTS* 1948, No. 387). With regard to the jurisdiction over British forces, the Agreement contained a provision almost identical to the Civil Affairs Agreement concluded between both states: consideration 8 of the Memorandum in the *Exchange of notes (with annexed Memorandum of Agreement) constituting an agreement concerning civil administration and jurisdiction in Belgium territory liberated by an Allied Expeditionary Force*; London, 16 May 1944 (Vol. 90 *UNTS* 1951, No. 266). Later on, a similar provision was included in the agreement between Belgium and the US: Article 9 *Memorandum of Agreement regarding the Status and Facilities Accorded in Belgium to the United States Forces Engaged in the Occupation of Germany and Austria* in the Exchange of Notes; Brussels, 29 April 1948 (5 Bevans 661 1968).

in Germany and Austria, in principle exercised jurisdiction over the foreign forces.[13] However, if both the suspect and victim were members of the sending States' forces (so-called *inter se* offences) or if the offence was not punishable under French law, France could refrain from exercising jurisdiction in favour of the UK and the US.[14] Furthermore, there was the option of requesting France to refrain from exercising jurisdiction. The US had also concluded agreements with other States, which generally remained unpublished and were of a temporal and informal nature pursuant to which the US forces allegedly enjoyed full immunity in a limited number of States.[15] In other cases immunity was limited in some way or other.[16]

On the whole the SOFAs concluded directly after World War II showed a wide diversity, each approach being supported in the literature. A number of SOFAs mirrored the practice of occupation law or the SOFAs that were concluded under wartime conditions, to the effect that the forces were subject to the exclusive criminal jurisdiction of the sending States. During and just after the war, King, a former American military lawyer, defended this practice as a generally accepted principle.[17] In the post-war literature, Barton had a contradictory point of view and stated that in principle on the basis of international customary law forces from sending States were subject to the criminal jurisdiction of the host State's courts and exceptions were only admissible in cases of "express privilege or concession".[18] With the establishment of NATO many States opted for a middle ground between the two approaches, as will be discussed below.

---

[13] The status of British forces was set out down in the Agreement of 19 April 1948, *UKTS*, 1948, No. 44, mentioned in Stanger 1957/1958, p. 143 (the date is mentioned in: Lazareff 1971, p. 34). The position of American forces was included in a series of partly classified agreements with France. Their content is reflected in a declaration of the French Minister of Justice in his response to questions of the National Assembly of 1952. Parts are included in Lazareff 1971, p. 35. See also Article X, *Agreement between the United States of America and the Republic of France regarding Facilities for United States Forces in France in Connection with the Occupation of Germany and Austria*; Paris, 16 February 1948 (7 Bevans 1230 1968).

[14] Article 4 Agreement of 19 April 1948 (*UKTS* 1948, No. 44, mentioned in Stanger 1957/1958, p. 143). Apparently, the US had to make a request to the French Minister of Justice; Lazareff 1971, p. 35.

[15] Letter of the Acting Secretary of State Smith to Senator Wiley, 22 April 1953: Stanger 1957/1958, p. 143.

[16] The Agreement concluded with Poland in 1946 only granted the American forces immunity in case they were 'in an official or other character' on Polish territory; *Exchange of notes constituting an agreement relating to criminal offences committed by members of the armed forces of the two countries*; Warsaw, 5 and 29 August 1946 (Vol. 160 *UNTS* 1953, No. 2097).

[17] See King 1942, p. 567. See also Bathurst 1946.

[18] Barton 1950, p. 234.

5.2.2 NATO

As a response to the increasing influence of the SU on the Central and Eastern European States after World War II, the Western European States decided to cooperate extensively in the area of defence and establish a common defence. To that end, Belgium, France, Luxembourg, the Netherlands and the UK adopted the *Treaty of Brussels* in 1948.[19] In order to facilitate the envisioned stationing of forces of one Member State on the territory of one of the other Member States also a SOFA was drafted.[20] In contrast to the practice at that time this particular SOFA took criminal jurisdiction of the host State over the visiting forces as a starting point (Article 7(2), first sentence):

> "Members of a foreign force" who commit an offence in the "receiving state" against the law in force in that state can be prosecuted in the courts of the "receiving state".

This provision, however, was not absolute in nature. Subparagraph 2 further reads that, if the offence were also an offence against the law of the sending States, these States could request the host State for the transfer of the accused to the sending States' court. The host State then should examine the request "...with the greatest sympathy...". Furthermore, with respect to some offences, such as offences against the security or properties of the sending State, or against a member of the sending State's forces, or offences that would involve disloyalty to the sending State, the host State would only prosecute, if special considerations required it to do so (Article 7(2), 3rd sentence). In the end, the treaty never entered into force. Nevertheless, the draft texts of the *NATO-SOFA* build on these provisions.

The continuing communist threat led the parties to the *Treaty of Brussels* to enter into negotiations with Canada and the US on the establishment of an Atlantic alliance soon after conclusion of the Treaty. As a result the *NATO Treaty* was signed on 4 April 1949.[21] With a view to future allied cooperation Member States acknowledged the importance of a framework SOFA. The US drafted a first text based on the principle set out in the *Treaty of Brussels*.[22] Subsequent negotiations resulted in the *NATO-SOFA*.

According to Article I(a) the SOFA applies to forces present on the territory of other Member States in connexion with their official duties.[23] This means, for

---

[19] *Treaty for Collaboration in Economic, Social and Cultural Matters and for Collective Self-Defence*; Brussels, 17 March 1948 (Vol. 19 *UNTS* 1948, No. 304).

[20] *Status of members of the armed forces of the Brussels Treaty Powers*; Brussels, 21 December 1949 (Department of State Bulletin, 20 March 1950).

[21] *North Atlantic Treaty*; Washington, 4 April 1949 (Vol. 34 *UNTS* 1949, No. 541). In the Cold War era NATO membership increased to 16 Member States pursuant to Article X *NATO Treaty*.

[22] The US provided the first draft, as it had the largest number of forces based on the territory of other NATO Members; Snee 1961, p. 7.

[23] In the literature this perspective had already been addressed to the extent that the host State generally refrained from exercising its jurisdiction only in relation to organised visiting forces of another sovereign State.

instance, that a soldier spending his holidays in another NATO Member State is not covered by the treaty.[24]

Article VII contains a comprehensive and balanced arrangement of criminal jurisdiction.[25] Subparagraph 1 respects both the flag principle (sub a) and the principle of territoriality (sub b). Consequently, the sending State can exercise criminal jurisdiction over its military personnel in the host State. Conversely, the host State can exercise jurisdiction over visiting units. Through the explicit inclusion of both principles the Member States express that neither the sending State nor the host State has exclusive jurisdiction and that, a priori, neither of the two principles has overriding force.

Subparagraph 1 does not specify which State can actually exercise jurisdiction in a particular case. This aspect is settled in the following subparagraphs of Article VII. Subparagraph 2 is the fist logical step in distributing the right to exercise criminal jurisdiction. The sending State has the exclusive right to prosecute offences that are only punishable under its own laws (sub a).[26] Vice versa, with regard to offences that only violate the laws of the host State, the latter is the sole competent authority to exercise jurisdiction (sub b).[27]

If offences are punishable under the laws of both States, either of them has jurisdiction. Until then, the majority of SOFAs took the exclusive jurisdiction of the sending State as starting point or had allocated jurisdiction on the basis of specific criteria or conditions. In the *NATO-SOFA* concurrent jurisdiction is the key feature, which means that a State cannot exercise its jurisdiction by exclusion of the other State, but has the primary right to exercise jurisdiction.

Subparagraph 3 regulates which State has the primary right to exercise its jurisdiction. The sending State has primary jurisdiction over (1) offences against the property or the security of the sending State or against the person or property of another member of the force and (2) offences that result from any act done or omission in the performance of official duty (see subparagraph 3(a) (i) and (ii)).[28] In all other cases the host State has primary jurisdiction (see subparagraph 3(b)). If not, it can request the State having primary jurisdiction for a waiver pursuant to subparagraph 3(c).[29]

---

[24] Unless otherwise agreed; e.g., *Agreement between the Federal Republic of Germany and the United States on the status of persons on leave*; 3 August 1959 (partly published in: Stanger 1957/1958).

[25] E.g., Lazareff 1971, pp. 128 et seq.; Fleck 2003a, pp. 108 et seq.

[26] This criterion was used in the Agreement between the UK and France of 19 April 1948 (*UKTS* 1948, No. 44, mentioned in Stanger 1957/1958, p. 143).

[27] National legislation may forestall this situation. E.g., Article 170 of the Dutch *Military Penal Code* stipulates that acts committed by Dutch military personnel that are criminal offences under foreign criminal law, but not under Dutch criminal law, will be punishable as minor offences under Dutch criminal law.

[28] This criterion had already been defined in case law and used in different SOFAs, such as the Anglo-French Agreement of 1948.

[29] States have concluded several additional agreements waiving their primary rights to exercise jurisdiction in advance (e.g., para 3 Annex to the *Exchange of Notes (with Annex) Constituting an Agreement Relating to the Stationing of United States Armed Forces in the Netherlands*; The Hague, 13 August 1954 (Vol. 251 *UNTS* 1956, No. 3535). As a result the sending State's forces enjoy almost full immunity.

The third subparagraph contains several elements that were also part of the balanced interpretation of the ground rule. Probably, the most important element is the position of the foreign forces as an organ of the sending State. When a member of the sending State's armed forces commits an offence while on duty, the interests of the sending State prevail and it has primary jurisdiction. In addition, if in any other way the interests of the sending States are affected, these interests outweigh the interest of the host State to maintain public order and the sending State will have the primary right to exercise its jurisdiction. Furthermore, offences between soldiers of the sending State, the so-called inter se offences, also fall under the primary jurisdiction allocated to the sending State.

The *NATO-SOFA* does not preclude host States to exercise jurisdiction over visiting forces within their military bases and camps. This can be explained by the post-war conditions under which the alliance operates; the stationing of forces is no longer confined to specific military installations, which makes such a provision almost obsolete. Furthermore, military installations such as camps and barracks are not the exclusive territory of visiting units, but are often also the working places of local personnel and of servicemen of the host State or other States. In many cases, however, the sending State will indeed have primary jurisdiction over offences committed on the military installations, because on-base offences will most likely be directed against the property and security of the sending State.

The reciprocal character of the *NATO-SOFA*, which underscores the equal position of the Member States, emphasises the balanced nature of the provision on criminal jurisdiction. It applies to a Member State in its capacity both as sending State and as host State. Furthermore, the regulation provides States with some level of flexibility, if so desired, since the State having primary rights can waive those rights at the request of another State. In practice, this provision can restrict the exercise of host State's criminal jurisdiction through the conclusion of additional bilateral treaties.

As mentioned above, not all of the elements contained in the *NATO-SOFA* are completely new. However, the combination of the elements and the reciprocal character of the agreement offer a new perspective on SOFAs.

A protocol to the *NATO-SOFA* addresses the status of NATO's military headquarters. In short, the *Paris Protocol*[30] extends the *NATO-SOFA* provisions to the headquarters and their staffs and settles how responsibilities of parties to the *NATO-SOFA* will be exercised with regard to these headquarters.[31]

---

[30] *Protocol on the status of International Military Headquarters set up pursuant to the North Atlantic Treaty*; Paris, 28 August 1952 (Vol. 200 *UNTS* 1954, No. 2678). The *Paris Protocol* is equally applicable with respect to activities of NATO military headquarters and their personnel carried out in the territory of a party to the *Further Additional Protocol to the PfP treaty: Further Additional Protocol to the Agreement among the States Parties to the North Atlantic Treaty and the other States participating in the Partnership for Peace regarding the status of their forces*; Brussels, 19 December 1997.

[31] The *NATO-SOFA* entails rights and obligations for the Member States; in some cases the Headquarters shall have to function as an independent entity instead of a State.

At the time NATO was established, the Federal Republic of Germany (FRG) was still occupied.[32] Ideas were brought forward to rearm Germany and to involve it in the defence of West Europe within the European Defense Community (EDC).[33] The Treaty establishing the EDC provided for an integrated defence force, the European Defense Forces.[34] It was the intention that, at the time of entry into force of the treaty, the Member States would transfer "their powers to mete out punishment for the penal offenses which may be committed by the members of the European Defense Forces" to the EDF,[35] which required a common military criminal law.[36] These far-reaching ideas have never been realised, as the Treaty never entered into force.[37] When the occupying forces withdrew from the FRG, it joined NATO on 5 May 1955[38] and acceded as a party to the *NATO-SOFA* on 1 July 1963.

Later many agreements were concluded supplementing the *NATO-SOFA*. One of the most important agreements is the *Supplementary Agreement* to the *NATO-SOFA* that applies to NATO forces stationed in the FRG.[39] Article 19(1) of the Agreement states that the FRG would waive its primary rights to prosecute a suspect when both States had jurisdiction, if requested to do so by a sending State. Subsequently, as the *Agreed Minutes* to the *Supplementary Agreement* show, it was agreed that the sending States could already request a waiver at the time the *Supplementary Agreement* became effective, to which the FRG had to respond favourably. Only under specifical conditions could the FRG exercise jurisdiction. In practice, this arrangement was almost synonymous with the absolute immunity

---

[32] In 1949 the four Occupying Forces divided Germany into two States. In May that year the territory consisting of the American, British and French zones obtained its independence as the Federal Republic of Germany (FRG). In October, the Russian zone became the German Democratic Republic (GDR).

[33] Trybus 2007, pp. 14 et seq.

[34] Article 9 *Treaty constituting the European Defense Community*; Paris, 27 May 1952 (aei.pitt.edu/5201/1/5201.pdf. Accessed November 2014. Parties to this agreement would have been Belgium, the FRG, France, Italy, Luxembourg and the Netherlands.

[35] Article 18 *Protocol concerning jurisdiction* to the *Treaty constituting the European Defense Community*; Paris, 27 May 1952 (aei.pitt.edu/5201/1/5201.pdf. Accessed November 2014).

[36] Article 19 *Protocol concerning jurisdcition*. For other elements normally contained in SOFAs, see *Convention relative to the Status of European Defense Forces and the tax and commercial regime of the European Defense Community*; Paris, 27 May 1952 (aei.pitt.edu/5201/1/5201.pdf. Accessed November 2014).

[37] The FRG acceded to the *Treaty of Brussels* at the moment the Treaty was modified and the organisation continued to exist as the West European Union (WEU); *Protocol modifying and completing the Treaty of Brussels*; Paris 23 October 1954 (Vol. 211 *UNTS* 1955, No. 304).

[38] *Protocol to the North Atlantic Treaty on the accession of the Federal Republic of Germany*; Paris 23 October 1954 (Vol. 243 *UNTS* 1956 No. 541).

[39] *Agreement to Supplement the Agreement between the Parties to the North Atlantic Treaty regarding the Status of their Forces with respect to Foreign Forces stations in the Federal Republic of Germany*; Bonn, 3 August 1959 (Vol. 481 *UNTS* 1963, No. 6986).

of visiting forces from the jurisdiction of German courts.[40] Conversely, however, the provision of the *NATO-SOFA* continued to apply to the German forces stationed in many other NATO member States, such as the Netherlands,[41] Canada, the UK and the US.[42]

In addition, in supplementary agreements with the FRG the US had secured that the provisions of the *Supplementary Agreement* would also apply to American personnel stationed in North Africa and elsewhere in Europe, who were on leave in the FRG.[43] Furthermore, the US concluded several bilateral supplementary agreements with a number of NATO Member States that set out in more detail the waiver-procedure of Article VII, subparagraph 3(c) of the *NATO-SOFA*. In these agreements, the host States waived their primary right to exercise jurisdiction pursuant to Article VII in advance.[44] The Netherlands was the first State to waive its primary right in this way, with the following reservation:

> except where they [the Netherlands authorities] determine that it is of particular importance that jurisdiction be exercised by the Netherlands authorities.[45]

These agreements gave American forces far-reaching, although not absolute, protection against the exercise of jurisdiction by local courts.

In summary, the stationing of forces in the context of the common Western military cooperation in their defence against the threat from the East was initially characterised by the right of host States to exercise jurisdiction. In the *SOFA* to the *Treaty*

---

[40] Lazareff 1971, p. 432. In case sending States did not exercise their jurisdiction, the FRG still disposed of the secondary right to exercise jurisdiction.

[41] Article 4 *Agreement regarding the stationing of military units of the Federal Republic of Germany in the Netherlands*; The Hague, 17 January 1963 (Vol. 474 *UNTS* 1963, No. 6877).

[42] E.g., *Agreement between the Department of Defense of the United States of America, referred to as "DoD" and the Federal Minister of Defense of the Federal Republic of Germany, referred to as "FMOD", on the stationing of training components of the FMOD in the United States (with annexes)*; Bonn, 24 May 1977 and Washington, 6 July 1977 (Vol. 1178 *UNTS* 1980, No. 18590) and *Exchange of notes constituting an agreement between the government of Canada and the government of the Federal Republic of Germany concerning German air flight training in the vicinity of Goose Bay, Labrador*; Bonn, 8 April 1981 (Vol. 1470 *UNTS* 1987, No. 24921). The UK applied a provision from the *NATO-SOFA* to the German forces present on its territory, before the FRG was a party to the Treaty: *Exchange of notes constituting an agreement between the government of the United Kingdom of Great Britain and Northern Ireland and the government of the Federal Republic of Germany applying to any force of the Federal Republic serving in the United Kingdom the provisions of the Agreement between the parties to the North Atlantic Treaty Organisation regarding the status of their forces, signed in London on 19 June 1951*; Bonn, 12 July 1961 (Vol. 421 *UNTS* 1962, No. 6109).

[43] *Agreement between the Federal Republic of Germany and the United States on the status of persons on leave*; 3 August 1959 (partly published in: Stanger 1957/1958).

[44] Moreover, it was American policy to obtain a waiver in case no supplementary agreement was concluded, in which they appeared to have been very successful; Stambuk 1963a, p. 110.

[45] Article 3 of the Annex to the *Exchange of Notes Constituting an Agreement Relating to the Stationing of United States Armed Forces in the Netherlands*; The Hague, 13 August 1954 (Vol. 251 *UNTS* 1956, No. 3535).

of Brussels the position of the host State in this matter was even the starting point. Shortly afterwards, States managed to balance the interests of both sending States and host States in the *NATO-SOFA* signifying a new approach to criminal jurisdiction.

5.2.3 Bilateral Cooperation Outside the Context of NATO

In Western Europe international military cooperation in general took place within the NATO framework. In other parts of the world several States continued their military presence in the former colonial territories.[46] France in particular maintained strong military relations with its former colonies in Africa.[47] In 1960 it concluded, for instance, a defence agreement with the Central African Republic (CAR), Congo and Chad on the use of military installations in these States.[48] The Annexes to the bilateral agreements that France concluded on the basis of the defence agreement[49] regulated the status of the French forces, stating that France could exercise its criminal jurisdiction:

> in respect of any offence with which a member of the French armed forces is charged and which is committed while he is on duty or committed within the bases or installations of such forces.

In other cases France could request the host States to waive its right to exercise jurisdiction. French agreements with other African States contained similar provisions.[50]

Compared to France the UK kept more distance from its colonial territories in military matters.[51] After their independence the UK continued its military presence in a few former colonies and by the end of the 1980s the UK only had forces stationed in Belize, Brunei en Cyprus. With regard to criminal jurisdiction the SOFAs concluded by the UK followed the *NATO-SOFA*.[52] Only the position of its

46 For a more detailed overview see Harkavy 2007, pp. 141–145 and Appendix IV.

47 Berman and Sams 2000, pp. 291 et seq. France reserved the right to base forces in, for example, the CAR, Djibouti, Gabon, Ivory Coast, Cameroon, Senegal and Chad: Gregory 2000, p. 438. Also mentioned are: Burkina Faso, Madagascar and Togo, Jacques Baillet, Tribunal aux Armées de Paris 2009.

48 Article 4 *Defence Agreement*; Brazzaville, 15 August 1960 (Vol. 821 *UNTS* 1972, No. 11761) and Article 5 of the Annex to the Agreement.

49 *Agreement concerning technical military assistance*; Bangui, 13 August 1960 (Vol. 821 *UNTS* 1972, No. 11759), *Agreement concerning technical military assistance*; Brazzaville, 15 August 1960 (Vol. 821 *UNTS* 1972, No. 11755) and *Agreement concerning technical military assistance (with annex and exchange of letters)*; Paris, 19 May 1964 (Vol. 653 *UNTS* 1969, No. 9443).

50 E.g., Cameroon 1960 and Djibouti 1977.

51 Berman and Sams 2000, p. 317; see also Woodliffe 1992, p. 68.

52 E.g., Annex 3, Section 1 *Agreement (with annexes and exchange of letters) on external defence and mutual assistance*; Kuala Lumpur, 12 October 1957 (Vol. 285 *UNTS* 1958, No. 4149) and Article 1 *Agreement regarding the status of the armed forces of the United Kingdom in Botswana*; Gaborone, 30 September 1966 (Vol. 595 *UNTS* 1967, No. 8646).

forces in Cyprus is somewhat exceptional, as since the establishment of the Republic of Cyprus the UK has retained sovereign rights over two areas (the Sovereign Base Areas (SBA) of Akrotiri and Dhekelia).[53] Within the SBA the UK can exercise exclusive jurisdiction over its forces, whereas outside the SBA it exercises jurisdiction over its forces in conformity with the jurisdiction provision of the *NATO-SOFA*.[54]

The US considered the NATO agreements merely as part of their entire security policy. In 1947 President Truman acclaimed the containment of communism as the leading principle of American foreign policy.[55] Against this backdrop, the US established defence alliances that encircled the European and Asian communist States.[56] An extensive network of military bases supported this policy, strengthening international political and economic relations at the same time.[57] In addition, the US concluded a number of bilateral defence agreements, often based on the *Mutual Defense Assistance Act*.[58]

Some States accepted that the US could exercise exclusive criminal jurisdiction over its forces on their territory.[59] However, the majority of SOFAs limited US jurisdiction to a certain extent. Some SOFAs, that originally provided for the exclusive criminal jurisdiction of the US over its forces, were modified at a later date. An example is Panama, where in 1977 the exclusive criminal jurisdiction of the US was restricted to military sites and outside these sites to offences committed against American property, security or personnel, or to offences resulting from the performance of official duties.[60] The US agreed to follow the *NATO-SOFA*

---

[53] Article 1 *Treaty concerning the establishment of the Republic of Cyprus*; Nicosia, 16 August 1960 (Vol. 382 *UNTS* 1960, No. 5476).

[54] Section 8, Annex C, *Treaty concerning the establishment of the Republic of Cyprus*; Nicosia, 16 August 1960 (Vol. 382 *UNTS* 1960, No. 5476). Within the SBA, Cyprus has similar rights on the basis of this reciprocal provision.

[55] 12 March 1947; Duke 1989, p. vii.

[56] Harkavy 2007, p. 96 and Mott 2002, p. 2. In addition to the NATO agreements, mention can be made of the *Inter-American Treaty on Reciprocal Assistance*, the Rio Pact; 1947, the *Australia-New-Zealand-US Security Treaty*, ANZUS; 1951 and the *Southeast Asia Collective Defence Treaty*, SEATO; 1954 and the bilateral agreements with Japan, South Korea and Taiwan.

[57] For an overview of American installations, see Harkavy 2007, pp. 98–124 and Appendix IV.

[58] *Mutual Defense Assistance Act of 1949, AJIL* 1950, pp. 68 et seq. Particularly in the 1950s the US concluded several bilateral treaties to this end.

[59] Sometime this was regulated explicitly. E.g., Article XVII of the agreement with Ethiopia stated that: "Members of the United States forces shall be immune from the criminal jurisdiction of Ethiopian courts"; *Agreement between the Government of the United States of America and the Imperial Ethiopian Government concerning the utilization of defense installations within the Empire of Ethiopia*; Washington, 22 May 1953 (Vol. 191 *UNTS* 1954, No. 2577). On other occasions, full jurisdiction resulted from granting military personnel a status equivalent to that of the administrative and technical staff of an embassy. These types of agreements were mostly concluded with respect to relatively small missions.

[60] Article VI *Agreement in implementation of article IV of the Panama Canal Treaty* (with annexes and agreed minutes); Washington, 7 September 1977 (Vol. 1280 *UNTS* 1982, No. 21088).

approach to criminal jurisdiction with other States, for instance Japan,[61] Korea[62] and the Philippines,[63] where the US has leased large military bases.

In sum, within the framework of military cooperation the *NATO-SOFA* approach to criminal jurisdiction was widely followed outside the NATO framework. Several States, though, granted sending States an extension of the right to exercise criminal jurisdiction over their forces and in some cases host States waived their criminal jurisdiction completely.

5.2.4 Eastern Europe

The FRG's participation in both the West European Union[64] and NATO led the SU to establish an Eastern European system of collective defence.[65] On 15 May 1955 the *Warsaw Pact Treaty* was signed, constituting the legal basis for military cooperation between the participating states.[66] Individual bilateral agreements with

---

[61] *Protocol to amend Article XVII of the Administrative Agreement under article III of the Security Treaty between the United States of America and Japan;* Tokyo, 29 September 1953 (Vol. 208 *UNTS* 1955, No. 2817). In 1960 Japan and the US adopted the *Treaty of Mutual Co-operation Security between Japan and the United States of America*; Washington, 19 January 1960. With regard to the criminal jurisdiction, the SOFA adopted on the same day, did not deviate from the *Administrative Agreement; Agreement under article VI of the Treaty of Mutual Co-operation and Security between Japan and the United States of America, regarding facilities and areas and the status of United States armed forces in Japan*; Washington, 19 January 1960.

[62] *Agreement under Article IV of the Mutual Defense Treaty between the United States of America and the Republic of Korea, regarding facilities and areas and the status of United States Armed Forces in the Republic of Korea* (with agreed minutes, agreed understandings and exchange of letters); Seoul, 9 July 1966 (Vol. 674 *UNTS* 1971, No. 9605). Moreover, the US can request South Korea to waive its criminal jurisdiction. This 'waiver-procedure' is in line with the *Supplementary Agreement* to the *NATO-SOFA,* and means in practice that Korea is severely restricted in exercising criminal jurisdiction over American soldiers, Wexler 2008, p. 62.

[63] *Exchange of notes (with Annex, agreed official minutes and agreed implementing arrangements) constituting an agreement amending the Agreement between the Republic of the Philippines and the United States of America concerning military bases*; Manila, 10 August 1965 (*UNTS* 1966, No. 6730). American jurisdiction over its forces remained almost complete, because in the *Agreed official minutes* the Philippines partly waived their rights in advance.

[64] On the occasion of FRG's and Italy's accession to the *Treaty of Brussels,* the treaty was modified and the organisation continued as the West European Union: *Protocol modifying and completing the Treaty of Brussels*; Paris 23 October 1954 (Vol. 211 *UNTS* 1955, No. 304).

[65] As there is little to no information on the status of Soviet forces based outside Europe, this will not be discussed here. For an overview of Russian bases, see Harkavy 2007, pp. 129–141 and Appendix IV.

[66] *Treaty of friendship, co-operation and mutual assistance between the People's Republic of Albania, the People's Republic of Bulgaria, the Hungarian's People's Republic, the German Democratic Republic, the Polish People's Republic, the Romanian People's Republic, the Union of Soviet Socialist Republics and the Czechoslovak Republic*; Warsaw, 14 May 1955 (Vol. 219 *UNTS* 1956, No. 2962). The Treaty entered into force on 6 June 1955.

Poland,[67] the GDR,[68] Romania[69] and Hungary[70] enabled the stationing of Soviet forces on their territory[71] and simultaneously regulated the status of these forces.[72]

Although these bilateral agreements were not completely identical, they hardly differed. Exercise of criminal jurisdiction by the host States was the starting point of the agreements: in case a member of the Soviet forces committed an offence, the host State could prosecute the suspect. This provision did not apply to offences "solely against the Soviet Union or against an individual serving with the Soviet forces or a member of the family of such individual" or offences "...in the performance of his official duties". In addition, the parties could request the transfer or the taking over of the jurisdiction.

This meant that also in Eastern Europe the position of the host State was given due attention in the regulation of the status of visiting foreign forces. Under conditions resembling the requirements of the *NATO-SOFA*, the SU could exercise jurisdiction over its own forces.[73] Besides, as the SU conscripts were hardly allowed to spend off-duty time outside the military bases, contacts between the foreign forces and the local population were less frequent than in NATO member States.

5.3 After the Cold War

At the end of the 1980s international tensions relaxed and the traditional East-West divide disappeared rapidly. In November 1989 this led to the fall of the Berlin Wall, symbolising the end of the Cold War. These developments changed

---

67 *Treaty concerning the legal status of Soviet forces temporarily stationed in Poland*; Warsaw, 17 December 1956 (Vol 226 *UNTS* 1957, No. 3830).

68 With a reference to the *Warsaw Pact Treaty* the status of forces was regulated in: *Abkommen zwischen der Regierung der DDR und der Regierung der UdSSR über Fragen, die mit der zeitweiligen Stationierung sowjetischer Streitkräfte auf dem Territorium der DDR zusammenhängen*; Berlin, 12 March 1957 (Vol. 285 *UNTS* 1958, No. 4150).

69 *Agreement concerning the legal status of Soviet forces temporarily stationed in the territory of the Romanian People's Republic;* Bucharest, 15 April 1957 (*UNTS* 1957, No. 3964). The agreement was not renewed after the withdrawal of the Soviet forces from the country in 1958.

70 *Agreement concerning the legal status of Soviet forces temporarily stationed in the territory of the Hungarian People's Republic*; Budapest, 27 May 1957 (Vol. 407 *UNTS* 1957, No. 5864).

71 The agreements were not reciprocal, as they did not allow for the basing of foreign forces in the SU.

72 The SU did not conclude an agreement with Bulgaria, as it withdrew its forces after the adoption of the *Peace Treaty* in 1947. With regard to Czechoslovakia, it was not until the Soviet invasion that put an end to the Prague Spring in 1968 that Russian forces were based there. Immediately after the invasion a SOFA legalising the basing of Russian Forces was adopted; mentioned in: Verona 1992, p. 190, fn 23.

73 From NATO's perspective, this would come down to the exercise of primary jurisdiction. However, in the context of the Warsaw Pact, host States waived their jurisdiction, which resulted in the immunity of Russian forces.

the international security situation dramatically and reduced the necessity to maintain the same number of forces stationed abroad.[74]

5.3.1 Partnership for Peace, the Extension of NATO and EU

On 1 July 1991 the Warsaw Pact ceased to exist. NATO, in its turn, adapted to the new international relations, also focussing on security and stability of the Euro-Atlantic region.[75] To this end it established friendly relations with Eastern and Central European States,[76] for instance through the Partnership for Peace (PfP) program.[77] In the context of PfP many common activities are taking place, such as international training and multilateral exercises.

The status of forces of both NATO and PfP member States is governed by the *NATO-SOFA*. Article I of the *PfP-SOFA* states that parties to the Treaty shall apply the *NATO-SOFA*, as if they were party to the latter.[78] Through the extension of NATO[79] and the accession of many PfP member States to the *PfP-SOFA*, the application of the *NATO-SOFA* has expanded to almost the entire territory of Europe and to parts of Asia.[80]

Most of the current supplementary agreements to the *NATO-SOFA,* in which host States waive their primary jurisdiction, remained unchanged, such as the *US-Netherlands Agreement* of 1954. After the reunification of Germany on 30 October

[74] E.g., the US closed 60 % of their bases abroad, see Strengthening the U.S. Global Defense Posture 2004, p. 10. They were also forced to withdraw their military forces from the Philippines; see Harkavy 2007, pp. 151–155. Only a handful of the Russian bases abroad remained in the States south of the Russian Federation; Harkavy 2007, pp. 147–148.

[75] Giegerich 2008, p. 120; see also the NATO Strategic Concept 1999. www.nato.int/cps/en/natolive/official_texts_27433.htm. Accessed November 2014.

[76] E.g., see the *London Declaration on a transformed North Atlantic Alliance*; 5–6 July 1990, www.nato.int/docu/comm/49-95/c900706a.htm. Accessed November 2014.

[77] In January 1994 NATO adopted a program to establish practical bilateral cooperation between individual Euro-Atlantic partner States and NATO; Partnership for Peace Framework Document 1994.

[78] *Agreement among the States Parties to the North Atlantic Treaty and the other States participating in the Partnership for Peace regarding the Status of their Forces*; Brussels, 19 June 1995.

[79] In the post-Cold War era enlargement of NATO to 28 member States, all party to the *NATO-SOFA*, took place in three steps: Hungary, Poland and the Czech Republic acceded on 12 March 1999; Bulgaria, Estonia, Latvia, Lithuania, Romania, Slovakia and Slovenia on 29 March 2004; Albania and Croatia on 1 April 2009. Currently, Bosnia and Herzegovina, Georgia, Montenegro and the former Yugoslav Republic of Macedonia are aspiring members.

[80] For an overview of the parties to the Treaty see: www.state.gov/documents/organization/91332.pdf. Accessed November 2014.

1990[81] the provisions in the *Supplementary Agreement* were somewhat revised.[82] Nevertheless, sending States retained their far-reaching rights over their forces stationed in Germany, so that in practice Germany could seldom exercise criminal jurisdiction over these forces.[83]

Conversely, the arrangement did not apply to German forces stationed in other NATO member States. Germany attempts to rectify this inequality through bilateral agreements. For example, since 1997 the *Supplementary Agreement* with the Netherlands has applied to the status of German forces stationed in the Netherlands.[84] In Article 14 of the Agreement the Netherlands waives the exercise of jurisdiction in cases of concurrent jurisdiction. However, the Netherlands can revoke the waiver in individual cases in special circumstances, such as seriously violent crimes.[85]

With a view to EU crisis management operations the *EU-SOFA* was signed in Brussels on 17 November 2003.[86] This SOFA regulates, inter alia, the status of EU Member States' forces that are stationed on other Member States' territory in preparation or execution of EU-led operations.[87] As the EU can make use of NATO

---

[81] On that day the GDR became part of the FRG on the basis of the *Vertrag zwischen der Bundesrepublik Deutschland und der Deutschen Demokratischen Republik über die Herstellung der Einheit Deutschlands*; Berlin, 31 August 1990 (*BGBl* 1990 II, 889); Fleck 2003c, p. 355.

[82] Germany was of the opinion that the existing SOFAs, i.e. the *NATO-SOFA* and the *Supplemetary Agreement,* should reflect a better balance between the rights of the sending State and those of Germany; Dutch Parliamentary papers 1999/00, 27 097, nrs. 224 and 1, p. 3.

[83] With regard to Dutch soldiers, it was not until 2007 that Germany revoked the waiver for the first time in a specific case and exercised its jurisdiction over the Dutch soldiers based in Germany; van den Bosch 2008, p. 195.

[84] *Supplementary Agreement to the Agreement of 19 June 1951 between the States that are party to the North Atlantic Treaty on the status of their armed forces in relation to German forces stationed in the Kingdom of the Netherlands*; Bergen, 6 October 1997 (Vol. 2401 *UNTS* 2006, No. 43364).

[85] Explanatory Note to the four defense treaties with Germany; Dutch Parliamentary Papers 1999/00, 27 097, nrs. 224 and 1, p. 8.

[86] *Agreement between the Member States of the European Union concerning the status of military and civilian staff seconded to the institutions of the European Union, of the headquarters and forces which may be made available to the European Union in the context of the preparation and execution of the tasks referred to in Article* 17(2) *of the Treaty to the European Union, including exercises, and of the military and civilian staff of the Member States put at the disposal of the European Union to act in this context* (*EU-SOFA*); Brussels, 17 November 2003 (OJ 2004, C 321). The Agreement has not come into force yet.

[87] Next, in April 2004, the *EU Claims Agreement* was signed and includes a supplementary provision to the SOFA for claims for damage sustained outside the territory of EU Member States of one Member State to another Member State in the context of an EU crisis management operation: *EU-claims agreement: Agreement between Member States of the European Union concerning claims introduced by each Member State against any other Member State for damage to any property owned, used or operated by it or injury or death suffered by any military or civilian staff of its services, in the context of an EU crisis management operation*; Brussels, 28 April 2004 (*OJ* 2004, C 116).

means,[88] it was necessary to gear the *EU-SOFA* to existing NATO arrangements. Therefore, Article 19(6(a)) of the *EU-SOFA* states that the Treaty is applicable in the absence of another agreement that regulates the status of personnel. In cases the status is regulated by other agreements States and organisations concerned can conclude specific arrangements on the applicability of the various agreements (subparagraph 6(b)), but if it is not possible to conclude such arrangements, the other agreements shall remain applicable (subparagraph 6(c)). This means that in many situations the NATO agreements, such as the *NATO-SOFA* or the *Paris Protocol*, remain applicable. The most important elements of the *NATO-SOFA*, including the provisions on criminal jurisdiction, have been incorporated in the *EU-SOFA* almost literally (Articles 17 and 18).

A special arrangement applies to personnel EU Member States contribute to the activities of the European Agency for the Management of Operational Cooperation at the External Borders (FRONTEX). Their status is set out in several EU regulations stating that personnel shall be treated as staff members of the host State with regard to criminal offences.[89] As a result it can be concluded that foreign officials fall under jurisdiction of the host State.

Furthermore, in 2007 some EU Member States established the European Gendarmerie Force (EGF) as a rapidly deployable police force with military status tasked to perform all police tasks within the scope of crisis management operations.[90] Article 25 of the *EGF Agreement* regulates the criminal jurisdiction of the EGF personnel stationed in the territory of the Member States in the same way as the *NATO-SOFA* and the *EU-SOFA* do (reference to both SOFAs is made in the preamble).

In summary, after the Cold War the *NATO-SOFA* approach to criminal jurisdiction was widely followed. PfP Member States applied the *NATO-SOFA*, as if they were party to the Agreement and the number of NATO member States increased through the enlargement of NATO. In addition, the *NATO-SOFA* approach was also applied following its implementation in other SOFAs by organisations such as the EU.

---

[88] The EU can use NATO means on the basis of the *'Berlin-Plus' agreements* of 17 March 2003. For instance, the EU has used this possibility during the Operation Concordia and EUFOR-Althea; Paulo 2008, pp. 23–24.

[89] Article 10 quarter *Regulation nr. 2007/2004* of 26 October 2004 on the establishment of FRONTEX (*OJ* 2004, L 349/1), modified by *Regulation nr. 836/2007* of 11 July 2007 (*OJ* L 2007, 199/30) and *Regulation nr. 1168/2004* of 25 October 2011 (*OJ* 2011, L 304/1) and Article 11 *Regulation nr. 836/2007* of 11 July 2007 establishing a mechanism for the creation of Rapid Border Intervention Teams (*OJ* L 2007, 199/30).

[90] *Treaty between the Kingdom of Spain, the French Republic, the Italian Republic, the Kingdom of the Netherlands and the Portuguese Republic, establishing the European Gendarmerie Force* (*EUROGENDFOR*); Velsen, 18 October 2007. www.eurogendfor.org/eurogendfor-library/download-area/official-texts/establishing-the-eurogendfor-treaty. Accessed November 2014.

5.3.2 The Security Situation After 11 September 2001

In the post-Cold War period it became clear that armed conflicts posed not the only threat to the international community. Poverty and contagious diseases, weapons of mass destruction, terrorism, cross-border organised crime, the threat of cyber attacks and climate change also play a role.[91] The attack on the US of September 2001 followed by serious attacks in other parts of the world made these threats very real.[92] States have to take into consideration that events occurring far outside their borders may have a direct effect on their national security situation.

This may mean that States have to deploy their forces more often and further away from their own region. As the network of foreign bases built during World War II and the Cold War has partly disappeared, more ad hoc provisions are necessary.[93] Today the US focuses on the arc of crisis running from North Africa, via the Horn of Africa and the Caucasus to Central Asia.[94] This approach means that the US still needs bases (Main Operating Bases) in Europe and Asia in support of operations taking place elsewhere in the world.[95] In and around the regions where operations are to take place Forward Operating Sites have been established, from where small-scale expeditionary units can operate.[96] In the area of operation itself the units conducting the operations must have access to airbases, naval bases and other facilities that are minimally equipped for use by the US forces. Like the Forward Operating Sites, these Cooperative Security Locations do not have a permanent US presence and are maintained by local forces.[97] The US units using these sites and locations rotate frequently and stay there for a short period of time.[98]

This approach means that the US has to conclude new agreements with respect to the installations to be used and the status of their forces and may have to revise existing agreements.[99] The content of these arrangements may diverge widely. Sometimes the US forces enjoy full criminal immunity, for example, when military personnel obtain a status equivalent to that of the administrative and technical

---

91 High-level Panel 2004 and European Security Strategy 2003, p. 3.

92 Bali (October 2002), Madrid (March 2004), London (July 2005) and Mumbai (November 2008).

93 Harkavy 2007, p. 158.

94 Id., pp. 150 and 154.

95 Strengthening the U.S. Global Defense Posture 2004, p. 10. E.g., Ramstein Air Force Base in Germany.

96 Lachowski 2007, pp. 8–9. E.g., Camp Lemonnier in Djibouti is the Forward Operational Site for the Combined Joint Task Force Horn of Africa (CJTF HOA), Ploch 2009, p. 8.

97 Id., p. 8.

98 Lachowski 2007, p. 15.

99 Peterson 2009, p. 197.

staff of an embassy.[100] In other cases the forces are partly subject to the exercise of criminal jurisdiction of the host State's courts, as the SOFA between Iraq and the US concluded when the UN mandate for the operation in Iraq expired on 31 December 2008 demonstrates.[101] On the basis of Article 12 of that treaty Iraq obtained the primary right to exercise jurisdiction over American soldiers for grave premeditated felonies committed outside agreed facilities and areas and outside duty status (subparagraph 1). The US obtained the primary right to exercise jurisdiction over members of the US forces with regard to "matters arising inside the agreed facilities and areas, during duty status outside agreed facilities and areas and in circumstances not covered by para 1" (subparagraph 3).[102]

Other States, such as the UK and France, maintain a more modest number of military bases abroad. For instance, on 26 May 2009, France opened a military basis abroad, the first in very long time.[103] From this strategically located base in Abu Dhabi its forces assist, for instance, the EU naval operation Atalanta. States without extensive military means will not be able to station forces abroad permanently. Still, the new international security situation is a challenge to them, as current operations are likely to take place in other regions and in more demanding circumstances than the forces have trained for over the last decades. In order to prepare their units, facilities for realistic training may have to be sought in States outside their region, with which there may not have been military relations so far. In addition, ongoing budget cuts are an incentive to Western forces to merge capabilities and consider far-reaching cooperation.[104]

Also, today States are more and more aware of the fact that international peace and security requires cooperation with unstable States to strengthen regional

[100] Palmer 2008, p. 79.

[101] *Agreement Between the United States of America and the Republic of Iraq on the Withdrawal of US Forces from Iraq and the Organisation of their Activities during their Temporary Presence in Iraq*; 17 November 2008 (www.state.gov/documents/organization/122074.pdf. Accessed November 2014).

[102] The SOFA between Iraq and the UK contained a similar arrangement in Article 6(1): "The United Kingdom Forces shall be subject to the jurisdiction of Iraq with the exception of crimes committed while on duty which are not committed with intent or do not arise from gross negligence, with the exception of those committed by them inside the United Kingdom Forces facility referred to in Article 4, in which case they shall be subject to the jurisdiction of the United Kingdom": *Agreement Concerning the Training and Maritime Support to the Iraqi Forces by and between the Government of the United Kingdom of Great Britain and Northern Ireland and the Government of the Republic of Iraq*, Bagdad 6 June 2009 ([2010] UKTS 4).

[103] *Accord entre le Gouvernement de la République Française et le Gouvernement de la République des Emirats arabes unis relatif à la coopération en matière de défense*; Abu Dhabi, 26 May 2009.

[104] E.g., *Dutch Parliamentary Papers II* 2011/12, 33 279 nr. 2 (Response of the Government to the advice of the Dutch Advisory Council on International Affairs on 'European defense cooperation') en *Dutch Parliamentary Papers II* 2011/12, 33 279 nr. 3 (International military cooperation).

Table 5.1 Criminal jurisdiction over Dutch forces

Bilateral military cooperation	Dutch Jurisdiction over its forces	
Belize (2004–2005)	Exclusive[a]	–
Benin, exercise (2009–….)	Exclusive[b]	–
Brunei (2004–2005)	Shared[c]	cfm. *NATO-SOFA approach to criminal jurisdiction*
Burundi, SSD (2009–….)	Functional immunity[d]	Reciprocal
Cameroon, exercise (2006)	Exclusive[e]	–
EASBRICOM, capacity building (2011–….)	Functional immunity[f]	–
Egypte, exercise (2005)	Limited[g]	–
Gabon, cooperation (2009–….)	Exclusive[h]	Reciprocal
Mali, cooperation (2010–….)	Functional immunity[i]	Reciprocal
Morocco, cooperation (2013–…)	Shared[j]	cfm. *NATO-SOFA approach to criminal jurisdiction*
Ruanda, cooperation (2009–….)	Functional immunity[k]	Reciprocal
Senegal, exercise (2005–2006)	Exclusive[l]	–
Senegal, training (2010)	Exclusive[m]	–
South Africa, cooperation (2007–….)	Functional immunity[n]	Reciprocal
Surinam, capacity building (1975–1981)	Exclusive jurisdiction[o]	Status cfm. Diplomatic Relations Treaty
Surinam, education and training (2004–2010)	Full immunity[p]	Status cfm. Diplomatic Relations Treaty
Tanzania, training (2002)	Shared[q]	cfm. *NATO-SOFA approach to criminal jurisdiction*
Uganda education and training (2012–…)	Functional immunity[r]	–
Zwitzerland (2007–….)	Shared[s]	cfm. *NATO-SOFA approach to criminal jurisdiction*; reciprocal

[a] Article III(2) *Exchange of notes constituting an agreement between the Kingdom of the Netherlands and Belize concerning the status of Netherlands military and civilian personnel related to training*; Mexico City, 21 January 2005 (*Dutch Treaty Series* 2005, 41)

[b] Article III(3) *Exchange of notes constituting an agreement between the Kingdom of the Netherlands and the Republic of Benin concerning the status of civilian and military personnel of the Netherlands Ministry of Defence, present on the territory of Benin for the exercise "DASSA 2009"*; Cotonou, 7 July 2009 (Vol. 2743 *UNTS* No. 48474)

[c] Article III *Exchange of notes constituting an agreement between the government of the Kingdom of the Netherlands and government of His Majesty the Sultan and Yang Dipertuan of Brunei Darussalam concerning the status of Netherlands military personnel realting training*; Singapore, 21 December 2004 (*Dutch Treaty Series* 2005, 40)

[d] Article 3(3) *Agreement between the Kingdom of the Netherlands and the Republic of Burundi concerning the status of civilian and military personnel of the Netherlands and Burundian Ministries of Defence, present in the territory of the other State in the framework of the partnership for the development of the Burundian security sector*; Bujumbura, 17 August 2009 (Vol. 2637 UNTS 2013, No. 46976)

[e] MOU ('Arrangement Technique'); not published

Table 5.1 (continued)

[f] Article 2(5) *Exchange of notes constituting an agreement between the Kingdom of the Netherlands and the Eastern Africa Standby Brigade Coordination Mechanism (EASBRICOM) concerning cooperation in support of the Eastern Africa Standby Force*; Nairobi, 21 Januaryi 2011 (*Dutch Treaty Series* 2011, 69) refers to the *Host Country Agreement between EASBRICOM and the Government of the Republic of Kenya for the purpose of hosting EASBRICOM and its subordinate structures in Kenya*; Nairobi, 28 May 2008

[g] MOU, not published. Jurisdiction of the Netherlands was limited to offences related to the exercise or committed in the training area

[h] Article 3(3) *Exchange of notes constituting an Agreement between the Kingdom of the Netherlands and the Republic of Gabon concerning the status of military and civilian personnel of the Ministry of Defence of the contracting parties, present in each other's territory for activities related to bilateral military cooperation*; Yaoundé, 16 October 2009 (Vol. 2653 *UNTS* 2009 No. 47208)

[i] Article III(3) *Exchange of notes constituting an agreement between the Kingdom of the Netherlands and the Republic of Mali concerning the status of military and civilian personnel of the Netherlands and Malian Ministries of Defence, present in each other's territory for activities related to bilateral military cooperation*; Koulouba, 17 June (Vol. 2711 *UNTS* No. 48007)

[j] Article 3 *Agreement between the Kingdom of the Netherlands and the Kingdom of Morocco concerning the status of forces*; Rabat, 21 May 2013 (*Dutch Treaty Series* 2013, 96)

[k] Article 3(3) *Agreement between the Kingdom of the Netherlands and the Republic of Rwanda concerning the status of military and civilian personnel of their Ministry of Defence present in each other's territory for activities related to bilateral military cooperation*; Kigali, 13 May 2009 (Vol. 2787 *UNTS* No. 49014)

[l] Article III(3) *Agreement between the Government of the Kingdom of the Netherlands and the Republic of Senegal concerning the status of Netherlands military and civilian personnel relating to multilateral military exercises*; Dakar, 26 October 2005 (*Dutch Treaty Series* 2005, 287)

[m] Article III(3) *Agreement between the Government of the Kingdom of the Netherlands and the Republic of Senegal concerning the status of forces*; Dakar, 18 October 2010 (*UNTS* No. 49254)

[n] Article 3(3) *Agreement between the Government of the Kingdom of the Netherlands and the Government of the Republic of South Africa concerning the status of military and civilian personnel of their department/ministry of defence present in each other's territory for activities related to military cooperation*; Tshwane (Pretoria), 8 June 2007 (Vol. 2594 UNTS 2013, No. 46157)

[o] Article 2 *Agreement establishing rules concerning the legal status of military and civilian personnel of the Kingdom of the Netherlands under the authority of the Department of Defence*; Paramaribo, 25 November 1975 (Vol. 1041 *UNTS* 1984 No. 15699)

[p] Article II(2) *Exchange of notes constituting an agreement between the Kingdom of the Netherlands and the Republic of Surinam on the status of Dutch military and civilian personnel stationed in the Republic of Surinam for training purposes*; Paramaribo, 29 June and 26 August 2004 (Vol. 2647 UNTS 2010, No. 47158)

[q] Article 12 *Agreement between the Kingdom of the Netherlands and the Government of the United Republic of Tanzania concerning the Status of the Netherlands Armed Forces in the United Republic of Tanzania participating in the exercise TANZANITE* 2002; Dar es Salaam, 29 January 2002 (*Dutch Treaty Series* 2002, 31)

[r] Article III(3) *Agreement between the Kingdom of the Netherlands and the Republic of Uganda concerning the status of personnel of the ministry of defence of the Kingdom of the Netherlands present on the territory of the Republic of Uganda for multilateral training and educational activities*; Kampala, 18 September 2012 (*Dutch Treaty Series* 2012, 191)

[s] Article VI *Agreement between the Government of the Kingdom of the Netherlands and the Swiss Federal Council concerning military exercises, training and education*; The Hague, 12 April 2007 (*Dutch Treaty Series*, 174)

stability and security. To this end concepts like Security Sector Reform (SSR) and Security Sector Development (SSD) emerged,[105] focussing on reform of the security sector of a State, in particular the military, the police force, the justice system and the security agencies.

The increased level of international military cooperation is also reflected in the growing number of bilateral SOFAs concluded with respect to activities, such as training, Host Nation Support etc. As an example Table 5.1 shows an overview of SOFAs the Netherlands has concluded in the framework of military cooperation. The content of the SOFAs differs on the aspect of criminal jurisdiction. In a number of States, the Dutch forces are subject to exclusive Dutch criminal jurisdiction. In some other States the exercise of criminal jurisdiction by Dutch authorities is limited to offences committed while military personnel are on duty, or the *NATO-SOFA* approach to criminal jurisdiction is followed. On some occasions host States seem more reluctant to waive their jurisdiction. For example, Egypt only agreed to refrain from exercising its criminal jurisdiction over Dutch forces participating in the biennial multinational exercise in cases of offences related to the exercise or committed in the military training areas.[106] Eventually, Egypt's perseverance to hold on to this provision, was reason for the Netherlands to withdraw from the exercise.

5.4 Analysis

Since World War II the stationing of forces within the framework of international military cooperation has led to the conclusion of a large number of SOFAs. The agreements continued the practice established by the allied forces in both World Wars to set out status arrangements in treaties, like SOFAs. In my opinion, the use of treaties can be explained by the unprecedented large-scale and semi-permanent peacetime military presence on the territory of friendly States. Besides, military personnel were often accompanied by their families and lived among the local population, which promoted the interaction between the two groups. These circumstances required clear and detailed arrangements.[107]

Another explanation for the increasing use of SOFAs can be found in the changing views on the exercise of criminal jurisdiction over visiting forces. With respect

---

[105] Exercise program Flintlock, for instance, aims amongst others to develop African security sector capacity and capacity to combat terrorism; Appendix to *Dutch Parliamentary Papers II* 2010/11, 2711, p. 4.

[106] On the basis of an MOU from 2005 the Netherlands had jurisdiction with regard to offences committed by Dutch servicemen "during the exercise or exercise related activities" (Article 4(3)); outside the context of the exercise or outside the military training areas the servicemen were subject to the jurisdiction of Egypt (Article 4, Subparagraph 2, *Memorandum of Understanding (MOU) between the Ministry of Defense of the Arab Republic of Egypt and the Ministry of Defense of the Kingdom of Netherlands on exercise Bright Star 2005* (not published).

[107] Rouse and Baldwin 1957, p. 30.

to military cooperation the strict application of the ground rule does not seem self-evident. In general visiting forces are to a certain extent subject to the jurisdiction of the sending States. However, to what extent and under what conditions sending States can exercise jurisdiction will have to be established by mutual consent. To that end SOFAs are an appropriate instrument to set out the arrangements.[108]

As was discussed in the previous chapters, in a situation of an armed conflict or in a crisis management operation forces abroad are in general subject to the exclusive criminal jurisdiction of the sending State which entails immunity of the forces from the exercise of jurisdiction by the host State's courts. However, under different circumstances, like peacetime military cooperation, this appears not necessarily to be the case. Although visiting forces may still be subject to the exclusive criminal jurisdiction of the sending State, generally only under certain specified conditions are host States prepared to waive their right to exercise criminal jurisdiction or to grant sending States the primary right to exercise jurisdiction, for example, with respect to *inter se* offences or offences committed in the performance of official duty.

In practice, States thus allow for application of the ground rule while taking into account host States' interests. Never before had these interests been so explicitly included in States' practice, although to a certain extent sending States did retain the right to exercise jurisdiction over their forces. A reason for this shift could be the reluctance of States in the post-World War II period to grant other states extraterritorial rights while at the same time arrangements tending towards colonialism were critically reviewed.[109] The right to exercise jurisdiction over foreign forces was considered as an expression of State sovereignty; a topic particularly sensitive for States that had recently gained their independence.[110]

Furthermore, within the framework of international cooperation, the interests of the States working together are more balanced,[111] which is, for instance, reflected in the reciprocal nature of the *NATO-SOFA*. The balance can be described as a sort of *quid pro quo* commitment between two equal States. The host State grants the sending State certain rights, for example, to use a foreign base or training area, thus accepting a certain restriction on the exercise of its sovereign rights. In return the sending State provides the host State with collective defence, military support or financial benefits.[112] Under these circumstances the element of dependency can still be relevant and sending States may have a stronger bargaining position than host States, resulting in arrangements that are more favourable to the sending

[108] Re 1956, p. 392.

[109] Rouse and Baldwin 1957, p. 32. This applied to Asia and Africa in particular.

[110] Moore 1959, p. 276.

[111] See Spies 2008, p. 239.

[112] See Stambuk 1963b, p. 474, Harkavy 2007, p. 156 and Munoz-Mosquera 2011, p. 3. Stambuk 1963a, p. 8 mentions that in contrast to what had previously been the case, during the 1960s sending States were interested in the security of the host State.

States' forces, for example, with respect to the exercise of jurisdiction by the sending States' authorities.

In addition, the specific circumstances under which the stationing of forces abroad takes place will have an impact on the SOFAs. Since World War II, these circumstances have become fundamentally different from those of the period before that, during which the impact of visiting foreign forces was limited both in time and place. Today States often accept the long-lasting and large-scale foreign military presence on their territory, which is not just restricted to a single garrison or base, but sometimes extends to the whole territory of the host State. Forces and individual soldiers can freely travel between the locations where they are stationed. The servicemen and their families often live amongst the local population and can spend their period of leave in the host State. Interaction with the host State's civilians increases even further, as local personnel are employed at the bases and camps or work for the sending State's forces.

Under these circumstances there is an increasing chance that by committing criminal offences foreign military personnel violate the legal order of the host State and affect the civilian population's interests. Consequently, the host State's interest to exercise criminal jurisdiction over foreign military personnel grows stronger. Besides, as offences may occur off base and outside the performance of official duties, the exercise of jurisdiction by the sending State seems less logical. On the other hand, prosecution of all offences committed by foreign visiting forces may become a burden to the judicial institutions of the host State. Therefore, sharing the right to exercise criminal jurisdiction is in the interest of either States. To what extent a State can exercise these rights will depend on their mutual trust and dependency.

Military cooperation can in part overlap with situations that have been discussed in the previous chapters. For example, a sending State that has deployed forces in support of a crisis management operation taking place in a third State will consider its deployed forces as part of the operation, which would call for full immunity of its forces. This point of view may be less evident for the host State, which can consider the foreign military presence as a form of cooperation, warranting a less far-reaching restriction of its jurisdiction.[113] In these situations it is hard to draw a clear line between the different legal bases for foreign military presence, resulting in room for negotiations on the exercise of criminal jurisdiction over the visiting forces.

Besides, the nature of the cooperation can change over time, for example, when an armed conflict arises. These circumstances can justify revision of SOFAs. Article XV(1) of the *NATO-SOFA* starts by stating that the treaty remains applicable during hostilities that fall under the scope of the *NATO Treaty*. Article XV(2) then continues that in that situation each of the parties to the *NATO-SOFA* has the right to suspend the application of any of the provisions of the agreement. Moreover, they will immediately review Article VII on criminal jurisdiction. The

[113] See also the examples mentioned in Chap. 4.

travaux préparatoires of this provision shows that under those conditions the US deemed it necessary to exercise exclusive criminal jurisdiction over its forces.[114] In this way the Treaty provides States with the possibility to apply the ground rule more rigorously, if required.[115]

5.5 Conclusion

This chapter has analysed the scope of the ground rule within the framework of international military cooperation. Right after World War II, States seemed to find it hard to cope with the status of the large numbers of foreign forces still present on or in transit through their territory. In occupied States the situation was quite clear. Occupation law applied and when there was a need for a prolonged foreign military presence, the States concluded agreements on the basis of which forces were subject to the exclusive criminal jurisdiction of the sending State.

The first SOFAs concluded by allied States in the aftermath of the war, gave the impression that, on the one hand, some States were eager to oblige their allies with respect to criminal jurisdiction and, therefore, agreed to continue the wartime arrangements[116]; on the other, States were searching for a new balance, as the emergency situation that served as justification for the exclusive jurisdiction over foreign friendly forces was no longer in existence. To that end States emphasised the principle of territoriality and thus the jurisdiction of the host State.[117] This principle was pivotal, for instance, in the SOFA to the *Treaty of Brussels*, which meant that the provision on jurisdiction accorded a key position to the host State. The host State did not automatically waive its jurisdiction when approving the visit of the foreign forces, but it could do so at the request of the sending State.

The *NATO-SOFA* offers sending States more clarity, because it explicitly states under which circumstance sending States will have primary jurisdiction: offences committed by its forces that, in short, are directed against the interests of the sending State, or committed in the performance of official duty. In other cases host States retain primary criminal jurisdiction. As the *NATO-SOFA* meets the interests of both host States and sending States, this balanced approach is also widely applied outside NATO.

However, other provisions are often agreed upon, pursuant to which some host States almost completely waive their criminal jurisdiction, while other host States only waive their jurisdiction under certain conditions. The different approaches

---

114 Snee, p. 221.

115 See Fleck 2003b, pp. 255–256.

116 This may also have been due to the incapacity of the liberated States' judiciary to fulfil their tasks just after the liberation.

117 E.g., Barton concluded that there was a rule of international law, determining in principle that the members of the visiting forces are subject to the criminal jurisdiction of local courts; Barton 1950, p. 234.

States take can be explained by the fact that they not always share the same interests and that the circumstances under which the foreign forces are present may differ. What all arrangements have in common is that sending States will always retain a certain level of jurisdiction over their forces.

References

Barton GP (1950) Foreign armed forces: immunity from criminal jurisdiction. Br Yearb Int Law 27:186–235

Bathurst ME (1946) Jurisdiction over friendly foreign armed forces: the American law. Br Yearb Int Law 23:338–341

Berman EG, Sams KE (2000) Peacekeeping in Africa, capabilities and culpabilities. United Nations Institute for Disarmament Research, Geneva

Duke S (1989) United States military forces and installations in Europe. Oxford University Press, Oxford

Fleck D (2003a) (ed) The handbook of the law of visiting forces. Oxford University Press, Oxford

Fleck D (2003b) The development of the law of stationing forces in Germany: five decades of multilateral cooperation. In: Fleck D (ed) The handbook of the law of visiting forces. Oxford University Press, Oxford, pp 349–364

Fleck D (2003c) Applicability during crisis or war. In: Fleck D (ed) The handbook of the law of visiting forces. Oxford University Press, Oxford, pp 255–256

Giegerich B (2008) Europe: looking near and far. In: Peace operations. Trends, progress and prospects. Georgetown University Press, Washington, pp 119–136

Harkavy RE (2007) Strategic basing and the great powers. Routledge, Oxon, pp 1200–2000

King A (1942) Jurisdiction over friendly foreign armed forces. AJIL 36(4):539–567

Lachowski Z (2007) Foreign military bases in Euroasia. SIPR Policy paper No. 18. Stockholm International Peace Research Institute, Sweden

Lazareff S (1971) Status of military forces under current international law. Sijthoff, Leiden

Moore FT (1959) Criminal jurisdiction in overseas areas. J Politics 21(2):276–302

Munoz-Mosquera A (2011) Host nation support arrangements: the NAC-approved military-to-military tools. NATO Legal Gazette 24:2–8

Palmer JS (2008) Legal impediments to USAFRICOM operationalization. Joint Force Q 51:79–85

Peterson JE (2009) Foreign military presence and its role in reinforcing regional security: a double-edged sword. Arabian Gulf Security: Internal and external challenges, Dubai, pp 183–205

Ploch L (2003) Africa command: U.S. Strategic interests and the role of the US military in Africa. CRS Report for Congress, Congressional Research Service

Re ED (1956) The NATO status of forces agreement and international law. Northwest Univ Law Rev 53(8):349–394

Rouse JH, Baldwin GB (1957) The exercise of criminal jurisdiction under the NATO status of forces agreement. AJIL 51(1):29–62

Snee JM (1961) NATO Agreements on status: traveaux préparatoires. International law studies, vol 54. Naval War College, Newport

Spies SC (2008) On the legal status of foreign armed forces, with a focus on the interrelation between ius ad praesentiam and ius in praesentia. Mil L and L War Rev 47:235–251

Stambuk G (1963a) American military forces abroad: their impact on the western State system. Ohio State University Press, Columbus

Stambuk G (1963b) Foreign policy and the stationing of American forces abroad. J Politics 25(3):472–488

Stanger RJ (1957/1958) Criminal jurisdiction over visiting armed forces. International law studies, vol LII. Naval War College, Newport

Trybus M (2007) The vision of the European Defence Community and a common defence for the European Union. In: Trybus M, White ND (eds) European security law. Oxford University Press, Oxford

van den Bosch B (2008) Jurisdictie over Nederlandse militairen in Duitsland, een nieuwe wending? Militair Rechtelijk Tijdschrift 101:193–196

Verona S (1992) Military occupation and diplomacy. Soviet troops in Romania. Duke University Press, Durham

Wexler I (2008) A comfortable SOFA: the need for an equitable foreign criminal jurisdiction agreement with Iraq. Naval Law Rev 56:43–86

Woodliffe J (1992) The peacetime use of foreign military installations under modern international law. Martinus Nijhoff Publishers, Dordrecht

Part II
The International Law Perspective

The previous Part on the historical analysis of the development of criminal jurisdiction over visiting armed forces cannot fully clarify to what extent and in what situations States have the right to exercise jurisdiction over those forces. For a proper understanding it is necessary to look at international law first. Part II focuses on the role and development of criminal jurisdiction over soldiers stationed abroad from the International Law Perspective.

When discussing the scope of criminal jurisdiction under international law, several elements of international law, which are all related to the position of the sovereign State in the international legal order, are fundamental. For example, sovereign States are independent and equal and cannot exercise power over each other. As a consequence, the States' rights to exercise extraterritorial jurisdiction is not unrestricted.

In the last few decades international organisations have become more important in international law. As States were facing a growing number of transnational problems, they intensified their cooperation and chose to have international governmental organisations deal with a number of the issues. To enable the effective execution of their tasks, international organisations and their staff have been accorded immunities that restrict the host States' exercise of jurisdiction.

Being organs of sovereign States, armed forces derive their status largely from the sovereign position of their own States. At the same time, armed forces can participate in activities of international organisations, which in part may also affect the legal status of military personnel involved.

This Part addresses a number of international law issues, which will be analysed in relation to the armed forces. Chapter 6 discusses the sovereign State and its jurisdiction, whereas Chap. 7 focuses on the immunity of the State and its organs. Chapter 8 combines the conclusions of the two preceding chapters to analyse the status of soldiers in the context of international law. Finally, international organisations will be discussed in Chap. 9.

Chapter 6
The Sovereign State and the Exercise of Jurisdiction

Abstract The status of visiting armed forces and especially criminal jurisdiction over those forces is firmly based in international law. States are the most important legal persons in international law, exercising their sovereign powers as equals. That sovereignty of States, as reflected in the concept of jurisdiction, is central to understanding the status of forces. Although jurisdiction is primarily territorial in nature, a State can exercise its legislative jurisdiction extraterritorially when founded on the principles of jurisdiction. Extraterritorial exercise of adjudicative and enforcement jurisdiction is generally more limited and depends on an explicit legal basis or the consent of another State.

Contents

6.1 Introduction

Traditionally, public international law has focused upon the relationship between States as the most important legal subjects within the international system. The Peace of Westphalia of 1648 is generally regarded as a milestone and as the starting point of the modern European State system. Although new legal subjects have gradually made their entry into the international legal system, today the State remains the principal bearer of rights and obligations under international law.

© T.M.C. ASSER PRESS and the author 2015

J. Voetelink, *Status of Forces: Criminal Jurisdiction over Military Personnel Abroad*,
DOI 10.1007/978-94-6265-057-2_6

Initially international law was still largely European oriented. However, since the end of the nineteenth century more non-European States have entered the international system.[1] Since World War II the number of States has increased exponentially and the international legal system has acquired a truly universal character.[2]

State sovereignty is reflected in the concept of jurisdiction with which a State exercises its power and authority. Jurisdiction (and the exercise thereof) is an essential characteristic of a State and consists of three elementary State powers: the legislative, enforcement and adjudicative power.[3] A State can decide to apply its laws to persons and activities on the basis of its legislative power, referred to as legislative or prescriptive jurisdiction. A State can use its enforcement jurisdiction to secure or compel compliance with the laws (enforcement jurisdiction). Likewise, a State has the power to subject persons and goods to the process of its courts based on its adjudicative jurisdiction. The State's jurisdiction is primarily territorial in nature, but it can to a certain extent be exercised outside the State's borders based on criteria such as nationality.

This chapter explores various forms of jurisdiction and their underlying principles, while addressing the question to what extent jurisdiction can be exercised extraterritorially. Starting with a description of the development of States within international law (Sect. 6.2), it is followed by a discussion of the sovereign position of a State in its relation with other States (Sect. 6.3) and ends with an analysis of the extraterritorial exercise of jurisdiction (Sect. 6.4).

In Chap. 8, these sections serve as a basis for defining the armed forces position within the sovereign State and this chapter discusses several principles of jurisdiction that are specifically relevant to the military forces.

6.2 The Origin and Development of the Concept of State

International law as we know it today is originally a product of reflection and developments in Europe starting in mediaeval society and continuing from the sixteenth to the eighteenth centuries. Under the influence of the Reformation and the Renaissance the idea that the State was subordinate to a higher worldly and ecclesiastic authority, represented by the Emperor and the Pope, was progressively abandoned.[4] The idea emerged that the State should not depend on a higher order, but instead, should constitute the highest sovereign authority administering its territory. The State should be able to exercise this authority free from any external influence

---

[1] Sucharitkul 2005, pp. 3 and 5.

[2] E.g., when it was first founded, the UN had 51 Members. The number of UN member States increased from 60 (1950) to 99 (1960) to 127 (1970) and to 154 members in 1980. On 14 July 2011 the Republic of South Sudan became the 193rd member State. www.un.org/en/members/growth.shtml. Accessed November.

[3] Restatement of the Law, Third, Foreign Relations Law of the United States, pp. 230 et seq.

[4] Gross 1948, p. 28.

and in a position of equality vis-à-vis other States. This sovereign equality is captured in the maxim '*par in parem non habet imperium*' (an equal has no power over his equal).[5] These reflections were embedded in the previously mentioned Westphalia Peace Treaties of 1648,[6] often considered the formal ending of the mediaeval feudal political order and the beginning of the modern State system.[7]

The sovereign State exercises exclusive authority over its own territory and population, which, however, does not imply that it does not affect the interests of other States. The use of the high seas, the establishment of diplomatic relations, or the conclusion of international treaties are examples of activities which involve other States. For this reason States agreed to certain rules, or accepted the existence of such rules, that primarily aimed to curtail sovereign power and to regulate their mutual relations.

These international legal rules were primarily the result of mutual agreements between States, either in the form of treaties or as usage and customs accepted as law. Although the national law element, such as justice and equality, played a role in the formulation of international law, these have become integrated into positive sources of legal obligations. Hence, international law is largely the product of the free will of States.[8]

6.3 The Sovereign State

When considering the concept of State, the definition often referred to is formulated in Article 1 of the *Montevideo Convention*[9]:

> The State as a person of international law should possess the following qualifications: (a) a permanent population; (b) a defined territory; (c) government; and (d) capacity to enter into relations.

---

[5] The maxim originates from Canon law and was later applied to feudal rulers, who were considered to be each other's equals; Schneider 1964, p. 15.

[6] *Instrumentum Pacis Osnabrugensis*; Osnabrück, 14/24 October 1648 (www.lwl.org/westfaelischegeschichte/portal/Internet/finde/langDatensatz.php?urlID=740&url_tabelle=tab_quelle) and *Instrumentum Pacis Monasteriensis*; Münster, 24 October 1648 (avalon.law.yale.edu/17th_century/westphal.asp. Accessed November 2014).

[7] Wessel 2007, p. 3.

[8] "The rules of law binding upon States therefore emanate from their own free will as expressed in conventions or by usage generally accepted as expressing principles of law", PHIJ 7 September 1927, *The case of the S.S. Lotus*, Series A. No. 10.

[9] *Convention on the rights and duties of States*; Montevideo, 26 December 1933 (Vol. 165 *LNTS* 1936, No. 3802). Even though the *Montevideo Convention* is an old treaty signed by only few American States, it constitutes the best-known wording of the criteria of Statehood; Werner 2007, p. 166.

An entity will have to fulfil the first three factual criteria to be considered a State. Fulfilment of these criteria entails the fulfilment of the fourth criterion: the State can establish relations with other States.[10]

With regard to the criteria of a permanent population, the Convention only requires that the population consists of people having the State's nationality. It does not impose any condition on its size or composition. Likewise, the territory has to be defined, but borders may still be subject to discussion or dispute.[11] Furthermore, the mere existence of a government does not suffice; it must be capable of effectively and independently exercising its authority.

The requirements set out in Article 1 of the *Montevideo Convention* lack the element of sovereignty that is inherent to the existence of a State.[12] Sovereignty literally means the 'highest power' (*suprema potestas*) of a State. Originally it indicated either the absence of a worldly or an ecclesiastical authority over States. This independent position was formulated by the Permanent Court of Arbitration in the *Island of Palmas* case:

> Sovereignty in the relations between States signifies independence. Independence in regard to a portion of the globe is the right to exercise therein, to the exclusion of any other State, the functions of a State.[13]

Sovereignty, however, does not imply that a State is above the law. International law arises from the States' will and consent, which restricts the exercise of their sovereign powers. In its advice *Customs régime between Germany and Austria (Protocol of March 19th, 1931)* the Permanent Court of Arbitration considered:

> Independence as thus understood is really no more than the normal conditions of States according to international law; it may also be described as sovereignty (suprema potestas), or external sovereignty, by which is meant that the State has over it no other authority than that of international law.[14]

From a legal point of view sovereignty implies equality of States; there is no hierarchical order in the relations between States.[15] This means that a State does not have authority over any other State, because the latter is considered as its equal. This vision is included in the above-mentioned maxim *par in parem non habet imperium*. Viewed from other perspectives, States can differ widely in such areas

---

[10] The capacity to enter into relations is a consequence of the recognition as a State. It is not a requirement; Werner 2007, p. 166.

[11] ICJ 20 February 1969, *North Sea Continental Shelf*, Judgement, I.C.J. Reports 1969, 3, para 46.

[12] Nollkaemper 2011, p. 66.

[13] PCA 4 April 1928, *The Island of Palmas case (or Miangas)*, United States v. The Netherlands, Award of the tribunal, p. 8. www.pca-cpa.org. Accessed November 2014.

[14] Individual opinion of Judge Anzilotti in: PCIJ 5 September 1931, *Customs régime between Germany and Austria (Protocol of March 19th, 1931)*, Advisory Opinion, Series A/B, No. 41, p. 57.

[15] This is one of the principles on which the UN is based: "The Organisation is based on the principle of sovereign equality of all its Members" (Article 2(1) *UN Charter*).

as their political, economic and military capacity. These factual power relations influence their legal relations and can be reflected in, for instance, the provisions of a treaty.

6.4 Jurisdiction of a State

6.4.1 Jurisdiction

Sovereignty of a State is one of the basic principles of international law and is reflected in the concept of jurisdiction.[16] The latter concept is a collective term generally referring to the legislative, enforcement and adjudicative powers of a State.[17] A State has full jurisdiction within the borders of its territory[18] only if it is not restricted by international law. Outside its territory a State can use its legislative power in accordance with recognised principles of jurisdiction, (to be discussed in the following sections), if a sufficiently strong nexus exists between the State and the specific fact.[19] In principle a State cannot subject another State to its adjudicative or enforcement jurisdiction (*par in parem non habet judicium*).[20] Therefore, the extraterritorial exercise of these forms of jurisdiction depends on either the consent of the State involved or an explicit international legal basis.[21]

Jurisdiction is relevant in the areas of both private and public law. The former is largely regulated by rules of private international law, while the exercise of public law jurisdiction is primarily focused upon criminal jurisdiction. This is the area most regulated by public international law, since the exercise of criminal jurisdiction is a sovereign attribute of any State and it will be the area of jurisdiction dealt with here.

---

16 See Mann 1964, p. 30: "Jurisdiction is an aspect of sovereignty, it is coextensive with and, indeed, incidental to, but also limited by, the State's sovereignty".

17 Restatement of the Law, Third, Foreign Relations Law of the United States, pp. 230 et seq.

18 On the development of these ideas, see: Mann 1964, pp. 26 et seq.

19 The idea that jurisdiction can be exercised in all cases unless prohibited under international law, as was accepted in the *Lotus Case*, is no longer accepted, e.g., Mann 1964, p. 35 and Fox 2004, p. 46. Today, the more restrictive approach prevails; in general States are not permitted to expand their jurisdiction, unless international law allows that under specific circumstances; Liivoja 2011, pp. 55 et seq.

20 Kokott 2007, p. 6, para 35. Also referred to as '*par in parem non habet jurisdictionem*' see: Voskuil 1981, p. 46.

21 Mann 1964, pp. 129–131 and 138 on enforcement jurisdiction; Brownlie 2010, p. 309; Oxman 2007, Sect. 4.

6.4.2 Principles of Jurisdiction

An unrestricted exercise of a State's jurisdiction may conflict with the sovereign rights of other States.[22] Therefore, extraterritorial application of national legislation must be based on one of the principles of jurisdiction. These principles are mainly defined in relation to criminal law and lay down the nexus between a State and a fact[23] based on territory, nationality, universality, and the protection of the State's interests.[24]

6.4.2.1 The Territorial Principle

In principle the legislative jurisdiction is territorial.[25] Each State can decide which acts are punishable within its own territory. The territory of a State includes its land territory, internal waters, the territorial sea and the airspace over these areas.[26] For instance, the Netherlands' borders with its neighbouring States are treaty-based[27] and the breadth of its territorial sea is established at twelve miles in accordance with Article 3 of the *United Nations Convention on the Law of the Sea* (*UNCLOS*). As Article 1 in conjunction with Article 2 of the *Chicago Convention*[28] determines that each State has sovereignty over the airspace over its territory, no separate action is required in this domain.

---

[22] Mann 1964, p. 30. See ECHR 12th December 2001, *Bankovic and others v. Belgium and 16 others* [GC], Application no. 52207/99, para 59: "While international law does not exclude a State's exercise of jurisdiction extraterritorially, the suggested bases of such jurisdiction (including nationality, flag, diplomatic and consular relations, effect, protection, passive personality and universality) are, as a general rule, defined and limited by the sovereign territorial rights of the other relevant States".

[23] Mann 1964, pp. 44–49.

[24] These principles form the basis for, for example, the Harvard *Draft Convention on Jurisdiction with Respect to Crime*, General Comment, AJIL, Supplement: Research in International Law 1935, p. 445 and are partly derived from the factual criteria mentioned in Article 1 Montevideo *Convention*, Oxman 2007, para 11; see also Mann 1964, pp. 82–94.

[25] ECHR 12 December 2001, *Bankovic and others v. Belgium and 16 others* [GC], Application no. 52207/99, para 59. See also: Fox 2008, p. 73.

[26] See Articles 1 and 2 *Convention on International Civil Aviation*; Chicago, 7 December 1944 (Vol. 15 *UNTS* 1948, No. 102) and Articles 2(2) and (3) *United Nations Convention on the Law of the Sea*; Montego-Bay, 10 December 1982 (Vol. 1833 *UNTS* 1994, No. 31363).

[27] van Elst and Orie 2008, p. 46.

[28] *Convention on International Civil Aviation*; Chicago, 7 December 1944 (Vol. 15 *UNTS* 1948, No. 102).

6.4.2.2 The Nationality Principle

The enactment of legislation implies its territorial application, unless the laws are specifically intended for extraterritorial application. From State practice other principles have developed, such as the principle of nationality, which enables the adoption and application of extraterritorial legislation. The principle of nationality further evolved in the principle of active nationality (or the principle of personality) and the principle of passive personality. On the basis of these principles States can exercise their legislative jurisdiction over their citizens,[29] even when they are abroad.

Nationality is also relevant in relation to vessels and aircraft. Vessels and aircraft registered in a particular State, and entitled to fly its flag, are considered to possess the nationality of that State. The 'flag State' principle is, therefore, a derivative from the active nationality principle.[30] Vessels and aircraft, however, are not part of a State's territory. A vessel sailing in foreign territorial waters is subject to the territorial jurisdiction of the State to which the waters belong,[31] although on the high seas the vessel is under the exclusive jurisdiction of the flag State.

Nationality is also part of the principle of passive personality. This principle focuses on the nationality of the victim of offences committed abroad and allows a State to claim jurisdiction for these offences against their nationals abroad. In March 2005 at a military checkpoint in Iraq an American soldier killed an Italian State official, accompanying Italian reporter Giuliana Sgrena who had just been released by Iraqi insurgents and was underway to Bagdad airport.[32] Italy initiated criminal procedures against the soldier on the basis of the principle of passive personality.[33]

Passive personality as a basis for jurisdiction was and is, to a certain extent, still somewhat controversial.[34] The reason for this is that it extends a State's criminal jurisdiction to non-resident foreign citizens and can, therefore, interfere with other States' sovereignty. However, in recent years it has become more acceptable with regard to certain types of offences, such as aerial hijacking, which are often aimed

---

[29] In some cases the extraterritorial jurisdiction can also apply to citizens of another State; see International Bar Association 2009, p. 145.

[30] Article 92(1) *UNCLOS* determines that a State has exclusive jurisdiction over vessels on the high seas under its flag.

[31] In 1948 the Supreme Court decided that criminal acts committed on board a foreign ship in a Dutch port or in the Dutch territorial waters fall under Dutch jurisdiction on the basis of Article 2 *Dutch Criminal Code*; HR 20 April 1948, NJ 1948, 344. However, this provision does not apply to warships.

[32] Cassese 2008, p. 1078.

[33] Court of Cassation 24 July 2008, *Lozano v. Italy*, Case No 31171/2008, ILDC 1085 (IT 2008).

[34] ICJ 14 February 2002, *Arrest warrant of 11 April 2000* (Democratic Republic of the Congo v. Belgium), Judgment, I.C.J. Reports 2002, p. 3, separate opinion of Judges Higgins, Kooijmans and Buergenthal, Para 47. Terrorist attacks on people because of their nationality have been the main reason for a wider acceptance of the application of the principle of passive nationality (on the basis of explicit treaty provisions); Engdahl 2007, pp. 33–34.

at the nationals' parent State. This has led to a number of multinational conventions, in which multiple bases for jurisdiction can be recognised, including passive personality. See for example the *Convention on the Safety of United Nations and Associated Personnel* and the *Convention on the Prevention and Punishment of Crimes Against Internationally Protected Persons*.[35]

6.4.2.3 The Protective Principle

Another basis to establish extraterritorial jurisdiction is provided by a State's essential interests: A State must be able to protect itself against actions abroad that may affect its security and financial solvency. However, application of the protective principle may easily conflict with other States' interests. Consequently, similar to the principles discussed above, the application of this principle calls for some caution. Only protection of specific and essential interests, such as national security and financial and monetary stability, allows establishment of extraterritorial jurisdiction.[36]

6.4.2.4 The Universality Principle

All principles discussed above imply either a direct or indirect link between a fact and the State establishing jurisdiction. This is not necessarily the case with the principle of universality based on the idea that the nature of the crimes, or of the circumstances under which they take place, affect the international legal order as a whole, which warrants action by any State. Acts of piracy on the high seas are a classic example of such crimes. As these acts already constituted a threat to all seafaring nations and international commerce at an early stage of the development of international law, a practice emerged that enabled any State to prosecute pirates.

Since World War II several treaties have been concluded that instruct States to extend their jurisdiction over the crimes included in the treaties under their national legislation. Immediately after World War II there was major concern about criminalising the type of acts that had occurred during the war. Crimes, such as genocide and grave violations of the laws of war,[37] were made subject to uni-

---

[35] *Convention on the Safety of United Nations and Associated Personnel*; New York, 9 December 1994 (Vol. 2051 *UNTS* 1999, No. 35457) and *Convention on the Prevention and Punishment of Crimes Against Internationally Protected Persons, including Diplomatic Agents*; New York, 14 December 1973 (Vol. 1035 *UNTS* 1977, No. 15410).

[36] de Hoogh and Molier 2007, pp. 218 and 219.

[37] E.g., Articles 49 and 50 *Convention (I) for the Amelioration of the Condition of the Wounded and Sick in Armed Forces in the Field*; Geneva, 12 August 1949 (Vol. 970 UNTS 1950, No. 970). Similar provisions are included in the other three Geneva Conventions and the *Protocol Additional to the Geneva Conventions of 12 August 1949, and relating to the Protection of Victims of International Armed Conflicts (Protocol I)*; Bern, 12 December 1977 (Vol. 1125 *UNTS* 1979, No. 17512) and *Convention on the Prevention and Punishment of the Crime and Genocide*; 9 December 1948 (Vol. 78 *UNTS* 1951, No. 1021).

versal jurisdiction (pure jurisdiction). Since then other crimes have been made subject to universal jurisdiction, such as attacks on civil airliners, aerial hijacking and attacks on international officials.[38] These, while not universal offences in the true sense, are subject to multiple bases of jurisdiction and States have agreed either to prosecute or extradite suspects of such offences (quasi-universal jurisdiction).[39]

In all cases it is important to note that the State on whose territory the crime has been committed, and which consequently has the primary rights to prosecute the suspects, may not always wish to proceed with the prosecution, for instance, in situations where the State itself is involved in the crime. To prevent that a crime remains unpunished, other States must be able to establish jurisdiction. In general, a link will be required between the State that exercises universal jurisdiction and the crime in question, for instance, because the victim or the offender is a citizen of the State that exercises jurisdiction, or if the offender finds himself on the territory of that State. Unrestricted universal jurisdiction can be established in special cases.[40]

6.5 Conclusion

This chapter has discussed the jurisdiction of a State and the underlying principles based on the following question: What encompasses the jurisdiction of a State and to what extent can it be exercised extraterritorially?

States are still the key players in international relations. In the past centuries they have developed into sovereign entities that exercise their power as equals. The sovereignty of a State is reflected in its legislative, enforcement and adjudicative jurisdiction. Although jurisdiction is primarily territorial in nature, a State can exercise its legislative jurisdiction extraterritorially when founded on the principles of jurisdiction based on nationality, the State's essential interests, and crimes against the international legal order. The possibilities to exercise adjudicative and enforcement jurisdiction are generally more limited and depend on an explicit legal basis or the consent of another State.

---

[38] An overview of the treaties can be found in *EU Doc* 8672/09 of 16 April 2009, The AU-EU Expert Report on the Principle of Universal Jurisdiction, para 9, fn. 5.

[39] Shaw 2003, pp. 597 et seq. ICJ, 14 February 2002, *Arrest warrant of 11 April 2000* (Democratic Republic of the Congo v. Belgium), Judgment, I.C.J. Reports 2002, p. 3, separate opinion of President Guillaume, para 4. The judgment uses the terminology 'subsidiary, universal jurisdiction'.

[40] E.g., the former Belgian *Law on Genocide and Crimes against Humanity* of 16 June 1993, modified on 10 February 1999, allowed Belgian courts to prosecute suspects of genocide, war crimes and crimes against humanity even if there was no connection between the crime and Belgium and even without any attention given to the location of the crime, the nationality of the offender, or the victim; Wouters and Panken 2002, p. 4. The *Law on Serious Violations of International Humanitarian Law* of 5 August 2003 replaced this act.

As mentioned in the Introduction, Chap. 8 assembles all relevant parts of international law related to the status of military personnel abroad. On the basis of this chapter it can be concluded that it is necessary to start with defining the position of the armed forces within a State. Furthermore, it is important to know how far the State's legislative jurisdiction extends over military personnel stationed abroad. A final step is to establish whether and to what extent international law allows for the extraterritorial exercise of the State's enforcement and adjudicative jurisdiction.

References

Cassese A (2008) The Italian Court of Cassation misapprehends the notion of war crimes. J Int Crim Justice 6(5):1077–1089

de Hoogh A, Molier G (2007) Jurisdictie. In: Horbach N, Lefeber R, Ribbelink O (eds) Handboek internationaal recht. T.M.C Asser Press, The Hague, pp 195–229

Engdahl O (2007) Protection of personnel in peace operations: the role of the safety convention against the background of general international law. Martinus Nijhoff Publishers, Leiden

Gross L (1948) The Peace of Westphalia, 1648–1948. AJIL 42(1):20–41

Kokott J (2007) States, sovereign equality. In: Max Planck encyclopedia of public international law. www.mpepil.com. Accessed November 2014

Liivoja R (2011) An axiom of military law. Applicability of national criminal law to military personnel and associated civilians abroad. Centre of Excellence in Global Governance Research, Helsinki

Mann FA (1964) The doctrine of jurisdiction in international law. The Hague Academy of International Law, Recueil des Cours 111:1–158

Nollkaemper A (2011) Kern van het internationaal publiekrecht. Boom, Den Haag

Oxman BH (2007) Jurisdiction of States. Max Planck encyclopedia of public international law. www.mpepil.com. Accessed November 2014

Restatement of the Law (1987) Third, Foreign relations law of the United States. American Law Institute

Schneider G (1964) Die Exterritorialität der Truppen in strafrechtlicher Hinsicht, unter besonderer Berücksichtigung der das deutsche Territorium betreffenden Truppenverträge. Albert-Ludwig Universität, Saarbrücken

Shaw MN (2003) International Law. Cambridge University Press, Cambridge

Sucharitkul S (2005) Jurisdictional immunities in contemporary international law from Asian Perspectives. Chin J Int Law 4(1):1–43

van Elst R, Orie AMM (2008) Strafrechtsmacht. In: van Sliedregt E, Sjöcrona JM, Orie AMM (eds) Handboek internationaal strafrecht. Schets van het Europese en internationale strafrecht. Kluwer, Deventer

Voskuil CA (1981) Summary of a report submitted to the Netherlands International Law Association. In: Jurisdictional immunities of states and their property, *UN Doc* A/CN.4/343/Add.1 (1981) pp 46–56

Werner W (2007) De staat. In: Horbach N, Lefeber R, Ribbelink O (eds) Handboek internationaal recht. T.M.C Asser Press, The Hague, pp 159–193

Wessel R (2007) Internationaal recht in ontwikkeling. In: Horbach N, Lefeber R, Ribbelink O (eds) Handboek internationaal recht. T.M.C Asser Press, The Hague, pp 1–17

Wouters J, Panken H (2002) Waar naartoe met de Genocidewet? Working Paper Nr. 30 - Sept 2002, Instituut voor Internationaal Recht

Chapter 7
Immunity

Abstract State immunity is a well-established principle of customary international law, enabling States to carry out their functions effectively. Under the restrictive doctrine of State immunity acts of a State of a purely public or sovereign nature enjoy immunity from another State's adjudicative and enforcement jurisdiction. State officials, acting on behalf of their States, benefit from the immunity of the State and enjoy a certain level of immunity, depending on their functions and the nature of their acts.

Contents

7.1 Introduction

In mediaeval feudal society a king ruled his territory and subjects as if they were his personal property. In this sense he personified the kingdom over which he exercised his royal powers. The inviolability of his person in the relations with befriended entities was one of the elements on which the doctrine of State

© T.M.C. ASSER PRESS and the author 2015

J. Voetelink, *Status of Forces: Criminal Jurisdiction over Military Personnel Abroad*,
DOI 10.1007/978-94-6265-057-2_7

immunity was based when sovereign States developed.[1] The *Exchange v. McFaddon* case (see Chap. 2) can be considered as one of the first court cases in which this doctrine was expressed.[2] The US Supreme Court's considerations in this case leaned heavily on the sovereign position of States and over a long period of time they influenced the legal proceedings in the US and the UK.[3]

Originally State immunity, based on the long-existing and accepted immunities of ambassadors,[4] was absolute in nature and did not seem to allow for any exception. In the course of the twentieth century this situation changed with respect to civil law, as States were becoming more and more active in the field of commerce. State officials, such as Heads of State or diplomats, represent their State abroad and as such they benefit from the immunity of the State. However, over time, their immunity developed into a self-contained legal regime, next to the regime of State immunity.[5] Yet, immunity of these officials is not self-evident under all circumstances and can be restricted. Developments in this area of law are still ongoing and may further define immunity of States and State officials in the future.

This chapter examines the immunity of the State and its officials and focuses on the question to what extent they enjoy immunity under international law. First, the chapter describes the development from the absolute doctrine of State immunity towards the restrictive doctrine and focuses on how the latter has been codified in treaties (Sect. 7.2). Second, the chapter discusses the immunities of Heads of State, Heads of Government, Ministers and envoys (Sect. 7.3). On the basis of these sections the next chapter explores the connection between State immunity and the immunities granted to the States' armed forces. The status of military forces will then be reviewed in the light of this chapter's findings on the status of State officials.

7.2 State Immunity

State immunity is a principle that has its origins in the principles of independence, sovereign equality and dignity of States[6] and enables a State to carry out its functions effectively.[7] Overall State immunity is a well-established principle of

[1] Caplan 2003, p. 745. Immunities of the heads of State, warships and diplomats were the basic elements of the development of State immunity, Fox 2008, pp. 201 and 223.

[2] Ibid. See also: van Alebeek 2008, p. 12.

[3] Bankas 2005, p. 23.

[4] Brownlie 2008, p. 326.

[5] Fox 2008, p. 665.

[6] Sinclair 1980, p. 121.

[7] Fox 2008, p. 1.

customary international law and is currently being further developed in case law, mostly due to the increasing attention given to the rights of individuals under international law. In part these rules are also codified in international treaties and national legislation. The following sections discuss the absolute doctrine of State immunity, the restrictive doctrine of State immunity, and the codification of the latter.

7.2.1 General Overview

Generally speaking, immunity is a restriction of the exercise of the adjudicative and enforcement jurisdiction within the territory of the State. It constitutes an exception to the principle that a State has exclusive jurisdiction over its territory. As a result, under international law, immunity provides States, natural and legal persons, or their goods, protection against the exercise of the sovereign rights of a State. However, the latter State does not refrain from its jurisdiction completely; the legislative function of that State remains in place, which means that national legislation continues to apply to persons enjoying immunity.[8] Consequently, such persons are not exempted from the obligations that local regulations impose,[9] but the State refrains from exercising its right to enforce the rules and to adjudicate the persons enjoying immunity.

7.2.2 Absolute Doctrine of State Immunity

In the early nineteenth century, partly due to the rise of nationalism, the equality of sovereign States was expressed in the absolute doctrine of State immunity. It implies that a State and its organs enjoy immunity from a foreign State's exercise of adjudicative and enforcement jurisdiction regardless of the nature or intention of the acts. In this doctrine, the maxim 'par in parem non habet imperium' applies in its purest form. A State can only be subjected to the jurisdiction of another State on a voluntary basis.

In the 1880 case of *The Parlement Belge* concerning a Belgian vessel, property of the Belgian King and manned by Belgian naval officers, the judge made what is regarded a classic statement of the absolute doctrine of immunity[10]:

> …as a consequence of the absolute independence of every sovereign authority, and of the international comity which induces every sovereign State to respect the independence and dignity of every other State, each and every one declines to exercise by means of its

---

[8] *UN Doc* A/CN.4/601 (2008), ILC preliminary report on immunity of State officials from foreign criminal jurisdiction, 29 May 2008, para 64.

[9] Schermers and Blokker 2003, p. 1025, para 1612.

[10] Cited in: Sinclair 1973, p. 256.

> courts any of its territorial jurisdiction over the person of any sovereign or ambassador of any other State, or over the public property of any State which is destined to public use, or over the property of any ambassador, though such sovereign, ambassador or property be within its territory and therefore, but for the common agreement, subject to its jurisdiction.

During a long period of time the absolute view on State immunity was the prevailing doctrine in international law. It was not until the twentieth century, when international commercial activities undertaken by States increased significantly, that the doctrine lost its standing. When States are involved in commercial and financial transactions, they enter the sphere of civil law consisting mainly of civil parties. The absolute doctrine of immunity led to inequality between the parties due to the privileged position of the foreign State because of which the affected civil party could not bring a case before a local court against the will of the foreign State.[11] With the rise of private transactions performed by States the absolute doctrine of immunity was increasingly perceived as a prejudice to the protection of the civil parties with whom the State had entered into legal transactions.[12]

7.2.3 Restrictive Doctrine of State Immunity

The situation described above was not very satisfactory and already in the early nineteenth century courts in Belgium and Italy, and the Mixed Courts of Egypt, started interpreting State immunity in a less strict sense. Courts in other States soon followed suit.[13] The ensuing restrictive doctrine of State immunity continued to define acts of States and State organs of a purely public or sovereign nature (*acta jure imperii*) as enjoying immunity from another State's adjudicative jurisdiction. However, when a State participated in civil life in the same manner as a private or legal person (*acta jure gestionis*), the State no longer enjoyed immunity before the courts of a foreign State (the forum State).

After WW II the restrictive doctrine was widely recognised and confirmed in the case law in an increasing number of States.[14] In 1952 the US State Department announced in the Tate letter the Department's policy to follow the restrictive doctrine of State immunity.[15] In 1976 the US enacted the *Foreign Sovereign Immunities Act,* which provided a statutory basis for the restrictive doctrine. This

[11] The only remaining possibility was to process a claim through diplomatic channels; Fox 2008, p. 26.

[12] Kokott 2011, p. 6, para 35.

[13] Mentioned are, for example, France, Greece, Austria, Romania and Switzerland; van Alebeek 2008, p. 14.

[14] Sinclair 1973, pp. 263–265; Fox 2008, p. 224 et seq.

[15] Letter from the Acting Legal Advisor of the Department of State, Jack Tate of 19 May 1952.

initiative was followed by many other States, such as the UK, Canada and Australia.[16] A first treaty having the same intentions was adopted in 1972 (see next Section).[17] Today the majority of States applies the restrictive doctrine of State immunity, although States differ as to the precise scope of the exceptions to immunity.[18]

It is not always easy to distinguish between sovereign acts (*acta jure gestionis*) and non-sovereign acts (*acta jure imperii*). To this end different criteria can be applied, focussing on the nature of the act or the purpose of the act. An example often used to clarify the complexity is the State's purchase of boots or cigarettes for its armed forces.[19] The purchase of goods to be used by armed forces can be classified as a typical governmental act, if one considers its purpose: the sustainment of the armed forces as a State organ. However, the nature of the act is purely civil in nature, i.e. an act that could also be carried out by an individual. Most States tend to emphasise the nature of the act to decide whether an act is sovereign or non-sovereign. There are certain acts, for which the State generally cannot claim immunity from the forum State's adjudicative jurisdiction. These are: conflicts arising from employment contracts; participation in legal entities; commercial transactions; intellectual and industrial property rights; ownership, possession, and the use of immovable property in the forum State; and claims arising from a tort that occurred in the forum State.[20]

Besides immunity from another State's adjudicative jurisdiction States also enjoy immunity from enforcement jurisdiction. For example, State property that serves sovereign and public goals, such as warships or military aircraft, are exempted from enforcement measures.[21] This type of immunity persists longer in its absolute form than the immunity from adjudicative jurisdiction and, under international law, exceptions to immunity from enforcement jurisdiction are rare.[22] To a certain extent upholding immunity from enforcement jurisdiction can render the exercise of adjudicative jurisdiction less effective under the restrictive doctrine.

---

[16] van Alebeek 2008, pp. 17–18.

[17] *European Convention on State Immunity*; Basel, 16 May 1972 (Vol. 1495 *UNTS* 1988, No. 25699).

[18] Fox 2008, pp. 235–236. A small number of States, for example, China and Brazil, still adhere to the absolute doctrine. In general, the absolute doctrine of State immunity still applies to criminal law procedures; Fox 2008, pp. 33 and 85.

[19] Dutch Supreme Court 26 October 1973, *NJ* 1974, 361, fn 2 by H.F. van Panhuys.

[20] Fox 2004, pp. 257–260.

[21] Sinclair 1980, p. 242. See Article 19(c), *United Nations Convention on Jurisdictional Immunities of States and Their Property;* New York, 17 January 2005 (*UN Doc* A/RES/59/38 (2004) van 16 December 2004) and Article 26 *European Convention on State Immunity* (both conventions are discussed below in Sect. 7.2.4).

[22] Fox 2008, pp. 35 and 56.

For instance, if a foreign State would not act on a court ruling, that ruling could only be enforced in a small number of cases with respect to State property.[23]

Although State immunity is particularly discussed in the field of civil law, it also applies to criminal law. In this field of law States enjoy absolute immunity from the adjudicative and enforcement jurisdiction of foreign States.[24] Yet, the absolute nature of the immunity does not fully extend to all State officials, as is explained in Sect. 7.3.

7.2.4 Codification

The development of the restrictive doctrine put a strain on international relations.[25] States still adhering to the absolute doctrine and granting other States immunity, did not enjoy similar immunities before foreign courts applying the restrictive doctrine. At an early stage initiatives were taken to solve this problem.[26] Although the core rules on State immunity are still customary in nature, some conventions on this issue have been adopted.

The first convention was adopted with respect to international sea transport. The 1926 *International Convention for the Unification of Certain Rules concerning the Immunity of State-owned Ships* and the 1934 *Additional Protocol*[27] subject State-owned vessels, their cargo and passengers, as regards claims, to the same obligations that apply to privately owned vessels, cargoes and equipment (Article 1). The most important exception to this rule concerns warships and other vessels that are used by, or in the possession of, a State for non-commercial purposes. These vessels:

> ...shall not be subject to seizure, arrest or detention by any legal process, nor to any proceedings in rem (Article 3, Subparagraph 1).

However, according to the same provision, claims may be brought before the courts of the State that owns or uses the vessel in case of collision or other nautical accidents, claims related to assistance, salvage or average, and in case of contracts relating to the vessel, such as repairs and supplies.

---

[23] Sinclair 1973, p. 255. There may be exceptions to enforcement jurisdiction in case the State involved gives its consent in relation to specific goods and if these goods serve "other than government non-commercial purposes"; Sun 2011, p. 701; see, e.g. Article 23 *European Convention on State Immunity*.

[24] Fox 2008, pp. 33 and 84.

[25] Explanatory Report 1972, Sect. 2.

[26] In 1891, the 'Institut de Droit International' made an attempt: *International regulations on the jurisdiction of courts in proceedings against sovereign States or heads of foreign States*, cited in the Explanatory Report 1972, Sect. 3.

[27] *Convention for the Unification of Certain Rules concerning the Immunity of State-owned ships*; Brussels, 10 April 1926 and *Additional Protocol*; Brussels, 24 May 1934 (Vol. 176 *LNTS* 1937, Nr. 4062).

It took until 1972 before a convention on immunity with a broader scope was adopted: the *European Convention on State Immunity*. The Convention is based on the restrictive doctrine, as is reflected in Articles 5–14 describing cases in which States are not entitled to immunity from adjudicative jurisdiction. The Convention is ratified by eight States[28] and only applies to civil procedures leaving the field of criminal law untouched.

The *UN Convention on State Immunity,* adopted by the UN General Assembly in 2004, has a much wider scope.[29] Although the treaty has not yet entered into force, its principles can be considered as reflecting customary law.[30] Similar to previous treaties the Convention does not include criminal procedures and, instead, focuses on the civil law actions of States.[31] The doctrine of the relative State immunity is also the basis for this Convention and is clearly reflected in Articles 10–17, which stipulate when a State cannot invoke its immunity.

A number of States, in particular those having an Anglo-Saxon legal tradition, have enacted rules on State immunity in their national laws.[32] In 1976 the US laid down the doctrine of relative immunity in the *Foreign Sovereign Immunities Act* (FSIA). Also, the act transferred the power to decide whether a situation concerns a case of State immunity from the executive branch to the judicial branch.[33] In 1978 the UK accepted the doctrine of relative State immunity and enacted the *State Immunity Act* (SIA). More importantly, the Act enabled the ratification of the *Convention for the Unification of Certain Rules concerning the Immunity of State-owned ships* and its protocol and the *European Convention on State Immunity*.[34] Besides, the Act also applies to other States that are not party to the above-mentioned conventions.

7.3 Immunity of State Officials

A State is an abstraction, an artificial body that acts through its organs, such as its Head of State, Head of Government, Ministers and envoys. In foreign States these officials enjoy immunity, exempting them from the adjudicative and enforcement

28 Belgium, Cyprus, Germany, the Netherlands, Luxembourg, Austria, the UK and Switzerland. Portugal is co-signatory, but has not ratified the convention yet.

29 *United Nations Convention on jurisdictional immunities of States and their property*; New York, 17 January 2005 (*UN Doc* A/RES/59/38 (2004).

30 Nollkaemper 2011, p. 121.

31 *UN Doc* A/RES/59/38 (2004), Sect. 2.

32 Dickinson et al. 2004, pp. 217 et seq. See also: *UN Doc* A/CN.4/596 (2008), Memorandum by the Secretariat, Immunity of State officials from foreign criminal jurisdiction, 31 March 2008, p. 31, fn 119.

33 Ibid.

34 Id., 329.

jurisdiction of the host State. These immunities follow from the relations that States maintain with each other, which are based on the international legal principles of sovereignty, equality and independence of States. The same principles are also the legal basis for immunity of State officials.[35] However, immunity does not have the same scope for all categories of officials. It depends on the function of the officials and the nature of their acts.

The following subsections address the functional and personal immunity of State officials, followed by a discussion on the immunities of the most important categories of officials. This section concludes with analysing immunity with respect to international crimes.

7.3.1 Functional and Personal Immunity

Officials can be entitled to immunity for acts performed in an official capacity. In this context the focus is on the features of the acts and this form of immunity is therefore referred to as functional immunity or immunity *ratione materiae*. As a State acts through its organs, officials can be considered instruments of the State and their official acts can only be attributed to the State.[36] They act in name of the State, which means that they are not individually responsible for these acts.[37] Each official acting in an official capacity, whether a Minister, police officer or member of the armed forces, enjoys functional immunity[38] from the enforcement and adjudicative jurisdiction of a foreign State (see Fig. 7.1).[39] As it concerns the immunity of the State, the functional immunity does not cease when an official vacates his office.[40]

[35] *UN Doc* A/CN.4/601 (2008), para 95.

[36] See *UN Doc* A/CN.4/631 (2010), ILC Second report on immunity of State officials from foreign criminal jurisdiction, 10 June 2010, para 26 and ICTY Appeals Chamber 29 October 1997, *Prosecutor v. Blaskić*, IT-95-14-AR108bis, Judgement on the request of the Republic of Croatia for review of the decision of the trial chamber II of 18 July 1997, paras 38 and 41. www.icty.org/x/cases/blaskic/acdec/en/71029JT3.html. Accessed November 2014.

[37] van Alebeek 2007, p. 251.

[38] Cassese 2002, p. 862 et seq; *UN Doc* A/CN.4/596 (2008), Memorandum by the Secretariat, para 166; I. Roberts 2009, p. 185. *UN Doc* A/CN.4/631 (2010), ILC Second Report on immunity of State officials from foreign criminal jurisdiction, 10 June 2010, para 18. Immunity also applies to the officials' acta jure gestionis, for which the State does not enjoy civil law immunity; ibid para 28.

[39] Some authors consider functional immunity as "…a principle of non-attribution of conduct rather than a bar to proceedings…", which means that it does not include individual responsibility for the act; e.g. Liivoja 2011, p. 113.

[40] *UN Doc* A/CN.4/601 (2008), para 85.

Fig. 7.1 Functional immunity

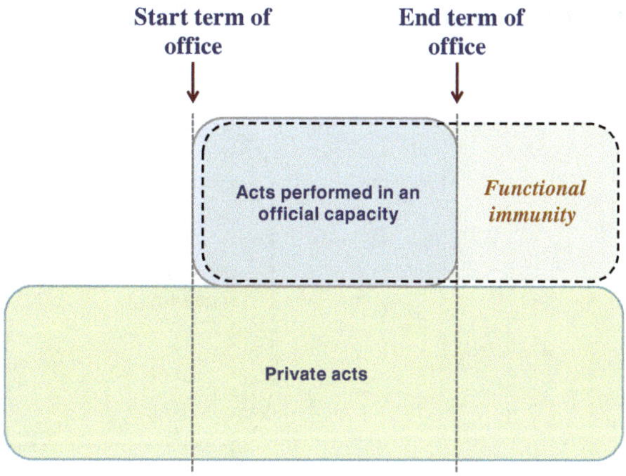

To decide if functional immunity exists, it is important to distinguish official from private acts. The commentary to Article 4 of the *Draft Articles on State Responsibility*[41] makes clear that it does not matter whether an act is committed out of ulterior or improper motives or whether the official abused his powers. In both cases the acts are attributable to the State if the official has acted "in an apparently official capacity, or under a colour of authority".[42]

During their term of office some high-ranking officials also enjoy immunity for other than official acts. Immunity then depends on the position of the official and is therefore referred to as personal immunity or immunity *ratione personae* (see Fig. 7.2). The nature of the act is no longer important and immunity extends to private acts as well. This type of immunity completely shields the officials from another State's exercise of jurisdiction while serving in office. It expires the moment the official vacates his post[43]; however, he continues to enjoy functional immunity (again, see Fig. 7.1).[44]

---

[41] *Draft Articles on Responsibility of States for Internationally Wrongful Acts, UN Doc* A/RES/56/83 (2002) of 28 January 2002.

[42] *UN Doc* A/56/10 (2001), ILC Report on the work of its fifty-third session, Chap. IV, State Responsibility, commentary to Article 14, para 13. Another approach is to exclude the acts that are mainly performed out of personal motives; *UN Doc* A/CN.4/596 (2008), Memorandum by the Secretariat, para 158.

[43] ICJ 14 February 2002, *Arrest warrant of 11 April 2000* (Democratic Republic of the Congo v. Belgium), Judgment, I.C.J. Reports 2002, p. 3, paras 54 and 61.

[44] *UN Doc* A/CN.4/596 (2008), Memorandum by the Secretariat, para 90.

Fig. 7.2 Personal immunity

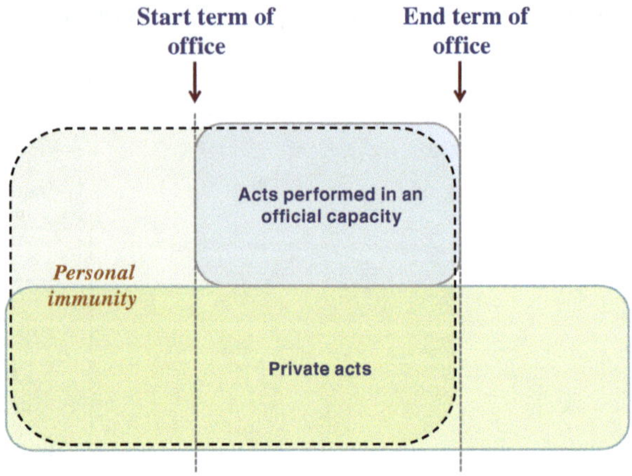

The rationale of affording personal immunity is at present based on ideas of functional necessity.[45] Stability and predictability are important elements to maintain international relations. Politically motivated foreign legal procedures can impede the activities of officials who act on behalf of a State.[46] For this reason the officials' immunity is in the interest of the orderly conduct of international relations[47] and to permit the effective performance of the functions of State officials.[48]

Immunity is a bar to a State's jurisdiction and can only be invoked if this jurisdiction actually exists.[49] This means that immunity and jurisdiction are closely related, as has been discussed in Sect. 1.4.4. The fact that officials enjoy immunity does not create jurisdiction for another State, nor does it trigger the obligation for the State already having jurisdiction to exercise it. Immunity simply exempts an official from the adjudicative and enforcement jurisdiction of the host State. The fact that the State sending the official possibly has jurisdiction over its official and may exercise that power on his return can be the consequence of immunity, but is in principle independent thereof.

---

45 *UN Doc* A/CN.4/596 (2008), Memorandum by the Secretariat, Immunity of State officials from foreign criminal jurisdiction, 31 March 2008, paras 22–23. Formerly the idea of representation was a central feature and the official was seen as the representative of the King or State; Liivoja 2011, p. 107.

46 *UN Doc* A/CN.4/601 (2008), para 96.

47 Fox 2008, p. 1.

48 Article II(1) *Immunity from Jurisdiction of the State and Persons Who act on Behalf of the State in Case of International Crimes*; Resolution, Naples 2009.

49 ICJ 14 February 2002, *Arrest warrant of 11 April 2000* (Democratic Republic of the Congo v. Belgium), Judgment, I.C.J. Reports 2002, 3, separate opinions of Judges Higgins, Kooijmans and Buergenthal para 70.

For some acts that breach the sovereign position of the State,[50] immunity cannot be invoked with respect to officials who do not operate with the consent of that State[51]; for instance, in case of espionage[52] and sabotage.[53]

7.3.2 State Officials

The following sections discuss some specific categories of State officials, starting with high-ranking officials, such as the Head of State, the Head of Government and Ministers. This subsection will be followed by a discussion on officials that represent the State in their capacity as diplomatic or consular agents. As any government official they all enjoy criminal immunity for acts performed abroad in their official capacity, although not all officials are entitled to personal immunity. The status of military personnel is discussed in the next chapter.

7.3.2.1 Heads of State

Heads of State are the highest-ranking officials of a State. Historically they personify the State they represent.[54] This approach is still reflected in the relations with other States, as the Head of State can represent his State in

---

[50] *UN Doc* A/CN.4/596 (2008), Memorandum by the Secretariat, paras 163–165.

[51] E.g. *EU Doc* 8672/09 of 16 April 2009, The AU-EU Expert Report on the Principle of Universal Jurisdiction, para 85. However, members of a diplomatic mission who are suspected of conducting espionage activities, are entitled to immunity on the basis of their diplomatic status, which has been approved by the host State; see Bundesverfassungsgericht 15 May 1995 in a case against East German spies. However, the host State can declare the diplomat 'persona non grata' in accordance with Article 9 *Vienna Convention on Diplomatic Relations*; Vienna, 18 April 1961 (Vol. 500 *UNTS* 1964, Nr. 7310); see Roberts 2009, pp. 206–225.

[52] 15 May 1995 Bundesverfassungsgericht in a case against East German spies: "There is no rule of international law according to which spies who are prosecuted by the State against which the espionage was directed could rely on the principles of sovereign immunity"; mentioned in Hafner et al. 2006, p. 374.

[53] E.g. Ruling by the Secretary-General of the United Nations, 6 July 1986, *Case concerning the differences between New Zealand and France arising from the Rainbow Warrior affair*, United Nations Reports of International Arbitral Awards, Vol. XIX, pp. 199–221.

[54] E.g. *UN Doc* A/CN.4/601 (2008), para 108. The King was identified with the State, as the words attributed to Louis XIV express "L'état, c'est moi"; *UN Doc* A/CN.4/596 (2008), Memorandum by the Secretariat, para 28.

all fields.[55] The legal position of Heads of State is above all a customary matter. Criminal immunity *ratione personae* of Heads of State has been widely accepted both in theory and in practice (also, see Sect. 7.3.3 on human rights and immunity).[56]

Personal immunity of the Heads of State ceases when their term of office has come to an end, although functional immunity continues to apply.[57] Therefore, former Heads of State can still be prosecuted by a foreign judge for acts committed prior to or after their term of office and for private acts committed during their term of office (see Sect. 7.3.3). Personal immunity of a Head of State is without prejudice to the competence of an international criminal court.[58] Such international proceedings do not subject a Head of State to the jurisdiction of another State, but to the jurisdiction of a body that has jurisdiction based on an international mandate.[59] Its jurisdiction obviously does not concern any offence, but covers serious crimes under international law.

---

[55] ICJ 3 February 2006, *Case concerning Armed Activities on the Territory of the Congo* (Democratic Republic of the Congo v. Rwanda), Judgment, I.C.J. Reports 2006, p. 6, para 46: "it is a well-established rule of international law that the Head of State, the Head of Government and the Minister for Foreign Affairs are deemed to represent the State merely by virtue of exercising their functions, including for the performance, on behalf of the said State, of unilateral acts having the force of international commitments. The Court moreover recalls that, in the matter of the conclusion of treaties, this rule of customary law finds expression in Article 7, para 2, of the Vienna Convention on the Law of Treaties".

[56] *UN Doc* A/CN.4/601 (2008), para 110; see also Article 3(2) *UN State Immunity Convention.* Several older examples: U.S. District Court, Eastern District of New York, 27 January 1994, *Lafontant v. Aristide*, p. 844 F Supp 128 (EDNY 1994); ILDC 1677 (US 1994) and Federal Supreme Court 14 December 1994, *Re Honecker*, ILR 80. More recently, the Spanish judge has recognised the immunity of Fidel Castro (Cassese 2002, p. 860, fn 21), the French judge has recognised the immunity of Colonel Gaddafi (Court de Cassation 13 March 2001, *Affaire Kadhafi*, Judgement No. 1414, ILR 125, 509), the British judge has recognised the immunity of Mugabe (District Court (Bow Street) Judgment, 14 January 2004, *Robert Mugabe*, Int Comp Law Q, Vol. 53 (2004), 770) and the judge in The Hague has recognised the criminal immunity of President Bush as the incumbent Head of State of the US (District Court The Hague 4 May 2005, *President Bush*, ECLI:NL:RBSGR:2005:AT5152) and of President Yudhoyono of Indonesia (District Court The Hague 6 October 2010, *Indonesian President,* ECLI:NL:RBSGR:2010:BO0384).

[57] See Article 13 of the Resolution of the 'Institut de Droit International': *Immunities from Jurisdiction and Execution of Heads of State and of Government in International Law*; Resolution, Vancouver 2001.

[58] E.g. Article 27 *Rome Statute of the International Criminal Court*; Rome, 17 July 1998 (Vol. 2187 *UNTS* 2004, No. 38544). In addition, a Head of State can be prosecuted by his own national court or his State can waive his immunity: see, e.g. U.S. District Court, Southern District of Florida 14 January 1993, *Paul and others v. Avril*, ILR 103.

[59] SCSL, Appeals Chamber 31 May 2004, The Prosecutor v. Charles Ghankay Taylor, Case No. SCSL-2003-01-I, *Decision on immunity from jurisdiction*, www.sc-sl.org/LinkClick.aspx?fileticket=7OeBn4RulEg=&tabid=191; mentioned in *UN Doc* A/CN.4/596 (2008), Memorandum by the Secretariat, para 72.

Furthermore, immunity can also be restricted in the area of civil law.[60] A Head of State enjoys full immunity in civil proceedings related to acts performed in the exercise of his public functions.[61] When it comes to private acts, international practice varies.[62] For instance, the US grant foreign Heads of State absolute immunity, while other States tend to restrict immunity to enforcement measures during State visits.[63] In the view of the 'Institut de Droit International' immunity of Heads of State in civil and administrative law is restricted to acts performed in the exercise of official functions.[64]

7.3.2.2 Heads of Government and Ministers

Today, not just Heads of State represent the interests of their States at the highest international level, but so do Heads of Government and Ministers for Foreign Affairs. For this reason international law provides these officials with immunity from jurisdiction in the area of civil and criminal law.[65] Generally speaking, similar to the Heads of State they enjoy criminal immunity *ratione personae.*

In the *Arrest Warrant* case the ICJ focussed particularly on the position of the Ministers for Foreign Affairs.[66] In this particular case, concerning a Belgian arrest warrant issued to the Minister for Foreign Affairs of the Democratic Republic of the Congo, the Court stated that no distinction could be made between acts performed in a private capacity and acts performed in an official capacity. If an incumbent Minister for Foreign Affairs would be arrested in a foreign State, he would no longer be able to exercise his functions. Consequently,

---

[60] In *The Exchange v. McFaddon*-case the judge remarked that exceptions to the immunity of a Prince can exist in case he acts as a private individual, such as in case of purchasing private property in a foreign State; *The Schooner Exchange v. McFaddon,* 145.

[61] Roberts 2009, p. 180; see Article 3 of the Resolution of the 'Institut de Droit International': *Immunities from Jurisdiction and Execution of Heads of State and of Government in International Law*; Resolution, Vancouver 2001.

[62] Fox 2008, p. 690, e.g. Civil Court of Brussels, 29 December 1988, *Mobutu v SA Cotoni,* ILR 91.

[63] van Alebeek 2007, p. 254. E.g. the French judge stated that the President of the former Republic of Zaire, Mobutu, did not enjoy immunity in respect of proceedings over the delivery of tents bearing his personal initials; Court of Appeal of Paris 31 May 1994, *Mobutu and Republic of Zaire v Société Logrine*, ILR 113.

[64] Article 3 *Immunities from Jurisdiction and Execution of Heads of State and of Government in International Law*; Resolution, Vancouver 2001.

[65] ICJ 14 February 2002, *Arrest warrant of 11 April 2000* (Democratic Republic of the Congo v. Belgium), Judgment, I.C.J. Reports 2002, p. 3, para 51.

[66] ICJ *Arrest warrant*, para 55.

Ministers for Foreign Affairs enjoy immunity *ratione personae*.[67] Their personal immunity ends when they have left their office, but they continue to enjoy functional immunity.[68]

Other high officials, such as Ministers of other departments, may also enjoy immunity.[69] In 2004, for instance, the British court considered that the roles of foreign affairs and defence are very much intertwined, as:

> …many States maintain troops overseas and there are many United Nations missions to visit in which military issues do play a prominent role between certain States.[70]

The court concluded that a Minister of Defence automatically acquires immunity in the same way as that pertaining to a Minister for Foreign Affairs. On this basis the judge declined issuing an arrest warrant to the Israeli Minister of Defence.[71] The same judge refused to issue an arrest warrant to a Chinese Minister of Commerce. He concluded that as the latter's functions were equivalent to those exercised by a Minister for Foreign Affairs, he enjoyed immunity 'ratione personae' to enable him to exercise his official functions effectively.[72]

Even though these high-ranking officials do not have the ultimate responsibility for the international relations of their State, today they have an important function to fulfil. The exercise of jurisdiction by a foreign State could impede the independent exercise of their official functions.

---

[67] In accordance with this decision the Belgian judge considered that Ariel Sharon enjoyed immunity *ratione personae,* being a foreign Head of Government, Court of Cassation 12 February 2003, *Re Sharon and Yaron*, Cass no P 02 1139 F/1, ILDC 5 (BE 2003); Journal des Tribunaux 2003, p. 250, para 21.

[68] See the obiter dictum in the *Arrest Warrant* case, para 61: "*after a persons ceases to hold the office of Minister for Foreign Affairs, he or she will no longer enjoy all the immunities accorded by international law in other States. Provided that it has jurisdiction under international law, a court of one State may try a former Minister of Foreign Affairs of another State in respect of acts committed prior or subsequent to his or her period of office, as well in respect of acts committed during that period of office in a private capacity*".

[69] National case law and the literature do not reflect a clear, coherent approach. In some cases national judges decided that the immunity of high-ranking foreign officials, such as Ministers, was limited; *UN Doc* A/CN.4/596 (2008), Memorandum by the Secretariat, para 134. The ICJ concluded that there are no grounds in international law upon which two high-ranking officials of Djibouti (the 'procureur de la République' and the Head of National Security) were entitled to personal immunities; ICJ 4 June 2008, *Certain Questions of Mutual Assistance in Criminal Matters* (Djibouti v. France), Judgment, I.C.J. Reports 2008, p. 177, para 194. The fact that Djibouti did not claim immunity for both officials contributed to the decision (see para 196).

[70] District Court (Bow Street), 12 February 2004, *Application for arrest warrant against General Shaul Mofaz*, Judgement, Int Comp Law Q, Vol. 53 (2004), 771.

[71] *Application for arrest warrant against General Shaul Mofaz,* 771.

[72] District Court (Bow Street) 8 November 2005, *Re Bo Xilai*, ILR 128.

7.3.2.3 Diplomats

In addition to Heads of State, Heads of Government and Ministers, diplomatic and consular agents and members of special missions also enjoy immunity in the host State. Diplomacy is essential in the official relations between the governments of sovereign States. Therefore, at an early stage rules concerning diplomatic relations have developed into the law as we know it today.[73]

The status of diplomatic and consular agents is first and foremost based on international customary law.[74] Other important sources are the *Vienna Convention on Diplomatic relations*[75] of 1961 and the *Vienna Convention on Consular Relations.*[76] The position of members of special missions does not have a customary basis, but is regulated in the *Convention on special missions* of 1969.[77] The status of the representatives to international organisations is set out in treaties between their member States and in the headquarters agreements (see Sect. 9.5).

Well before ideas on State immunity developed, immunity of envoys was part of international law.[78] Originally the ruling opinion was that envoys were to be considered as representatives of the King and that the immunity of the King would extend to his envoys. Today, fundamental for diplomatic immunity is the concept that diplomatic agents must be able to represent their State without impediments (the principle *ne impediatur legatio*)[79] "... to ensure the efficient performance of the functions of diplomatic missions as representing states".[80]

Thus, diplomatic immunity and State immunity have a different origin. State immunity is based on the principle of equality of sovereign States, whereas diplomatic immunity is derived from the role of envoys as representatives of a foreign State and is based on the necessity to safeguard the liberty in the exercise of their functions.[81]

Article 1 of the *Vienna Convention on Diplomatic Relations* distinguishes three categories of agents. The most important category consists of diplomatic agents:

---

[73] The rules on diplomatic law described by Vattel in 1758 in 'Le Droit des Gents' remained unchanged for the next two centuries, Denza 2004, p. 1.

[74] Roberts 2009, p. 10.

[75] *Vienna Convention on Diplomatic Relations*; Vienna, 18 April 1961 (Vol. 500 *UNTS* 1964, Nr. 7310).

[76] *Vienna Convention on Consular Relations*; Vienna, 24 April 1963 (Vol. 596 *UNTS* 196, No. 8638).

[77] *Convention on Special Missions*; New York 8, December 1969 (Vol. 1400 *UNTS* 1985, No. 23431).

[78] Bankas 2005, p. 41.

[79] Supreme Court 13 November 2007, *Criminal immunity EURATOM*; ECLI:NL:PHR:2007:BA9173, note N. Keijzer para 3.

[80] Preamble, *Vienna Convention on Diplomatic Relations.*

[81] Fox 2008, pp. 710 and 711.

the head of the diplomatic mission and the members of the diplomatic staff. They hold a diplomatic rank and pursuant to Article 31 they enjoy far-reaching immunities from local jurisdiction. The only exception to these immunities can be found in the area of civil jurisdiction with respect to actions related to private immovable property and commercial transactions.

The second category consists of administrative and technical staff, such as members of the secretariat, cypher clerks and communications experts. As their duties may involve the handling of diplomatic secrets, immunity is needed to guarantee a proper exercise of their functions.[82] The immunities laid down in Article 37(2) are not customary in nature, but are the consequence of ongoing developments in the area of immunity.[83] These immunities largely draw on immunities of diplomatic agents. Exceptions can be found in the area of civil and administrative law, in which immunity is limited to acts performed in the course of their duties.

The last category consists of members of the service staff[84]: persons who are in domestic service of the mission, such as drivers, kitchen and cleaning personnel. They are not directly involved in the official activities of the diplomatic mission and for that reason do not enjoy personal immunity. Instead, pursuant to Article 37 they are entitled to immunity for all acts performed in the course of duty.[85]

Diplomacy means conducting foreign policy of a State.[86] The deployment of military personnel abroad may serve the same purpose and may be supportive of that policy. A case in point is a commissioned officer attached to a diplomatic mission as military attaché whose status is based on the *Vienna Convention on Diplomatic Relations*. Other military officials may be entitled to diplomatic status as well. Personnel involved in small-scale military missions supporting foreign policy need sufficient freedom to perform their duties abroad and will therefore need immunity.[87] In general, SOFAs covering these missions will not grant members of the mission diplomatic status, but will offer similar immunities as the technical and administrative staff of a diplomatic mission are entitled to.

---

[82] Roberts 2009, pp. 158–159.

[83] Id., p. 159.

[84] In contrast to 'private servants', who are employed by a member of the diplomatic mission, members of the service staff are employed by the sending State.

[85] According to the Dutch Supreme Court, a servant of the Italian Embassy in The Hague, who had committed a traffic offence, enjoyed immunity because he committed the offence during the performance of his duty as a servant of the Embassy; Dutch Supreme Court 9 September 1975, *NJ* 1976, p. 69.

[86] Roberts 2009, p. 3.

[87] E.g. the Dutch military mission in Surinam tasked with the transfer of military material to Surinam; *Agreement establishing rules concerning the legal status of military and civilian personnel of the Kingdom of the Netherlands under the authority of the Department of Defence*; Paramaribo, 25 November 1975 (Vol. 1041 *UNTS* 1984, No. 15699).

On occasion SOFAs also refer to the immunity of diplomatic agents when regulating the status of specific military officials responsible for the conduct of crisis management operations. For example, in accordance with section 19 of the *Convention on Privileges and Immunities of the United,* section 24 of the *UN Model-SOFA* grants the Force Commander and the members of his staff the immunities "...accorded to diplomatic envoys in accordance with international law." The same applies to the Chief Military Observer in charge of an observation mission. Sometimes SOFAs accord a similar status to military observers (see Chap. 4).

In addition to diplomatic missions, States may have consular missions abroad. The most important difference between diplomatic and consular agents is that the former carry out their duties interacting directly with officials of the central government of the host State. The consular officers' activities are aimed at the lower administrative levels of government,[88] as they are mostly of an administrative and legal nature helping and assisting their nationals (see Article 5 of the *Vienna Convention on Consular Relations*). The different degree of representation is reflected in the immunities that are needed for the performance of the consular functions. On the basis of Article 43(1) of the *Vienna Convention on Consular Relations,* career consular officers enjoy functional immunity, except for several civil actions enumerated under para 2 of the same article.

A diplomatic mission is a State's permanent representation in the receiving State. Sometimes States send a temporary mission for particular purposes.[89] To regulate those situations the 1969 *Convention on special missions* was adopted. In summary, the Convention grants members of a special mission similar immunity as is granted to permanent missions under the *Vienna Convention on Diplomatic Relations*. Although the importance of the Convention may be somewhat limited,[90] some of its rules are customary by nature.

7.3.3 International Crimes and Immunity

At the end of the nineteenth century, when State participation in commercial transactions abroad had steadily increased, the disadvantageous position of their civil counterparties had led to exceptions to State immunity. In the course of time the position of individuals has been strengthened further and the question has

[88] Roberts 2009, p. 259. However, in practice these distinctions are not always easy to make.

[89] Id., pp. 187–188.

[90] Many States have second thoughts when it comes to administrative problems that could occur as a consequence of protecting the immunity or granting tax-free allowances to the temporary missions. This means that only a small number of States is party to the Convention.

arisen to what extent States and their officials should continue to enjoy immunity in case of alleged violations of the individuals' fundamental rights.[91]

In the field of civil law State immunity barred victims of human rights violations from bringing civil actions before their national courts against a foreign State involved in the human rights violation.[92] Under these circumstances, however, State immunity has been criticised from a jus cogens perspective. When a State violates the peremptory norms under international law, this State should not be entitled to immunity.[93] However, in the *Al-Adsani* case the European Court of Human Rights (ECtHR) rejected this position with respect to Al-Adsani's claim of alleged torture[94]:

> … the Court is unable to discern in the international instruments, judicial authorities or other materials before it any firm basis for concluding that, as a matter of international law, a State no longer enjoys immunity from civil suit in the courts of another State where acts of torture are alleged.[95]

So far States[96] or national courts have only in exceptional cases rejected State immunity with regard to human rights violations.

Over the past few years, the Greek and Italian courts have denied Germany immunity with respect to claims based on the violation of international law in World War II. In the *Voiotia* case a Greek court ordered Germany to pay damages for the burning of the village of Distomo and for summary executions of a number of inhabitants in 1944.[97] However, the Greek Minister of Justice refused execution

---

[91] For an overview of, and a discussion on, the various arguments, see *UN Doc* A/CN.4/631 (2010), ILC Second report on immunity of State officials from foreign criminal jurisdiction, 10 June 2010, para 56 et seq.

[92] For an overview of court decisions, see O'Keefe 2011, pp. 1013–1019. The *UN Convention on State Immunity* does not contain any exceptions to immunity in these cases either.

[93] Caplan 2003, p. 741.

[94] ECtHR 21 November 2001, *Al-Adsani v. the United Kingdom*, Application no. 35763/97, para 61.

[95] The Court upheld the immunity of foreign States in a number of judgement: e.g. ECtHR 12 December 2002, *Kalogeropoulou and others v. Greece and Germany*, Application no. 59021/00 and recently, ECtHR 14 January 2014, *Jones and others v. The United Kingdom*, Application no. 34356/06 and 40528/06.

[96] E.g. the US *Anti-terrorism and Effective Death Penalty Act 1996* is a modification to the FSIA, which rejects immunities related to claims of American citizens of torturing or extrajudicial killings; Fox 2008, p. 364. The Act only applies to the States designated by the US as State sponsors of terrorism; Gattini 2011, p. 174. In March 2012 Canada in a similar way modified the *State Immunity Act* by adopting the *Justice for Victims of Terrorism Act*. As a result, Canadian citizens who have fallen victim to terrorism can bring a civil proceeding against the relevant State, if the State is on the black list of States suspected of sponsoring terrorism; Provost 2012.

[97] Supreme Civil and Criminal Court (Areios Pagos) 4 May 2000, *Germany v Prefecture of Voiotia*, ILDC 287 (GR 2000).

of the sentence. In the following procedure before the ECtHR the Court referred to the *Al-Adsani* case and stated:

> The Court does not find it established, however, that there is yet acceptance in international law of the proposition that States are not entitled to immunity in respect of civil claims for damages brought against them in another State for crimes against humanity.[98]

In subsequent decisions the Greek courts followed this reasoning of the ECtHR.[99]

In the *Ferrini* case the Italian court allowed a civil claim brought against Germany with respect to the deportation and forced labour of an Italian citizen in 1944, because it found that immunity could not bar a claim in the case of an international crime.[100] In *Mantelli,* a similar case, the court confirmed this ruling.[101]

These decisions caused Germany to start a procedure before the ICJ.[102] The Court had to answer the question "whether customary international law had developed to the point where a State is not entitled to immunity in the case of serious violations of human rights law or the law of armed conflict" (para 83 of the judgment). After thorough analysis the Court concluded that a State is still entitled to immunity under current international customary law (para 91). In its opinion the fact that the case concerned violations of jus cogens did not affect the applicability of the customary international law on State immunity (para 97).

In the field of criminal law the discussion focuses on the question whether immunity of Heads of State, Heads of Government and Ministers for Foreign Affairs can be upheld in cases of crimes, such as genocide, war crimes, crimes against humanity, or other crimes under international law. The growing attention of the international community for compliance with fundamental human rights puts pressure on criminal immunity of these State officials. As a result, there is a tendency in international law to penalise international crimes,[103] as the jurisdiction

---

98 ECtHR 12 December 2002, *Kalogeropoulou and others v. Greece and Germany*, Application no. 59021/00, 8.

99 Special Supreme Court 17 September 2002, *Germany v Margellos*, 1 AED 11–19, 3 March 2003, ILDC 87 (GR 2002).

100 Court of Cassation 11 March 2004, *Ferrini v. Federal Republic of Germany*, no 5044/4, ILDC 19 (IT 2004).

101 Court of Cassation 29 May 2008, *Germany v Mantelli and ors*, No 14201/2008, ILDC 1037 (IT 2008).

102 ICJ 3 February 2012, *Jurisdictional Immunities of the State* (*Germany v. Italy*: Greece Intervening), Judgment. The decision did not prevent the Italian court in the *Milde* case from convicting Germany once more to pay indemnity for crimes committed by a German soldier in WWII; Court of Cassation 13 January 2009, *Criminal proceedings against Milde*, Case no 1072/2009, ILDC 1224 (IT 2009).

103 Hirsch Ballin 2002, p. 741.

of the International Criminal Court over incumbent Heads of State and other high-ranking officials demonstrates.[104]

However, as can be concluded from the *Arrest Warrant* case, international law does not provide national courts with a clear legal basis for prosecuting these officials. In general this approach is reflected in national legislation, case law and, partly, the literature.[105] Nevertheless, at national level there is a search for openings and possibilities to make national prosecution of international crimes possible. One of the main arguments to restrict immunity is that the principle of jus cogens is considered to be hierarchically of a higher ranking than rules on immunity. Following this thought means that the violation of higher rules has primacy over the applicability of immunity.[106] Another argument is based on the idea that an international crime cannot constitute an official activity of the State.[107]

These arguments have occasionally led courts to deny former Heads of State immunity, when they were accused of having committed international crimes.[108] Likewise, some States have adopted rules stating that foreign officials cannot be entitled to immunity in case of genocide, crimes against humanity and war crimes.[109] In its resolution *Immunities from Jurisdiction and Execution of Heads of State and of Government in International Law* of 2001, the 'Institut de Droit

[104] Article 27(2) *Statute of Rome* states that no government official can claim immunity before the International Criminal Court. Statutes of other international tribunals determine that the official position of government members shall not free them from criminal responsibility; see Article 7, *Charter of the International Military Tribunal* (Nuremberg Tribunal); Article 6 *Charter of the International Military Tribunal for the Far East* (Tokyo Tribunal); Article 7(2) *Statute of the International Criminal Tribunal for the former Yugoslavia* (Yugoslavia Tribunal) and Article 6(2) *Statute of the International Criminal Tribunal for Rwanda* (Rwanda Tribunal).

[105] *UN Doc* A/CN.4/596 (2008), Memorandum by the Secretariat, para 145 et seq. See also the recommendation that national criminal law authorities are obliged to respect the immunities of foreign government officials, in: *EU Doc* 8672/09 van 16 April 2009, The AU-EU Expert Report on the Principle of Universal Jurisdiction, para 46, R8.

[106] E.g., see Court of Cassation 24 July 2008, *Lozano v Italy*, Case No 31171/2008, ILDC 1085 (IT 2008).

[107] See van Alebeek, who States that in case of international crimes immunity ends and individual responsibility starts; van Alebeek 2012, p. 36. Functional immunity is based on the idea that personal responsibility is absent. In case of international crimes, the offenders are responsible, which means that crimes are not considered as official acts for which government officials can claim functional immunity; Ibid., p. 19.

[108] *UN Doc* A/CN.4/596 (2008), Memorandum by the Secretariat, paras 184–187 and 200 and *EU Doc* 8672/09 16 April 2009, The AU-EU Expert Report on the Principle of Universal Jurisdiction, para 24 punt (vii).

[109] *EU Doc* 8672/09 of 16 April 2009, The AU-EU Expert Report on the Principle of Universal Jurisdiction mentions Niger, the Congo and South Africa, para 17. *UN Doc* A/CN.4/596 (2008), Memorandum by the Secretariat, para 150, fn 419 refers to the national legislation of, inter alia, Croatia and South Africa to implement Article 27 *Statute of Rome*. Neither document contains any details on the national legislation.

Fig. 7.3 Functional immunity and international crimes

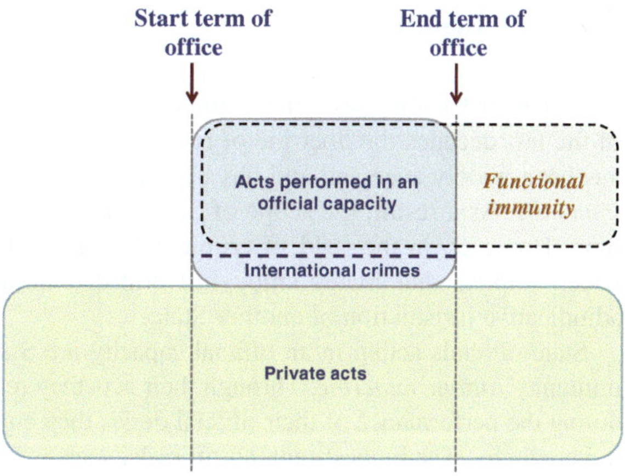

International' indicated that a former Head of State can be prosecuted for an international crime when it has been committed:

> ...exclusively to satisfy a personal interest, or when they constitute a misappropriation of the State's assets and resources.[110]

With regard to international crimes committed by government officials the 'Institut' stated in 2009 that:

> No immunity from jurisdiction other than personal immunity in accordance with international law applies with regard to international crimes.[111]

This means that in case of international crimes there is no immunity *ratione materiae*. Consequently, national courts can prosecute former Heads of State and other State officials for international crimes committed during their term of office (see Fig. 7.3).[112]

In practice, there is still uncertainty about the topic of immunity relating to international crimes. As the emphasis on the position of the individual under international law is of growing importance, this topic will most likely receive more attention in the future[113] and functional immunity might have to make way for criminal responsibility for international crimes.

---

[110] Article 13(2) *UN Doc* A/CN.4/631 (2010), ILC Second report on immunity of State officials from foreign criminal jurisdiction, 10 June 2010, para 89 emphasises that this is not the prevailing doctrine.

[111] Article III(1) Resolution on *Immunity from Jurisdiction of the State and Persons Who act on Behalf of the State in Case of International Crimes*; Naples 2009. However, this is not the prevailing doctrine, as emphasised in: *UN Doc* A/CN.4/631 (2010), ILC Second report on immunity of State officials from foreign criminal jurisdiction, 10 June 2010, para 80.

[112] Bellal 2011, p. 238, see also Dutch Advisory Committee on Issues of Public International Law 2011, p. 15.

[113] *UN Doc* A/CN.4/596 (2008), Memorandum by the Secretariat, para 151.

7.4 Conclusion

This chapter has discussed the immunity of State officials under international law. In the last decades the doctrine of relative State immunity in the field of civil law has been widely accepted and has been integrated in the *UN Convention on State Immunity.* As a result, the scope of State immunity was limited over the course of time. However, in the field of criminal law absolute immunity has been upheld, which implies that States enjoy full criminal immunity from enforcement and adjudicative jurisdiction of another State.

State officials acting in an official capacity are State organs that generally enjoy immunity *ratione materiae*. Through their acts they represent the State, meaning that during the performance of their official duties they enjoy their State's immunity as if it were theirs. The highest-ranking officials, such as Heads of State and Government and Ministers for Foreign Affairs also enjoy immunity for acts performed in a private capacity: immunity *ratione personae*. Other officials, such as Ministers, who play a more important part in international relations nowadays, seem to be entitled to similar immunities. After their term of duty has finished, the officials partly lose immunity *ratione personae*, but remain entitled to immunity *ratione materiae*.

Envoys represent their State abroad and should be able to perform their duties independent from the receiving State. They represent their State and as a consequence enjoy the necessary immunities that are related to their level in diplomatic relations. On the basis of existing treaties diplomats and members of the diplomatic staff enjoy full immunity in the field of criminal law. When it comes to civil law there are some exceptions.

The increasing attention for the rights of individuals puts pressure on the immunity of State officials and a trend can be discerned towards a denial of immunity in case of serious international crimes committed by State officials. For the moment, personal immunity is upheld in national and international legal proceedings, but there seems to be growing support for denying functional immunity in respect of serious international crimes after the term of office has come to an end.

The next chapter links the position of the armed forces to the immunity of the State and its officials. Previous sections of this chapter have illustrated that the position of the military has to be analysed in the light of the transition from the absolute doctrine of State immunity to the restrictive doctrine of State immunity. Although it seems that the armed forces are also covered by immunity of the State, it will have to be examined whether immunities of military personnel serving abroad has developed wholly or partly independently from the immunity of other State officials.

References

Advisory Committee on Issues of Public International Law (2011) Immunity of foreign state officials. www.cavv-advies.nl/Publications. Accessed Nov 2014

Bankas EK (2005) The state immunity controversy in international law. In: Private suits against sovereign states in domestic courts. Springer, Berlin

Bellal A (2011) The 2009 resolution of the Institute of International Law on immunity and international crimes. J Int Crim Justice 9(1):227–241
Brownlie I (2008) Principles of public international law. Oxford University Press, Oxford
Caplan LM (2003) State immunity, human rights, and jus cogens: a critique of the normative hierarchy theory. AJIL 97:741–781
Cassese A (2002) When may senior state officials be tried for international crimes? some comments on the Congo v. Belgium case. EJIL 13(4):853–875
Dickinson A, Lindsae R, Loonam JP (2004) State immunity. In: Selected materials and commentary. Oxford University Press, Oxford
Fox H (2008) The law of state immunity. Oxford University Press, Oxford
Hafner G, Kohen MG, Breau S (2006) State practice regarding State immunities. La pratique des états concernant les immunités des états. Martinus Nijhoff Publishers, Leiden
Hirsch Ballin EMH (2002) Yerodia. Rechtsmacht, immuniteit en vervolgingsbeleid. Ars Aequi 51(10):741–751
Kokott J (2011) States, sovereign equality. In: Max Planck encyclopedia of public international law. www.mpepil.com. Accessed Nov 2014
Nollkaemper A (2011) Kern van het internationaal publiekrecht. Boom, Den Haag
O'Keefe R (2011) State immunity and human rights: heads and walls, hearts and minds. Vanderbilt J Transnatal Law 44(4):999–1045
Provost R (2012) Canada's Alien Tort Statute. EJIL: Talk. www.ejiltalk.org
Roberts I (ed) (2009) Satow's diplomatic practice. Oxford University Press, Oxford
Schermers HG, Blokker NM (2003) International institutional law. Martinus Nijhoff Publishers, Leiden
Sinclair IM (1973) The European Convention on State Immunity. Int Comp Law Q 22(2):254–283
Sinclair IM (1980) The law of sovereign immunity. Recent developments. In: Recueil des cours. Collected courses of the Hague Academy of International Law 1980, II, Tome 167 de la collection, Sijthoff, Noordhoff, Alphen aan den Rijn, The Netherlands
van Alebeek R (2007) Staatsimmuniteit. In: Horbach N, Lefeber R, Ribbelink O (eds) Handboek internationaal recht. T.M.C. Asser Press, The Hague, pp 231–273
van Alebeek R (2008) The immunity of States and their officials in international criminal law and international human rights law. Oxford University Press, Oxford
van Alebeek R (2012) National courts, international crimes and the functional immunity of State officials. NILR 59:5–41
Zieck M (2007) Diplomatiek en consulair recht. In: Horbach N, Lefeber R, Ribbelink O (eds) Handboek internationaal recht. T.M.C. Asser Press, The Hague, pp 275–308

Chapter 8
The State, the Armed Forces and the Concept of Immunity

Abstract The armed forces are State organs and keep that status when deployed abroad and under command and control of an international commander, as sending States retain the highest political and military command and control over their forces. Also, when sending States have extended their legislative jurisdiction with respect to the armed forces they may be able to exercise criminal jurisdiction over their deployed forces, as military personnel is at least entitled to functional immunity. Warships, military aircraft and their crews traditionally enjoy a special status under international law and are entitled to absolute immunity.

Contents

8.1 Introduction

As States depend on their national armed forces to protect their external security, armed forces and the State are closely interrelated in spite of the increasing international military cooperation and use of civilian contractors. When considering criminal jurisdiction over forces stationed abroad from an international law perspective, it is essential to analyse the relationship between the State and its

© T.M.C. ASSER PRESS and the author 2015
J. Voetelink, *Status of Forces: Criminal Jurisdiction over Military Personnel Abroad*,
DOI 10.1007/978-94-6265-057-2_8

armed forces. In this context two aspects need to be addressed: the State's jurisdiction over its forces abroad and the immunity that the forces enjoy in a foreign State. This chapter determines the position of the armed forces within the State and analyzes to what extent the sending State can exercise its jurisdiction over its deployed forces.

As an organ of a sovereign State the armed forces benefit from the immunity of the State. However, over the years immunities of armed forces have developed into a regime with special features next to the immunity regime of the sovereign State.[1] Due to the close relationship between the State and its armed forces developments in the field of immunities cannot be considered separately. A clear example are warships that since long have called at foreign ports, representing their State. Immunities of high-ranking State officials, such as Heads of Government, as discussed in the previous chapter, are also closely related to State immunity and, with a view to this shared background, are also relevant to understand the development of immunities of the armed forces.

This chapter commences with an analysis of the armed forces as an organ of the State, and addresses the extraterritorial exercise of criminal jurisdiction over the armed forces (Sect. 8.2). This section is followed by a study of the legal basis of immunity of armed forces under international law considered from the view of the absolute doctrine of State immunity doctrine and the restrictive doctrine of State immunity (Sect. 8.3). The discussion includes the status of warships and military aircraft.

8.2 The State, the Armed Forces and Jurisdiction

Apart from the requirement for a sovereign State to have a government,[2] international law does not attach any conditions to the State's organisation and administration. In the *Western Sahara* case, the ICJ concluded that international law does not require a State to be organised in accordance with a particular structure.[3] As a result, disposing of armed forces is not a constitutive element of the State's existence under international law.[4] Conversely, the existence of armed forces is closely related to the State.[5] This section focuses on the relation between the State and its armed forces, followed by the discussion on the criminal jurisdiction over the armed forces.

---

[1] See Fox and Webb 2013, p. 570; Sari 2008, pp. 98–100.

[2] See Article 1 of the *Montevideo Convention*.

[3] ICJ 16 October 1975, *Western Sahara*, Advisory Opinion, I.C.J. Reports 1975, pp. 43–44, para 94.

[4] Some small States, such as Costa Rica and NATO member Iceland, do not or hardly possess military means.

[5] E.g., Article 97(1) of the *Dutch Constitution*.

8.2.1 Relationship Between the State and Its Armed Force

Although States may be organised and administered differently, the government's exercise of public authority is essential for a State.[6] The most important function of the State is protection of its citizens and national legal order. For this reason the government has at its disposal a police force and armed forces to exercise its 'right of the sword',[7] making the armed forces one of the fundamental State security institutions.[8]

Originally, the relationship between the State and the armed forces was not as strong and close-knit as it is today. In the seventeenth century European States hired private entrepreneurs, who would not just provide logistic support, but fighting power as well.[9] Later States largely took over the entrepreneurs' position and concluded treaties that put complete regiments at the disposal of other States.[10] Since the nineteenth century under the influence of, inter alia, the French Revolution and the introduction of conscription, European States have come to rely on national armed forces instead of contracted foreign military personnel, thus tightening the bond between State and armed forces. As a consequence, nation armies became the primary means to wage wars with other States[11] to guarantee external security of the State[12] and to protect its vital interests.

In the past few decades the international security situation has changed dramatically. The ideological East-West division has made way for new dangers that threaten the international community as a whole, as a consequence, expanding the armed forces' tasks to include the protection of the international legal order. As a result, today's national armed forces are deeply involved in crisis management operations and assist in fighting terrorism and piracy, etc. Notwithstanding this international orientation, armed forces remain the States' exclusive means to project force[13] and its position and function are usually laid down in the Constitution or in an Act of Parliament.

There is no doubt that the armed forces are State organs. In the commentary to Article 2 of the *UN Convention on State Immunity* the ILC includes ministries, governmental departments and armed forces in the scope of the definition of State.[14]

---

[6] Dekker and Schrijver 2007, p. 31.

[7] Ibid.

[8] *Dutch Parliamentary Papers II* 2011/12, 33 279 nr. 2, p. 2.

[9] Amersfoort 1988, p. 4. Practice varied from State to State, which was also true for to the armed services.

[10] In particular, German, Scottish, Walloon and Swiss units were 'hired'; Ibid., p. 2.

[11] Werner 2007, p. 162.

[12] Ducheine 2008, p. 15 et seq. In the post-modern state armed forces still remain a means of power of the State, even though parts of its powers have been transferred to international institutions.

[13] Ibid., p. 14.

[14] Report of the International Law Commission, *UN Doc* A/CN.4/415 (1991) included in: Dickinson et al. 2004, p. 85.

A memorandum written by the UN Secretariat considers the armed forces as one of the most important bodies of the State and their status of the utmost importance when it comes to immunities.[15] Likewise, in *McElhinney*, the ECtHR concluded that part of the "…core area of State sovereignty…" is:

> the acts of a soldier on foreign territory which, of their very nature, may involve sensitive issues affecting diplomatic relations between States and national security.[16]

A Greek court considered the acts of the armed forces one of the most important expressions of state sovereignty: "…state sovereignty, the main expression of which are acts carried out by its armed forces".[17] Furthermore, Article 4(1) of the *Draft Articles on Responsibility of States for Internationally Wrongful Acts*[18] stipulates that the acts of any organ of the State, including the executive organs, shall be considered as acts of that State.[19] Finally, the ILC derives from the fact that States exercise criminal jurisdiction over their forces participating in UN crisis management operations that the forces consequently act as an organ of the State.[20]

Although the armed forces are State organs, military tasks can be delegated to private contractors and command and control over military units can be transferred to an international commander. These situations will be briefly discussed in the next sections.

8.2.1.1 Private Contractors

The past two decades there has been an increasing trend of contracting out services formally belonging to the military domain to private companies. In particular during recent operations in Iraq and Afghanistan the use of these so called contractors has largely increased and included controversial tasks, like armed security services. This development can be partly explained by the increasing number of international crisis management operations established after the Cold War, which involve significant numbers of troops. As States lacked capacity to carry out these demanding tasks, they turned to the private market to fill the gap and contracted out services to private companies. These contractors in their turn could furnish the services, because of the large number of former military personnel that had become available due to the downsizing of armed forces.

---

[15] *UN Doc* A/CN.4/596 (2008), Memorandum by the Secretariat, para 16.

[16] ECHR 21 November 2001, *McElhinney v. Ireland*, Application no. 31253/96, para 38.

[17] Special Supreme Court 17 September 2002, *Germany v Margellos*, ILDC 87 (GR 2002).

[18] *Draft Articles on Responsibility of States for Internationally Wrongful Acts, UN Doc* A/RES/56/83 (2002) of 28 January 2002.

[19] The explanatory notes mentions the example of a military commander representing his State's government.

[20] *UN Doc* A/59/10 (2004), ILC Report on the work of its 56th session, Chap. V, Responsibility of International Organizations, p. 110.

These developments were in line with the worldwide tendency of States to privatise or contract out governmental services to private enterprises. Besides, operations were more and more undertaken in or from States with limited possibilities for Host Nation Support.[21] When such support was inadequate, States could rely on contractors to ensure execution of the operations.

However, the increasing use of private contractors cannot lead to the conclusion that the armed forces have lost their monopoly as the State's exclusive means of force. The contractors' services are auxiliary to military activities and in principle they are subordinated to the military authorities.[22] Besides, many States, organisations and interests groups are extremely critical of the use of contractors and they aim to regulate and control their activities. From that perspective the argument of the armed forces as a State's exclusive means of force can even be used to limit the activities of the contractors.

8.2.1.2 Delegation of Command Authority

During their foreign presence military units remain part of the State and stay under its State authority, which, however, does not exclude the possibility to partly transfer command and control authority over these units to a foreign military commander. When participating in international operations, sending States generally transfer Operational Control (OPCON) over the participating units to the commander of the international force. Although States transfer the authority

> [...] to direct forces assigned so that the commander may accomplish specific missions or tasks which are usually limited by function, time, or location; to deploy units concerned, and to retain or assign tactical control of those units to assign missions or tasks to subordinate commanders, to deploy units, to reassign forces, and to retain or delegate operational and/or tactical control as the commander deems necessary. [23]

they always retain the supreme command (Full Command)[24] over their units (see further Sect. 11.3). As such the unit remains an organ of the sending State.

The right of the sword of the armed forces constitutes an elementary part of the sovereign State's authority and is vital to its survival. Even when the sending State deploys forces abroad, for instance, to participate in a crisis management operation, they will continue to fulfil this elementary function. In case of emergency the

---

[21] E.g., the Netherlands has concluded mutual support agreements with the UK and the US, which also apply during military operations: MOU on *Provision of mutual logistic support* of 19 April 1999 with the UK and *Mutual Defense Assistance Agreement* of 27 January 1950, and the implementing agreements with the US.

[22] The subordination is merely of a contractual nature and does not concern military hierarchical relations.

[23] NATO Glossary of terms and definitions 2013.

[24] Full Command is: "The military authority and responsibility of a commander to issue orders to subordinates. It covers every aspect of military operations and administration and exists only within national services"; NATO Glossary of terms and definitions 2013.

forces must be kept at the disposal of the sending State for national tasks.[25] For this reason States want to be in the position to exercise authority and jurisdiction over the forces.

8.2.2 *Criminal Jurisdiction and the Armed Forces*

National criminal law can in part be applicable to citizens abroad (see Sect. 6.4.2). However, with respect to the military this claim can be broader. Many States, including 'common-law' States that normally do not favour extraterritorial jurisdiction, have either in part or entirely extended the applicability of national criminal law to military personnel stationed abroad.[26] It concerns the legislative jurisdiction only and not the executive or adjudicative jurisdiction and it should be stressed that this situation does not preclude the jurisdiction of the foreign State (see discussion below in Sect. 8.3).

The extension of jurisdiction over military personnel abroad cannot be exclusively based on the principle of active nationality, since the legislation of several States allows non-nationals to enlist in their armed forces. For instance, traditionally foreign nationals enlisted with the French Foreign Legion, the British Brigade of Gurkhas and the Royal Irish Regiment. Likewise, lawful foreign residents of the US can join the US armed forces regardless of their nationality.[27] Recently, several European States have enacted legislation to enable EU citizens to join their armed forces.[28]

In addition, the protective principle may also offer a reference point for extending the scope of national criminal law.[29] The application of domestic criminal law enables a State to maintain order and discipline over its forces when stationed abroad. Consequently, the extension of the national criminal legislation contributes to the coherence and efficiency of the military force as a whole.[30] Likewise, the

[25] E.g., in April 2010 the Dutch warship Tromp rescued the German cargoship 'Taipan' from pirates. As the action was beyond the EU mandate, the Netherlands continued the operation under national command and control; Lodder 2010, p. 15.

[26] Liivoja 2010, p. 310 mentions, *inter alia*, Australia, Denmark, Germany, the UK and the US. This practice appears not to be in conflict with international law: "we have not been referred to any rule of international law or international comity of nations which is inconsistent with a State exercising disciplinary control over its own armed forces, when those forces are operating outside its territorial limits"; Bombay High Court 9 May 1946, *Mohammad Mohy-Ud-Din vs Emperor*, (1946) 48 BOMLR 740. indiankanoon.org/doc/789276. Accessed November 2014. Other states, such as Canada and Ireland, remain more hesitant; Odello 2010, p. 377.

[27] Liivoja 2010, p. 319.

[28] Ibid., p. 320 mentions Belgium, Ireland, Spain and Luxembourg.

[29] See Liivoja 2011, pp. 236 et seq. who states that many authors base jurisdiction over armed forces on the security principle.

[30] Idem.

protection principle has been used to argue that when a State is unable to maintain order in a military unit the security of the State itself is at stake.[31] This argument considers the vital interests of the State and is as such related to the protection principle.[32]

The discussion above has led some authors to classify the jurisdiction over military personnel as a hybrid form of a jurisdiction principle, based on the principle of active nationality and the protection principle, supplemented with its own specific features.[33] For instance, with this special nature in mind, Liivoja argued that this 'service jurisdiction' should be considered as *sui generis* principle allowing a State to establish its legislative jurisdiction.[34]

Likewise, Sari's principle of 'organic jurisdiction' defends the desirability of a principle independent from the traditional principles of jurisdiction and elaborates on the State's authority to exercise jurisdiction over its organs and officials. His point of departure is the unalienable right of any State under international law to organise its government and to submit the operation of its bodies to its legislations.[35] This right comprises a "reserved domain of domestic jurisdiction", which includes in its turn the exercise of the jurisdiction over its armed forces.[36]

The applicability of national criminal law to military personnel abroad makes their position different from other State officials. The possibility to extend the applicability of the national legislation abroad was created specifically for military personnel,[37] enabling the courts of the sending State to effectively deal with criminal offences of members of the national armed forces on their return to their home State. However, when exercising these powers abroad, the sending State will have to take into account international law or the explicit consent of the foreign State.

8.3 Armed Forces and the Concept of Immunity

From the discussion above it cannot be concluded that a serviceman suspected of having committed an act punishable under the laws of the sending State will always appear before the sending State's criminal court. When the host State has penalised the same act on the basis of the principle of territory, the legislative jurisdiction of the sending State and the host State concur. As mentioned above, the extraterritorial

[31] Enthoven and van der Maas 2008.

[32] Stanger takes the principle of protection as a starting point, because of the armed forces' duty to protect national security; Stanger 1957/1958, p. 86.

[33] Iain Cameron, The Protective Principle of International Criminal Jurisdiction, 1994; mentioned in Liivoja 2010, p. 331.

[34] Liivoja 2011 pp. 238 et seq.

[35] Sari 2008, p. 77.

[36] Ibid., p. 86.

[37] See Liivoja 2011, pp. 32–33.

application of the sending State's legislative jurisdiction does not imply that this State can then exercise its executive and adjudicative jurisdiction with the exclusion of the host State. Immunities under international law are decisive for such a situation.

The host State will have to respect immunities when exercising its executive and adjudicative jurisdiction. Therefore, military personnel enjoying immunity abroad are exempted from the host State's executive and adjudicative jurisdiction. This enables sending States to exercise their jurisdiction over them to the extent that their criminal legislation is applicable to them. The next sections explore the position of armed forces from the perspectives of the doctrines of State immunity, functional immunity of military personnel and the status of warships and military aircraft.

8.3.1 Position of the Armed Forces Under the Absolute and Restrictive Doctrine of State Immunity

Being an organ of the State, the armed forces historically benefit from the immunity of the State when deployed abroad with the host State's consent. In the past jurisdiction over these forces was based on the absolute doctrine of State immunity as the considerations in *The Exchange v. McFaddon* case illustrate. At least until the first developments towards the restrictive doctrine of State immunity at the beginning of the twentieth century, the armed forces enjoyed full immunity from the jurisdiction of the local courts, as did the States they served. Because of the applicability of the absolute doctrine of State immunity there was no real need for States to make arrangements on the status of the visiting forces, which can help to explain the lack of specific SOFAs at that time.

The balanced view on the ground rule as expressed in nineteenth century literature and case law was related to this approach, as the immunity of visiting armed forces was assumed to exist with respect to military units deployed abroad as State organs. Exceptions to their immunity brought forward in the literature and case law merely concerned the circumstances that influenced the relation between a serviceman and his unit, for example, a sailor on leave in a foreign port or a soldier off-duty outside his military garrison. Under these circumstances, the soldier was not considered to be part of the State organ and would be denied immunity.

In the early twentieth century the absolute doctrine of State immunity came under pressure. Treaties reflecting the relative doctrine, did, however, not affect immunity of the armed forces in the field of civil law. As mentioned above, the 1926 *Convention for the Unification of Certain Rules concerning the Immunity of State-owned Vessels* excluded warships from foreign States' jurisdiction. In addition to this Convention,[38] Article 31 of the *European Convention on State Immunity* states the following with regard to deployed forces:

---

[38] The *European Convention on State Immunity* does not apply to cases falling under the scope of the *Convention for the Unification of Certain Rules concerning the Immunity of State-owned Vessels* (Article 30 *European Convention on State Immunity*).

> Nothing in this Convention shall affect any immunities or privileges enjoyed by a Contracting State in respect of anything done or omitted to be done, or in relation to, its armed forces when on the territory of another Contracting State.

The Explanatory Report to the Convention clarifies that this provision precludes uncertainties over immunities from jurisdiction as a result of visits by naval forces and that the Convention cannot be invoked for stationing of armed forces, to which other more specific agreements apply.[39] With regard to the latter the Explanatory Report refers to Article 33 that reads:

> Nothing in the present Convention affects existing or future international agreements in special fields which relate to matters dealt with in the present Convention.

The applicability of the *UN Convention on State Immunity* to military activities is less clear.[40] When presenting the draft of this Convention to the UN General Assembly, the chairman of the *Ad Hoc* Committee on Jurisdictional Immunities of States and their Property indicated that it was the Committee's understanding that military activities did not fall under the scope of the Convention.[41] States have not opposed this interpretation; some States have even ratified the Convention and made explicit declarations stating that it did not apply to military activities.[42] Nonetheless, the Convention contains several provisions referring to the military.[43] Further, Article 26 is of interest, stating:

> Nothing in the present Convention shall affect the rights and obligations of States Parties under existing international agreements which relate to matters dealt with in the present Convention as between the parties to those agreements.[44]

The three conventions mentioned above acknowledge the possibility to make different arrangements with respect to armed forces by means of SOFAs. Furthermore, case law shows that acts concerning the armed forces enjoy immunity to the extent they can be classified as *acta jure imperii*.[45] This leads to the conclusion that civil

---

[39] Explanatory report, para 116. In the same vein: ICJ 3 February 2012, *Jurisdictional Immunities of the State* (Germany v. Italy: Greece Intervening), Judgment, para 67.

[40] Fox and Webb 2013, p. 314.

[41] *UN Doc* A/C.6/59/SR.13 of 25 October 2005. Article 3 of the Convention, listing the immunities and privileges not falling under the Convention's scope, does not mention visiting military units or navy vessels.

[42] ICJ 3 February 2012, *Jurisdictional Immunities of the State* (Germany v. Italy: Greece Intervening), Judgment, para 69.

[43] Article 16(1) excludes immunity of a State from jurisdiction related to the operation of vessels if "the ship was used for other than government non-commercial purposes." The following para, however, provides an exception for e.g. warships. Article 21(1) defines categories of property not considered as property specifically in use or intended for use by the State for other than government non-commercial purposes and exempted from post-judgment measures of constraint. Under (b) it enumerates the "property of a military character or used or intended for use in the performance of military functions." These provisions do not add to the clarity of the Convention with regard to military activities.

[44] Existing SOFAs fall under the scope of this provision and may contain arrangements deviating from the Convention; Hafner and Köhler 2004, p. 47.

[45] Examples are mentioned in: ICJ 3 February 2012, *Jurisdictional Immunities of the State* (Germany v. Italy: Greece Intervening), Judgment, paras 72–77.

law immunity can be restricted for *acta jure gestionis*, such as the purchase of cigarettes for the military. In general, however, most acts related to the armed forces will concern the sovereign function of the State.[46]

8.3.2 Armed Forces and the Concept of Functional Immunity

In the previous chapter it was concluded that State officials benefit from State immunity in the performance of their official duties. This means that they enjoy functional immunity from the jurisdiction of the courts of foreign States. Military personnel, as State officials, are not excluded from this rule and should at least be entitled to functional immunity in the performance of their official duties abroad.[47] From the discussion above it can now be concluded that, from an international law perspective, the ground rule as defined in Part I of this book points at the functional immunity of the armed forces.

In the course of time, a special regime for armed forces has developed, just like there has evolved a special regime for diplomats and Heads of State. Today this regime seems to be conventional in nature, as it is reflected in the numerous treaties analysed in Part I of this book. The question is whether this special regime respects the functional immunity of military personnel abroad.[48]

The SOFAs analysed in Part I show that military personnel always enjoy immunity from criminal jurisdiction of the local courts in the extraterritorial performance of their official duties. During crisis management operations and military operations in support of allied States in armed conflict, military personnel virtually

---

[46] E.g., the British court concluded that medical treatment in an American military hospital in the UK (High Court, Queen's Bench Division 8 June 1992, *Littrell v. USA (No. 2)*, ILR 100, pp. 438–464) and a report written on the education of personnel of the American Department of Defence and their family members in the UK (House of Lords 20 July 2000, *Holland v Lampen-Wolfe*, UKHL 40; [2000] 3 All ER 833; [2000] 1 WLR 1573) had to be considered as *acta jure imperii*.

[47] Despite the differences in opinion on the status of forces that exist in the literature, generally, authors are in agreement that military personnel who obey instructions of the sending State enjoy criminal immunity; Lazareff 1971, p. 170. More recently, Fleck 2006, p. 144: "… in the absence of clear treaty provisions, core rules of functional immunity continue to apply to members of sending states' forces". Functional immunity can be further restricted in case of war crimes. In the past this was the object of various cases. This could be explained by the fact that the sending States did not invoke immunity; see *UN Doc* A/CN.4/631 (2010), ILC Second report on immunity of State officials from foreign criminal jurisdiction, 10 June 2010, para 69. In *Certain Questions of Mutual Assistance in Criminal Matters* the ICJ stated that when a State wants to claim immunity for its organs, it should inform the other State; ICJ 4 June 2008, *Certain Questions of Mutual Assistance in Criminal Matters* (Djibouti v. France), Judgment, I.C.J. Reports 2008, p. 177, para 196.

[48] Some authors give a negative response to the question, assuming that foreign forces are fully subject to the exclusive criminal jurisdiction of the host State's courts in case no SOFA has been concluded; e.g., Priest-Hamilton 2000, p. 610 and Conderman 2013, para 1(2).

enjoy absolute immunity, because they are subject to the exclusive criminal jurisdiction of their own States. SOFAs in the context of international military cooperation generally contain stricter arrangements with respect to immunities of foreign forces. Nevertheless, virtually all SOFAs respect the functional immunity of forces and exceptions are rare.

Examples of these exceptions were the SOFAs concluded by the UK and some Commonwealth States with sending States during World War II. They contained a provision specifying that some specific crimes would be subject to the jurisdiction of host State civil (non-military) courts. These agreements did not contain exceptions for offences committed during the performance of official duties. Other examples are the treaties the SU concluded in World War II, in which the SU retained jurisdiction over crimes committed against the SU. These treaties do not contain an exception for offences committed on duty either.

Post-war examples of SOFAs that do not recognise functional immunity are a number of SOFAs Canada concluded with respect to foreign units visiting Canada for military training purposes. The SOFAs stipulated that military personnel participating in the training were fully subject to the criminal jurisdiction of the Canadian civil courts.[49] Another example is the 2002 SOFA concluded between the Netherlands and Qatar, which allowed Qatar courts to exercise jurisdiction over crimes committed by Dutch military personnel, except for cases in which these crimes were committed against Dutch interests, personnel or property.

These SOFAs contain very specific exceptions to the functional immunity of armed forces' personnel and do not affect the validity of the functional immunity rule in general. In my opinion these examples cannot lead to the conclusion that functional immunity of State officials would not apply to military personnel. In other words, in the absence of a formal SOFA military personnel abroad continue to enjoy at least functional immunity. This conclusion is supported by, often poorly documented, State practice and case law, which also shows that military personnel is often granted more extensive criminal law immunities.

For example, a Dutch service regulation of 1971 contains a section on situations not covered by a SOFA,[50] which instructs commanders to take into account that Dutch military personnel abroad continue to be subject to the exclusive jurisdiction of the Dutch authorities provided that criminal offences have been committed on board a Dutch warship, within a Dutch military camp or base, or outside that base when personnel are on duty. Although somewhat outdated, this regulation it is still in force. A Dutch manual written by the Ministry of Justice contains an instruction that military personnel from non-NATO member States who are present in the Netherlands in an official capacity are

[49] E.g., *Agreement for the training in Canada of personnel of the armed forces of Nigeria*; Lagos, 3 July 1963 (Vol. 529 *UNTS*, 1965 No. 7656) and *Agreement for the training in Canada of personnel of the armed forces of Barbados*; Bridgetown, 12 November 1985 (Vol. 1469I *UNTS* 1987, No. 24897).

[50] *Reglement toepassing straf-en tuchtrecht ten aanzien van Nederlandse militairen, geplaatst buiten het Koninkrijk*, 17 June 1971, published in Van den Bosch c.s., Part II, Annex V.

entitled to criminal immunity.[51] The manual seems to imply that this concerns a situation not covered by a SOFA.

Case law with respect to situations not covered by SOFAs is also rare. Several World War II cases show diverging views. In the *Reference re Exemption* case[52] the Canadian Supreme Court was divided on the government's question on the legal status of American forces. Two out of five judges were of the opinion that Canadian courts had full criminal jurisdiction over foreign forces. Two other judges concluded that there existed a rule under international law providing immunity to organised forces present on the territory of the host State with its consent. The fifth judge considered that the forces enjoyed immunity for offences committed in their own camps or on board their warships, except for offences against persons who are not subject to US service law or their property.

These diverging opinions in the *Reference re Exemption* case were reflected in later court cases. In the *In re Gilbert* case[53] a Brazilian judge decided that the American court martial had exclusive jurisdiction over an American soldier who had killed an intruder while on guard duty,[54] due to the fact that the Brazilian government had classified this particular location as an American military area.[55]

In the *Panos Stamatopoulos v. Ministère Public* case,[56] the Mixed Courts of Egypt referred to the fact that Greek military courts were only allowed to exercise military criminal law "within the limits of the Greek armed forces".[57] In the *Malero Manuel v. Ministère Public* case the same Mixed Courts considered that the principle of immunity from jurisdiction for armed forces abroad was no longer disputed with regard to offences committed on duty, disciplinary offences, military offences, or to violations of common law committed within military premises.[58] The Court further noted that in the literature there was still disagreement with respect to disturbance of the public order and security outside the military

[51] *Handleiding ten behoeve van de praktijk inzake delicten begaan door vreemde militairen (waaronder begrepen burgerpersoneel en gezinsleden)* 19 February 1981, nr. 137/281, para V.

[52] The Supreme Court of Canada 3 August 1942, *Reference re Exemption of United States Forces from Proceedings in Canadian Criminal Courts*, ILR 12.

[53] Supreme Federal Court 22 November 1944, *In Re Gilbert (Admiral Ingram Camp Case)*, ILR 13. The judge implicitly applied Article 299 of the *Bustamante Code,* which stated: "Nor are the penal laws of the State applicable to offences committed within the field of military operations when it authorizes the passage of armed forces of another contracting State through its territory, except offences not legally connected with the said armed forces"; *Bustamante Code Annexed to the Convention on Private International Law*; Havana, 20 February 1928 (*AJIL* 29:642).

[54] King 1946, p. 262.

[55] Barton 1950, p. 229.

[56] The Mixed Courts of Egypt, established in 1871, had jurisdiction over nationals from Western States visiting Egypt (Brinton, pp. 675 et seq). The decisions of the Mixed Courts are particularly interesting due to the fact that these courts had an internationally mixed composition.

[57] Court of Cassation 23 November 1942, *Panos Stamatopoulos v. Ministère Public*, *AJIL* 1945.

[58] Court of Cassation 8 March 1943, *Malero Manuel v. Ministère Public*, *AJIL* 1945.

premises while not on duty.[59] After analysing the State practice, case law of national courts and the literature, the Court considered that:

> outside of the case of service on duty, there exists no international system of a character sufficiently general to be obligatory which extends the principle of immunity from jurisdiction in the case of a permitted sojourn of foreign troops within the territory, as regards violations of the common law committed outside of the military premises;

In the civil law case *Wright v Cantrell*[60] partly concerning the criminal jurisdiction over visiting forces, an Australian judge considered that the decision in *The Exchange v McFaddon* case did not lead to the conclusion that visiting forces would have exclusive jurisdiction over their own personnel. Immunity of the forces could only be granted in cases where the exercise of jurisdiction by local courts would impede the military activities of the visiting forces. Shortly after World War II a Greek judge took a different stance in the *In re A.F* case[61] and concluded, on the basis of the principles of public international law, that stealing British soldiers were exempted from the jurisdiction of the Greek courts.

In the post-war period only a limited number of decisions were published in which the exercise of jurisdiction could not be based on a SOFA or any other formal arrangement.[62] One such case concerned a Senegalese soldier on trial in Israel.[63] The judge concluded that the UN soldier was not stationed in Israel, but was visiting Israel for personal motives and for that reason could not claim immunity.

In the *Lozano* case, an Italian judge considered that:

> Under a well-established rule of customary law….acta jure imperii performed by organs of a state in the discharge of their functions were covered by immunity and therefore could not be subjected to the civil or criminal jurisdiction of a foreign state.[64]

Therefore, an American soldier, member of the Multinational Force Iraq who had killed an Italian citizen at one of the checkpoints, was exempted from the jurisdiction of the Italian courts.

The discussion above leads to the conclusion that the evolving special regime on the immunity of armed forces does not exempt military personnel from the rule that State officials enjoy functional immunity abroad. In other words, similar to

---

[59] According to the Court it was only the American doctrine that decisively rejected territorial jurisdiction.

[60] Supreme Court of New South Wales 2, 3 and 22 September 1943, *Wright v Cantrell*, ILR 12, pp. 133–141.

[61] Tribunal Correctionnel of the Isle of Chios 1945, *In re A.F.*, ILR 12, p. 163.

[62] ECtHR 21 November 2001, *McElhinney v. Ireland*, Application no. 31253/96 concerned a civil claim resulting from a case in which a British serviceman was present in Ireland without that State's consent. The court accepted the Irish point of view that the acts of the serviceman were 'acta jure imperii' and that the soldier enjoyed immunity.

[63] District Court of Haifa 10 May 1979, *Israel v. Papa Ben Coli Dista Saar*, UN Juridical Yearbook 1979.

[64] Court of Cassation 24 July 2008, *Lozano v Italy*, Case No 31171/2008, ILDC 1085 (IT 2008), H3.

State officials, military personnel enjoy functional immunity from foreign courts' jurisdiction, regardless of the framework in which they operate.[65]

8.3.3 *Warships*

In this section on the armed forces and the concept of immunity, warships[66] merit special attention. For centuries they have frequently called at foreign ports for purposes of resupply and repair, or for paying a formal visit. During these foreign visits the ships, their commanders and crews benefitted from the absolute immunity of the State.[67] In the case *The Exchange v. McFaddon* the immunity of warships was analysed. According to the judge, such vessels constitute:

> [...] a part of the military force of her nation; acts under the immediate and direct command of the sovereign; is employed by him in national objects. He has many and powerful motives for preventing those objects from being defeated by the interference of a foreign state. Such interference cannot take place without affecting his power and his dignity. The implied license, therefore, under which such vessel enters a friendly port may reasonably be construed, and it seems to the Court ought to be construed, as containing an exemption from the jurisdiction of the sovereign within whose territory she claims the rites of hospitality.[68]

The judge concluded by saying:

> It seems then to the Court to be a principle of public law that national ships of war entering the port of a friendly power open for their reception are to be considered as exempted by the consent of that power from its jurisdiction.[69]

In 1898 the 'Institut de Droit International' expressed itself in similar vein in the *Règlement sur le régime légal des navires et de leurs équipages dans les ports étrangers*[70] stating that a warship in a foreign port was not subject to host State jurisdiction and criminal offences committed on board fell under the scope of the criminal jurisdiction of the ship's State. However, local courts had jurisdiction to prosecute crewmembers who had committed offences against the laws of the host

---

[65] See Sari 2008, pp. 264–264.

[66] "a ship belonging to the armed forces of a State bearing the external marks distinguishing such ships of its nationality, under the command of an officer duly commissioned by the government of the State and whose name appears in the appropriate service list or its equivalent, and manned by a crew which is under regular armed forces discipline" Article 29 *UNCLOS*.

[67] Immunity of warships already existed prior to the doctrine of absolute State immunity; see Fox 2008, p. 131.

[68] *The Schooner Exchange v. McFaddon*, 144.

[69] Ibid, 145–146.

[70] *Règlement sur le régime légal des navires et de leurs équipages dans les ports étrangers*; The Hague, 23 August 1989. This Regulation, which is not legally binding, aimed to capture the current state of law. In 1928 the Regulation was repeated in similar words in the *Règlement sur le régime des navires de mer et de leurs équipages dans les ports étrangers en temps de paix.*

State when ashore,[71] except when the offence was committed on duty (*service commandé*).[72]

Subsequent international agreements respected these traditional immunities of warships and their crews, also in the field of civil law,[73] and as a result, today warships and crews continue to enjoy full immunity abroad. Accordingly, in 1987 a Dutch court decided that it was not lawful to seize the 'Almirante Grau', a Peruvian warship visiting the Netherlands for maintenance purposes.[74]

8.3.4 Military Aircraft

In contrast to the status of warships, international law is less clear when it comes to the status of military aircraft and their crews.[75] Although many agreements regulating aviation have been adopted, their applicability to military aircraft remains

---

[71] See Part I, Sect. 1 of the Regulation.

[72] Article 18(4) of the 1898 Regulation; Articles 20(3) and (4) of the 1928 Regulation. With regard to immunities of warships and their crews in general, see; Stanger 1957/1958, pp. 55–78. In 1926, in accordance with the provisions mentioned above, a British court convicted a crewmember of the American warship 'Sharkey', who had killed a colleague in a British port; Stanger 1957/1958, p. 74. The provision was also the basis for the decision of the Mixed Courts in Egypt in the *George Triandoufilou v. Ministère Public case*; Court of Cassation 29 June 1942, *AJIL* 1945, pp. 345–347. According to the Court, whether a crewmember was on duty, did not depend on the intrinsic nature of the offence, but on the nature of the orders; Brinton 1944, p. 379. In this case, the suspect had orders to purchase supplies ashore. As a result, the Court considered that Triandoufilou was on duty when committing the offence and that the Court had no jurisdiction in this case. In *Japan v. Smith and Stinner*, the Japanese judge based his jurisdiction over two British crewmembers, who had robbed a taxi-driver during a city trip of Kobe, by considering that the act was not committed during the performance of their duty; High Court of Osaka, 5 August 1952, *Japan v. Smith and Stinner*, ILR 19. The case *Chung Chi Cheung v. The King* is somewhat different in the sense that the UK itself prosecuted a British citizen for committing a murder on board of a Chinese armed customs ship, apparently for the reason that China had not requested the suspect's extradition; Adjudicative Committee of the Privy Council 2 December 1938, *Chung Chi Cheung v. The King*, ILR 9.

[73] Article 3 *Convention for the Unification of Certain Rules concerning the Immunity of State-owned Vessels*, Article 30 *European Convention on State Immunity*, Article 16 *UN Convention on State Immunity* and Articles 32 and 236 *UNCLOS*.

[74] The ship visited the Netherlands for extensive repairs, but remained under Peruvian command and navigating tests were executed with a partly Peruvian naval crew, which meant that the vessel remained in Peruvian service; President District Court Amsterdam 19 November 1987, *Almirante Grau*.

[75] Under international law, despite various attempts the wording 'military aircraft' has not been defined in a uniform manner; Williams 2007, pp. 106–109, see e.g. Article 13(j), *San Remo Manual on International Law Applicable to Armed Conflicts at Sea*, 12 June 1994, www.icrc.org/ihl.nsf/FULL/560?OpenDocument. Accessed November 2014: "military aircraft means an aircraft operated by commissioned units of the armed forces of a State having the military marks of that State, commanded by a member of the armed forces and manned by a crew subject to regular armed forces discipline". *Manual on International Law Applicable to Air and Missile Warfare*; Bern 14 May 2009. www.ihlresearch.org/amw/. Accessed November 2014 does not contain a definition.

mostly restricted.[76] The act of entering the airspace of a foreign State and landing on its territory are without doubt subject to the foreign State's explicit consent.[77] Consent, in the form of a specific diplomatic clearance or general permission, can be subject to conditions related to the immunity of the aircraft.[78] However, in practice the scope of these conditions seems to be limited.

In general it is assumed that immunities for military aircraft are comparable to those that apply to warships.[79] As a result aircrews enjoy criminal immunity for acts committed on board the aircraft.[80] Continuing the comparison with warships, it can be concluded that a crewmember of a military aircraft, who has committed an offence when on duty outside the aircraft, also enjoys immunity from the local courts' jurisdiction.[81]

In accordance with the discussion above, several aviation agreements indeed explicitly exclude the possibility of restricting immunity of military aircraft. Article 3(1)(a) of the 1933 *Convention of Certain Rules Relating to the Precautionary Arrest of Aircraft* determines that aircraft that are exclusively designated for the execution of a public service cannot be subject to precautionary arrest.[82] According to Article

---

[76] Treaty provisions are often expressed in the negative in the sense that they enumerate the provisions that do not apply to military aircraft or the acts that are prohibited for aircraft; Milde 2001, pp. 152–153.

[77] Article 3(c) *Chicago Convention*. In case of *force majeure* or distress no consent is required. However, entering foreign airspace requires an agreement with the State; Schmitt 2010, p. 306. See Articles 23 and 24 *Draft Articles on Responsibility of States for Internationally Wrongful Acts*, *UN Doc* A/RES/56/83 (2002) of 28 January 2002. The text with its commentary can be found in: *UN Doc* A/56/10 (2001), ILC Report on the work of its fifty-third session, Chap. IV, State Responsibility, pp. 59 et seq.

[78] E.g., the consent to search an aircraft, AAP1003 (2004) Royal Australian Air Force, Operations Law for RAAF Commanders 2004, p. 15. In this case the sending State actually renounces only part of its immunity. Clearance can also be laid down in a SOFA; Geraci 1994, p. 160.

[79] See Article 32 *Convention Relating to the Regulation of Aerial Navigation*; Paris, 13 October 1919 (11 *LNTS* p. 173): "No military aircraft of a contracting State shall fly over the territory of another contracting State nor land thereon without special authorisation. In case of such authorisation the military aircraft shall enjoy, in principle, in the absence of special stipulation, the privileges which are customarily accorded to foreign ships of war." Although the provision does not appear in the Chicago Convention, it can "be considered as still part of international air law"; Cooper 1968, p. 243, for further discussion, see e.g. Brownlie 2008, p. 372; Williams 2007, p. 105. Spiegel notes that the statements on State vessels are largely applicable to state aircraft; Spiegel 2001, p. 208. Schmitt 2010, p. 311 states that generally: "…military aircraft, enjoy sovereign immunity".

[80] Petras 2010, p. 70.

[81] Article 46 of the Proposal to the International Convention, adopted during the diplomatic conference of Paris, May–June 1910, accorded full immunity to both the military aircraft itself and to its crew. The Convention never entered into force; see Cooper 1968, pp. 224 and 225. Later agreements do not specifically regulate the status of the crew of military aircraft.

[82] *Convention on the Unification of Certain Rules relating to the Precautionary Arrest of Aircraft*; Rome, 29 May 1933. Military aircraft are classified as designated for public services.

XIII of the *Convention on the International Recognition of Rights in Aircrafts*,[83] which regulates, *inter alia*, the sale in execution of aircraft, does not apply to "...aircraft used in military ...services."

In the 2003 case *Airport Linz v. United States*[84] about payment of landing fees and airport user charges with respect to US Air Force flights to and from the Austrian airport of Linz in the course of the NATO operations in the Balkans, the Austrian judge concluded that the US and its aircraft enjoyed full immunity.[85] His decision was based, *inter alia*, on the consideration that the flights were made in the exercise of governmental and sovereign authority.

8.4 Conclusion

This chapter has analysed the position of the armed forces within the State and discussed to what extent sending States can exercise jurisdiction over their forces abroad. During the development of the sovereign State the armed forces have acquired a special position. It is part of the State's executive power and, as a consequence, can be defined as an organ of the State with the special competence to use armed force to protect the State's interests. During the extraterritorial execution of sovereign tasks, the relation between the State and the military remains in place, even if the forces are deployed as part of an international force to ensure international peace and security.

In addition to the supreme authority and full command, States will also be adamant to continue exercising their criminal jurisdiction over their forces abroad. On the basis of the 'law of the flag', national legislation may include a provision declaring national criminal law applicable to these forces. The resulting concurrence of the host and sending State's jurisdiction will partly be solved by functional immunity military personnel abroad is entitled to like any other State official. As host States thus refrain from the exercise of their jurisdiction, sending States will be able to exercise theirs.

When it comes to the immunity of warships and their crews, it can be concluded that under international law immunity is absolute. Only crewmembers who are ashore and not on duty will not be able to successfully claim immunity when there is no formal SOFA with the host State regulating the contrary. The same can be assumed to apply to military aircraft and their crews.

---

83 *Convention on the International Recognition of Rights in Aircraft*; Genève, 19 June 1948 (Vol. 310 *UNTS* 1958, No. 4492).

84 Oberster Gerichtshof 28 August 2003, *Airport Linz v. United States*, 2 Ob 156/03 k, ILDC 3 (AT 2003).

85 The decision of the judge was also based on the fact that the flights were carried out under binding UN Security Council resolutions and were within the scope of on international treaty; Wittich 2005, p. 250.

References

Amersfoort H (1988) Koning en Kanton. De Nederlandse staat en het einde van de Zwitserse krijgsdienst hier te lande 1814–1829. Sectie Militaire Geschiedenis Landmachtstaf, The Hague

Barton GP (1950) Foreign armed forces: immunity from criminal jurisdiction. Br Yearb Int Law 27:186–235

Brinton JY (1944) Jurisdiction over members of allied forces in Egypt. AJIL 38(3):375–382

Brownlie I (2008) Principles of public international law. Oxford University Press, Oxford

Conderman PJ (2013) Status of armed forces on foreign territory agreements (SOFA). In: Max Planck encyclopedia of public international law. http://www.mpepil.com Accessed Nov 2014

Dekker I, Schrijver N (2007) Internationale rechtssubjecten. In: Horbach N, Lefeber R, Ribbelink O (eds) Handboek internationaal recht. T.M.C. Asser Press, The Hague, pp 19–46

Dickinson A, Lindsae R, Loonam JP (2004) State immunity. In: Selected materials and commentary. Oxford University Press, Oxford

Ducheine PAL (2008) Krijgsmacht, geweldgebruik & terrorismebestrijding. Een onderzoek naar juridische aspecten van de rol van strijdkrachten bij de bestrijding van terrorisme. Wolf Legal Publishers, Nijmegen

Enthoven V, van der Maas HJ (2008) Zorrug dat je erbij komt. Recrutering over de grens. Militaire Spectator 177(10):524–534

Fox H (2008) The law of state immunity. Oxford University Press, Oxford

Fox H, Webb P (2013) The law of state immunity. Oxford University Press, Oxford

Geraci TA (1994) Overflight, landing rights, customs, and clearances. Air Force Law Rev 37:155–168

Hafner G, Köhler U (2004) The United Nations Convention on Jurisdictional Immunities of States and Their Property. Neth Yearb Int Law 35:3–49

Harkavy RE (2007) Strategic basing and the great powers, 1200–2000. Routledge, Oxon

Koekkoek AK (2000) De Grondwet. Een systematisch en artikelsgewijs commentaar. W.E.J. Tjeenk Willink, Deventer

King A (1946) Further developments concerning jurisdiction over friendly foreign armed forces. AJIL 40(2):257–279

Lazareff S (1971) Status of military forces under current international law. Sijthoff, Leiden

Liivoja R (2010) Service jurisdiction under international law. Melbourne J Int Law 11(2):309–337

Liivoja R (2011) An axiom of military law. Applicability of national criminal law to military personnel and associated civilians abroad. Centre of Excellence in Global Governance Research, Helsinki

Lodder R (2010) Tromp versus de piraten. De bevrijding van MS Taipan. Carré 9:13–19

Milde M (2001) Status of military aircraft in international law. In: Luft-und Weltraumrecht im 21. Jahrhundert. Heymann, Köln

Odello M (2010) Tackling criminal acts in peacekeeping operations: the accountability of peacekeepers. J Confl Secur Law 15(2):347–391

Petras CM (2010) The law of air mobility—the international legal principles behind the U.S. mobility air forces' mission. Air Force Law Rev 66:1–76

Priest-Hamilton KC (2000) Who really should have exercised jurisdiction over the military pilots implicated in the 1998 Italy gondola accident. J Air Law Commer 65(3):605–638

Sari A (2008) The jurisdictional immunities of visiting forces under public international law. A case study of the European security and defence policy (not published; on file with author)

Schmitt MN (2010) Air law and military operations. In: TD Gill, Fleck D (eds) The handbook of international law of military operations. Oxford University Press, New York, pp 303–323

Spiegel J (2001) Vreemde staten voor de Nederlandse rechter. Amsterdam University, Amsterdam

Stanger RJ (1957/1958) Criminal jurisdiction over visiting armed forces, vol LII. Naval War College, International law studies, Newport

Werner W (2007) De staat. In: Horbach N, Lefeber R, Ribbelink O (eds) Handboek internationaal recht. T.M.C. Asser Press, The Hague, pp 159–193

Williams AS (2007) The interception of civil aircraft over the high seas in the global war on terror. Air Force Law Rev 59:73–152

Wittich S (2005) Airport Linz v. United States, decision no. 2 Ob 156/03 k. 126 JBt. 390 (2004). Oberster Gerichtshof (Supreme Court of Austria), August 28, 2003. AJIL 99(1):248–252

Chapter 9
International Organisations

Abstract International organisations are established by treaty or other international instrument governed by international law and have legal personality. The extent of their legal rights and obligations depends on the organisations' purposes and functions and their constituent instruments. They can, inter alia, conclude treaties that are necessary for the exercise of their functions and the fulfilment of their purposes. Most organisations operating in the framework of international military cooperation and crisis management, like UN, NATO and EU, possess legal personality and are entitled to conclude treaties, including SOFAs. International organisations and their staffs enjoy the immunities necessary to independently perform their duties.

Contents

© T.M.C. ASSER PRESS and the author 2015

J. Voetelink, *Status of Forces: Criminal Jurisdiction over Military Personnel Abroad*,
DOI 10.1007/978-94-6265-057-2_9

9.1 Introduction

Initially international law developed within the community of States in order to manage their bilateral and multilateral relations while preventing, as far as possible, breaches of the States' sovereignty. Although this continues to be an important matter in international law today, the transnational nature of the problems that States increasingly have had to face obliged them to strengthen international cooperation. Consequently, since the nineteenth century States have delegated part of their functions to international institutions. From World War II on the institutions have undergone an explosive growth and developed into international governmental organisations (IGOs), which act in the interests of the cooperating States.

As international organisations vary in purpose, establishment, membership, functions and proceedings, they constitute a heterogeneous group. For the purpose of this chapter an international organisation is understood to be established by treaty or another instrument governed by international law and to have legal personality. As a consequence, non-governmental organisations are not included in the discussion in this chapter. Despite their legal personality international organisations do not possess the same rights and obligations as States do; for example, their capacity to conclude international agreements is more limited. Furthermore, they do not share the immunity accorded to States, but they possess similar rights on the basis of treaties and customary law.

For tasks such as national security, crisis management and the enforcement of international peace, States increasingly depend on international (military) cooperation. Since World War II military cooperation has to a large extent taken place under the auspices of international organisations, such as UN, NATO and EU. The functions of the organisations are diverse and may vary from coordination of the use of a particular military weapon system to the common defence of the member States' territory. Within this broad framework of military cooperation some organisations conclude SOFAs. Military personnel can become part of the staff of such an organisation and international military forces enjoy an internationally recognised status.

This chapter discusses the status of international organisations and their staffs under international law, paying particular attention to UN, NATO and EU. In addition, the position of military personnel executing tasks within the framework of activities of international organisations is analysed.

The first sections identify the most important elements of the definition of international organisations (Sects. 9.2 and 9.3), followed by a discussion of the position of UN, NATO and EU (Sect. 9.4). The subsequent section focuses on the immunities of international organisations and their staffs (Sect. 9.5). The chapter concludes with a discussion on the status of military personnel temporarily assigned to, or employed by, an international organisation (Sect. 9.6).

9.2 Definition of International Organisations

Shortly before World War I the notion of international organisations emerged,[1] but has subsequently never been clearly defined.[2] This is partly due to the diversity of organisations, which complicates the definition of such a heterogeneous group. In general a distinction is made between, on the one hand, organisations that have a membership consisting of States and are established by treaty (IGOs) and, on the other, different organisations (non-governmental organisations, NGOs).[3] This distinction is also made in the *Vienna Convention on the Law of the Treaties*, in which an international organisation is described as an intergovernmental organisation (Article 2, subparagraph 1(i)), implicitly excluding NGOs.[4]

As this definition was too broad for the purpose of the study of the International Law Commission (ILC) on the responsibility of international organisations,[5] Article 2(e) of the *Draft articles on the responsibility of international organizations 2011*[6] defines an international organisation as:

> an organization established by a treaty or other instrument governed by international law and possessing its own international legal personality. International organizations may include as members, in addition to States, other entities.

In the literature other definitions are proposed in which the emphasis may vary depending on the purpose for which they are adopted. In the context of this book it suffices to conclude that the core elements contained in the various definitions are also part of the ILC definition,[7] which covers the organisations discussed below. Therefore, the ILC definition is used as starting point.

---

[1] Brölmann 2007, p. 44.

[2] Schermers and Blokker 2003, p. 22.

[3] First Report on Responsibility of International Organizations; 26 March 2003, UN Doc A/CN.4/532, p. 7.

[4] The same formulation can be found in other treaties, such as the *Vienna Convention on the Law of Treaties between States and International Organizations or between International Organizations*; Vienna, 21 March 1986 (*UN Doc* A/CONF.129/15; not yet in force), the *Vienna Convention on the Representation of States in their Relations with International Organizations of a Universal Character*; Vienna, 14 March 1975 (Vol. 1035 *UNTS* 1984, No. 15410) and Article 2(1)(n) of the *Vienna Convention on the Succession of States in respect of Treaties*; Vienna, 23 August 1978 (Vol. 1946 *UNTS* 1996, No. 33356).

[5] First Report on Responsibility of International Organizations; 26 March 2003, UN Doc A/CN.4/532, p. 13.

[6] *UN Doc* A/66/10 (2011), ILC Report on the work of its 63rd session, Chap. V, Responsibility of International Organizations.

[7] The definitions contain the following core elements: "…established by international law, or by subjects of international law; …governed by international law, …degree of autonomy", Brölmann 2007, p. 20.

9.3 Establishment of International Organisations and Their Legal Personality

The last sentence of the ILC definition specifies that the membership of international organisations does not merely consist of States. This approach is in accordance with international practice that international organisations can also be members of other international organisations.[8]

The first sentence of the definition focuses on the establishment of an international organisation, which must take place either by treaty or by an "other instrument governed by international law." Most organisations mentioned in Part I of this book, such as EU, NATO and UN, meet this requirement, as they were established by treaty. Only a few international organisations have been established by other international legal instruments, such as a decision of a Conference of States.[9] The definition of international organisations excludes institutions formed on the basis of national law, such as multinational corporations and NGOs.[10]

Meeting the requirement of being established by an international instrument does not automatically entail that the international organisation actually falls under the ILC definition. The second element contained in the first sentence of the definition requires the international organisation has a legal personality. This means that, under international law, it possesses rights and obligations that enable it to operate independently from its members and to participate in the international legal order.[11] Without this capacity organisations cannot be held responsible for their acts under international law.[12] As a result, international legal personality is essential to the ILC definition on the responsibility of international organisations.

The subjective approach to international legal personality holds that legal personality depends on the will of the member States[13] as expressed in the constituent instruments of the organisation. However, in most cases such an explicit provision is absent.[14] The considerations of the ICJ in the *Reparation for Injuries* case suggest that legal personality of an international organisation may be implicit in case

---

[8] *UN Doc* A/58/10 (2003), ILC Report on the work of its fifty-fifth session, Chap. IV, Responsibility of International Organizations, p. 44.

[9] E.g. the Organization for Security and Co-operation in Europe (OSCE) falls within the scope of the definition, as it was been established by the Conference of participating States in Budapest in 1995; *UN Doc* A/58/10 (2003), ILC Report on the work of its fifty-fifth session, Chap. IV Responsibility of International Organizations, p. 40.

[10] See Schermers and Blokker 2003, pp. 37–38, paras 46–47.

[11] Blokker 2007, p. 443. According to the ICJ, 'legal personality' means that an entity is "capable of possessing international rights and duties, and that it has capacity to maintain its rights by bringing international claims", ICJ 11 April 1949, *Reparation for Injuries Suffered in the Service of the United Nations*, Advisory Opinion, I.C.J. Reports 1949, pp. 9, 179.

[12] Zwanenburg, 2005, pp. 53 et seq.

[13] The objective approach of international personality holds that legal personality depends on several specific objective criteria; Zwanenburg 2005, p. 66 referring to Seyersted 1964.

[14] Schermers and Blokker 2003, p. 988, para 1565.

the organisation can exercise specific functions and possesses specific rights. With regard to the UN, the Court concluded that:

> […] the Organization [UN] was intended to exercise and enjoy, and is in fact exercising and enjoying functions and rights which can only be explained on the basis of the possession of a large measure of international personality and the capacity to operate upon an international plane.[15]

The Court also specified that the UN possessed "objective international personality",[16] implying that the legal personality is effective vis-à-vis members and nonmembers alike, even in case the legal personality has not been explicitly recognised.[17] The Court's conclusion was based on the consideration that the fifty States constituting the UN represented the vast majority of the international community. This consideration has led some authors to conclude that the number of member States is one of the elements determining the existence of objective international legal personality.[18]

The legal personality international organisations possess is derived from the legal personality originally accorded to States. Therefore, the rights and obligations of international organisations are more limited than those of the States and depend on the organisations' purposes and functions.[19] They possess powers provided by their member States or flowing from their purposes. In the *Nuclear weapons* case, the ICJ considered that:

> …the necessities of international life may point to the need for organizations, in order to achieve their objectives, to possess subsidiary powers which are not expressly provided for in the basic instruments which govern their activities. It is generally accepted that international organizations can exercise such powers, known as "implied" powers.[20]

Legal personality of international organisations entails the capacity to conclude treaties;[21] however, this does not mean that all international organisations actually can. In general, their powers are limited to treaties that are "…necessary for the exercise of their functions and the fulfilment of their purposes."[22]

---

[15] ICJ 11 April 1949, *Reparation for Injuries*, p. 174, pp. 8 and 9; see also Sect. 9.4.1.

[16] *Reparation for Injuries* case, p. 185, p. 15. In its commentary to the *Draft Articles on the Responsibility of International Organisations*, the ILC interpreted the ICJ's opinion in a fairly broad sense: "when legal personality of an organization exists, it is an "objective" personality"; commentary to Article 2, second reading in: *UN Doc* A/66/10 (2011), ILC Report on the work of its 63rd session, Ch. V, Responsibility of International Organizations.

[17] Shaw 2003, p. 1189.

[18] Restatement of the Law, Third, Foreign Relations Law of the United States, p. 141.

[19] *Reparation for Injuries* case, p. 174, p. 10. Later the ICJ re-emphasised this point: "The Court need hardly point out that international organizations are subjects of international law which do not, unlike states, possess a general competence" in IGH 8 July 1996, *Legality of the Use by a State of Nuclear Weapons in Armed Conflict*, Advisory Opinion, I.C.J. Reports 1996, p. 66, para 25.

[20] Ibid.

[21] Schermers and Blokker 2003, p. 114, para 17480, see also the Preamble to the 1986 *Vienna Convention on the Law of Treaties*. So, an international organisation's capacity to conclude treaties may imply it has international personality.

[22] Preamble to the *Vienna Convention on the Law of Treaties between States and International Organisations or between International Organisations*.

Legal personality under international law is not the same as legal personality under national law. The capacity of taking legal actions under national law, such as renting a building or purchasing materials, requires legal personality under the laws of a particular State. In general, the constituent instruments of the international organisation include a provision on the legal personality of the organisation under the laws of (one of) the member States.[23]

9.4 UN, NATO and EU

Part I of this book discusses several organisations that operate in the field of international military cooperation and crisis management, such as UN, NATO and EU. If they possess legal personality and have the capacity to conclude treaties, they can adopt SOFAs for the benefit of armed forces from member States. The following sections briefly touch on the international legal status of these organisations and their treaty-making powers.

9.4.1 UN

Shortly after the establishment of the UN the legal personality of international organisations became the subject of the ICJ's *Reparation for Injuries* case. In this case the ICJ considered that international personality is indispensable to enable UN to meet its purposes and principles as laid down in the *UN Charter*.[24] However, the *Charter* does not explicitly provide for the UN's international personality. In the opinion of the ICJ it is nevertheless undeniable that the functions and rights allocated to UN can only be explained by the intention of its founding members to grant it a large measure of international personality.[25]

The *UN Charter* contains several provisions, in which the UN's capacity to conclude international agreements is laid down. For example, Article 43, subparagraph 1, enables UN to conclude agreements with States on the contribution of armed forces to crisis management operations and on related assistance and facilities.[26] With a view to the international personality of UN it can be assumed that Article 43 concerns treaties. The Charter remains tacit on the possibility to conclude international agreements with respect to other issues, such as SOFAs in the context of crisis management operations.

---

[23] Blokker 2007, p. 443. See, e.g. Article 104 *UN Charter* obliging member States to recognise the legal personality of the UN in their national law; *UN Doc* A/58/10 (2003), ILC Report on the work of its fifty-fifth session, Chap. IV, Responsibility of International Organizations, p. 41. This enables the UN to participate in the legal order of that particular state.

[24] *Reparation for Injuries* Case, pp. 8, 174.

[25] Ibid., p. 9.

[26] However, such treaties have never been concluded, Schermers and Blokker 2003, p. 1115, para 1749. See also, e.g. Article 63(1) on the capacity of the UN Economic and Social Council (ECOSOC) to conclude treaties.

Whenever such a capacity has not explicitly been provided for, it may be implicit. In the *Reparation for Injuries* case the ICJ observed the following with regard to UN:

> Under international law, the Organization must be deemed to have those powers which, though not expressly provided in the Charter, are conferred upon it by necessary implication as being essential to the performance of its duties.[27]

One of UN's main tasks is to promote international peace and security. To this end UN have established a number of crisis management operations. This activity implies the capacity to conclude agreements, such as SOFAs, with the States where the operations take place. UN's broad practice in this field confirms the organisation's authority to conclude international agreements. Furthermore, as mentioned in the preceding section, the UN possesses objective personality, which means that its personality applies to all States and international organisations.

9.4.2 NATO

The establishment of NATO is related to the 1949 *NATO Treaty,* although this agreement does not explicitly define NATO as an international organisation. As a consequence there are hardly any institutional provisions in the *NATO Treaty*. These provisions can be found in additional agreements, such as the *Ottawa Agreement*,[28] regulating the civilian institutions and the *Paris Protocol*,[29] defining NATO's military headquarters.[30]

Article I(a) of the *Ottawa Agreement* defines the 'organisation' NATO as consisting of the North Atlantic Council (NATO Council) and its subsidiary bodies. Article IV determines that NATO possesses both the juridical personality and the capacity "to conclude contracts, to acquire and dispose of movable and immovable property and to institute legal proceedings." The nature of the enumerated capacities refers, however, to NATO's legal personality under national law. Other provisions of the agreement imply that NATO has international personality as well. For example, the organisation enjoys immunities that are comparable to those of diplomatic missions and it has the capacity to conclude treaties (see discussion below).[31] Considering these aspects, NATO's legal advisor rightly remarked[32]:

---

[27] *Reparation for Injuries* Case, pp. 12, 174.

[28] *Agreement on the Status of the North Atlantic Treaty Organisation, National Representatives and International Staff*; Ottawa, 20 September 1951 (Vol. 199 *UNTS* 1954, No. 2691).

[29] *Paris Protocol*: *Protocol on the status of International Military Headquarters set up pursuant to the North Atlantic Treaty*; Paris, 28 August 1952 (Vol. 199 *UNTS* 1954, No. 2678). Article II *Ottawa Agreement* excludes military headquarters from the scope of the Convention, bringing along that a separate agreement had to be concluded.

[30] Johnson 2001, p. 260.

[31] Zwanenburg also refers to the arguments of the member States in ECHR 12 December 2001, *Bankovic and others v. Belgium and 16 others*, Application no. 52207/99; Zwanenburg 2005, p. 67.

[32] See also: Naert 2005, p. 9.

> NATO, as an intergovernmental organization, is a subject of international law … entitled to rights, duties or powers established in international law, and, generally, the capacity to act on the international scene.[33]

The international personality is necessary to achieve the organisation's purpose, which is: "…the further development of peaceful and friendly international relations…".[34] Therefore, the organisation has, inter alia, treaty-making powers. Article XXV of the *Ottawa Agreement* covers the NATO Council's capacity to represent the organisation and to conclude complementary agreements in its name. The Council has used this capacity to conclude agreements on the status of the organisation's bodies in member States.[35]

In addition, Article XVI of the *Paris Protocol* enables NATO's Supreme Headquarters[36] to conclude supplemental agreements with receiving States on the Protocol's application.[37] The fact that NATO's subordinate headquarters have these powers implies that the organisation itself also possesses such a capacity. In any case NATO's tasks and functions with respect to international military cooperation require the capacity to conclude agreements regarding those tasks and functions. This line of reasoning is confirmed by NATO's practice of concluding treaties with States and international organisations[38] on various topics related to military cooperation, such as status of forces.

NATO's decision-making procedure deserves particular attention, because its member States retain almost all decision-making powers and are directly involved

[33] De Vidts 2004, p. 4, para 12. Also, see the note of the Secretary-General of NATO, in which he explicitly indicates that the NATO Airlift Management Organisation will benefit from the international personality of NATO; Note by the Secretary-General, Strategic Airlift Capability (SAC)—Initiative Adoption of the NAMO Charter, 20 June 2007, para 2; see also *UN Doc* A/CN.4/637 (2011), Responsibility of International Organizations. Comments and observations received from international organisations, 14 February 2011, p. 11 in which NATO indicates that it "…possesses international legal personality as well as treaty-making power".

[34] Article 2 *NATO Treaty.*

[35] E.g. the *Agreement between the Kingdom of the Netherlands and the North Atlantic Treaty Organisation concerning privileges and immunities of the staff of the NAPMA Agency in the light of the Netherlands Government Policy Framework on Attracting and Hosting International Organisations*; The Hague/Brussels, 29 September 2006 (Vol. 2420 UNTS 2010, No. 43672).

[36] Article I(b) *Paris Protocol* refers to the NATO headquarters SHAPE and HQ SACT as the "Supreme Headquarters'. They possess national legal personality on the basis of Article X. The agreements concluded by SHAPE, such as the one concerning the headquarters in Brunssum, the Netherlands, imply that also headquarters at this level possess international personality; see also: Naert 2005, p. 10.

[37] For example, see *Agreement between the Kingdom of the Netherlands and the Supreme Headquarters Allied Powers Europe on the Special Conditions Applicable to the Establishment and Operation of International Military Headquarters Within the European Territory of the Kingdom of the Netherlands*; Paris, 25 May 1964 (Vol. 544 *UNTS* 1967, No. 7920).

[38] An example of an agreement between NATO and another international organisation is the *Agreement between the European Union and the North Atlantic Treaty Organisation on the Security of Information*; Athens, 14 March 2003 (*OJ* 2003, L 80/36).

in the administration and operation of NATO.[39] Decisions are taken by consensus, which means that a decision is only adopted when all States accept it:

> Decisions are thus the expression of the collective will of the Sovereign member States, arrived at by common consent and supported by all.[40]

This decision-making process also applies to the Council's decisions on NATO-led operations.

Whether NATO also possesses an objective international personality has not clearly been established yet. The current number of 28 NATO Member States constitutes a minority within today's international community, which consists of more than 190 States. Therefore, the assertion that NATO possesses objective personality does not seem to be very convincing. Nevertheless, the organisation does not only fulfil an important regional task, but has also been influential in the field of international peace and security further afield.[41] In this respect mention can be made of the UN authorization to take over its crisis management operations (IFOR/SFOR), or to execute major operations (ISAF, the anti-piracy operations near Somalia and the operations with respect to Libya in 2011). In the context of these operations, NATO has concluded international agreements with third States and international organisations, without its legal personality being disputed. Therefore, it seems plausible to conclude that NATO possesses objective international personality.

9.4.3 EU

Today the position of the EU is well established. Initially, and similar to UN and NATO, an explicit conventional provision on its legal personality did not exist. In 1997 the *Treaty of Amsterdam* added Article 24 to the *Treaty on European Union* (hereafter *TEU*),[42] enabling the EU to conclude treaties within the field of the common foreign and security policy. Since 2001 this legal basis has frequently been used by the EU Council, as a EU institution,[43] to conclude a number of SOFAs for EU crisis management operations,[44] which leads to the conclusion that

[39] *UN Doc* A/CN.4/637 (2011), Responsibility of International Organizations. Comments and observations received from international organisations, 14 February 2011, p. 11, para 1. This procedure, however, has not been set out formally, but evolved out of practice.

[40] *UN Doc* A/CN.4/637 (2011), Responsibility of International Organizations. Comments and observations received from international organisations, 14 February 2011, p. 12, para 4.

[41] See Sects. 4.4.2 and 5.2.2.

[42] *Treaty on European Union*; Maastricht, 7 February 1992 (*OJ 1992*, C 191).

[43] It has to be noted that the EU does not represent its member States when concluding agreements, but acts in its capacity as the EU; Verwey 2004, pp. 6, 59 and 74.

[44] The capacity to conclude international agreements returned in the *Treaty of Lisbon*, see Article 37 (ex Article 24) in the chapter on the Common Foreign and Security Policy: "The Union may conclude agreements with one or more States or international organisations in areas covered by this Chapter."

the EU has legal personality.[45] Any remaining controversy on the issue was put to rest with the adoption of the *Treaty of Lisbon*,[46] which added Article 47 to the *TEU* stating: "The Union shall have legal personality." Furthermore, a sentence was added to Article 1 of the TEU determining that the Union "shall replace and succeed the European Community (EC)." Article 281 of the EC Treaty saw to the legal personality of the EC,[47] although it did not specify whether it concerned personality under national or international law. However, due to the capacities attributed to the EC in the same treaty, it was generally accepted that it included international personality.[48] So, it is beyond doubt that the EU has acquired this status. From the discussion above on the objective international personality of NATO, it can be concluded that the same applies to the EU.

9.5 The Status of International Organisations

Generally speaking, the status of international organisations and their staffs has been laid down in multilateral international agreements that stipulate the member States' mutual duties and define the functions and the status of the organisations and their staffs. An international organisation is a functional entity, which, unlike a State, does not have territorial sovereignty. Therefore, such an organisation will generally have its seat on the territory of a member State and will have to conclude an agreement with this host State.[49] In general international organisations[50] themselves have the capacity to conclude these so-called Host State Agreements.[51]

9.5.1 Organisation

States establish international organisations that in their own name serve the agreed common interests of the participating member States. In this sense they embody

45 Schermers and Blokker 2003, p. 992, para 1569; see also: Verwey 2004, p. 59. In 2001 the EU concluded the first agreement: *Agreement between the European Union and the Federal Republic of Yugoslavia on the activities of the European Union Monitoring Mission (EUMM) in the Federal Republic of Yugoslavia; Belgrade, 25 April 2001* (*OJ* 2001, L125/2–4).

46 *Treaty of Lisbon Amending the Treaty on European Union and the Treaty establishing the European Community*; Lisbon, 13 December 2007 (*OJ* 2007, C 306; *Trb.* 2008, 11).

47 *Treaty Establishing the European Economic Community*; Rome, 25 March 1957 (Vol. 294 *UNTS* 1958, No. 4300).

48 Naert 2010, p. 286.

49 There is an exception for the bodies of the OSCE. As the organisation does not possess international personality, the Netherlands, as host State of the High Commissioner for National Minorities (HCNM), determined by statute law (Law on HCNM) that the organisation is regarded as an international organisation for the purposes of that law.

50 Schermers and Blokker 2003, p. 1131, para 1770.

51 Also referred to as 'Host state agreement'; Herbst 2008, para 1.

the member States' sovereign powers reflected in the purposes and functions of the organisations. Therefore, the international organisations will have to be able to function without the unilateral interference of member States, in particular of the State on whose territory the organisation is located.[52] Essentially for this reason host States grant international organisations immunities necessary to guarantee the independent exercise of their functions (doctrine of functional necessity).[53] As the purposes and the functions of international organisations vary widely, so does the status of organisations and their staffs.

Treaties on the status of international organisations generally grant the organisations absolute immunity from jurisdiction[54] and as a result they do not distinguish between *acta jure gestionis* and *acta jure imperii*.[55] Furthermore, it is common to exclude certain forms of responsibility from immunity, such as damages arising from traffic accidents.[56] Likewise, in the field of commercial transactions the treaties often provide for arbitration as an alternative means to settle disputes[57] in order to ensure that parties entering into legal relations with the international organisations can take legal action, if necessary. Lastly, the international organisations may refrain from immunity altogether.

In the absence of a treaty most national courts will not accept immunity of an international organisation.[58] An exception is a Dutch Supreme Court's case, in which it was considered that under international customary law an international organisation is entitled to immunity of jurisdiction in the State where it has its seat with the consent of the host State.[59]

9.5.2 Staff

The special position of international organisations requires that both organisations and their staffs can execute their functions independently from the host State.[60] This means that also staff members need to be entitled to immunities. The scope of

52 Schermers and Blokker 2003, p. 252, para 324.

53 Id., pp. 252–253, para 324.

54 Sands and Klein 2009, p. 494. For example, see Sect. 2, *Convention on the Privileges and Immunities of the United Nations*.

55 Gaillard and Pingel-Lenuzza 2002, p. 5; Ryngaert 2003, p. 125. In case of some financial organisations that actively operate on the international financial market, such as the World Bank, immunity may be restricted in the field of civil law, I. Roberts 2009, p. 299 and Sands and Klein 2009, p. 495.

56 Protocol Guide 2012, p. 42.

57 Gaillard and Pingel-Lenuzza 2002, p. 3.

58 Wickremasinghe 2009, para 33; Ryngaert 2003, p. 124.

59 Dutch Supreme Court 20 December 1985, *Criminal Immunity Iran—United States Claims Tribunal* para 3.3.4. However, this decision seems to be exceptional; Ryngaert 2003, p. 125.

60 Schermers and Blokker 2003, p. 369, para 529.

these immunities depends on the functions of the organisation. As States grant immunities to staff members in the interest of the organisation, these immunities are not for the personal benefit of the individuals themselves.

In the past States granted staff of international organisations a diplomatic status, or they treated them as if they were diplomats. However, the position of the staff of an international organisation fundamentally differs from the position of diplomats.[61] The latter are official representatives of their State in the host State, where they normally stay for a limited period of time. In contrast, the staff of an international organisation consists of officials, who are employed by the organisation and stay in the host State either for an unlimited period of time or for the period of their employment.

This distinction is reflected in treaties regulating the position of the staff of international organisations. Usually immunities accorded to the staff are more restricted than those granted to diplomats,[62] which does not preclude staff members, depending on their responsibilities, from being accorded immunities similar to those granted to diplomatic agents of comparable rank.

One of the most important requirements for an independent execution of the international organisation's functions is the restriction of the host State's criminal jurisdiction over the organisation's staff members. Normally host States grant high-ranking officials of an international organisation, such as the Head of the Secretariat, immunity *ratione personae*[63] to avoid that the host State may put undue pressure on these officials.

Other staff members of international organisations normally enjoy immunity *ratione materiae*.[64] The *Convention on the Privileges and Immunities of the United Nations* (see Chap. 4 with respect to the status of UN observers) often functions as a model agreement for other large organisations with broad responsibilities. The Convention sees to functional immunity with respect to words spoken or written and all acts performed. Organisations that mainly have a technical or commercial focus run less risk of being influenced by the host State, which may further restrict immunities.[65]

The international organisation is in the best position to decide whether an official has acted in an official capacity. Although in its advisory opinion in the *Cumaraswamy* case, the ICJ considered that the conclusion of the UN Secretary-General, finding that a UN expert on mission had acted in the performance of his duty, was not binding to a national court,[66] the conclusion does:

> create[s] a presumption which can only be set aside for the most compelling reasons and is thus to be given the greatest weight by national courts

[61] Id., p. 370, para 29.

[62] See I. Roberts 2009, pp. 294 and 308.

[63] Schermers and Blokker 2003, pp. 375–376, para 535.

[64] Id., p. 374, para 534.

[65] I. Roberts 2009, pp. 301–304.

[66] ICJ 29 April 1999, *Difference Relating to Immunity from Legal Process of a Special Rapporteur of the Commission on Human Rights* (*Cumaraswamy case*), Advisory Opinion, I.C.J. Reports 1999, 62, para 61.

The host State grants functional immunity to the staff of an international organisation with the view to protect the organisation's interests. However, if criminal proceedings do not prejudice the organisation's interest, it may waive immunity, if so requested by the host State.

9.5.3 National Representatives

To serve their interests, States can establish representations to the international organisations and their bodies and institutions. On the basis of a host State agreement or another international agreement representatives of the member States normally enjoy immunities comparable to those accorded to a diplomatic mission.[67] Sometimes the member States' representations are hosted by their local embassy in the receiving State. Organisations may also send staff members to member States, for which they shall have to make separate arrangements.

9.6 Immunities of Armed Forces Seconded to International Organisations

Increased international cooperation has also led to intensive international military contacts and establishment of international organisations with military functions. However, in contrast to States, these international organisations do not have armed forces of their own. Thus, to execute their military tasks, they will have to call upon the member States' armed forces. This Section focuses on the status of military personnel temporarily employed by international organisations.

It has to be noted that a number of military partnerships, such as multinational units, cannot be classified as international organisations. In general they are based on non-legally binding Memoranda of Understanding and are not established by treaty or another legally binding international instrument.[68] Although some military partnerships are established by treaty, they do not necessarily possess international personality.[69] The status of participating military personnel is often regulated in, or based on, the existing SOFAs, such as the *NATO-SOFA*.[70]

[67] Schermers and Blokker 2003, p. 1155, para 1811.

[68] For instance, several European States have established a partnership to expedite the deployment of combined F-16 detachments to crisis management operations. The partnership was based on the MOU on "*the establishment of the European Participating Air Forces' Expeditionary Air Wing* (EEAW)"; Voetelink 2009, p. 326.

[69] E.g. the partnership between several European air forces, the European Air Group: *Agreement concerning the European Air Group and Amending Protocol*; London, 16 June 1999 (Vol. 2077 *UNTS* 2002, No. 46089). The Dutch Explanatory Memorandum to the act approving the convention mentions that it does not accord (international) legal personality to the EAG; *Dutch Parliamentary Papers* 2000–01, 27 479, nrs. 68 and 1, p. 3.

[70] E.g. see the second paragraph of the preamble to the *EAG-Treaty*.

9.6.1 The Staff

Officials who work for an international organisation are part of the staff and are normally employed for an unlimited period of time. Military personnel assigned to an international organisation continue to be members of the sending State's armed forces. This means that they actually perform tasks for the organisations without being employed by them, which makes their position comparable to national representatives to the organisation.

When a large number of military personnel is assigned to an organisation, it may be practical to make specific arrangements. For instance, the secondment of military personnel to the EU Military Staff was one of the main reasons for drafting the *EU-SOFA* (see Part II of the Treaty; "Provisions applicable only to military or civilian staff seconded to the EU institutions").[71] When the agreement enters into force, military personnel seconded to EU institutions will enjoy functional immunity.[72]

NATO has a somewhat more complex arrangement, as the civilian structure and the military headquarters each have their own legal basis (see Sect. 9.4.2).[73] The introduction and subparagraph b to Article XIII of the *Ottawa Agreement* accord immunity to any representative of a NATO member State to the NATO Council or its subsidiary bodies with regard to words spoken or written or acts done in an official capacity. As the wording 'any representative' does not exclude military personnel, they are entitled to functional immunity on the basis of the *Ottawa Agreement*.[74] Article II of the *Paris Protocol*, applicable to military headquarters, stipulates that the *NATO-SOFA* applies to military personnel working at those headquarters.

There are no UN arrangements specifically detailing the status of military personnel from member States temporarily working for the organisation. They are considered to be member States' representatives who enjoy criminal immunities on the basis of Article IV, Section 11(a) of the *Convention on the Privileges and Immunities of the United Nations*:

> …in respect of words spoken or written and all acts done by them in their capacity as representatives…

Military personnel participating as military observers in a UN operation are not part of the UN staff or national representatives of a State.[75] They are considered

---

[71] Voetelink 2005, p. 22.

[72] The same applies to EU personnel on the basis of the *Protocol on the Privileges and Immunities of the European Communities*; Brussels, 8 April 1965 (*OJ* 2004, C 310); see Chapter V (Officials and other staff members of the European Communities) and Chapter VII (General Provisions).

[73] The *Ottawa Agreement* regulates the civilian structure of NATO. Military headquarters are exempted from this Agreement on the basis of Article II and are covered by the *Paris Protocol*.

[74] The negotiations preceding the adoption of the Agreement confirm that this was indeed the intention of the parties; Snee 1961, p. 143.

[75] Memorandum to the Director, Question of whether contractor's personnel could be considered as "experts on mission"—Article VI, Section 22, of the 1946 *Convention on the Privileges and Immunities of the United Nations*, 1998, p. 481.

experts on mission and on the basis of Article VI, Section 22(b) they too enjoy functional immunity (see Sect. 4.3.1).

The status of military personnel working for international organisations primarily depends on the functions of the organisation involved and is not derived from the immunity of the sending State. As the functions must be exercised independently from the host State, functional immunity of the soldiers normally suffices.

9.6.2 International Forces

In the context of this chapter forces established by international organisations deserve special attention. As has already been mentioned above, the organisations do not have military units of their own and depend on member States and third States to provide these international forces. To this end States in principle delegate Operational Control (see Sect. 11.3) over their national military contingents participating in an international force to the international commander of that mission. However, the contingents, as military units, remain under national command and control.

An international force as a whole constitutes a subsidiary body of the organisation, as the ICJ stated in its advisory opinion in *Certain Expenses* with regard to the United Nations Mission in the Congo, ONUC.[76] This also seems to apply to NATO[77] and EU missions.[78] Such subsidiary bodies primarily serve the interests of the international community and not necessarily the interests of an individual State or a region.[79] The establishment of an international force as a subsidiary body of an organisation, for instance by the UN, confirms the international nature of the missions.[80]

If international or regional peace and security are threatened, the States' participation in crisis management operations is primarily in the interest of the international community and not necessarily merely in the interest of the individual States. Furthermore, in the course of time operations have changed and are more demanding of the participating forces. As a result they are tasked to do a wide variety of tasks and sometimes have to support, or even temporarily replace, the local government. Within this framework military operations, including the possible use of armed force, must be conducted independently and without interference from the host State.[81]

---

[76] ICJ 20 July 1962, *Certain Expenses of the United Nations* (Article 17, paragraph 2, of the Charter), Advisory Opinion I.C.J. Reports 1962, p. 151, p. 177. Article 29 *of the UN Charter* is its legal basis. The General Assembly can proceed with establishing subsidiary organs on the basis of Article 22 of the *UN Charter*.

[77] Zwanenburg 2005, pp. 44, 45 and 47.

[78] Naert 2010, pp. 355–356.

[79] Chapman 1958, p. 72.

[80] *UN Doc* A/3943 (1958), Summary study of the experiences derived from the establishment and operation of the Force, report of the Secretary-General, 9 October 1958, paras 14 and 19.

[81] Oswald et al. 2010, p. 377.

The forces' independent execution of their tasks can be secured, for instance, by exempting them from the jurisdiction of the host State's courts. For this purpose, mission specific SOFAs include provisions subjecting the forces to the exclusive criminal jurisdiction of the sending States. Section 1.4.4 explained that such provisions emphasise the special relation between the sending State and its forces abroad.

The UN assumes exclusive criminal jurisdiction to be a customary rule. The *Model UN-SOFA*, IV. *Application of the status agreement,* reads:

> 5. Accordingly, the military and/or civilian personnel provided by [the Participating State] shall enjoy the privileges and immunities, rights and facilities and comply with the obligations provided for in the status agreement.
>
> 6. Pending the conclusion of such an agreement, the United Nations shall apply the customary principles and practices which are embodied in the model status-of-forces agreement.

The Office of Legal Affairs (OLA) confirmed this position in a legal opinion of the Secretariat of the United Nations. Responding to a question on the status of military members of the military component of a peacekeeping operation, the OLA stated:

> Military personnel of military components who serve in United Nations peacekeeping operations under the authority of the Secretary-General are, in accordance with the customary principles and practices applicable to peacekeeping, subject to the exclusive criminal jurisdiction of their respective national authorities…[82]

The existence of a customary rule may also explain why the UN Security Council sometimes provisionally applies the *Model UN-SOFA*'s provision on jurisdiction. Thus, a Security Council resolution does not impose additional obligations on the host State, but makes the existing customary rule explicit.

The ILC seems to implicitly accept the existence of a customary rule as well. Without any further reservation the ILC states in its commentary to Article 4 of the *Draft Articles on the responsibility of international organizations*, that "…the State retains disciplinary powers and criminal jurisdiction over the members of the national contingents".[83] In the literature there is some ambiguity.[84] After having analysed the different opinions of several authors, Burke concludes that, despite the fact that several authors seem to accept the existence of such a customary rule, there is insufficient State practice and *opinio juris*.[85] This conclusion does not seem to be accurate as Burke discusses SOFAs in general. Indeed, for instance within the framework of international military cooperation military personnel are hardly ever subject to the exclusive jurisdiction of the sending States.[86]

[82] 'Letter to the Acting Chair of the Special Committee on Peacekeeping Operations, United Nations, regarding immunities of civilian police and military personnel', 14 April 2004.

[83] *UN Doc* A/59/10 (2004), ILC Report on the work of its 56th session, Chap. V, Responsibility of International Organizations.

[84] Engdahl mentions: "customary principles applicable in peace operations"; Engdahl 2007, p. 153; see also his discussion of the opinions, pp. 193 et seq.

[85] Burke 2011, p. 99.

[86] This also appears to be the basis of Burke's conclusion.

However, when it comes to crisis management operations forces are almost without any exception subject to the exclusive criminal jurisdiction of the sending States, as can be concluded on the basis of numerous SOFAs adopted by the UN. Furthermore, no State has opposed the repetitive UN conclusion that the exclusive jurisdiction of the sending States was to be considered as a legal rule. On the contrary, in some cases States have even explicitly supported such a conclusion. On the occasion of the imprisonment of two Italian marines by India, who were suspected of having killed two Indian fishermen during anti-piracy operations, Italy declared that:

> the immunity of peacekeepers working within the framework of UN resolutions must be reasserted, along with "assertion of immunity and national jurisdiction as general and broadly recognized principles".[87]

The above leads to the conclusion that the exclusive jurisdiction sending States can exercise over their forces participating in UN crisis management operations, which entails the forces' full criminal immunity from the jurisdiction of the host State's courts, has acquired the status of a customary norm to which the UN refers (as noted above).

The crisis management operations led by other organisations or coalitions of States do not have the long tradition of UN operations. Nevertheless, these operations are based on similar principles, which entails that their interests prevail over the interests of individual States. Furthermore, it has to be noted that the majority of the operations takes place with UN authorization. Therefore, it can be concluded that the customary principles on which crisis management operations are based extend to operations undertaken by other entities.[88] This can be illustrated by the opinion of New Zealand on the status of its forces participating in INTERFET in East Timor. New Zealand did not recognise the authority of Indonesia over the territory. Consequently, New Zealand could not base the status of its forces on the SOFA between Australia and Indonesia. Instead, New Zealand took the position that international customary law had developed to the point where, inter alia, exclusive criminal jurisdiction of the sending State over its forces could confidently be asserted.[89]

The sending States' exclusive criminal jurisdiction over their forces can also in part be the result of the treaty-making powers of international organisations. This capacity derives from member States combining their interests, so to speak, through the organisations, thus reinforcing their negotiating position *vis-à-vis* the host State. In this way, organisations, such as EU, UN and NATO, have a stronger bargaining position than a single State in persuading the host State to accept a SOFA that precludes the latter's exercise of criminal jurisdiction over the foreign forces.

---

[87] Press report of the Italian Ministry of Foreign Affairs, 30 March 2012. www.esteri.it/MAE/EN/Sala_Stampa/ArchivioNotizie/Approfondimenti/2012/03/20120330_prosue.htm?LANG=EN. Accessed November 2014.

[88] Cf. Sari 2008, p. 264.

[89] Rogers 2005, p. 571; Riordan 2001, p. 23.

9.7 Conclusion

This chapter sought to define the status of international organisations, such as UN, NATO and EU, under international law, and to determine the position of military personnel functioning within the boundaries of the mandates of these organisations. In the course of time, States have created international organisations based on a treaty or any other instrument governed by international law and possessing international legal personality. Based on the legal personality and to the extent the constituent instrument or the functions of the international organisations permit, the organisations can conclude treaties that are necessary to exercise their functions and to fulfil their purposes. These requirements are fulfilled by UN, NATO and EU.

On the territory of the State where the headquarters are located, international organisations enjoy the immunities as agreed upon in the Headquarters Agreement necessary for the unimpeded exercise of their functions. Similarly officials employed by the organisations enjoy the immunities necessary to independently perform their duties. This means that in the area of criminal law they at least enjoy functional immunity. In fact, it is not unusual to grant staff members, especially higher ranking officials, personal immunity.

Forces participating in crisis management operations are subject to the exclusive criminal jurisdiction of the sending State while in the State where the operation takes place. This allows the sending State to continue exercising its authority over its forces while, at the same time the participating military personnel enjoy full criminal immunity from the host State's jurisdiction. In my opinion this long lasting practice is widely accepted today and can now be considered a rule of international customary law.

References

American Law Institute (1987) Restatement of the law, third, foreign relations law of the United States. American law institute publishers, Philadelphia

Blokker N (2007) Recht van internationale organisaties. In: Horbach N, Lefeber R, Ribbelink O (eds) Handboek internationaal recht. T.M.C. Asser Press, The Hague, pp 437–468

Brölmann C (2007) The institutional veil in public international law. International organisations and the law of treaties. Hart Publishing, Portland

Burke R (2011) Status of forces deployed on UN peacekeeping operations: jurisdictional immunity. J Conflict Secur Law 16(1):63–104

Chapman H (1958) International law: the United Nations Emergency Force: legal status. Mich Law Rev 57(1):56–81

de Vidts B (2005) Aspects related to the legal status of the North Atlantic Treaty Organization, speaking notes 22 November 2004. NATO document CJ 2004:0910

Engdahl O (2007) Protection of personnel in peace operations: the role of the safety convention against the background of general international law. Martinus Nijhoff Publishers, Leiden

Gaillard E, Pingel-Lenuzza I (2002) International organisations and immunity from jurisdiction: to restrict or to bypass. Int Comp Law Q 51(1):1–15

Herbst J (2008) Host State agreements. Max Planck encyclopedia of public international law. www.mpepil.com. Accessed Nov 2014
Johnson MS (2001) NATO military headquarters. In: Fleck (ed) The handbook of the law of visiting forces. Oxford University Press, Oxford, pp 257–320
Naert F (2005) De bevoegdheid van de NAVO inzake het sluiten van internationale overeenkomsten. FOD Personeel en Organisatie, Brussel
Naert F (2010) International law aspects of the EU's security and defence policy with a particular focus on the law of armed conflict and human rights. Intersentia, Antwerpen-Oxford-Leuven
Oswald B, Durham H, Bates A (2010) Documents on the law of peace operations. Oxford University Press, Oxford
Protocol Guide for International Organisations (2012) Netherlands ministry of foreign affairs, The Hague www.government.nl/documents-and-publications/leaflets/2012/12/01/protocol-guide-for-international-organisations.html
Riordan K (2001) Operations law—peacekeeping operations in East Timor: A New Zealand military perspective. New Zealand Armed Forces Law Review 2001:19–24
Roberts I (ed) (2009) Satow's diplomatic practice. Oxford University Press, Oxford
Rogers F (2005) The international force in East Timor. Legal aspects of maritime operations. Univ New South Wales Law J 28(2):566–580
Ryngaert C (2003) The immunity of international organizations before domestic courts: recent trends. J Int Crim Justice 7(1):121–148
Sands P, Klein P (2009) Bowett's law of international institutions. Thomson Reuters, London
Sari A (2008) The jurisdictional immunities of visiting forces under public international law. A case study of the European security and defence policy (not published; on file with author)
Schermers HG, Blokker NM (2003) International institutional law. Martinus Nijhoff Publishers, Leiden
Shaw MN (2003) International law. Cambridge University Press, Cambridge
Snee JM (1961) NATO agreements on status: Traveaux préparatoires. Int Law Stud vol 54, Naval War College, Newport
Verwey DR (2004) The European Community, the European Union and the international law of treaties. T.M.C. Asser Press, The Hague
Voetelink JED (2005) The EU SOFA: the European Union status of forces agreement. The Military Law and Law of War Review 44:17–38
Wickremasinghe C (2009) International organizations or institutions, immunities before national courts. Max Planck encyclopedia of public international law. www.mpepil.com. Accessed November 2014
Zwanenburg M (2005) Accountability of peace support operations. Martinus Nijhoff Publishers, Leiden

Part III
Military Operational Law

The discussion in Part II on the international legal framework for criminal jurisdiction over armed forces abroad shows that the forces enjoy at least functional immunity from the foreign courts' exercise of criminal jurisdiction. The historical analysis in Part I has already demonstrated that in practice, immunity of the armed forces generally extends beyond functional immunity. Part III on *Military Operational Law* builds on these previous parts and provides an insight into the backgrounds of this extended immunity.

International law requires an adequate legal basis allowing military forces, vessels and aircraft to enter foreign territory.[1] In the absence of another generally recognized legal basis,[2] the entry of foreign armed forces must be founded on the consent of the host State in order to be considered lawful under international law. SOFAs, including the core provisions on criminal jurisdiction, build on this legal basis.

From a military operational law perspective SOFAs can accommodate the extraterritorial visit of armed forces, in the sense that they expedite the entry into the host State and facilitate day-to-day operations of the units during their foreign presence. When taking the requirement of explicit consent as a point of departure, three general bases can be recognised that run parallel with the three different frameworks discussed in Part I: the stationing of armed forces in the territory of allied States during armed conflict, the participation in crisis management operations, and peacetime international military cooperation.

---

[1] See, Ducheine PAL (2008) Krijgsmacht, geweldgebruik & terrorismebestrijding. Een onderzoek naar juridische aspecten van de rol van strijdkrachten bij de bestrijding van terrorisme. Wolf Legal Publishers, Nijmegen p. 24 et seq.

[2] E.g., peace enforcement operations based on Chap. VII, UN Charter and operations on the basis of the right of self-defence (Article 51 UN Charter).

While analysing the history of criminal jurisdiction over military personnel abroad, Part I has taken into account the circumstances under which the soldiers are stationed abroad, the interests of the States involved and their relationships. Part III also takes the different frameworks for the stationing of forces abroad as a starting point for further discussion with a special focus on the purpose and the duties of the forces.

Chapter 10 explains the concept of military operational law and clarifies the position therein of the law of visiting forces. Chapter 11 analyses several terms relevant to SOFAs and with a specific meaning within the military context, such as performance of official duty and command and control. This is followed by Chap. 12, which analyses the three frameworks for the stationing of forces taking operational considerations as a starting point, such as the fundamental principles of military action. Chapter 13 concludes Part III with a discussion of the provisions of SOFAs that do not directly regulate criminal jurisdiction over soldiers, but do have an influence thereon.

Chapter 10
Law of Visiting Forces as Part of Military Operational Law

Abstract Military operational law is a relatively new, hybrid discipline of law, which concentrates on national and international law related to the planning and conduct of military operations. SOFAs are one of the core themes of military operational law and are instrumental to the commander in accomplishing his mission. Viewed from a military operational law perspective, SOFAs support the effective execution of a military mission by expediting the entry into a foreign State and by facilitating and supporting the forces' presence and operations.

Contents

10.1 Introduction

Military operational law is a relatively new sub-discipline of military law, which concentrates on the law related to military operations. One of the components of the discipline is the status of armed forces serving abroad. The rule of law requires that military operations take place on the basis of and in accordance with the law, which encompasses both national and international law. In this context, the ele ments of international law, as discussed in Part II of this book, are of particular importance to military operational law. This does not prevent military operational

© T.M.C. ASSER PRESS and the author 2015

J. Voetelink, *Status of Forces: Criminal Jurisdiction over Military Personnel Abroad*,
DOI 10.1007/978-94-6265-057-2_10

practice from having an impact on military operational law; this practice gives it a specific and often underrated dynamic.

This chapter introduces the concept of military operational law and discusses the position therein of SOFAs. It starts with a short introduction to military operational law (Sect. 10.2). Within the context of military operational law status of forces is not a self-contained element; it is part of the so-called law of visiting forces.[1] International law requires armed forces, naval vessels and military aircraft to have an adequate legal basis for entering and operating in the territory of a foreign State. If there is no other generally recognised legal basis, the military presence depends on the explicit consent of the receiving States. This consent comes with specific requirements that are closely related to the purpose of the foreign deployment and the specific duties the forces are ordered to fulfil.

All arrangements dealing with the consent to the entry and presence of the sending State's forces and the conditions attached to them constitute the legal basis for the presence of the foreign forces in the host State, also referred to as *jus ad praesentiam* (Sect. 10.3.1).[2] This legal basis is closely connected with the status of visiting foreign soldiers, the so-called *jus in praesentia* (Sect. 10.3.2).[3] The whole of legal bases and SOFAs will be referred to as the law of visiting forces.

10.2 Military Law and Military Operational Law[4]

Military action requires an unambiguous legal basis and demands conformity with the law.[5] This concept of the rule of law applies to all military operations, whether at home or abroad. Most rules applying under normal peacetime conditions remain in force during military operations. However, some rules may then apply in a different way, whereas other rules will simply not be applicable. Certain specific circumstances may even require the entry into force of special regulations. The whole of these rules, of which the law of visiting forces is one of the core elements, constitutes military operational law and is part of the broader discipline of military law. The following subsections further describe military operation law, focusing on the development of the discipline.

[1] Fleck 2003.

[2] Id., p. 351.

[3] Id., p. 353.

[4] This Chapter is partly based on Voetelink and Walgemoed 2009, pp. 195–212.

[5] *Dutch Parliamentary Papers* 2006/07, 29 521, nr. 41. See for an elaborate explanation, Ducheine 2008, pp. 24 et seq.

10.2.1 A Description of Military Operational Law

Military operational law is hard to define as it is an umbrella term that comprises all parts of the law related to military personnel and the armed forces.[6] Whereas military law has a broad scope covering the relation between military personnel and the law at large, military operational law concentrates on military operations. It can be defined as:

> the various bodies of national and international law which are applicable to and regulate the planning and conduct of military operations.[7]

Questions relating to military operational law arise during both national and international operations. It is in particular the latter operations that have left their mark on military operational law due to their increasing complexity, which has been decisive for the development of military operational law.[8]

As follows from the description above, military operational law (like military law) is a hybrid discipline of law which covers several areas of law of both sending States and host States and in which international law in particular plays a decisive role. In this sense military operational law is not entirely new. However, it is new in:

> ....the way and extent to which these various areas of law interact with each other and influence and regulate and shape the way in which contemporary operations are planned and conducted.[9]

Thus, military operational law is a collection of coherent legal elements with core themes, like the States' right to use force (*jus ad bellum*), the law of armed conflict (*jus in bello*), human rights law, guidelines for the use of force (the Rules of Engagement) and SOFAs. All these themes cannot be separated from the military operational environment, which has a strong influence on military operational law.

Compliance with the rules provides military operations with the necessary legal legitimacy.[10] This means that military operational law applies from the moment the deployment of the armed forces is decided upon. Commanders then have to apply it within the dynamic context of military operations by integrating it into the planning and execution of their operations. In this way military operational law contributes to the operations (force multiplier) and is instrumental in achieving the commander's missions (mission accomplishment).

Military operational law is a discipline, which is relatively new and developing and not yet firmly incorporated in military doctrine and still lacking a conclusive

[6] Gill 2006, p. 184.

[7] Gill and Fleck 2010, p. 3.

[8] Id., p. 5.

[9] Id., p. 5.

[10] Ducheine uses this concept next to the concept of social legitimacy, which refers to the support of the population and the government; Ducheine 2008, pp. 26–27.

theory. Be that as it may, it goes without saying that it is applied as an integral part of an operation in conformity with the basic principles of military operations, which are the "....rules of a fundamental nature for the use of military means",[11] e.g.: maintenance of morale, security, concentration of force, selection and maintenance of the aim, unity of effort, simplicity, flexibility and sustainability.[12]

10.2.2 Historical Development of Military Operational Law

As mentioned above, military operational law is a relatively new dynamic discipline whose evolution correlates with changes in the international security situation and developments in the field of crisis management operations. For example, in the international context operations are increasingly focussing on the reconstruction of a State in a post-conflict situation.[13] In those circumstances armed forces cooperate with a growing number of civilian partners from various backgrounds. At the same time the role of the law becomes more prominent within our regulated society, a tendency which also affects military operations. In addition, military operations receive more and more public attention while, legal accountability for, and political control over, military action has become a matter of course.[14] All these factors give military operational law a dynamic character, although the core of the discipline is firmly founded in both theory and operational practice, despite these developments.

The development of military operational law originates from US involvement in the Vietnam War and subsequent operations.[15] In the late 1950s, when US forces got enmeshed in the Vietnam War, military commanders were confronted with a wide variety of operational issues that would require a legal response.[16] The most pressing legal problems, however, occurred in the field of the law of armed conflict. Crimes committed by US soldiers received a large amount of media attention.[17] As a consequence, the Department of Defence (DoD), under great political pressure, launched the DoD Law of War Program for the entire US armed forces in 1974. The Program, which still runs today, provides, inter alia, a uniform,

[11] Netherlands Defence Doctrine 2013, p. 97.

[12] Id., pp. 97 et seq.

[13] E.g., Voorhoeve 2007.

[14] E.g., Ducheine et al. 2010.

[15] Graham 1987, pp. 9–12.

[16] E.g., the processing of claims for damages of Vietnamese citizens and the settlement of wrongful acts of civilian contractors hired by the armed force.

[17] The US public was particularly shocked by the tragedy at My Lai in March 1968, when US soldiers killed and tortured hundreds of Vietnamese civilians; see Addicott et al. 1993, pp. 153 et seq.

compulsory training in the field of the law of armed conflict for all military personnel.[18]

More important to the development of military operational law was the decision that all operational plans were to be checked on their compliance with the law of armed conflict.[19] As a result, military legal advisors were given a role in an early phase of the operational planning process and could assist the commander in applying the law of armed conflict. This also meant that during the preparation and execution of operations both the commander and his staff could easily and quickly obtain legal advice on other issues outside the field of the law of armed conflict as well. On the basis of the experiences gained during the Vietnam War and subsequent operations, legal operational matters were collected under the heading of Operational Law.[20]

After the Cold War altered international political relations made it easier for the UN Security Council to establish crisis management operations. Those operations became more complex and made commanders increasingly conscious of operational legal matters. Within the armed forces around the world those aspects received more and more attention and were soon applied as a coherent set of rules within the specific operational context.

10.3 Law of Visiting Forces Within the Context of Military Operational Law

Foreign visits of armed forces are based on a decision of the sending State. The commander of the visiting forces is responsible for the execution of the decision and is required to act in accordance with, inter alia, the provisions of the SOFA in force. Consequently, SOFAs are unmistakably part of the legal framework that regulates the preparation and execution of military operations.[21] They are part of the core themes of military operational law and instrumental to the commander in executing his duties abroad.

SOFAs constitute the rights and obligations of armed forces when abroad, the *jus in praesentia*, and as such they are not a legal basis for armed forces to enter the territory of a foreign State. This is regulated by the rules on the entry and presence of foreign forces, the so-called *jus ad praesentiam*. This means that SOFAs are not

[18] Lohr and Gallotta 2003, p. 470.

[19] Borch 2001, p. 31.

[20] Graham 1987, pp. 9–12.

[21] Failure to conclude a SOFA may lead to cancellation of postponement of planned military activities; see e.g., the negotiations between the NATO and Bahrein, Qatar and the United Arabic Emirates; Munoz-Mosquera 2011, pp. 2–3 and the withdrawal of the US forces and the NATO Training Mission from Iraq at the end of 2011 when no agreement could be reached with Iraq on a new SOFA; Gutman 2011; Lekic 2011.

self-contained entities, but must be considered in connexion with the host State's consent and related legal bases for the presence of the visiting forces. The *jus ad praesentiam* and the *jus in praesentia* together constitute the law of visiting forces.[22]

The following subsections discuss the host State's consent and the legal bases for the visits of armed forces, followed by an explanation of SOFAs that are based upon them. Consent, legal bases and SOFAs are closely related and provide the law of visiting forces with a layered structure, which will be clarified in the last section of this chapter.

10.3.1 The Legal Basis for the Visiting Forces

The presence of foreign forces, which are as executive State organs charged with carrying out the national duties of their sending State in the host State, in principle infringes on the latter's sovereignty. However, the host State's consent removes the wrongfulness of the entry and presence of the foreign forces.[23] For this reason, consent is the basis of the law of visiting forces.

Consent has to be accorded lawfully[24] in the sense that the State organ or official giving the consent has to be authorised thereto and that consent has been granted in accordance with national legal procedures. For example, some States require an explicit legal basis[25] for allowing the entry of foreign armed forces or require the involvement of Parliament[26] or Government.[27] Furthermore, consent must be unambiguous and cannot be merely assumed on the basis of implicit actions.[28] Finally, consent can in specific situations be invalid due to error or fraud, or corruption or coercion of a representative of the host State.[29]

When the host State grants consent, it simultaneously accepts the execution of specific military activities by a foreign State's executive organ within its boundaries. Despite the granted consent the foreign military activities, depending on their nature and scope, may still affect the host State's sovereignty. This means that they require a clear legal basis that formalises the host State's consent and expresses the purpose of the foreign forces' entry and presence (the '*ius ad praesentiam*').

---

[22] Fleck 2003, pp. 351 and 253.

[23] See Article 20 *Articles on Responsibility of States*.

[24] Article 20 *Articles on Responsibility of States* includes the wordings "valid consent by a State…".

[25] E.g., Belgium: Article 185 Belgian Constitution.

[26] E.g., Hungary, see Barsony 2001, p. 1.

[27] E.g., Latvia, Sect. 3 of the 1997 Law, *Status of Foreign Armed Forces in the Republic of Latvia*. www.mfa.gov.lv/en/security/basic/ForeignForces/. Accessed November 2014.

[28] See Commentary on Article 20 *Articles on Responsibility of States*, *UN Doc* A/56/10 (2001), ILC Report on the work of its fifty-third session, Chap. IV, State Responsibility, p. 73.

[29] *Cf.*, Articles 48–52 of the *1969 Vienna Convention on the Law of Treaties*.

To that end the host State will generally conclude specific agreements with the Sending State, which may further detail the duties of the visiting forces, the size of the forces, the duration of the visit, the sites to be used etc.

Within this framework the agreements are sometimes referred to as basing agreements or, in reference to the specific nature of the duties, as training agreements, transit agreements etc. For reasons of clarity this book will refer to all of these agreements with the generic term 'visiting forces agreements'. It must be noted that in respect of crisis management operations in general no specific visiting forces agreement is needed, as the decision of the UNSC authorising the operation forms a sufficient legal basis for the foreign military presence.

Continuing the foreign presence after the visiting forces agreement has expired or violating the SOFA provisions constitutes a breach of the host State's sovereignty. The UNGA has declared that such actions can under certain circumstances even be considered as acts of aggression.[30]

The visiting forces agreements provide a specific legal basis for the foreign forces' presence in the host State. Often these agreements build on a more general treaty, for example a defence agreement or a military cooperation agreement, which holds the general principles that apply when forces are deployed to another State that is party to the agreement.

NATO practice shows some excellent examples. The *NATO Treaty* can be considered as the general legal basis for the stationing of forces in NATO member States. This treaty does not include an explicit right of visit, but opens the possibility thereto by mentioning the resolve "…to unite their efforts..." (Preamble) and the option of rendering "...mutual aid…" (Article 3). The actual presence of NATO forces in another NATO-State requires a separate specific legal basis. The 1997 German–Netherlands *Basing* Agreement, for example, provides such a basis explicitly allowing Germany to base its forces on Dutch territory.[31]

10.3.2 The SOFA

The law of visiting forces shows a close connexion between the law on entry and presence (*jus ad praesentiam*) and the resulting legal rights and obligations during the presence (*jus in praesentia*). The SOFA in which these rights and obligations

---

[30] See Article 3(5) in conjunction with Article 2 Annex 'Definition of Aggression' to *UN Doc* A/9631 (1974), Resolution 3314 (XXIX), 14 December 1974. For a detailed discussion of this provision see Aurel Sari, Ukraine Insta-Symposium: When does the Breach of a Status of Forces Agreement amount to an Act of Aggression? The Case of Ukraine and the Black Sea Fleet SOFA, 6 March 2014 at Opinio Juris. opiniojuris.org/2014/03/06/ukraine-insta-symposium-breach-status-forces-agreement-amount-act-aggression-case-ukraine-black-sea-fleet-sofa/. Accessed November 2014.

[31] Article 1 *Vertrag zwischen dem Königreich der Niederlande und der Bundesrepublik Deutschland über die Stationierung von Truppen der Bundesrepublik Deutschland im Königreich der Niederlande*; Bergen, 6 October 1997 (*Dutch Treaty Series* 1998, 123).

are set out is a technical and legal document, which also carries political weight due to its connexion with the *jus ad praesentiam*.[32]

The previous section has given the example of German soldiers stationed in the Netherlands, for which the *NATO Treaty* provided a general legal basis and the *1997 Basing Agreement* served as the specific legal basis. However, the status of the German forces in the Netherlands is not regulated in either agreement. Instead, it is laid down in the *NATO-SOFA* and an additional and more specific SOFA (see Part I).[33] Without the specific legal basis, the *NATO-SOFA* would not apply.[34] Sections 2 and 3 of the Preamble to the *NATO-SOFA* emphasise the distinction within the NATO context between the entry of the forces and the conditions for their stay and operations:

> Considering that the forces of one Party may be sent, by arrangement, to serve in the territory of another Party;
> Bearing in mind that the decision to send them and the conditions under which they will be sent, in so far as such conditions are not laid down by the present Agreement, will continue to be the subject of separate arrangements between the Parties concerned;

This entails the multi-layered structure of the law of visiting forces as indicated in Fig. 10.1.

For various reasons, however, this structure may not always be recognisable. The legal basis and the SOFAs are sometimes either combined in one single agreement,[35] or to be found in different types of agreements, such as treaties or the non-legally binding MOUs[36], or not made public at all. Furthermore, practice may even often be more complex due to the conclusion of additional multilateral and bilateral agreements.

---

[32] E.g., After Operation Desert Storm, Saudi Arabia strongly questioned the continued basing of the US forces on its territory. To emphasise the temporary nature of the US presence, Saudi Arabia refused to conclude a SOFA with the US, Copeland 2007, pp. 108 and 132. In Afghanistan in response to the high number of civil victims resulting from the operations taking place on its territory, Present Karzai instructed his ministries to reconsider the presence of the foreign forces and to amend the SOFA accordingly; Human Rights Watch 2008, p. 3.

[33] *Zusatzabkommen zu dem Abkommen vom 19. Juni 1951 zwischen den Parteien des Nordatlantikvertrags über die Rechtsstellung ihrer Truppen hinsichtlich der im Königreich der Niederlande stationierten deutschen Truppen*; Bergen, 6 October 1997 (*Dutch Treaty Series* 1998, 124).

[34] E.g., Turkey was of the opinion that foreign forces based on its territory to provide humanitarian aid to North Iraq in the context of Operation Provide Comfort in 1991, did not fall under the scope of the *NATO-SOFA*; see Meek 1994, p. 236.

[35] E.g., In 1954 the Netherlands and the US agreed on the *Exchange of Notes (with Annex) Constituting an Agreement Relating to the Stationing of United States Armed Forces in the Netherlands*; The Hague, 13 August 1954 (Vol. 251 *UNTS* 1956, No. 3535). The Agreement allows the US to base its forces on Dutch territory and at the same time supplements the *NATO-SOFA* with bilateral arrangements.

[36] E.g., Dutch Security Sector Reform activities in Burundi are based on the Mémorandum d'entente entre le gouvernement de la République du Burundi et les ministres des affaires étrangères, de la coopération au développement et de la defense des Pays-Bas sur le développement du secteur de la sécurité; The Hague and Bujumbura, 10 April 2009 (not published). At a later stage the status of Dutch military personnel was laid down in the Accord entre le Royaume des Pays-Bas et la République du Burundi concernant le statut du personnel civil et militaire des

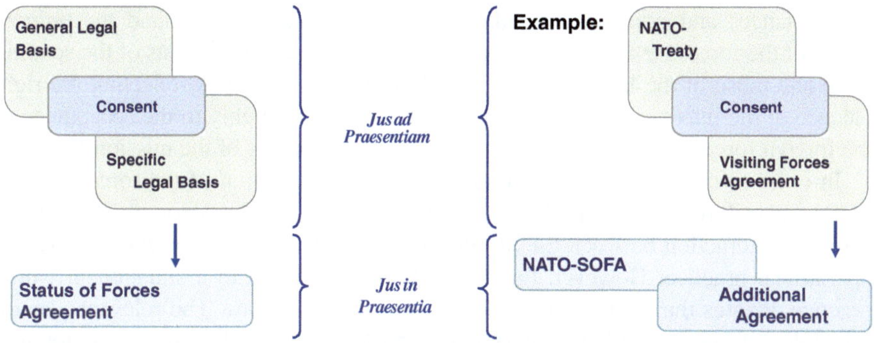

Fig. 10.1 The multilayered structure of the law of visiting forces

Criminal jurisdiction over armed forces is a key aspect in the structure of the law of visiting forces. In practice it can be the breaking point in negotiations, which may have consequences for the stationing of forces abroad. For example, NATO planned to base personnel in Bahrain, Qatar and the United Arab Emirates in support of its operations in Afghanistan and the anti-piracy operation 'Ocean Shield'. However, the essential visiting forces agreements could not be concluded due to the insurmountable difference of views on the provisions on the exercise of criminal jurisdiction.[37] The failure to reach an agreement required the revision of the operational plans and repositioning of units. Another example is the withdrawal of the US forces and the NATO Training Mission from Iraq at the end of 2011, the prime reason being Iraq's refusal to grant full immunity to US and NATO personnel after this year.[38]

SOFAs define the legal position (status) of the sending State's forces on the territory of an allied State. Viewed from a military operational law perspective, SOFAs should also create a practical framework to shore up the effective execution of the mission. For that reason the SOFA provisions should cover all aspects related to the foreign deployment of the forces and should respond to the operational

Footnote 36 (continued)

Ministères de la Défense néerlandais et burundais, présent sur leurs territoires respectifs, dans le cadre du Partenariat pour le développement du secteur de la sécurité au Burundi; Bujumbura, 17 August 2009 (Dutch Treaty Series 2009, 134).

[37] Munoz-Mosquera 2011, p. 3.

[38] Gutman 2011 and Lekic 2011. At the end of 2011 the US forces had to leave Iraq on the basis of previous arrangements adopted in the *Agreement Between the United States of America and the Republic of Iraq on the Withdrawal of US Forces from Iraq and the Organisation of their Activities during their Temporary Presence in Iraq*; 17 November 2008 (www.state.gov/documents/organization/122074.pdf. Accessed November 2014). The Agreement was also applicable to the NATO mission; see *Dutch Parliamentary papers* 2010/11, 29 521, nr. 148, pp. 6–7.

circumstances and practice at hand.[39] The nature of the mission and the ordered duties of the forces have a clear impact thereon. However, the interests of the sending State and those of the host State are equally important. A SOFA reflecting the right balance of the interests of all parties involved contributes highly to the acceptance of the foreign forces' presence and, consequently, to the success of the mission.[40]

In order to make an effective contribution to the execution of the forces' duties, SOFAs also have to take military operational practice into account. This brings about an interaction between the SOFA, being part of military operational law, and operational practice. However, this interaction cannot lead to a situation in which practice dictates the content of the SOFA, and hence the law. The relevant general principles of law, on which military operational law is based, will remain applicable. Consequently, operational practice remains subordinate to the law.

Viewed from a military operational law perspective, SOFAs aim to support the effective execution of the mission by expediting the forces' entry into a foreign State and facilitating their stationing and operation on foreign territory.[41] Therefore, SOFAs should preferably be adopted well before the foreign stationing takes place,[42] in order to support the execution of the foreign activities. Experience with various crisis management operations demonstrates that delay in adopting a mission-specific SOFA may result in a delayed launch of the mission and impede its execution.[43]

---

[39] On 25 June 1996 an attack took place on a US barracks in Dhahran, Saudi Arabia, resulting in nineteen casualties. According to Copeland cooperation with respect to Force Protection was inadequate due to the absence of a SOFA between Saudi Arabia and the US, which contributed to the opportunity to the launch the attack; Copeland 2007.

[40] Failure to establish the right balance can have far-reaching consequences. For example, at the end of the 1980s, when the US presence in the Philippines met with increased resistance, the Philippines sought to modify the SOFA in order to widen jurisdiction over the US forces. The US rejected the proposal, which lead to the termination of the permanent basing of its forces on the Philippine territory; see Egan 2006, pp. 324–325. However, the US continued to assist the Philippines in its combat against rebel forces partly affiliated to al-Qaeda; Feickert 2005, p. 9. In order to enable US forces to provide training and to participate in combined military exercises, a new SOFA was concluded, which included a provision on criminal jurisdiction over the US forces that corresponds with the approach in the *NATO-SOFA* (Article V *Agreement between the government of the United States of America and the government of the Republic of the Philippines regarding the treatment of United States Armed Forces visiting the Philippines*; Manila, 10 February 1998 (*TIAS* 12931)).

[41] E.g., the Explanatory Memorandum to the Dutch *Law approving the NATO-SOFA* stresses, in addition to Treaty's object to balance protection of the legal interests of the citizens of the host State with the interests of the sending States' servicemen, to achieve the utmost speed and flexibility in the mutual relations and to subject armed forces personnel to national regulations as much as possible; *Dutch Parliamentary papers* 1952/53, 2881, nr. 3, p. 1. Also Engdahl 2007, p. 15, stating that the aim of the mission-specific SOFAs established by the UN "…is to facilitate the implementation of the operation's mandate".

[42] Smith 2003, p. 14.

[43] Background Paper on UN Peacekeeping and The Model Status of Forces Agreement 2010, p. II. For Dutch experiences with the delay in the commencement of the missions caused by the negotiations on SOFAs with states in the Gulf region, see the Final Evaluation of the OEF; *Dutch Parliamentary papers* 2003/04, 27 925, nr. 135, p. 33.

10.4 Conclusion

Military operational law consists of different parts of national and international law that are applicable to the planning and execution of military operations. It cannot be considered separated from the operational context in which the commander and his staff apply and interpret the law. It contributes to the execution of the mission and is, therefore, an instrument at the commander's disposal. An important component of military operational law is the law of visiting forces, which includes the legal status of the forces.

The host State's consent to the stationing of foreign forces on its territory is the cornerstone of the law of visiting forces. If consent or any other recognised legal basis is absent, the entry of the foreign forces can be considered as an internationally wrongful act, for which the sending State can be held accountable. In contrast, if a host State grants its consent, the foreign forces are free to enter its territory, stay and execute the duties the sending State and the host State have agreed upon.

Therefore, it is essential for the States involved that the purpose of the foreign military presence and the conditions attached to the entry of the forces into the host State are absolutely clear. In general, the States involved set out their understandings on these issues in treaties, which are referred to in this work as 'visiting forces agreements'. This term is a generic reference to all agreements allowing the entry of foreign forces, which carry a wide diversity of labels referring to the specific nature of the stationing at hand, such as training agreement. Visiting forces agreements constitute the specific legal basis for the foreign presence of military forces. Likewise, these agreements are often based on other, more general agreements. Together these agreements, in combination with the consent of the host State, constitute the legal basis for the extraterritorial presence of the forces; the *jus ad praesentiam.*

These agreements are the foundation of SOFAs that define the legal status of forces; the *jus in praesentia*. Viewed from a military operational law perspective, SOFAs function to support the effective execution of the mission by expediting the entry into a foreign State and by facilitating and supporting the forces' presence and operations. In this way, the legal bases and SOFAs together embody the multilayered structure of the law of visiting forces.

References

Addicott JF, Hudson WA (1993) The twenty-fifth anniversary of My Lai: a time to inculcate the lessons. Mil Law Rev 139:153–185

Barsony A (2001) The problems of stationing foreign military forces in Hungary either temporarily or permanently, its supervision by parliament and legal regulation. In: International workshop on the experiences of South East European states in the parliamentary control of armed forces: achievements and problems, Kiev, pp 1–16

Borch FL (2001) Judge advocates in combat. Army lawyers in military operations from Vietnam to Haiti. Office of the Judge Advocate General and Center of Military History United States Army, Washington

Copeland TE (2007) Fool me twice: intelligence failure and mass casualty terrorism. Brill, Leiden

Ducheine PAL (2008) Krijgsmacht, geweldgebruik & terrorismebestrijding. Een onderzoek naar juridische aspecten van de rol van strijdkrachten bij de bestrijding van terrorisme. Wolf Legal Publishers

Ducheine P, van der Meulen J, Moelker R (2010) Legitimacy and surveillance: shifting patterns of external control. In: Soeters J, Venema P van, Beeres R (eds) Managing military organizations: theory and practice (Cass military studies). Routledge, London, pp 29–41

Egan JW (2006) The future of criminal jurisdiction over the deployed american soldier: four major trends in bilateral U.S. status of forces agreements. Emory Int Law Rev 20:291–343

Feickert A (2005) U.S. military operations in the global war on terrorism: Afghanistan, Africa, the Philippines, and Colombia. CRS Report for Congress. Congressional Research Service, 26 Aug 2005

Fleck D (2003) The development of the law of stationing forces in Germany: five decades of multilateral cooperation. In: Fleck D (ed) The handbook of the law of visiting forces. Oxford University Press, Oxford, pp 349–364

Gill TD (2006) Voordracht ter gelegenheid van de oprichting van de Gezamenlijke Militaire Juridische Dienst. Militair Rechtelijk Tijdschrift 99:184–189

Gill TD, Fleck D (2010) The handbook of international law of military operations. Oxford University Press, New York

Graham D (1987) Operational law (OPLAW)—a concept comes of age. Army Lawyer, pp 9–12

Gutman R (2011) NATO ends iraq mission as drama unfolds in Green Zone. www.mcclatchydc.com/2011/12/17/133410/nato-ends-iraq-mission-as-drama.html. Accessed Nov 2014

Lekic S (2011) NATO to end its training mission in Iraq. The Washington Times 12 Dec 2011. www.washingtontimes.com/news/2011/dec/12/nato-end-its-training-mission-iraq/. Accessed Nov 2014

Lohr MF, Gallotta S (2003) Legal support in war: the role of military lawyers. Chicago J Int Law 4(2):465–478

Meek PA (1994) Operation provide comfort: a case study in humanitarian relief and foreign assistance. Air Force Law Rev 37:225–238

Munoz-Mosquera A (2011) Host nation support arrangements: the NAC-approved military-to-military tools. NATO Legal Gazette 24:2–8

Netherlands Defence Doctrine (2013) www.defensie.nl/documenten/publicaties/2013/11/20/defence-doctrine-en. Accessed Nov 2014

Smith WC (2003) Lawyers at war. Am Bar Assoc J 89:14–16

Voetelink JED, Walgemoed GJ (2009) De totstandkoming van het hedendaags militair operationeel recht. Militair Rechtelijk Tijdschrift 102(5):195–212

Voorhoeve J (2007) From war to the rule of law. Peacebuilding after violent conflict. Study for the Scientific Council for Government Policy, Amsterdam University Press, Amsterdam

Chapter 11
Terminology

Abstract The phrase 'in performance of official duty', often used with respect to the law of immunities, can be translated as 'on duty' within the context of military operational law. In SOFAs 'on duty' is hardly ever defined, but logically a nexus is required between a specific act and the nature of the ordered tasks. In general, the visiting commanding officer will decide whether an act was performed 'on duty'. Military command and control over the armed forces can be exercised at various levels and a part of that authority may be transferred to a foreign, international commander. However, the sending States will always retain Full Command over their deployed forces.

Contents

11.1 Introduction

Viewed from a military operational law perspective, the basic principles for conducting military operations play a leading role in executing assigned military tasks. Before elaborating on this aspect in the next chapter, the present chapter discusses terminology specific to the field of military operational law. In general, it can be stated that legal terminology consists of a variety of terms, to which the different disciplines of law each can attach a specific meaning. Terms are not always strictly defined, leaving room for various interpretations. Needless to say, military operational law leans heavily on existing legal terminology, in particular

© T.M.C. ASSER PRESS and the author 2015

J. Voetelink, *Status of Forces: Criminal Jurisdiction over Military Personnel Abroad*,
DOI 10.1007/978-94-6265-057-2_11

terminology used in international law. However, it also contains specific terms derived from military practice. This chapter aims to clarify some of these specific legal military terms.

Section 11.2 clarifies the phrase 'in performance of official duty', a phrase often used in SOFAs, which mainly has a functional application. Section 11.3 concentrates on command and control over the deployed armed forces. From a legal point of view, command and control include authority and control over forces, which touches upon the concepts of accountability and liability.

11.2 In Performance of Official Duty

In the field of the international law regarding immunities the phrase 'in performance of official duty' is used frequently, which can be paraphrased within the military context as 'on duty'. In SOFAs variations of this phrase are used mainly in relation with the exercise of criminal jurisdiction and settlements of claims (Chap. 13). This section concentrates on its meaning in respect of criminal law and its procedures.[1]

With respect to the functional immunity of State officials, the sending States will as a matter of course reserve the right to exercise criminal and disciplinary authority over members of their forces acting in performance of their duties. Military personnel present on the territory of a foreign State with its consent and acting in accordance with sending States' instructions, act on behalf of these States and consequently cannot be prosecuted by a local criminal court. In the military context this form of immunity reflects the sending States' authority and control over their armed forces and the servicemen's accountability before the sending States' courts. Armed forces stationed in another State are under the orders and under political control of the sending States' authorities, emphasising that members of the armed forces do not visit the host State in a personal capacity, but as State organs functioning under the mandate and political authority of the sending States. Members of the visiting forces continue to be in the service of the sending States and their presence in the host State results directly from the sending States' orders to execute their tasks in the host State.

The latter aspect, however, does not imply that members of the forces are continuously on duty. During their foreign stay they can temporarily be relieved from their duties or be on leave. Depending on the circumstances, they can travel in the host State and be in contact with the local population and so on.

SOFAs that explicitly connect the exercise of criminal jurisdiction with on duty acts seldom define the scope of the term. Furthermore, most regulations do not specify who has the authority to determine whether an act has been carried out

[1] With a view to the different criteria applicable to criminal and civil procedures, interpretation of the phrase 'on duty' may vary in both procedures; see Mullins 1966, p. 81.

while on duty. As a result, the term 'on duty' has further developed in practice. Both the scope of the term and the authority to determine if an act is performed while on duty are discussed in the following sections.

11.2.1 The Scope of 'on Duty'

Even though armed forces are stationed abroad on sending States' orders, this does not mean that every activity which is undertaken during a foreign visit qualifies as being 'on duty'. The scope of 'on duty', however, is not unambiguous, as many SOFAs, including the *NATO-SOFA* and the *EU-SOFA*, do not specify the meaning of the term. Draft proposals for the *NATO-SOFA* initially spoke of "in performance of official duty" and "pursuant to a lawful order issued by the military authorities of the sending State".[2] The examples provided at the time of the negotiations related to members of the armed forces one of whom, injured a civilian of the host State, when driving a service vehicle on duty while another, an over-zealous sentry, injured an intruder.

In the negotiations, Italy proposed a more detailed definition of 'on duty' by including the phrase "within the limits of that official duty". The example was given that a driver making a detour with a service vehicle for personal reasons does not act within the limits of his official duty.[3] The US seemed to prefer a broader interpretation of the concept, but apparently refrained from bringing forward their ideas during the negotiations of the *NATO-SOFA*.[4] However, neither points of view can be found in the agreement, leaving the interpretation to the Contracting Parties.

However, even though SOFAs generally do not provide a definition of 'on duty', several additional agreements clarify the concept to some extent.[5] The *Agreed Minutes* to the SOFA between Korea and the US determine that the term official duty does not cover each act conducted during official duties.[6] The term is applicable to "acts which are required to be done as functions of those duties which the individuals are performing".[7] Furthermore, the *Agreed Understandings* specify that acts deviating considerably from acts normally necessary to execute

---

[2] Snee 1961, p. 131 (document D-R(51) 15).

[3] Id., p. 173 (document MS-R (51) 14, para 30).

[4] Snee and Pye 1957, p. 47.

[5] Not all additional agreements have been published.

[6] *Agreement under Article IV of the Mutual Defense Treaty between the United States of America and the Republic of Korea, regarding facilities and areas and the status of United States Armed Forces in the Republic of Korea*; (with agreed minutes, agreed understandings and exchange of letters); Seoul, 9 July 1966 (Vol. 674 *UNTS* 1971, No. 9605).

[7] *Agreed Minutes*; Re Para 3(a)(1).

the specific tasks, can be regarded as an indication that the person has acted beyond the scope of official duty.[8]

This interpretation rules out that each act performed by a soldier while in service automatically falls under the scope of an on duty activity and puts more emphasis on the actual performance of the duties. Thus, the act is related to the nature of the duties rather than merely to the time during which it is committed.[9] This approach was followed in the *Girard*-case.[10] Girard, a US soldier based in Japan, was ordered to guard a machine gun on a shooting range. During the execution of this task, he fired empty shell cases with his rifle-mounted grenade launcher. One of the cases killed a Japanese woman, who was collecting spent cartridge cases on the range.

On the basis of the 1951 *Japan-US Security Treaty* the US and Japan had concluded a SOFA including criminal jurisdiction provisions similar to relevant provisions of the *NAVO-SOFA*. The US were of the opinion that Girard had acted "in performance of official duty", as meant in Article XVII, para 3 of the *Administrative Agreement*,[11] entailing primary jurisdiction for the US. This approach would be in accordance with the interpretation that Girard had acted to protect the machine gun, even though the performance was excessive in nature. However, Japan was of the opinion that Girard had acted "beyond the scope of official duty", which would follow another version of the incident: Girard had supposedly encouraged the woman to enter the range and had jokingly fired an empty shell case.

Notwithstanding their legal argumentation in the *Girard*-case, other documents reveal that, in their interpretation of the term official duty included in the *Administrative Agreement*, the US followed the same reasoning as adopted in the agreements with Korea[12] (a definition that refers to the acts required to be done as functions of the duties which the individual are performing). Bearing in mind the Japanese interpretation of the facts, it can be concluded that the acts performed by Girard deviated considerably from acts normally necessary to perform

---

[8] *Agreed Understandings*; *Agreed minutes*, Re Para 3(a), under 1. In *Girard* (U.S. Supreme Court 11 July 1957, *Wilson v Girard*, 354 U.S. 524 (1957). supreme.justia.com/us/354/524/case.html. Accessed November 2014. This interpretation was also applied with respect to the SOFA concluded with Japan.

[9] See Stanger 1957/1958, p. 218.

[10] U.S. Supreme Court 11 July 1957, *Wilson v Girard*, 354 U.S. 524 (1957). supreme.justia.com/us/354/524/case.html. Accessed November 2014.

[11] *Administrative Agreement under article III of the Security Treaty between the United States of America and Japan*; Tokyo, 28 February 1952 (Vol. 208 *UNTS* 1955, No. 2817). Shortly thereafter this agreement's provisions on criminal jurisdiction were amended to be in conformity with the *NATO-SOFA*: *Protocol to amend Article XVII of the Administrative Agreement under article III of the Security Treaty between the United States of America and Japan*; Tokyo, 29 September 1953 (Vol. 208 *UNTS* 1955, No. 2817).

[12] Stanger 1957/1958, p. 229, fn. 33.

guard duties and, consequently, indicate that the act was conducted beyond the scope of duty.[13]

A somewhat different approach can be found in the agreement between France and the United Arab Emirates (UAE), which defines the concept 'en service' ('on duty') as:

> Les membres du personnel de l'Etat d'envoi, lorsqu'ils se trouvent sur le territoire de l'Etat d'accueil, sont considérés comme étant en service sur les lieux d'accomplissement de leurs missions et activités liées à la mise en oeuvre du présent accord et à l'occasion des trajets qui s'y rattachent. Ils sont considérés comme n'étant pas en service lorsqu'ils exercent une activité dépourvue de tout lien avec la mise en oeuvre de l'accord.[14]

However, an extensive description as included in the Agreement between France and the UAE is exceptional in SOFAs. In my opinion, due to the ambiguity over the scope of the term 'on duty', a more precise definition in a SOFA linking the act with the nature of the duty is preferable.

11.2.2 Competence to Determine Application of the Term 'on Duty'

Most SOFAs do not define who is authorised to decide whether a criminal offence has been committed within the limits of official duty.[15] Usually, it will be the commanding officer who is in the best position to determine whether a serviceman was on duty at a particular moment. He is in charge of all units and orders to perform specific duties have been given by him or a commander subordinate to him. This approach was reflected in the negotiations on the *NATO-SOFA* when the chairperson of the legal Sub-Committee argued that as part of normal allied cooperation it would be for the sending State to decide whether a soldier was on duty or not.[16] At a later stage, the US reemphasised in the working group that it was the sending State that could take such a decision.[17]

The decision whether a soldier is on duty or not can be expressed in a certificate. In early NATO practice the use of these certificates was not always rational.

---

[13] However, the US refrained from exercising criminal jurisdiction without expressing whether the act was conducted within the limits of official duty.

[14] Article 11(2) *Accord entre le Gouvernement de la République Française et le Gouvernement de la République des Emirats arabes unis relatif à la coopération en matière de défense*; Abu Dhabi, 26 May 2009.

[15] Exceptions are, inter alia, Article 18 of the *Supplementary Agreement* to the *NATO-SOFA* and the *Agreed Minutes* to the SOFA between Korea and the US. E.g., the *Agreed Minutes* state that a duty certificate of the military authorities of the US is sufficient evidence of the situation of 'official duty' (Para 3(a)(1)). If the Korean Chief Prosecutor is of the opinion that there is evidence demonstrating the contrary, both states shall proceed to diplomatic negotiations (Para 3(a)(2)).

[16] Snee 1961, p. 103 (document MS(J)-R(51) 5).

[17] Id., pp. 172 and 173 (document MS-R(51) 14).

Stambuk remarks that sometimes the certificates of sending States were based on unconvincing grounds and that host States were pressed to accept these unfounded declarations.[18] In the course of time, within the context of the bilateral relations between the States involved, a practice emerged that did justice to the position and interests of both the sending State and the host State. This experience implies that in respect of a multilateral agreement, such as the NATO-SOFA, practice between States may vary.

For example, in the UK a formal certificate of the commanding officer stating that the serviceman acted while on duty is generally sufficient. However, a British court has the authority to review evidence suggesting the contrary. In this way, the certificate constitutes a refutable assumption.[19] This practice is in accordance with the considerations of the ICJ in its advisory opinion in *Cumaraswamy*, stating that the findings of the UN Secretary-General that a UN expert on mission had acted in the performance of official duty, creates an assumption that a national court can only disregard for compelling reasons.[20] In general, the practice within the context of NATO appears to be that a certificate suffices. If a difference of opinion arises between parties, they will then try to resolve the issue through bilateral negotiations.[21]

Occasionally, the competence to determine whether an act has occurred during the performance of official duty, is left to the discretion of the host State.[22] An agreement between Turkey and the UK states that, in case a difference of opinion arises during military activities taking place outside the context of NATO, a bilateral Committee decides.[23] If the Committee cannot reach an agreement, the opinion of the host State shall prevail. Likewise, in an exchange of letters on the interpretation of the SOFA between France and the UAE, both states agree that the host State decides after deliberations with the sending State.[24]

Despite the fact that these agreements deviate from general international practice, they do provide the clarity absent in most SOFAs. In my opinion, SOFAs

---

[18] Stambuk 1963, p. 88.

[19] Mullins 1966, p. 79; Rouse and Baldwin 1957, p. 44.

[20] ICJ 29 April 1999, *Difference Relating to Immunity from Legal Process of a Special Rapporteur of the Commission on Human Rights* (*Cumaraswamy case*), Advisory Opinion, I.C.J. Reports 1999, 62, para 61.

[21] Mullins 1966, p. 80; see also e.g., Article 18 *Supplementary Agreement (with Protocol of Signature) to the NATO regarding the Status of their Forces with respect to Foreign Force stationed in the Federal Republic of Germany*; Bonn, 3 August 1959 (Vol. 481 *UNTS* 1963, No. 6986).

[22] The Philippines' wish to determine as host State whether a US soldier acted within the limits of official duty was one of the breaking points of the negotiations between the Philippines and the US on the modification of the SOFA; Porreta-Doria 1992, p. 99.

[23] Article VII(5) *Framework Agreement between the Government of the United Kingdom of Great Britain and Northern Ireland and the Government of the Republic of Turkey on Military Cooperation*; London, 23 November 2011 (Cm. 8344, May 2012).

[24] *Accord sous forme d'échange de lettres relatif à l'interprétation de l'Accord de coopération en matière de défense*; Paris, 15 December 2010.

should, alongside determining and apportioning the exercise of jurisdiction over visiting forces, devote equal attention to authority to determine the official nature of acts performed by members of visiting forces. If such a provision is lacking, it must be assumed that the sending State is most capable of determining whether the act was performed on duty, which can only for compelling reasons be refuted by a national court of the host State.

11.3 Command and Control

As explained in Chap. 8, armed forces are an integral part of the State and, as such, can be deployed abroad by the competent national organ, which has the ultimate political authority over the armed forces under national law. Within the armed forces, command and control is exercised by the military chain of command. In short, command relates to the commander's authority[25] and the term control to the exercise of the authority.[26] Three main levels of command and control can be recognised: the strategic, operational, and tactical level. At the strategic level, a State or international organisation translates its political aims into military objectives and assigns military capabilities accordingly. At the operational level these objectives are implemented by the actual deployment of military units. The underlying tactical level focuses on directing the conduct of operations in accordance with the operational objectives.[27]

Command and control as military terms are closely linked and complement each other. The supreme authority is referred to as Full Command and entails the authority to command military units in general.[28] Full Command is always a national responsibility, just like the political authority over the armed forces.[29]

Even though States retain Full Command over their armed forces, parts of the command authority can be transferred. That concerns in the first place Operational Command (OPCOM): "The authority granted to a commander to assign missions

[25] NATO Glossary of Terms and Definitions-06, 2013 (AAP-06, 2013): "The authority vested in an individual of the armed forces for the direction, coordination, and control of military forces". A footnote to the definition of Full Command emphasises that in the international context, command "implies a lesser degree of authority than when it is used in a purely national sense".

[26] AAP-06, 2013: "That authority exercised by a commander over part of the activities of subordinate organisations, or other organisations not normally under his command, that encompasses the responsibility for implementing orders or directives".

[27] Cathcart 2011, p. 238.

[28] Although states and international organisations use the same terms, in practice their meaning may differ; see Cathcart 2010, pp. 236–237. AAP-06, 2013: "Full Command: The military authority and responsibility of a commander to issue orders to subordinates. It covers every aspect of military operations and administration and exists only within national services".

[29] With regard to Full Command the AAP-06, 2013, p. 2-F-7 specifies that "No NATO or coalition commander has full command over the forces assigned to him since, in assigning forces to NATO, nations will delegate only operational command or operational control".

or tasks to subordinate commanders, to deploy units, to reassign forces, and to retain or delegate operational and/or tactical control as the commander deems necessary".[30] During these missions a commander may assign tasks and orders to the units based on Operational Control (OPCON).[31]

During crisis management operations OPCON will generally be transferred to the international commander (Transfer of Authority, TOA), whereas the national commander will retain OPCOM over his units. The international commander can then direct the units in accordance with the operations plan. As States retain Full Command over the units, a State can withdraw units from the international command if necessary, also referred to as 'reverse TOA'. As the international commander then loses control over a part of his military capabilities, reverse TOA should be the exception and only applied in close coordination with the international commander.[32]

The underlying level of the command structure is Tactical Command (TACOM): "The authority delegated to a commander to assign tasks to forces under his command for the accomplishment of the mission assigned by higher authority".[33] Lastly, the Tactical Control (TACON) consists of the "detailed and, usually, local direction and control of movements or manoeuvres necessary to accomplish missions or tasks assigned".[34] Similar to OPCOM and OPCON, both TACOM and TACON can be transferred.

In general, command and control authority is hard to translate into legal terms. Notwithstanding, law imposes consequences on the exercise of command and control. For example, on the basis of Article 7 of the *Draft Articles on the responsibility of international organisations* an organisation can be held accountable for the conduct of armed forces placed at the disposal of the organisation for a crisis management operation, insofar as the organisation exercises effective control over the conduct. The extent to which the organisation has command and control over the forces is one of the factors to determine if the organisation has effective control.

---

30 Ibid, 2013.

31 Ibid.: "The authority delegated to a commander to direct forces assigned so that the commander may accomplish specific missions or tasks which are usually limited by function, time, or location; to deploy units concerned, and to retain or assign tactical control of those units. It does not include authority to assign separate employment of components of the units concerned. Neither does it, of itself, include administrative or logistic control".

32 Also referred to as 'Change of Operational Control'. An example is the rescue of the commercial vessel 'Taipan' in 2010 that was attacked and taken over by pirates. The Dutch warship 'Tromp', participating in EU operation 'Atalanta' and operating under EU command, was near the area where the 'Taipan' was located. However, the Tromp could not proceed under the European command, because the 'Taipan' was outside the EU Area of Operations. The Dutch Commander in Chief then decided to temporarily withdraw the Tromp from EU command to allow the rescue operation of the 'Taipan' under Dutch command.

33 AAP-06, 2013.

34 Ibid.

Maintenance of order and discipline within the unit is one of the tasks of a military commander.[35] For this purpose he has disciplinary power over soldiers under his command. This task is not part of the above-mentioned authorities, but falls under Administrative Control (ADMINCON or ADCON), which concerns administrative matters, such as personnel management.[36] Disciplinary power is incorporated in the national law of States and, therefore, cannot be transferred to an international commander.

Many states and international organisations use the above-mentioned or similar terminology. However, in practice the terms give rise to diverse interpretations and applications. Therefore, participating forces will have to coordinate the scope of command and control authority in accordance with to the situation at hand and lay that down in operational documents. Despite these differences, the general scope is not subject to ambiguity. In the context of this book on the status of forces, it should be emphasised that a sending State cannot transfer its highest political authority or its highest military command over its forces based abroad, whether it be in the context of international military cooperation or an armed mission.

11.4 Conclusion

Military operational law uses several military terms in a specific legal context. This chapter has analysed two such terms. The first term is 'on duty', a term that is frequently used in SOFA provisions on criminal jurisdiction. As such, 'on duty' is a concept that resembles terminology, like performance of official duty, frequently used in international law on immunities. In the military operational context the scope of the term is not firmly established and the term is seldom defined in SOFAs. The lack of definition should by no means be an excuse to interpret the term as broadly as to include all acts conducted during the period of military service abroad; a certain link between the act and the nature of the tasks performed seems to be necessary.

This leads to the question who has the authority to decide whether an act has been conducted on duty. The allocation of this authority is seldom included in SOFAs. After a period of cooperation, host State and sending State are generally able to reach a practical balance. The basic assumption related to the allocation of authority is that the commanding officer in question is the most capable official to decide whether a soldier has acted while on duty. For this reason, many

[35] This is based on the assumption that the conduct does not violate the national order of the host State and, as a result, does not constitute a criminal offence.

[36] AAP-06, 2013: "Direction or exercise of authority over subordinate or other organizations in respect to administrative matters such as personnel management, supply, services, and other matters not included in the operational missions of the subordinate or other organization".

states have accepted a decision from the foreign commanding officer to that effect without requiring further justification. The decision must be considered a refutable presumption, which the national courts of the host State may only disregard for compelling reasons. In NATO practice States have often chosen to resolve differences of opinion through bilateral negotiations.

This leads to the conclusion that, when connecting the exercise of criminal jurisdiction over the soldiers based abroad with the performance of official duty, SOFAs must equally define the term of 'on duty' in more detail and must also determine who has the authority to decide whether an act has been performed on duty.

The second term discussed in this chapter is command and control over military units. Laws may contain provisions that impose consequences on the exercise of the different types of authority, such as in the case the command is connected with the term effective control over the units. The general authority to give orders to units, also referred to as Full Command, is a sovereign authority, which in principle the State cannot transfer. Parts of this command authority may be transferred to the international commander when forces are deployed during international operations. Generally, OPCON over the participating forces is delegated to the Force Commander of these operations.

References

Cathcart B (2010) Command and control in military operations. In: Gill TD, Fleck D (eds) The handbook of international law of military operations. Oxford University Press, New York, pp 235–244

Mullins WR (1966) The international responsibility of a State for torts of its military forces. Mil Law Rev 34:59–100

Porrata-Doria RA (1992) The Philippine bases and status of forces agreement: lessons for the future. Mil Law Rev 137:67–102

Rouse JH, Baldwin GB (1957) The exercise of criminal jurisdiction under the NATO status of forces agreement. AJIL 51(1):29–62

Snee JM, Pye KA (1957) Status of forces agreement: criminal jurisdiction. Oceana publications, New York

Stambuk G (1963) American military forces abroad: their impact on the western state system. Ohio State University Press, Columbus

Stanger RJ (1957/1958) Criminal jurisdiction over visiting armed forces. International law studies, vol. LII. Naval War College, Newport

Chapter 12
Analysis of the Frameworks for Foreign Presence from an International Operational Perspective

Abstract In general, sending States can exercise criminal jurisdiction over their deployed forces for offences committed either on- or off-duty, to the exclusion of, or priority over, the host State. Viewed from an operational law perspective, this practice can be explained by a general desire of the host States to protect their armed forces' members against a foreign legal system. Moreover, the operational tasks of the deployed forces may entail the functional necessity of subjecting them to the exclusive criminal jurisdiction of the sending States.

Contents

12.1 Introduction

Part I discussed foreign stationing of armed forces within three specific frameworks: when stationed on co-belligerent territory during armed conflict, when participating in crisis management operations and when partaking in international military cooperation activities abroad. Based on this overview subsequent chapters focused on explaining the exercise of criminal jurisdiction over armed forces abroad by looking more closely at the circumstances under which the forces are stationed abroad, the interests of the States involved and their mutual relations. In addition, this chapter focuses on objectives and tasks of visiting forces arising from the legal bases and frameworks for their foreign presence.

© T.M.C. ASSER PRESS and the author 2015

J. Voetelink, *Status of Forces: Criminal Jurisdiction over Military Personnel Abroad*,
DOI 10.1007/978-94-6265-057-2_12

Military operational law is partly instrumental in supporting armed forces abroad in executing their tasks. In order to do justice to this function, the law has to be aligned with operational military practice and applied in accordance with the so-called basic principles of military operations,[1] which implies that military practice influences developments within this discipline of law, including the law of visiting forces. However, the latter aspect can by no means subordinate the law to operational practice. This chapter discusses the exercise of criminal jurisdiction over forces based abroad, looking more closely at objectives and tasks resulting from the legal bases discussed in the previous chapter. It addresses the question to what extent operational practice can explain the sending States' exercise of jurisdiction over their armed forces.

Viewed from a military operational law perspective, various general arguments may be brought forward to justify the exercise of criminal jurisdiction over visiting forces by sending States. These arguments are connected with the protective function of SOFAs (Sect. 12.2). In that context we will briefly reflect on the international legal instruments that have been adopted in view of Article 98 of the *Rome Statute* establishing the International Criminal Court. Other more specific arguments justifying the sending States' criminal jurisdiction over their forces can be derived from military operational considerations resulting from the tasks the forces are ordered to carry out abroad.[2] To this end, exercise of criminal jurisdiction is analysed on the basis of the three different frameworks for stationing forces abroad (Sect. 12.3).

In case SOFA provisions lead to criminal immunity of visiting forces, that immunity should not result in impunity. If a sending State decides not to prosecute a soldier who has committed a crime abroad, it will undermine the credibility of both the forces and the mission as a whole. Therefore, we will take a closer look at experiences of the UN with offences committed by peacekeepers, which will be discussed specifically (Sect. 12.4).

12.2 The Protective Function of SOFAs

In the performance of their official duties abroad State officials benefit from State immunity and thus enjoy functional immunity from the jurisdiction of the foreign States' courts. Military personnel, as State officials, are not exempted from this rule and are entitled to functional immunity while on duty abroad.

[1] Basic principles of military operations are rules of a fundamental nature for the use of military means, Netherlands Defence Doctrine 2013, p. 97.

[2] See the statement in an EU note made in the context of a generic SOFA for police missions, declaring that immunities as point of departure should primarily be accorded in order to give personnel the necessary protection and independence while at work, para II, *EU Doc* 15711/02 of 17 December 2002; Note from the Presidency, Generic Status of Force Agreement for police missions—Immunities and privileges for EU Mission personnel.

Part I has already indicated that military personnel often enjoy broader immunities than required by the rule of functional immunity. In general, the broader immunities can be explained by the sending States' preference to protect servicemen from foreign legal systems.[3] This preference arises from a certain sense of uneasiness or even a lack of trust in the host State's legal system. Sometimes this feeling can be explained by the clear failure of that foreign system[4] which may occur when the local legal system is not fully developed or does not function properly due to a crisis situation. Under these circumstances sending States will not be prepared to subject their forces to the host State's jurisdiction[5] and contribute forces to a crisis management operation.[6] Also, sending States may fear that host State judiciary bodies will be prejudiced towards foreign servicemen, jeopardising the conduct of a fair trial.[7]

Furthermore, uneasiness may be caused by the fact that the foreign legal system is different from the familiar national system,[8] reducing legal certainty for a soldier accustomed to the rights he enjoys under his national legal system. Parties can resolve this issue by introducing a provision in the SOFA guaranteeing certain (fundamental) rights. For instance, Article VII(9) of the *NATO-SOFA* enumerates several rights that aim to ensure a fair trial. If such an arrangement still does not provide sufficient certainty, practical measures may take away the final concerns. For example, the US adopted internal procedures that protect the interests of US servicemen who may be subject to the host State's jurisdiction.[9]

Viewed from a military operational law perspective, the argument to protect the interests of visiting forces is highly relevant. The fact that servicemen can partly be subject to the criminal jurisdiction of foreign courts within a legal system that is insufficient or does not adequately correspond to the rights servicemen enjoy in

---

[3] For example, the EU mentioned the "...protection needed to ensure the legal security..." as general argument for the adoption of a SOFA on EU police missions; *EU Doc* 15711/02 of 3 October 2002, Framework for drafting a document on the Status of Forces Agreement (SOFA) to be used in the event of EU led Police operation.

[4] See Wexler 2008, pp. 85–86, on the Iraqi legal system in 2008.

[5] Hemmert 1999, p. 238.

[6] See Oswald and Bates 2011, p. 395.

[7] The fear of politically inspired criminal procedures against US servicemen was a reason for the US to prevent extradition of servicemen to the International Criminal Court by treaty.

[8] For differences in legal tradition and language, see Stone 2006, p. 238, who finds that the Japanese legal system "...is structurally deficient and incompatible with the American idea of due process and an individual's right to defend themselves".

[9] DoD Directive 5525.1, para 2. This Directive regulates that commanders are to examine the criminal legal system of the host State, in particular by comparing the system with the procedural safeguards for fair trial in accordance with US law (para 4.4.1.). If a commander is of the opinion that a US soldier runs the risk of being subject to an unfair trial (in comparison with US procedures, which does not mean that a trial is necessarily unfair if not identical to the US system, DoD Directive 5525.1, para 4.5.2.), he can consider to request the host State to refrain from its jurisdiction; para 4.5. DoD Directive 5525.1.).

the sending State, can affect the morale of the troops.[10] Maintenance of morale is an important element contributing to the success of an operation and is, therefore, one of the basic principles of military operations.[11]

If, in a sending State's opinion, a SOFA fails to sufficiently protect the deployed forces, that State can take practical measures to meet the concerns. This may lead to restrictions when executing their tasks or to restrictions during their presence abroad in general. For example, the Netherlands was required to adopt supplementary codes of conduct for its forces stationed in Qatar and the UAE, when the two host States did not accept full Dutch jurisdiction over its deployed forces, in order to "reduce the legal risks" to the extent that the "legal risks linked with the interests of the mission" were generally acceptable.[12] The aim of the measures was to reduce the "contact with the local population to the extent strictly necessary for the operation".[13] In practice, the measures required personnel to remain on base or to employ local personnel for purposes such as transport outside the base, reducing possible risks for the Dutch servicemen.[14] Such practical measures are in conformity with the basic principles of military operations and require the necessary flexibility from the commander.[15]

The 'Article 98 Agreements' adopted by the US under the Presidency of G.W. Bush constitute a special version of the protective function of SOFAs.[16] The title of the agreements refers to Article 98(2) of the *Rome Statute,*[17] stating that the International Criminal Court may not:

> proceed with a request for surrender which would require the requested State to act inconsistently with its obligations under international agreements pursuant to which the consent of a sending State is required to surrender a person of that State to the Court.

The aim of Article 98(2), as proposed by the US, was to protect the applicability of SOFA provisions that reserved the right to exercise criminal jurisdiction of the courts of the sending State, as these agreements constituted "the U.S. military's security blanket for its global deployment of military personnel".[18] It was

---

[10] See Re 1961, p. 320, who indicates that the absence of a SOFA with Iran and the Iranian prosecution of US servicemen had a negative impact on the morale of the forces.

[11] Netherlands Defence Doctrine 2013, p. 100.

[12] *Dutch Parliamentary Papers II* 2003/04, 27 925, nr. 135, p. 33.

[13] *Dutch Parliamentary Papers II* 2003/04, 27 925, nr. 135, p. 37.

[14] *Dutch Parliamentary Papers II* 2001/02, 26 122 and 27 925, nr. 39, p. 21 and *Dutch Parliamentary Papers I* 2005/06, 30 300 X, A, p. 5.

[15] Flexibility is one of the basic principles of military operations, Netherlands Defence Doctrine 2013, p. 98.

[16] Approximately one hundred of these 'Bilateral Immunity Agreements' or 'Non-Surrender Agreements' have been concluded.

[17] *Rome Statute of the International Criminal Court*; Rome, 17 July 1998 (Vol. 2187 *UNTS* 2004, No. 38544).

[18] Scheffer 2003, pp. 602 and 603.

generally assumed that Article 98(2) only applied to agreements already in force and that the article could only cover new agreements, if the application of existing agreements, such as the *NATO-SOFA*, was extended to new member States.[19]

However, the literal formulation of the provision leaves room for a wider interpretation that does not exclude application to new agreements. The US explicitly indicated that it considered the provision to be applicable to new agreements and adopted a series of 'Article 98 Agreements'.[20] The aim of these agreements is primarily to ensure that US servicemen remain subject to US jurisdiction[21] by preventing the host State from surrendering them to the International Criminal Court.[22] The conclusion of the agreements derives from, inter alia, the fear for politically inspired procedures against US forces involved in military or humanitarian missions worldwide, which are not always widely supported.[23]

As host of the International Criminal Court, the Netherlands, like many European States, is critical to agreements that run counter to the spirit of *Rome Statute*.[24] However, also the Netherlands had to accept provisions related to Article 98 of the *Rome Statute* in a multilateral context. For example, Section 1(4)4 of the *ISAF SOFA* included a provision, stating that Afghanistan may not surrender ISAF personnel to the International Criminal Court. The Netherlands accepted the provision, as rejection of the provision could have jeopardised the vital contribution of the US.[25]

12.3 The Different Frameworks for Extraterritorial Presence

In addition to the argument of protection discussed above, there are other elements that can explain a sending State's preference for a more extensive right of criminal immunity of its servicemen. To be successful, a military operation requires

[19] Zappalà 2003, p. 122.

[20] These agreements do not appear to be in conflict with international law, at least to the extent that they do not result 'de facto' in impunity; Knoops 2004, p. 310.

[21] Rosenfeld 2003, p. 291. The agreements also aim to prevent that other US officials and citizens are surrendered to the International Criminal Court, van den Wilt 2005, p. 107.

[22] For an unofficial text of the model agreement, see Zappalà 2003, p. 123.

[23] Meyer 2005, p. 109. Reference can also be made to resolutions of the UN Security Council, adopted under US pressure, in which the Security Council requested the Court on the basis of Article 16 *Statute*: "if a case arises involving current or former officials or personnel from a contributing State not a Party to the Rome Statute over acts or omissions relating to a United Nations established or authorised operation … not commence or proceed with investigation or prosecution of any such case, unless the Security Council decides otherwise": *UN Doc* S/RES/1422 (2002) of 12 July 2002: period 1 July 2002–30 June 2003; *UN Doc* S/RES/1487 (2003) of 12 June 2003: period 1 July 2003–30 June 2004.

[24] *Dutch Parliamentary Papers II*, 2002/03, 28 498, nr. 3.

[25] *Dutch Parliamentary Papers II*, 2001/02, 27 925, nr. 62, p. 2.

Fig. 12.1 Connection between the legal bases and status of forces

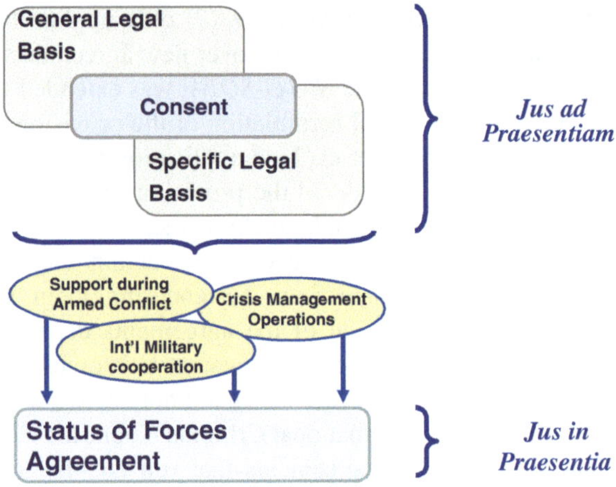

absolute authority and control over the armed forces, which is reflected in the preference of sending States to be able to exercise jurisdiction over their forces. Indeed, in many SOFAs not the immunity of the forces is key but the sending State's exclusive or primary right to exercise jurisdiction over its own forces.

Furthermore, servicemen may commit specific military offences, such as absence without official leave or disobedience of lawful orders, which, in principal, do not affect the legal order of the host State.[26] Moreover, military offences are part of the military criminal law of a State, to which only its own servicemen are subject. Under these circumstances, it makes no sense for the host State to restrict the jurisdiction of the sending State with regard to military offences.

To what extent the need for the effective execution of the tasks has an effect on SOFAs depends on the purpose of the foreign presence of armed forces. Building on the three different frameworks for foreign stationing of forces, discussed in Part I, the development of SOFAs can be further analysed and discussed from the perspective of military operational practice (Fig. 12.1).

Initially, this section discusses criminal jurisdiction over visiting forces within the framework of stationing allied forces on co-belligerent territory during an armed conflict. Then follows a review of the issue of criminal jurisdiction within the framework of international crisis management operations. The section 3 ends

[26] In this context, the term 'organic jurisdiction' is sometimes used, referring to specific issues that, on the basis of their nature, can only be regulated by the sending State; see Sari 2008, pp. 78 et seq; Liivoja 2011, p. 239.

by looking at forces operating abroad under peacetime conditions within the framework of international military cooperation.[27]

12.3.1 Support During Armed Conflict

After analysing the application of the ground rule within the framework of stationing allied forces on co-belligerent territory during armed conflict in Chap. 3 it was concluded that the scope of the ground rule during armed conflict is not fixed, contributing to the practice of dealing with criminal jurisdiction over the foreign forces by treaty. These SOFAs illustrate that the wartime application of the ground rule is almost absolute; in general, the forces are subject to the exclusive criminal jurisdiction of the sending States. Exceptions to exclusive criminal jurisdiction are allowed for forces outside the area of operation and whose tasks do not directly contribute to the military effort.

As already discussed, State officials enjoy functional immunity. The question in this section is whether and to what extent operational practice can explain the armed forces' more extensive immunities from criminal jurisdiction. The point of departure is that when States deploy their forces on allied territory during armed conflict, the host State will have given its consent to the use or armed force by the visiting forces. Thus, the host State also has implicitly acknowledged that the foreign forces remain under the highest political authority and military command of the sending States.

One of the basic principles of military operations is the unity of effort.[28] This principle requires the commander to synchronise assets and activities to achieve his objective. The most solid basis for unity of effort is single command. The armed forces operate under Full Command of the respective sending States (see Sect. 11.3), within which subordinate commanders lead their units. In order to operate effectively, the commanders must be able to lead their units without interference of foreign authorities and the military chain of command must be maintained at all times.

The host State's exercise of criminal jurisdiction over visiting forces would affect the military command lines and the execution of the operations. The commander must be able to carry out his operational tasks, independently of the host State. The same applies to activities in direct support of the operations, such as supply activities or the repair of equipment. Such activities are elementary to the success of combat operations, meaning that also with regard to these activities the military lines of command must be respected.

This leads to the conclusion that the operational tasks of the deployed forces bring about the functional necessity of full criminal immunity of these forces. Full immunity is essential to the effective execution of the operation. Therefore, it must

[27] Peacetime international military cooperation contributes to maintaining a sufficient level of military training and as such it can be considered as a preparation to actual operational deployment.

[28] Netherlands Defence Doctrine 2013, p. 101.

apply to all acts and not only the acts performed on duty. At the same time, the operational tasks demand that sending States retain full control over the forces and are able to exercise their criminal jurisdiction accordingly. For this reason, as mentioned above, SOFAs emphasise the exclusive jurisdiction of the sending States, instead of concentrating on immunity of forces. In other words, because of operational necessity forces are subject to the exclusive criminal jurisdiction of the sending States and enjoy full criminal immunity from the host State's courts.

Already in 1879, in the *Dow v. Johnson* case, restrictions on the sending State's exercise of criminal jurisdiction were considered undesirable. The judge noted that the local tribunals' possibility to summon servicemen would destroy the efficacy of an armed force.[29] This approach can also be recognised in the negotiations of the Civil Affairs Agreements at the end of World War II (see Sect. 3.3). At the start of the negotiations Norway proposed to shape the arrangements on the exercise of criminal jurisdiction over Allied forces in Norway in the same manner as provisions applicable to foreign forces in the UK.[30] The UK did not accept the proposal and emphasised that in Norway UK forces would operate under different circumstances than the Norwegian forces in the UK. When conducting combat operations, British commanders would have to have full control over their forces[31] and to be able to take all measures necessary for the execution of the mission,[32] which required exclusive jurisdiction of the UK over its forces.

Article XV of the *NATO-SOFA* is based on a similar reasoning. This provision states that in the event of hostilities to which the *NATO Treaty* applies, the Contracting Parties will immediately review Article VII on criminal jurisdiction and make modifications, if desirable. Initially, it was the intention that the *NATO-SOFA* would remain applicable without any modification during armed conflict.[33] However, during the negotiations the US expressed the wish to exercise exclusive jurisdiction over its forces:

> In time of war, it would be inadvisable that members of the Force or assimilated personnel should be withdrawn from the control of their military authorities by reason of their subjection to the jurisdiction of the receiving State.[34]

The final version of the provision is a compromise between the two ideas. In a commentary, Lazareff remarks that the sending State's exercise of criminal jurisdiction contributes to the maintenance of discipline and prevents servicemen

[29] U.S. Supreme Court October 1879, *Dow v. Johnson*, 100 U.S. 158 (1879). supreme.justia.com/us/100/158/case.html. Accessed November 2014.

[30] Donnison 1961, p. 39.

[31] Stanger 1957/1958, p. 114.

[32] Donnison 1961, p. 37.

[33] See Lazareff 1971, p. 415.

[34] Snee 1961, p. 173 (document MS-R (51) 4, para 3). During further negotiations and during the period the Treaty was reviewed by the US Congress, the US emphasised the necessity to exercise criminal jurisdiction in the event of hostilities, Lazareff 1971, p. 418.

eluding their national commanders' authority by committing minor offences.[35] According to Lazareff, the compromise reflected in Article XV does not do justice to this concern. He holds that the *NATO-SOFA* should contain the provision that the sending State has exclusive criminal jurisdiction over its forces in the event of hostilities.[36]

Notwithstanding the discussion above, it has to be noted that today exercise of criminal jurisdiction may take place outside the military chain of command. Many legal systems have abolished the system of courts martial as the only courts responsible for military criminal trials. Instead, hybrid civilian courts are responsible for the prosecution of military personnel, taking into account operational circumstances and developing and securing a sufficient level of operational situational awareness.[37]

Today, a consistent and widely accepted international practice exists that military personnel deployed abroad enjoy full criminal immunity and are subject to the exclusive criminal jurisdiction of the respective sending States. It is difficult to identify and to prove to what extent States regard this practice as a legal obligation. However, in my opinion, the existence of a rule of international customary law can be assumed, as there are strong operational arguments pleading for immunity and exclusive criminal jurisdiction, which have not been contradicted by States.

12.3.2 Crisis Management Operations

As discussed in Chap. 4, during the execution of crisis management operations, armed forces of the participating States are subject to the exclusive jurisdiction of Sending States resulting in full immunity of the forces. It has been explained that these extensive rights result from, inter alia, the forces' international function. This begs the question whether and to what extent operational practice supports broad immunity of the forces.

When answering this question, special attention should be paid to the changing nature of crisis management operations, which have become more complex in the course of time. The possibility to use force has increased due to, inter alia, more extensive mandates. Besides, the military are now required to carry out tasks traditionally of a non-military nature, such as law enforcement. These developments have led to situations in which, from a criminal law perspective, servicemen have become more vulnerable and can increasingly be held accountable for their acts.[38]

[35] Lazareff 1971, p. 417.

[36] Lazareff 1971, p. 418.

[37] Brouwer 2011, p. 133.

[38] Knoops 2004, pp. 73–75.

The crisis management operations discussed in this book have taken place with host State consent.[39] As a consequence, host States have accepted the possible use of armed force by the participating forces on their territory and, implicitly, they have recognised that the foreign forces operate under national command and control or that of the international organisation in charge of the operation. In the latter situation the forces remain under the highest political authority and military command of the relevant national bodies. Thus, the host States have consented to have no command and control over the forces.

If forces are under the command of an international organisation, they constitute a subsidiary body of the organisation. As such the international forces must be able to carry out their tasks independently from host States and, from an international law perspective, are entitled to functional immunity. Units operating under national command also enjoy functional immunity, as bodies of the sending State. In practice, however, sending States have exclusive criminal jurisdiction over their forces, which implies full criminal immunity.

Similar to the stationing of allied forces on co-belligerent territory during armed conflict, as discussed above, the nature of the forces' tasks during crisis management operations must be taken into account. These forces operate in an unstable and possibly hostile environment. In general, they are armed and authorised to use force in self-defence or in accordance with the Rules of Engagement.

The final objective of the operations is not to defeat an enemy force, as is the case in armed conflict, but depends on the international mandates. Since the 1990s the scope of mandates has been extended, including the tasks of international forces[40]; a development that has increased the probability that in implementing the mandate the use of armed force is required. Even though the use of military force in the highest spectrum of violence is generally not the primary goal of contemporary crisis management operations, the possibility must be taken into account. Even in relatively peaceful situations with hardly any violence, or no violence at all, the commander implementing the international mandate must be able to immediately deploy armed units, if circumstances so require. Regardless of whether he is commander of an international force or a national unit, in such situations a commander must be able to make free use of his forces and give them orders. It is highly detrimental if in such situations the host State, by exercising criminal jurisdiction over the servicemen, would have the possibility to cut across the chain of command and possibly influence or even hamper the execution of the military mission.[41]

It is not unlikely that during crisis management operations international forces encounter obstruction from host States. Sometimes this is simply because local

[39] Certain types of crisis management operations, such as enforcement operations, may constitute an armed conflict and consent may not have been given.

[40] For example, the disarmament of armed groups, the definition of safe areas, the provision of disaster relief, and the protection of the civilians; Oswald et al. 2010, p. 4.

[41] See Naert 2008, p. 391.

authorities may not always be aware of the existing SOFAs.[42] Problems like these can quickly be resolved, in contrast to situations in which host States deliberately disregard the SOFA. Although host States may have consented to the presence of foreign forces, that may have been the result of international pressure and may not fully reflect the host State's interests. A reluctance to fully implement the SOFA, or even deliberate non-compliance with the SOFA, may be the consequence.

In practice, it regularly occurs that host States attempt to restrict the essential freedom of movement of the forces,[43] which is part and parcel of every crisis management SOFA.[44] Likewise, the host States do not always provide the agreed areas and premises required for conducting the mission in time.[45] The host States' attitude in such matters can have a negative impact on the mission.[46] If host States were also to have jurisdiction over foreign forces, they might abuse this right and further obstruct the operation.

This leads to the conclusion that the operational tasks of deployed forces entail the functional necessity of their full criminal immunity both within the framework of crisis management operations and when stationed on allied territory during armed conflict. Immunity is necessary for an effective execution of the operation, and, for this reason it cannot be restricted to acts performed on duty. At the same time, the operational deployment requires that sending States retain control over their forces and exercise criminal jurisdiction over their personnel. For this reason SOFAs emphasise the exclusive jurisdiction of the sending States instead of concentrating on the forces' immunity. In other words, out of operational necessity the forces are subject to the exclusive criminal jurisdiction of the sending State and they enjoy full criminal immunity from the courts of the host State.

In Sect. 9.6.2 it was concluded that the exclusive jurisdiction of sending States over their forces participating in crisis management operations, entailing the forces' full criminal immunity from jurisdiction of the host State's courts, has acquired the status of a customary norm. The operational reasons for full immunity and exclusive criminal jurisdiction put forward in this section shore up that conclusion.

[42] Rubin 2004, p. 178.

[43] An example is the failure to provide a flight clearance in time, which significantly hampered the transport of wounded UN troops participating in the United Nations Interim Security Force for Abyei (UNISFA) by air; *UN Doc* S/2011/603 (2011), Report of the Secretary General on the situation in Abyei, 29 September 2011.

[44] E.g., see Section 12, *Model UN-SOFA* and Article 4, para 5, *Model EU-SOFA*.

[45] E.g., see Section 16–19, *Model UN-SOFA*.

[46] There are other ways host States can obstruct the execution of a mission, for example, by imposing charges and taxes without a legal basis; for example, see Rubin 1999, p. 32. These activities may raise the costs of the mission, but do not endanger the mission's execution.

12.3.3 International Military Cooperation

During armed conflicts and crisis management operations forces remain subject to the sending State's exclusive criminal jurisdiction, which implies that the forces enjoy immunity when executing their extraterritorial tasks. Although the same is true for the framework of international military cooperation (see Chap. 5), there is room for an approach allowing the host State to exercise criminal jurisdiction over foreign forces to some extent.

Similar to the frameworks discussed above, during international military cooperation the visiting forces remain under the political authority and the highest military command of the sending State. Depending on the nature of the cooperation part of the command and control authorities may be transferred to an international commander, for instance, in the context of an international exercise or a multilateral partnership. As a sending State organ the units retain their right to functional immunity.

Such units carry out their tasks in a host State under normal peacetime conditions. Viewed from an operational point of view, these tasks may contribute to keeping up a sufficient level of training and the operational readiness of the unit. To carry out this task, the commander must be able to exercise his command of the unit without interference. However, it is likely that in these circumstances a host State's exercise of its criminal jurisdiction has less impact on the execution of the forces' tasks and, consequently, immunity beyond functional immunity would not strictly be necessary.[47]

From an operational point of view the host State's exercise of criminal jurisdiction may even be preferable in certain circumstances. When the host State cannot exercise its criminal jurisdiction in criminal cases that have shocked a local community, it may affect the locals' acceptance of the foreign forces' presence. If, subsequently, a decision of a judge from the sending State does not meet the local sense of justice,[48] it can give rise to fierce reactions among the local population and authorities and may impede the execution of the forces' tasks. For instance, the acquittal by a US court of US servicemen in Korea,[49] who killed two school

---

[47] For example, at the end of the 1950s US research on the application of the *NATO-SOFA* concluded that "… the criminal jurisdictional arrangements concerning American servicemen abroad have operated satisfactorily, and that they have not adversely affected either the morale or the discipline of the American Forces. It follows clearly that they have not had a detrimental effect on the accomplishment of the important United States military mission in the various countries"; Re 1961, p. 310.

[48] Differences in the legal systems of the sending States, on the one hand, and the host States, on the other, may cause misunderstanding. For instance, the US legal system requires that an offence be proved 'beyond a reasonable doubt'. A host State may have a lower standard of accepting the evidence of an offence; see Lee 2003, p. 235.

[49] The US, having the primary right to jurisdiction, did not respond to the Korean request to waive the right to exercise jurisdiction. This was the first Korean request to the US to waive jurisdiction; Jung and Hwang 2002, p. 1104.

children with their armoured vehicle, led to protests and marches that were also directed against the US military presence in Korea in general.[50] In addition, the Court's decision led to direct actions against US bases and to other activities making the presence of the forces 'less pleasant'.[51]

If international military cooperation is based on defence and security agreements and when the risks of armed conflict increase, the host State's exercise of criminal jurisdiction may indeed impede the preparations of military operations. Cooperation between the host State and the sending State is based on the understanding that the sending State's forces may execute military actions from the territory of the host State, if the security situation so requires. In that case, and similarly in crisis management operations, the commander must be able to deploy his forces to carry out the agreed tasks without interference of the host State exercising criminal jurisdiction.

None of the SOFAs discussed in Part I include a provision that amends the SOFA in accordance with the actual security situation. Nor do SOFAs include a provision that restricts the exercise of criminal jurisdiction by the host State, if the risk of an armed conflict increases. However, some SOFAs allow certain provisions to be suspended or modified in case of hostilities. For instance, the *NATO-SOFA* contains such a provision,[52] but despite the sometimes high threat levels in the Cold War era NATO member States never suspended Art. VII in order to secure more extensive rights of criminal jurisdiction over their forces.

12.4 Misconduct During UN Crisis Management Operations

During crisis management operations the participating forces are subject to the exclusive criminal jurisdiction of the respective sending States. Thus, the jurisdiction of the sending State is emphasised rather than the immunity of the forces. This approach reflects the idea that (as follows from Sect. 12.3.2) the sending States will exercise their criminal jurisdiction, ensuring that servicemen committing crimes abroad will be prosecuted. In an operational setting immunity should not lead to impunity. A decision to refrain from prosecution would not only be difficult to justify legally and morally, but may run counter to the interest of the deployed armed force and the international mission and could damage the image and credibility of the States and international organisations involved as well.

[50] Lee 2003, pp. 215–217 explains that even the apologies of the US President and the Ministers of Foreign Affairs and of Defence could not stop the protests entirely.

[51] Lee 2003, p. 241 enumerates actions, such as the refusal to grant US servicemen entry to shops, but also more aggressive actions, such as firebomb attacks. These actions led to a curfew for US servicemen.

[52] In the event of hostilities the *NATO-SOFA* remains applicable. However the contracting parties may suspend the application of certain provisions (Article XV).

It is especially during the last decades that crisis management operations have been confronted with serious misconduct of participating personnel, which not always resulted in prosecution of the perpetrators by the sending States. This section discusses this topic and the resulting implications for the status of forces. Because of UN experiences in this field and the interest of effective crisis management operations to the organisation this section focuses on the UN practice.

Frequent misconduct, sometimes serious crimes against the local population by personnel participating in UN operations have been the subject of news reports since the 1990s.[53] Media and human rights organisations reports on misconduct in refugee camps in West Africa gave rise to a UN investigation. In the resulting report, the UN Secretary-General confirmed several cases of sexual abuse of girls and women by peacekeepers and civilian staff of the UN in the West African refugee camps.[54]

Some years later the UN was again confronted with reports of misconduct. This time the reports concerned the MONUC-mission in de Democratic Republic of Congo (DRC). An extensive investigation of the Office of Internal Oversight Services shed light on approximately 20 cases of sexual exploitation and abuse by UN peacekeepers from three different contingents[55] and revealed a pattern of sexual exploitation.

In addition to the afflictions suffered by the victims, the fact that the offenders were staff members of the peacekeeping mission, expected to bring relief to the suffering population, had huge negative implications. This is clearly expressed in the 2005 Zeid report, written by the special advisor to the Secretary-General appointed to define a strategy to prevent sexual exploitation and abuse in UN operations[56]:

> Sexual exploitation and abuse damages the image and credibility of a peacekeeping operation and damages its impartiality in the eyes of the local population, which in turn may well impede the implementation of its mandate. The ill discipline engendered by sexual exploitation and abuse also degrades the effectiveness of the peacekeeping operation, especially in times of crisis. Moreover, instances of sexual exploitation and abuse may constitute violations of international humanitarian law, international human rights law or both. Indeed, a peacekeeping operation cannot legitimately advise the Government on adherence to international human rights standards and legal and judicial reform if its own peacekeeping personnel are engaging in acts of sexual exploitation and abuse, including

[53] Odello 2010, p. 350; Background Paper on UN Peacekeeping and The Model Status of Forces Agreement 2010, p. 6. For example, see the reports on the misconduct of forces in, for example, UNOSOM and UNPROFOR; Schmalenbach 2004, pp. 448 et seq.

[54] *UN Doc* A/57/465 (2002), Report of the Secretary General on the activities of the Office of Internal Oversight Services. Investigation into sexual exploitation of refugees by aid workers in West Africa, 11 October 2002.

[55] *UN Doc* A/59/661 (2005), Report of the Secretary General on the activities of the Office of Internal Oversight Services. Investigation by the Office of Internal Oversight Services into allegations of sexual exploitation and abuse in the United Nations Organisation Mission in the Democratic Republic of the Congo, 5 January 2005.

[56] The Zeid report: *UN Doc* A/59/710 (2005), A comprehensive strategy to eliminate future sexual exploitation and abuse in United Nations peacekeeping operations, 24 March 2005, para 10.

> such crimes as rape. Sexual misconduct by peacekeeping personnel can also expose both them and the mission to blackmail and violent retaliation, especially during times of breakdown in law and order in the country. Moreover, such misconduct increases the incidence of medical problems, including the risk of contracting or transmitting sexually transmitted diseases and HIV/AIDS. Victims frequently suffer from psychological trauma as a result of their experiences. Victims and abandoned peacekeeper babies may face stigmatization by their families and communities, which deprive them of all support (economic, social, emotional, etc.). This in turn may push victims into further exploitative relationships with peacekeeping personnel and others in order for them and their children to survive.

Preventing misconduct is also in the interest of the mission. Moreover, officials who misbehave must be punished, which is not always the case, unfortunately.

In 2003, the UN Secretary-General drafted his *Bulletin on special measures for protection from sexual exploitation and sexual abuse,* which contained specific prohibitions on sexual exploitations and abuse.[57] However, the misconducts reported in the DRC demonstrated that the Bulletin did not suffice. The Zeid report drew attention to divergent rules applying to different categories of personnel involved in UN missions,[58] such as experts on mission and forces.[59] As the 2003 UN Secretary-General's Bulletin only applies to the UN Staff, experts on mission and forces fall outside the scope of the Bulletin.[60] Consequently, the report recommended that the Bulletin would apply to all categories.[61]

Section 4.3 already discussed the differences in status between experts on mission and forces. In short, forces are subject to the exclusive criminal jurisdiction of the sending States and experts on mission enjoy functional immunity on the basis of the *Convention on the privileges and immunities of the United Nations*.[62] The UN itself hardly has any possibilities to take action against misconduct and can only start an investigation into allegations of misconduct and repatriate the serviceman involved as an administrative measure.[63]

With respect to forces the initiative to prosecute members of the forces remains the sending States' prerogative, as they have exclusive criminal jurisdiction over their forces. As mentioned above, in practice States sometimes fail to prosecute.

---

57 *UN Doc* ST/SGB/2003/13 (2003), Secretary General's Bulletin on special measures for protection from sexual exploitation and sexual abuse, 9 October 2003.

58 For details, see the Annex to the Zeid report.

59 Like military observers, members of the civilian police falls under the category experts on mission. The other categories consist of the UN staff members, UN volunteers and individual contractors; *UN Doc* A/59/710 (2005), paras 14–18).

60 The Zeid report, para 14.

61 For further information, see the advisory report *UN Doc* A/61/645 (2008), making the standards contained in the Secretary-General's bulletin binding on contingent members and standardising the norms of conduct so that they are applicable to all categories of peacekeeping personnel, 18 December 2008.

62 Different general guidelines are applicable to behaviour and discipline; see the Zeid report, Annex, A14–A35.

63 On the basis of a recommendation of the Head of Mission the Department of Peacekeeping can decide that the serviceman or military observer be repatriated; id., Annex para A26 en A34.

The Zeid report observed that the usual assurances from sending States that they will exercise their jurisdiction in case of well-founded allegations were no longer included in the MOUs on the contribution of forces to the UN-mission and the report advised the reintroduction of such a provision.[64] Furthermore, it was recommended to oblige sending States to inform the UN on the measures taken.[65] In principle, the inclusion of such a clause should be redundant, as the exercise of authority and control over the forces, including the exercise of criminal jurisdiction, is essential for an effective military unit.

Moreover, the report proposed to involve experts from sending States, such as (military) prosecutors, in the investigation into allegations of misconduct. In this way, it can be ascertained that evidence is admissible in the sending State's legal proceedings.[66] In addition, the report recommended that sending States would conduct on-site courts martial[67] which would facilitate access to local witnesses and evidence and demonstrate to the population that misconduct does not go unpunished. Interestingly, the report did not dispute the exclusive criminal jurisdiction of the sending States at all. In other advisory reports and in the literature this jurisdiction also stands as a fact.[68] This confirms the customary nature of the sending States' exclusive criminal jurisdiction over visiting forces during crisis management operations.

In the meantime the UN is still lacking the means to take direct action against misconduct of forces. However, as a result of the report and the subsequent investigations the model-MOU on the contribution of forces to the UN-mission has been amended.[69] It now reads that the sending States' governments must ensure that the forces are required to comply with the standards of conduct included in the Annex to the MOU (Article 7 bis). The commander has to take reasonable measures to maintain the discipline and good order among the members of his contingent (Article 7 ter) and must cooperate in the investigations held by the UN (Article 7 quater). Moreover, the sending States' governments have to assure the UN that they will exercise their jurisdiction (Article 7 quinquiens).

The initiative to initiate criminal proceedings remains with the sending States. Because of the possible damage to the image and credibility of the sending States and the UN prosecution is highly desirable. Viewed from an operational perspective, it can even be considered necessary. The sending State must exercise its authority over the forces to reduce negative consequences for the operation as a whole and to ensure a successful execution of the mission.

---

[64] Id., paras 78–79.

[65] Id., para 79.

[66] Id., para 33.

[67] Id., para 35.

[68] See Odello 2010, p. 358.

[69] Model *Memorandum of understanding between the United Nations and* [*participating State*] *contributing resources to* [*the United Nations Peacekeeping Operation*], *UN Doc A/C.5/63/18* of 29 January 2009.

A somewhat different conclusion can be drawn with regard to the military observers with the status of experts on mission. As mentioned above, they enjoy functional immunity instead of full immunity.[70] Moreover, the Secretary-General can waive the right to immunity, which may not be in the interest of the UN, if the host State does not have an adequately functioning legal system, respecting basic human rights standards.[71] If the Secretary-General does not waive immunity, it remains to be seen whether the respective national courts of the sending States have jurisdiction to prosecute the observer concerned.[72] Filling this legal void is anything but easy. Consequently, the report recommends to establish a group of experts charged with providing further advice and, if considered feasible, with drafting of a new international legal instrument.

In 2006 as a consequence of the Zeid report an advisory group of legal experts recommended that, as far as is possible, host States should exercise jurisdiction over crimes committed by peacekeeping personnel in their territory.[73] If host States lacked that capacity, other States would have to take over the task to avoid impunity.[74] Because of the complexities to fill this jurisdictional gap the group of legal experts provided a draft proposal for a new convention.[75] States do not appear convinced that a new agreement would solve the problem and the issue is still being discussed.

12.5 Conclusion

This chapter has discussed the exercise of criminal jurisdiction over military personnel based abroad with reference to the objectives and tasks arising from the three frameworks for foreign military presence and clarified to what extent operational practice can explain the sending States' exercise of jurisdiction over their forces.

---

[70] Sexual abuse and exploitation do normally not fall under the scope of functional immunity; see *UN Doc* A/60/980, Report of the Group of Legal Experts on ensuring the accountability of United Nations staff and experts on mission with respect to criminal acts committed in peacekeeping operations, 16 August 2006, para 20.

[71] The Zeid report, para 87.

[72] Id., para 88. The UNGA has called upon states to establish jurisdiction over UN officials and experts on mission; *UN Doc* A/RES/62/63/ (2008), Criminal accountability of United Nations officials and experts on mission, 8 January 2008.

[73] *UN Doc* A/60/980, Report of the Group of Legal Experts on ensuring the accountability of United Nations staff and experts on mission with respect to criminal acts committed in peacekeeping operations, 16 August 2006, para 27.

[74] Id., para 46 et seq.

[75] Id., Annex III. This agreement has not yet entered into force; Background Paper on Peacekeeping and The Model Status of Forces Agreement 2010, p. 24.

One of the core themes of military operational law is the law of visiting forces. This discipline includes SOFAs which, apart from containing rights and obligations of the forces of the sending State during their extraterritorial presence, are also instrumental to the commander for mission accomplishment. Therefore, SOFAs must sufficiently take into consideration all aspects related to the foreign presence of the forces and be responsive to operational circumstances and practice. In this sense the SOFA and its provisions on the exercise of criminal jurisdiction over forces expedite access to the foreign host State and facilitate the presence and day-to-day operation of the forces in the host State.

Parts I and II have illustrated that, although functional immunity of State officials is the international standard, military practice gives a subtler view with respect to military personnel. In general, sending States can exercise jurisdiction over their own forces for offences committed either on- or off-duty, to the exclusion of, or priority over, the host State. This practice has been explained partly by arguments brought forward in Part I relating to the specific circumstances of the foreign deployment, on the one hand, and the interests of the States involved and their mutual relations, on the other.

From a military operational point of view additional arguments can be brought forward, which have priority over other considerations under operational conditions.[76] In general, it is pointed out that from the maintenance of morale, one of the basic principles of military operations, flows the necessity to protect forces against the host State's legal system. Furthermore, it has to be noted that specific military offences are normally only punishable by sending States.

In addition, the framework within which the forces operate abroad is of equal importance. If forces are or can be deployed for the execution of armed tasks or in direct support thereof, the military lines of command must be respected in accordance with the unity of effort as a basic principle of military operations. The host State's exercise of its criminal jurisdiction over visiting forces would cut across the military lines of command and can have a detrimental effect on the execution of the operations.

The preceding arguments lead to the conclusion that the operational tasks of the deployed forces bring about the functional necessity of full criminal immunity of these forces. Immunity is necessary to ensure the effective execution of the operation and is, therefore, not only restricted to acts performed on duty, but applies to all acts. In addition to the importance to grant immunity to military personnel, it is even more important for sending States to exercise criminal jurisdiction over their deployed forces. For that reason SOFAs emphasise the exclusive jurisdiction of sending States rather than immunity of the forces. Arguably, the exclusive criminal jurisdiction of the sending States has acquired the status of international customary law.

---

[76] In World War II during the negotiations on the Civil Affairs Agreements military considerations were given priority over any other consideration; Donnison 1961, p. 39.

Viewed from a military operational law perspective, international military cooperation adds to a sufficient level of training and operational readiness of the forces. Functional immunity fits the execution of tasks within this framework. The host State's exercise of jurisdiction over foreign forces does not necessarily conflict with a military commander's command of his forces. A more extensive level of immunity that goes beyond functional immunity would only be required if the risk of hostilities increases and the foreign forces would have to prepare for combat operations.

Immunity granted to military personnel committing offences in the host State must not lead to impunity: sending States must prosecute the servicemen involved. However, cases of sometimes very serious misconduct of military personnel participating in UN operations illustrate that sending States do not always respond adequately. This attitude can seriously hamper the mission and could damage the image and credibility of UN and participating States. Recent UN initiatives aim to ensure that the sending States take their responsibility. In spite of the UN's 'fight against impunity', the full immunity accorded to the servicemen participating in the operations remains beyond discussion.

References

Brouwer HN (2011) Pitbull of embedded prosecution? Het OM en de vervolging van militairen. Militair Rechtelijk Tijdschrift 104:125–135

Donnison FSV (1961) Civil affairs and military government North-West Europe 1944–1946. H.M. Stationery Office, London

Hemmert SG (1999) Peace-keeping mission SOFAs: US interests in criminal jurisdiction. Boston Univ Int Law J 17(1):215–239

Jung Y, Hwang JS (2002) Where does inequality come from? An analysis of the Korea-United States status of forces agreement. Am Univ Int Law Rev 18(5)1103–1144

Knoops GJ (2004) The prosecution and defense of peacekeepers under international criminal law. Transnational Publishers, Ardsley

Lazareff S (1971) Status of military forces under current international law. Sijthoff, Leiden

Lee YHA (2003) Criminal jurisdiction under the US-Korea status of forces agreement: problems to proposals. J Transnational Law Policy 13(1):213–249

Liivoja R (2011) An axiom of military law. Applicability of national criminal law to military personnel and associated civilians abroad. Centre of Excellence in Global Governance Research, Helsinki

Meyer EM (2005) International law: the comptability of the Rome Statute of the International Criminal Court with US bilateral immunity agreements included in the American Servicemembers' Protection Act. Okla Law Rev 58:97–133

Naert F (2008) Accountability for violations of human rights law by EU forces. In: Blockmans S (ed) The European Union and crisis management. T.M.C. Asser Press, The Hague, pp 375–393

Netherlands Defence Doctrine (2013) Defence staff. The Hague

Odello M (2010) Tackling criminal acts in peacekeeping operations: the accountability of peacekeepers. J Conflict Secur Law 15(2):347–391

Oswald B, Bates A (2011) Privileges and immunities of United Nations police. J Int Peacekeeping 14(3):375–402

Oswald B, Durham H, Bates A (2010) Documents on the law of peace operations. Oxford University Press, Oxford

Re ED (1961) Status of Forces Agreements: the American experience. St. John's Law Rev 35(2):306–322

Rosenfeld E (2003) Application of the US Status of Forces Agreements to article 98 of the Rome Statute. Wash Univ Global Studies Law Rev 2:273–293

Rubin GR (1999) Peace support operations and practical legal problems 'on the ground'. RUSI Journal 144(6):27–35

Rubin GR (2004) United Kingdom SOFAs and rules of engagement in Yugoslavia: some further reflections. In: Carey J, Dunlap W, Pritchard J (eds) International humanitarian law challenges. Transnational Publishers, Ardsley, pp 175–199

Sari A (2008) The jurisdictional immunities of visiting forces under public international law. A case study of the European security and defence policy (not published; on file with author)

Scheffer D (2003) Restoring US engagement with the International Criminal Court. Wis Int Law J 21(3):599–609

Schmalenbach K (2004) Die Haftung internationaler Organisationen im Rahmen von Militäreinsätzen und Territorialverwaltungens. Peter Lang, Frankfurt am Main

Snee JM (1961) NATO Agreements on Status: Traveaux préparatoires. International law studies, vol 54. Naval War College, Newport

Stanger RJ (1957/1958) Criminal jurisdiction over visiting armed forces. International law studies, vol. LII. Naval War College, Newport

Stone TD (2006) US–Japan SOFA: a necessary document worth preserving. Naval Law Rev 53:229–258

van den Wilt H (2005) Bilateral agreements between the United States and state parties to the Rome Statute: Are they compatible with the object and purpose of the Statute? Leiden J Int Law 18(1):93–111

Vandiver J (2011) Curfew put in place for all US troops in South Korea. In: Stars and stripes 7 Oct 2011

Wexler I (2008) A comfortable SOFA: The need for an equitable foreign criminal jurisdiction agreement with Iraq. Naval Law Rev 56:43–86

Zappalà S (2003) The reaction of the US to the entry into force of the ICC statute: comments on UN SC Resolution 1422 (2002) and Article 98 agreements. J Int Crim Justice 1(1):114–13

Chapter 13
Specific SOFA Provisions

Abstract Viewed from a military operational law perspective, SOFAs support the effective execution of a military mission by expediting the entry into a foreign State and by facilitating and supporting the forces' presence and operations. Therefore, SOFAs may address a wide range of subjects, including criminal jurisdiction, civil immunities, privileges and other rights and obligations. All provisions are closely linked and can have an impact on the exercise of criminal jurisdiction over the deployed forces, like provisions on the use of armed force and the settlement of claims for damages.

Contents

13.1 Introduction

The previous chapters concentrated on criminal jurisdiction as the central feature of SOFAs. In combination with other provisions SOFAs aim to expedite visiting armed forces' entry into foreign States and to facilitate the presence and operational activities of these forces on foreign territory. Viewed from a military operational law angle, SOFAs can be considered as an instrument that helps commanders achieve their foreign mission. To this end SOFAs, in addition to the provisions on criminal jurisdiction, include provisions on civil immunities, privileges and other rights and obligations. All provisions together are closely linked

© T.M.C. ASSER PRESS and the author 2015

J. Voetelink, *Status of Forces: Criminal Jurisdiction over Military Personnel Abroad*,
DOI 10.1007/978-94-6265-057-2_13

and form a coherent structure. Consequently, considering one element requires the consideration of the whole structure. As provisions on the use of armed force and settlement of claims are closely linked with criminal jurisdiction, these topics call for special attention. This chapter addresses the question how these specific SOFA-provisions may affect the exercise of criminal jurisdiction by sending States.

SOFAs often include a provision requiring members of armed forces to respect local law, which is subject to further consideration in Sect. 13.2. State armed forces constitute the State's right of the sword: the right to use armed force in executing their tasks is inherent to their military status. When stationed abroad, depending on the circumstances, use of force may sometimes be inevitable. If armed force is used, it has to have a clear legal foundation and be justified by special instructions on the use of force. The instructions must be in accordance with criminal law of the State that is entitled to exercise jurisdiction based on custom or treaty (Sect. 13.3).

In contrast to criminal immunity, civil immunity of foreign forces hardly causes any controversy. However, it has to be noted that the adoption of supplementary procedures for the settlement of claims is crucial to enhance the local population's acceptance of the foreign forces' presence (Sect. 13.4). In the course of time these claims procedures have progressively developed and claims-provisions ultimately became a standard element of SOFAs. Supplementary procedures may indeed have an impact on the exercise of criminal jurisdiction as a sending State's flexible and expedient approach to settle claims may cause host States to waive their exercise of criminal jurisdiction.

13.2 Respect for Local Law

Many SOFAs contain a provision that instructs soldiers from sending States in how to respect host State law.[1] For example, Article II of the *NATO-SOFA* reads:

> It is the duty of a force and its civilian component and the members thereof as well as their dependents to respect the law of the receiving State.[2]

This provision begs the question: What does respect for local law really mean?[3] In the literature experts sometimes refer to the psychological aim of the provision

[1] Some SOFAs contain a supplementary obligation to respect local customs, traditions and conventions; e.g., Article 3(1) *Agreement between the United States of America and the Republic of Iraq on the withdrawal of US forces from Iraq and the organisation of their activities during their temporary presence in Iraq*; 17 November 2008. www.state.gov/documents/organization/122074.pdf. Accessed November 2014.

[2] Other examples are: Section 6 *Model UN-SOFA* and Article 2(1) *Model EU-SOFA*. Moreover, this obligation is not a typical SOFA provision, but is also used in other international agreements, e.g., the *Vienna Convention on diplomatic relations* (Article 41).

[3] For example, Zwanenburg observes that in crisis management operations, it is not realistic to require the full respect for local laws. He holds that in these situations the law of the sending State may occasionally prevail, e.g., in the field of labour law; Zwanenburg 2008, p. 30.

that reflects the mutual respect between NATO States.[4] Such an interpretation seems to suggest that the provision is a mere duty of courtesy to take host State law into account. Other authors are of the opinion that host State law only applies to the extent in which it has been incorporated in the law of the sending States,[5] which reduces the scope of the duty to respect local laws.

In my opinion, the requirement to respect host State law is related to legislative jurisdiction and the applicability of law. In Chap. 6 it was established that on the basis of the territorial principle States have the power to apply their laws within the borders of their territory. Other jurisdiction principles allow them to extend application of their laws to a certain extent beyond their borders as well. However, extraterritorial application of legislative jurisdiction does not affect other States' laws. Host State law continues to apply and SOFA provisions dealing with respect for local laws are, strictly speaking, superfluous: visiting forces have to observe it.

However, parties to a SOFA may agree upon restrictions on the exercise and applicability of host State law by granting immunities and privileges.[6] Granting immunities does not imply that host States waive their legislative powers. Their laws continue to apply to the foreign visiting forces that enjoy immunity.[7] Therefore, officials who enjoy immunity are not exempt from the duties imposed by local law.[8] Immunity concerns adjudicative and enforcement jurisdiction resulting in host States refraining from enforcing their laws and starting legal proceedings against officials enjoying immunity. Therefore, immunity is not substantive law, but a formal, procedural rule.[9]

If this were different and host State law would not apply to officials enjoying immunity, this could cause problems. If, for instance, a sending State waived

[4] Lazareff 1971, pp. 100–101.

[5] According to Häussler, local law is only applicable to foreign military personnel to the extent they are integrated into the legal framework of an operation, such as the Operations Plan, including the Rules of Engagement and Standing Operating Procedures; Häussler 2007, p. 59; see also; Burke 2011, p. 67.

[6] See Lazareff 1971, p. 102.

[7] ILC preliminary report 2008, para 64. If the sending State declares its legislation applicable to the forces based abroad, servicemen have to comply with both legal systems.

[8] Schermers and Blokker 2003, p. 1025, para 1612.

[9] Wouters and Naert 2002, p. 5. The ECHR observed in this context: "The grant of immunity is to be seen not as qualifying a substantive right but as a procedural bar ...", ECHR 21 November 2001, *Al-Adsani v. the United Kingdom*, Application no. 35763/97, para 48. The Court considered that in case a State waives its immunity, the action will proceed to a hearing and judgment; see also: EHRM, 21 November 2001, *McElhinney v. Ireland*, Application no. 31253/96, para 25: "The grant of immunity is to be seen not as qualifying a substantive right but as a procedural bar on the national courts' power to determine the right".

immunity of a serviceman who committed murder in the host State, host State law would only become applicable when the sending State waives the immunity, meaning that at the moment the serviceman committed murder that crime would not have been punishable according to local host State law.[10]

Applicability of host State law to foreign officials or to staff members of international organisations is not always desirable and necessary. Therefore, host States may grant officials privileges with regard to specific regulations,[11] mostly in the field of customs, fiscal law, and social security law. Unlike immunities, privileges are not procedural but substantive in nature and exempt officials from certain host State obligations or rules. As these rules do not apply to officials adjudication and enforcement of these rules is not an issue.[12]

Closely connected to privileges are international practices based on international courtesy. Strictly speaking, these practices do not oblige host States to refrain from applying national rules, although this is what is generally the case. For example, on the basis of Article 27(3) of the *Vienna Convention on diplomatic relations*[13] a diplomatic bag of a diplomatic mission is not to be opened by a host State. This prohibition does not extend to a diplomat's suitcase. However, it is international practice to leave the suitcases untouched, unless there are reasonable assumptions that the diplomat has violated host State law.

As mentioned above, the requirement to respect local law is without prejudice to host State legislative jurisdiction and, therefore, foreign visiting forces are subject to local law. However, host State law may not be entirely applicable to the visiting forces as parties to SOFAs may agree upon exceptions to host State law that take the form of immunities or privileges. Consequently, the formulation in SOFA "to respect local law" means that forces are subject to the laws of the host States except where agreed immunities and privileges are exceptions in their favour. Use of the term 'respect', therefore, is not without obligation and reflects a legally binding duty.[14]

---

[10] In the literature reference is also made to complicity. For instance, if a person would aid another person enjoying immunity to commit a murder and immunity would imply non-applicability of the law, the other person could not have violated local law and the person not having immunity cannot be prosecuted as an accomplice, as there is no crime to begin with; Liivoja 2010, p. 48.

[11] Zieck 2007, p. 283.

[12] See Wouters and Naert 2002, p. 6.

[13] *Vienna Convention on diplomatic relations*; Vienna, 18 April 1961 (Vol. 500 *UNTS* 1964, Nr. 7310).

[14] Today, the duty to respect host State law reflects nothing less than a legal duty to obey these laws; Denza 2004, p. 374.

13.3 Use of Force

States have the exclusive right to use armed force.[15] They dispose of armed forces which are equipped and trained to exercise this right. National legislation provides the legal basis for deployment of these forces and regulates the use of force.[16] When deployed abroad, the visiting forces' right to carry arms and use armed force is also subject to host State law and international law. Generally, local law restricts or even prohibits the right to carry arms and use force. The following subsections discuss exceptions resulting from SOFAs, Rules of Engagement and the right to self-defence, and their link with criminal jurisdiction.

13.3.1 SOFA

Most SOFAs contain the right to bear arms,[17] to which the host State may attach conditions, for example, to carry arms only during specific activities.[18] However, few SOFAs deal with the use of arms or any other use of force. For instance, the Dutch-Ukrainian agreement concluded in the aftermath of the downing of flight MH17 on 17 July 2014 allowed members of the multinational International Mission "to possess and carry weapons and to use force in self-defense and for fulfillment of its activities under this Agreement".[19] Various SOFAs on crisis management operations include indirect references when emphasising respect for international humanitarian law.[20] Some SOFAs contain specific provisions. For

[15] In a democratic State governed by the rule of law the monopoly on the use of armed force is not absolute because self-defence of citizens is still an option in case the State cannot fully guarantee their security; see Advisory Committee on armed private protection against piracy, Chap. 2.

[16] See Ducheine 2008, p. 27.

[17] E.g., Article VI *NATO-SOFA*.

[18] E.g., the SOFA between the Netherlands and Rwanda allows military personnel to possess and carry arms only during their participation in exercises: Article 5 *Agreement between the Kingdom of the Netherlands and the Republic of Rwanda concerning the status of military and civilian personnel of their Ministry of Defence present in each other's territory for activities related to bilateral military cooperation*; Kigali, 13 May 2009 (*Dutch Treaty Series* 2009, 114).

[19] Article 3.1. *Agreement between the Kingdom of the Netherlands and Ukraine on the International Mission for Protection of Investigation*; Kiev, 8 July 2014 (*Dutch Treaty Series* 2014, 135).

[20] E.g., Section 3 of the Secretary-Generals's Bulletin Observance by United Nations Forces of International Humanitarian Law states that SOFAs adopted by the UN should require that operations are executed in accordance with humanitarian law (*UN Doc* ST/SGB/1999/13 (1999), Secretary-Generals's Bulletin Observance by United Nations Forces of International Humanitarian law, 6 August 1999). For an enumeration of SOFAs containing such a provision, see: Background Paper on UN Peacekeeping and The Model Status of Forces Agreement 2010, p. 33.

instance, Article 12 of the *Supplementary Agreement* with Germany states that personnel "responsible for safeguarding of cash or property or are particularly endangered by the special nature of their official position or activities" may carry and possess arms and use them in conformity with specially drafted provisions based on the German right to self-defence ('Notwehr').[21] The SOFA between the Netherlands and Rwanda allows the use of firearms only during training activities on locations specified by the host State. The 2008 SOFA between Iraq and the US is somewhat different in the sense that provisions were included on the execution of operations by US forces.[22] However, many SOFAs, such as the *NATO-SOFA*, do not mention the use of arms.[23]

13.3.2 Rules of Engagement

The lack of provisions on the use of armed force in SOFAs is striking in the sense that in general the use of force must conform to criminal law, to which end SOFAs provide for a balanced right to exercise jurisdiction.[24] This section analyses military directives on the use of force, the so-called Rules of Engagement (ROE), and the possible criminal implications of the use of force. Within this context the layered structure of the law of visiting forces must be kept in mind. As explained in Sect. 10.3.2, SOFAs do not stand alone, but, instead, build on the general and specific legal bases for the foreign presence of visiting forces. Authority to use force flows from the same legal bases. For instance, if the legal basis is a defence agreement, in which States agree to assist each other in the event of an armed attack, it is obvious that when a State is attacked and allied States send their armed forces to help, the sending States forces may use their fighting power. Or, if the legal basis is a UN mandate for a crisis management operation, the participating forces must be able to use arms when implementing the mandate. Also, the nature of the mission may require additional authority relating to the use of force, e.g. arrest and detention.

These legal bases do not specify the extent to which use of force is allowed. This can be found in another part of military operational law: the ROE, which NATO defines as:

> directives to military forces (including individuals) that define the circumstances, conditions, degree, and manner in which force, or actions which might be construed as provocative, may be applied.

[21] Article 12(1)(2) *Supplementary agreement to the NATO Agreement regarding the Status of Forces with respect to Foreign Forces stationed in the Federal Republic of Germany*; Bonn, 3 August 1959 (Vol. 481 *UNTS* 1963, No. 6986).

[22] In particular, see Article 4(5): "The Parties retain the right to legitimate self defense within Iraq, as defined in applicable international law."

[23] Mason 2012, p. 6.

[24] Moreover, this is a case of extraterritorial exercise of a State's enforcement jurisdiction that requires explicit host State consent.

ROE are a political and operational instrument to control the use of force within the applicable legal frameworks,[25] such as international law and national law of the States involved.[26] States involved in a joint mission shall individually[27] or jointly adopt ROE.[28] In case of crisis management operations, the organisations that are in charge of the operations will undertake this task.

Whether and to what extent States recognise the legal implications of ROE depends on the laws of the States involved.[29] For military personnel who may have to use force during operations abroad it is important that their actions are tested against the law on which their training on Tactics, Techniques and Procedures (TTPs) with respect to the use of force are based. As armed force should in principle be used in the line of duty, for which military personnel enjoy functional immunity, this should not cause any problems. If, however, military action would have to be tested against host State law every time States deploy their forces, TTPs and training would have to be geared to host State law as well. This aspect further reinforces the necessity to grant the sending States' forces (functional) immunity.

Another issue is the level of secrecy.[30] ROE are a commander's instrument to execute the mission, which, viewed from an operational perspective, may make secrecy necessary. If host States do not participate in that mission, which is normally the case in crisis management operations, they will not have access to classified operational documents, like ROE. As a result ROE cannot be taken into consideration during criminal procedures before host States' courts.

13.3.3 Right to Self-defence

Regardless of how and to what extent use of force is laid down in SOFAs or ROE, the individual right to self-defence constitutes an independent legal basis for the use of force. The formulation and interpretation of the right to self-defence depend on national law. This means that if a serviceman based abroad avails himself of his right of self-defence and if the host State exercises criminal jurisdiction under the applicable SOFA, the serviceman's action will be reviewed in accordance with

---

25 NATO Legal Deskbook 2010, p. 254.

26 E.g., Boddens Hosang 2003, pp. 354–370; van Diepenbrugge 2003, pp. 371–375.

27 In this case, implementation of the different ROEs must be coordinated at the highest level of command.

28 Cathcart 2010, p. 203.

29 NATO Legal Deskbook 2010, p. 257. For example, according to Article 38 Dutch *Military Penal Code* ROE may justify the individual serviceman's military action.

30 Dolman et al. 2005, p. 393.

host State law.[31] However, if the sending State has the right to exercise jurisdiction, the action will be judged on the sending States' rules on self-defence.

In general, military personnel will only be authorised to bear arms in the performance of their duties. Under these circumstances they enjoy at least functional immunity from the host States' jurisdiction and the sending States' courts will review the use of force as an act of self-defence. This is important because the visiting forces' TTPs and training are based on sending State law. If this were different, visiting military personnel would have to get acquainted with and trained in local self-defence procedures for every foreign mission.

The application of different rules of self-defence by foreign forces can entail certain risks for host States, if the local population gets in contact with visiting forces who in the exercise of their right to self-defence apply rules and procedures that are less strict than the rules and procedures the local population is accustomed to. The risks will be most apparent in peacetime conditions, when the use of force by foreign soldiers is unlikely. States can reduce the risks by, for instance, restricting the right to bear arms or leaving the armed protection of the sending States' personnel and equipment to host State authorities.[32]

13.4 Claims

Acts of sending States' forces, particularly in case of their enduring presence of large contingents, almost inevitably cause physical harm to local citizens and damage to their property.[33] These kinds of damages, often resulting from traffic accidents, can be a source of irritation and harm the relationship between the States involved. If damages are due by criminal offences, a flexible and fair settlement by the sending States may be an incentive for host States to waive their jurisdiction and reduce or take away negative feelings amongst the indigenous population.

As is the case with respect to criminal jurisdiction over visiting armed forces, State immunity plays a major role in the discussion on the settlement of claims. To the extent in which sending States' acts can be considered *acta jure imperii*, State

[31] Military personnel serving abroad must be aware of differences between host State law and sending State law. It could be an option to provide them with a pocket card describing their rights under the SOFA; a sort of 'emergency jurisdictional chit'; see Norman and Leary 2010, p. 39.

[32] MOUs on military cooperation often include the understanding that host States will be responsible for the security of specific sites or areas in use by the visiting forces. Sending States may then be authorised to guard and protect special objects within the secured sites.

[33] Host States, sending States and members of the sending State's forces may also suffer damage. However, damage to local host State citizens happens more frequently. It may have a considerable impact on host States and may also affect the exercise of criminal jurisdiction. Therefore, this section concentrates on the latter cases of claims.

immunity prevents the injured local citizen's access to host State courts. Although international law allows for exceptions to State immunity in case of wrongful acts, these exceptions normally do not apply to acts of the armed forces.[34]

Of course, injured citizens may initiate an action for damages before the sending States' courts.[35] In the case of minor damages, however, this option would hardly be worthwhile for an average person, leaving him without a viable option to compensate for the damage. If a realistic judicial process is not available to injured citizens, they may end up bearing the loss themselves. From a legal point of view this is not an acceptable outcome due to the general principle of law that "requires that those who cause an injury to others compensate them".[36] Furthermore, the situation does not contribute to the local population's acceptance of the foreign forces.[37]

Today settlement of claims is a common element of SOFAs, of which Article VIII(5) of the *NATO-SOFA* is a clear example.[38] In short, the NATO procedure provides that third-party claims, arising from acts or omissions of members of the forces done in performance of official duty, are processed by the host State in accordance with its national laws and regulations. Thus, host State residents having suffered damage can claim compensation from their own government. The costs incurred in satisfying the claims are divided between host State and Sending State in the proportion of 25 per cent to the host State and 75 per cent to the sending State. The drafters of the NATO SOFA deemed the distribution of costs necessary to prevent host States from sufficiently considering the sending State's interests.

Eventually, sending States have the final responsibility to pay money in compensation for damages. However, host States may take, as it were, the sending States' place in the legal procedures,[39] which prevents sending States from becoming directly involved in the claims process. This approach maintains the principle

[34] See Article 11 *European Convention on State Immunity* and Article 12 *UN Convention on Jurisdictional immunities of States and their property.* Both provisions are not applicable to activities of armed forces; see e.g., Gattini 2011, p. 175.

[35] See House of Lords 13 June 2006, *Al-Skeini and others (Respondents) v. Secretary of State for Defence*, [2007] UKHL 26. www.publications.parliament.uk/pa/ld200607/ldjudgmt/jd070613/skeini-1.pdf. Accessed November 2014 and the Court of Appeal of The Hague 5 July 2011, *Srebrenica, LJN* BR0132 en BR0133.

[36] Reisman and Sloane, p. 514.

[37] This aspect most likely contributed to the adoption of Article VIII(6) *NATO-SOFA*, which gives the sending State the possibility to propose an ex gratia payment for damages resulting from acts not done in the performance of duty; see Lazareff 1971, pp. 345 and 355.

[38] The draft texts of the claims provisions build on two principles: immunity of the sending State and, as a corollary, "a procedure for compensation to ensure that damage should not be caused without being covered by compensation"; see id., p. 277.

[39] However, the host State itself is not legally responsible for settling the claims. Therefore, the procedure of substitution seems purely procedural; id., p. 321.

of State immunity. With regard to the injured citizens, *NATO-SOFA* thus provides an accessible procedure conducted in their native tongue. Many bilateral SOFAs use similar or somewhat simplified arrangements, which all build on the same approach.[40]

Settlement of claims can affect the exercise of criminal jurisdiction over sending States' armed forces.[41] When foreign soldiers commit crimes causing damage in the process, the injured citizens' interests are best served by a fair and swift settlement of the claims. When sending States are able and willing to follow such procedures, that could be reason for a host State to consider waiving its jurisdiction depending on the nature of the offence and other circumstances.[42]

When damage is caused by a criminal offence and the sending State exercises its criminal jurisdiction, the court decision may not respond to the local population's sense of justice. A rapid claims settlement may take away possible negative feelings, which is well-illustrated by the tragic cable car incident near the village of Cavelese in northern Italy in 1998. A US EA-6B Prowler aircraft on a low-level training flight cut the line of a cable-car causing a gondola to crash, killing 20 people,[43] while the airplane itself managed to return safely to its base in Aviano.

An Italian court found that the US had primary jurisdiction pursuant to Article VII(3)(a)(ii) of the *NATO-SOFA*.[44] In the ensuing trial a US court martial acquitted the pilot charged with involuntary manslaughter and negligent homicide. The verdict was received with outrage in Italy and other NATO member States where the victims came from. The US countered criticism by emphasising that it accepted its responsibility and referred to the compensation granted to the relatives of the victims, who were offered an advance payment of $100.000 each to cover immediate expenses and additional claims would soon be settled on the basis of *NATO-SOFA*.[45]

---

[40] E.g., Article VII(3) *Accord entre le gouvernment du Royaume des Pays-Bas et le gouvernement de la Republique du Senegal portant sur le status des forces*; Dakar, 18 October 2010 (*Dutch Treaty Series* 2010, 320): "Les demandes d'indemnité de tiers pour toute perte, tout dommage ou toute blessure (autres que les indemnités contractuelles) causes par le personnel de l'Etat d'envoi seront réglées par l'Etat d'accueil pour le compte de l'Etat d'envoi conformément aux lois et réglementations de l'Etat d'accueil. Les coûts lies au règlement d'une telle demande seront remboursés par l'Etat d'envoi".

[41] Mullins 1966, p. 84.

[42] Stephenson 1994, p. 208.

[43] The victims came from Germany, Belgium, Italy, Poland, the Netherlands and Austria.

[44] Ciampi 1999a, pp. 220–224.

[45] Reisman and Sloane 2000, p. 509. A bill proposed by the US Senator Robb to offer funds to pay compensation was not approved. The Senator justified the bill by warning that the accident and the resulting acquittal of the pilot would harm the reputation of the US. In his opinion, an amount of $40 million in compensation funds would largely make up for the possible costs of the ruined reputation of the US with its forces being based worldwide.

In 1999, in accordance with Article VIII(5) of the *NATO-SOFA,* Italy paid $42 million compensation to the relatives of the victims.[46] In addition, the US reserved $20 million to rebuild the cable car line, although that was not required under the *NATO-SOFA*.[47] Such voluntary "supplementary strategic compensation procedures" can be decisive in avoiding the loss of local support for the foreign military presence.[48]

13.5 Conclusion

This chapter has analysed several specific topics that are directly or indirectly related to criminal jurisdiction over armed forces stationed abroad and may be part of SOFAs. SOFAs can be elaborate documents, containing the core provisions on criminal jurisdiction, as well as including provisions on a range of other topics. All these provisions do not stand alone, but have to be considered in relation to each other. Besides provisions on criminal jurisdiction, characteristic of SOFAs, contemporary SOFAs also include provisions on civil law immunities. Furthermore, host States may grant privileges to the sending States' forces to the effect that specific parts of host State law no longer apply to the foreign forces. As a consequence, they are not fully subject to local law, but have the duty to respect it.

Provisions on the use of force are less frequently included in SOFAs. One of the reasons is the multi-layered structure of the law of visiting forces, which means that the authorization for visiting forces to use force flows directly from the legal bases for their presence abroad. In that case, detailed provisions on the extent to which force can be used are generally set out in ROE. Moreover, in the event of direct attacks each serviceman has the inherent right to self-defence, which does not necessarily have to be included in SOFAs.

Viewed from an operational law perspective, it is important that in all these cases, the use of force is considered in accordance with sending State law. TTPs on the use of force are based on sending State law. Use of armed force will normally result from the performance of official duty, implying that the visiting forces enjoy immunity. If military personnel did not enjoy immunity the use of force would have to be judged against local law. This would entail that the visiting forces TTPs would have to be geared to host State law.

Next to provisions on criminal jurisdiction, current SOFAs always include a provision on the settlement of claims arising from the acts and omissions of the sending State's forces affecting citizens of the host State. Viewed from an

[46] The political pressure to reach a settlement was the reason to start a special procedure and to regulate the compensation by law; Ciampi 1999b, p. 118. Based on para e of the provision, the US paid 75 % of these costs to Italy; Reisman and Sloane 2000, p. 513.

[47] Id., p. 513. Article VIII(2) states that an arbitrator may determine the amount of damages to non-military properties of a State.

[48] Id., p. 516.

operational law perspective, procedures on the settlement of claims are paramount for the preservation of the local population's acceptance of the foreign forces' presence. Swift and fair settlements of claims may avert the emergence of a negative attitude due to harmful behaviour. Furthermore, settlement procedures may benefit criminal adjudication. If a sending State is able and willing to swiftly and fairly settle claims resulting from offences committed by the visiting forces, the host State may be less hesitant to waive the exercise of its jurisdiction if so requested.

However, a sending State's criminal proceedings may not respond to the sense of justice of the host State population. The possible resulting negative attitude may partly be taken away if the sending State demonstrates its responsibility and involvement by compensating any damage done to the local population in an expedient way.

References

Advisory Committee on Armed Private Protection Against Piracy (2011) The monopoly on the use of force and piracy (in Dutch). www.nvkk.nl/files/3113/6223/9641/Artikel20110901_Rapport_Commissie_de_Wijkerslooth_-_Geweldsmonopolie_Piraterij.pdf. Accessed November 2014

Boddens Hosang JFR (2003) Rules of Engagement, het politiek-juridisch struikelblok voor de militaire commandant. Militair Rechtelijk Tijdschrift 96:354–370

Burke R (2011) Status of forces deployed on UN peacekeeping operations: jurisdictional immunity. J Conflict Security Law 16(1):63–104

Cathcart B (2010) Application of force and rules of engagement in self-defence operations. In: Gill TD, Fleck D (eds) The handbook of international law of military operations. Oxford University Press, New York, pp 201–211

Ciampi A (1999a) Public prosecutor v. ashby. Judgement No. 161/98. AJIL 93(1):219–224

Ciampi A (1999b) Compensating victims of the cermis cable-car accident under NATO Status of forces agreement. Ital Yearb Int Law 9(1):113–123

Denza E (2004) Diplomatic law. A commentary on the vienna convention on diplomatic relations. Oxford University Press, Oxford

Dolman MM, Ducheine PAL, Gill TD, Walgemoed GF (2005) Functioneel geweldgebruik in internationale operaties: een spiegel van rechtspraak en praktijk. Militair Rechtelijk Tijdschrift 98:369–420

Ducheine PAL (2008) Krijgsmacht, geweldgebruik and terrorismebestrijding. Een onderzoek naar juridische aspecten van de rol van strijdkrachten bij de bestrijding van terrorisme. Wolf Legal Publishers, Oisterwijk

Gattini A (2011) The dispute on jurisdictional immunities of the State before the ICJ: is the time ripe for a change of the law? Leiden J Int Law 24(1):173–200

Häussler U (2007) The limits of law enforcement by peacekeeping operations in accordance with SOFAs, ROEs and SOPs. In: Arnold R (ed) Law enforcement within the framework peace support operations. Brill, Leiden, pp 53–73

Lazareff S (1971) Status of military forces under current international law. Sijthoff, Leiden

Liivoja R (2010) The criminal jurisdiction of states: a theoretical primer. J Extreme Legal Positivism 7:25–58

Mason RC (2012) Status of Forces Agreement (SOFA): What is it, and how has it been utilized. CRS Report for Congress, Congressional Research Service

Mullins WR (1966) The international responsibility of a State for torts of its military forces. Mil Law Rev 34:59–100

NATO Legal Deskbook 2010

Norman RE, Leary RW (2010) Making a molehill out of a mountain: the U.S. army counterinsurgency doctrine applied to operational law in Iraq. The Army Lawyer May 2010:22–42

Reisman WM, Sloane RD (2000) The incident at Cavalese and strategic compensation. AJIL 94(3):505–515

Schermers HG, Blokker NM (2003) International institutional law. Martinus Nijhoff Publishers, Leiden

Stephenson DP (1994) An introduction to the payment of claims under the Foreign and International Agreement Claims Act. Air Force Law Rev 37:191–210

van Diepenbrugge JA (2003) Geweldgebruik in het kader van vredesoperaties: Leidt integratie van politieke, juridische en operationele aspecten in de Rules of Engagement tot vage en multi-interpretabele regels? Militair Rechtelijk Tijdschrift 96:271–275

Wouters J, Naert F (2002) Internationale immuniteiten in de Belgische rechtspraktijk. Working Paper Nr. 34—oktober 2002, Instituut voor Internationaal Recht, Louvain, Belgium

Zieck M (2007) Diplomatiek en consulair recht. In: Horbach N, Lefeber R, Ribbelink O (eds) Handboek internationaal recht, T.M.C. Asser Press, The Hague, pp. 275–308

Zwanenburg M (2008) UN peace operations between independence and accountability. Int Organ Law Rev 5(1):23–47

Part IV
Synthesis and Conclusion

Chapter 14
Synthesis and Conclusion

Abstract The status of visiting armed forces and especially criminal jurisdiction over those forces has a firm basis in international law. Military operational law offers additional points of reference, further defining the theory on the status of forces with respect to forces deployed abroad in three different frameworks: during armed conflict, participating in crisis management operations and during international military cooperation. Building on that theory the development of a Status-of-Forces Compendium is proposed, as a practical tool for drafting and using SOFAs.

Contents

14.1 Introduction

This book focuses on the theory of criminal jurisdiction over military personnel stationed abroad with host State consent and has a twofold aim. First and foremost, it brings together the international law and military operational law perspective contributing within this common legal framework to the theory that forms the basis of criminal jurisdiction over armed forces during the

© T.M.C. ASSER PRESS and the author 2015

J. Voetelink, *Status of Forces: Criminal Jurisdiction over Military Personnel Abroad*,
DOI 10.1007/978-94-6265-057-2_14

extraterritorial execution of their tasks. Second, this book incorporates this theory in a proposal to develop a practical tool for drafting and using SOFAs.

Part I of the book keys in on the development of criminal jurisdiction over visiting forces over the past two centuries and the particular circumstances under which the forces are stationed abroad. Part II analyses the role and development of criminal jurisdiction over visiting armed forces from the international law perspective, while Part III takes military operational law as the point of departure for analysis.

This concluding chapter combines the results of these three parts and formulates a theory of criminal jurisdiction over military personnel stationed abroad (Sect. 14.2). Building on this theory, it is proposed to draft a Status-of-Forces Compendium that may serve as a guideline for drafting and applying SOFAs (Sect. 14.3). This chapter ends with a brief conclusion.

14.2 The Theory

State sovereignty is a central element of international law. Throughout the centuries the sovereign State has evolved into an entity functioning independently of a higher authority as an equal of other States. For the exercise of their duties sovereign States may have armed forces at their disposal: an institution that today constitutes the State's exclusive instrument of force to safeguard its internal and external security. Armed forces, therefore, are inextricably linked with the State, even if deployed outside its territory.

The next sections formulate the theory of criminal jurisdiction over military personnel stationed abroad. *The Exchange v. McFaddon* case is taken as point of departure leading to the identification of the ground rule on status of forces (Sect. 14.2.1). Next, functional immunity is addressed as a rule of international law applicable to all State officials, including members of the armed forces (Sect. 14.2.2). In Sect. 14.2.3 the role of SOFAs as a commanders' instrument is discussed. The final section puts criminal jurisdiction over visiting forces in a wider perspective by linking the points of departure for military operational law with the different frameworks for foreign military presence.

14.2.1 The Exchange v. McFaddon as Basis

Until approximately two centuries ago criminal jurisdiction over military personnel stationed abroad did not raise any issues in international State practice. Therefore, no case law on the issue was to be found until 24 February 1812 when the US Supreme Court in *The Exchange v. McFaddon* case touched upon the issue for the first time. This case serves as the point of departure for this book. In *The Exchange v. McFaddon* case Chief Justice Marshall considered that granting a free passage to foreign military forces implied a waiver of the host State's jurisdiction over the visiting forces and permitted its commander to exercise his jurisdiction. In later case law this consideration was extended from the transit of forces to the presence of foreign forces and was to play a key role in discussions and reflections on criminal jurisdiction over military personnel for a long time.

Many articles on status of forces refer to the 1812 Supreme Court's decision. The reference is remarkable if one considers that the case is very different from today's situation, as the decision in *The Exchange v. McFaddon* case was reached at a time when the peacetime presence of armed forces on foreign territory generally had a temporary and small-scale character. Furthermore, the decision fits the doctrine of absolute State immunity that was emerging in the early nineteenth century, granting State organs immunity from the exercise of adjudicative and enforcement jurisdiction of other States. According to this doctrine military forces, as organs of sending States, enjoy immunity from host State jurisdiction.

Chief Justice Marshall stated that immunity could only exist, if the host State had consented to the presence of the foreign forces. This is a legitimate point when viewed from an international law perspective, as the entry of armed forces into the territory of other States without their consent or any other international legal basis, such as a mandate of the UN Security Council, may constitute an international wrongful act. Obviously, in similar situations it cannot be assumed that States have waived their jurisdiction. Should incursions of foreign armed forces lead to an armed conflict, the situation would further develop and the presence of foreign forces would have to be considered in accordance with the law of armed conflict.

During the nineteenth century the doctrine of absolute State immunity, and within that context, the Supreme Court's decision in *The Exchange v. McFaddon* case, provided sufficient guidance to determine the legal status of visiting forces. As the foreign presence of armed forces was also limited in time, place and number of military personnel, specific legal arrangements on the status of forces were not necessary.

Although the nineteenth century literature and case law generally reflected the ideas described above, the relation between sending States and their armed forces was also emphasised. It was understood that immunity only applied to military personnel as members of an organised military unit, but not to individual soldiers who committed an offence while off-duty outside the military premises, such as a garrison or a ship. The idea seemed to be that only in these conditions was the military commander in the position to exercise his direct control over the force by taking disciplinary action.

This approach also reflects the doctrine of absolute State immunity. As States act through their organs and State officials, only their official acts are attributable to the States and, therefore, State officials benefit from the immunity of the State. What the literature and case law make clear is that in respect of military personnel the relation between their acts and the State is key and not just the military status of a person as such.

14.2.2 Functional Immunity of State Officials

Since the nineteenth century judges have accepted restrictions to immunity of States. This process of gradual modification of the absolute doctrine of State immunity evolved in the field of civil law, especially in respect of adjudicative jurisdiction, while immunity from enforcement jurisdiction largely remained untouched. The latter also applies to criminal immunity of States, which is without question absolute: a State cannot be held criminally responsible for its acts before a foreign court.

In the field of criminal law high-ranking State officials, such as Heads of State, Heads of Government and Ministers of Foreign Affairs, and high-ranking staff members of international organisations, are entitled to full immunity. They need to carry out their tasks undisturbed and without interference of other States to ensure the orderly conduct of international relations. Therefore, they are fully exempted from the foreign courts' exercise of criminal jurisdiction. A similar degree of immunity may apply to high-ranking military officers, such as the commander of an international peacekeeping force led by the UN. His claim to immunity is, by the way, not based on his military status, but on his specific international position.

The position of lower-ranking State officials and staff members of international organisations normally does not require that they enjoy full immunity under all circumstances. This category of officials, therefore, can be subject to the criminal jurisdiction of the host State, if offences are committed outside their official duties. International law does not distinguish between the various backgrounds of these officials and does not make a specific exemption for military personnel, either. Therefore, military personnel are also entitled to functional immunity. In general, this rule applies to all members of the sending States' armed forces and may also apply, under specific circumstances, to military personnel who serve an international organisation in a personal capacity, for example, as a UN expert on mission. Viewed from this perspective, it is no surprise that the historical analysis shows that foreign forces hardly ever enjoy a lower level of immunity than functional immunity from host State jurisdiction. The analysis further demonstrates that there is no uniform immunity rule applying to all military personnel stationed abroad, as the frameworks within which armed forces operate abroad are too diverse.

14.2.3 The Instrumental Role of SOFAs

In respect of the absence of a uniform immunity rule, military operational law can provide additional points of reference. Viewed from this particular legal perspective, SOFAs, as part of the *jus in praesentia*, do not stand alone, as they build on the *jus ad praesentiam* that encompasses the general and specific legal bases for foreign military presence. *Jus ad praesentiam* and *jus in praesentia* together constitute the law of visiting forces, which is part and parcel of the legal framework of military operations and is as such an essential part of military operational law. This makes SOFAs a commanders' tool when preparing and executing their missions, as SOFAs expedite entry into host State territory and facilitate day-to-day operations. From the perspective of military operational law, consent together with the legal bases for foreign military presence have great impact on the content of SOFAs, including the key provision on criminal jurisdiction.

Independently of the legal bases and based on the general principles of military operations, sending States will seek immunity for their deployed armed forces as protection against foreign legal systems. Often this endeavour is prompted by unfamiliarity with those legal systems or the plain fact that the system is different from the familiar national system. Sometimes, host State legal systems have not fully been developed yet, or do not function properly due to a crisis situation. Also, sending States may fear that host State criminal justice authorities will be prejudiced against foreign soldiers, which may jeopardise a fair trial.

Immunity from the host States' criminal jurisdiction is without prejudice to the sending States' control over their forces and must not lead to impunity. It is of paramount importance that sending States can prosecute military personnel who enjoy immunity abroad and to that end criminal law of the sending States must be applicable to them. Many States have adopted specific provisions thereto. In my opinion, extraterritorial application of the sending States' criminal law is a prerequisite for granting a level of immunity beyond functional immunity.

14.2.4 Status of Forces in Three Frameworks

The historical analysis of Part I has explored to what extent criminal jurisdiction over military personnel stationed abroad could be explained from three different frameworks: armed conflict, crisis management operations and international military cooperation, while taking into account the circumstances under which the forces are present abroad, the interests of the States involved and their mutual relations. In Part III military operational law considerations were added. The following subsections merge all elements for each framework, respectively, allied forces on co-belligerent territory during armed conflict (Sect. 14.2.4.1), participation in crisis management operations (Sect. 14.2.4.2), and international military cooperation during peacetime (Sect. 14.2.4.3).

14.2.4.1 Allied Forces on Co-belligerent Territory During Armed Conflict

In situations of consensual stationing during armed conflict foreign forces are subject to the exclusive criminal jurisdiction of the sending States. The sending States' jurisdiction may be restricted when military operations are not directly conducted on host State territory, or when the threat of an armed conflict has diminished; for instance, when forces are not based in or in the direct vicinity of the area of operation, or not directly involved in supporting combat operations. Such circumstances may give the foreign forces' presence the character of international military cooperation.

Under operational conditions the need for sending States to be able to exercise criminal jurisdiction over their armed forces to the exclusion of host States is paramount from a military operational law perspective. During armed conflict military units are tasked to support the host State in combatting its enemy. Within this operational framework effective and expedient military action requires units to operate as a unity under single military command without host State interference. From operational necessity forces must, therefore, enjoy criminal immunity; furthermore, sending States must be able to exert their authority and control over their forces abroad, inter alia, by exercising criminal jurisdiction over them.

Given the circumstances in armed conflict, it may not even be in the direct interest of host States to exercise criminal jurisdiction over foreign forces. In times of war sometimes massive armed forces can be concentrated in specific areas for a longer period of time. The armed forces' lasting and intensive contact with the local population will inevitably lead to violations of the host State's legal order. Although in such events the host State may want to be able to exercise its criminal jurisdiction, the vast and enduring presence of foreign armed forces may create a disproportionate burden to the local judiciary that may already be strained because of the ongoing war.

Also, the balance of power is of particular importance. Although States are equal under international law, they can be very different in an economical and military sense and may be dependent on one another. In times of war this inequality will have a massive impact on the negotiations about the status of forces. States whose forces are forced to flee their national territory because of an armed attack, or whose territorial integrity is threatened by such an attack, heavily depend on allied support. On the other hand, militarily and economically strong States that can make a decisive contribution to the war are in a much better bargaining position and host States will be more inclined to meet their demands in respect of the status of their forces.

Other interests of the States concerned have to be taken into account as well. Deployment of allied forces is in the direct interest of the host States whose existence is at stake because of their enemies' acts of war. Under those circumstances they will not easily consider the presence of foreign forces and loss of criminal jurisdiction over these forces as a disproportionate prejudice to their sovereignty. Moreover, the battle against a common enemy can be considered as an interest of the coalition as a whole that outweighs the individual interests of the States involved. By waiving criminal jurisdiction over allied forces host States recognise and respect this common interest.

In the operational phase in which military action is carried out, international war-time practice in respect of the status of allied forces mirrors the law of armed conflict, allowing States to exercise exclusive criminal jurisdiction over their forces in occupied territory. As the law of armed conflict does not address the stationing of allied forces on friendly States' territory, SOFAs may cover that.

The historical analysis of Part I has demonstrated the widespread international practice that military personnel enjoy full criminal immunity during the operational deployment of armed forces that are subject to the exclusive criminal jurisdiction of the sending States. In the course of time this international practice, which is shored up by military practice, has been widely accepted by States and is undisputed. This leads to the conclusion that there is an international customary rule that sending States' armed forces are subject to the exclusive criminal jurisdiction of the sending States, when preparing and executing military operations during armed conflict and thus enjoy full criminal immunity from host States' courts. However, this rule cannot be assumed to apply outside the operational phase, when the forces are not directly involved in planning and executing combat operations. The States involved may then negotiate additional arrangement in a SOFA. However, as it is hard to determine which servicemen are directly involved in the operational phase, and with a view to other circumstances and interests, sending States will in general continue to exercise exclusive jurisdiction over their forces.

14.2.4.2 Crisis Management Operations

The execution of crisis management operations is in nature not very different from the war-time military operations discussed above. Therefore, it will not come as a surprise that also within this framework the participating forces continue to be subject to the exclusive jurisdiction of the sending States. Their jurisdiction can be exercised without any restriction to all participating forces regardless of their activities and location within the host State.

Viewed from a military operational law perspective, this status can be justified by the nature of the foreign forces' activities. They are likely to operate in an unstable and possibly hostile environment and have the right to use armed force. Even in relatively peaceful situations, the commander must be able to deploy his units fully armed, if necessary, to implement the international mandate. These circumstances trigger the operational necessity for the commander to dispose of his forces without interference of host States exercising their jurisdiction, affecting or even hindering the execution of the international military mission.

The execution of crisis management operations requires the deployment of vast military forces, staying in a host State for a considerable period of time. Violations of host State law are, unfortunately, very likely to happen. Reference can be made to occurrences of sexual abuse and exploitation by UN personnel. These types of offences directly affect the legal order of the host States and would justify the exercise of their jurisdiction. Be that as it may, wholesale instability in the host State has necessitated the presence of foreign forces. If host States exercise their jurisdiction, it would seriously burden their legal system, which is probably already affected by the crisis circumstances.

As a practical element it can be noted that many sending States are not very comfortable with the host States' legal systems and are only prepared to contribute forces to the mission if criminal immunity can be guaranteed. Moreover, also in the framework of crisis management operations, power relations are likely to influence the negotiations. The organisations involved or States representing an international coalition will dominate the negotiations and can put pressure on the host State to accept the international demands.

The most important aspect related to the deployment of forces within the framework of crisis management operations is that troop contributing States do not primarily serve their own national interests, but those of the international community as a whole. The international character of the operation requires that the forces are able to operate independently and without host State interference and stand above the parties involved. Therefore, criminal immunity of the foreign forces is paramount. The common interests of the international community outweigh the interests of individual host States to exercise criminal jurisdiction over foreign forces.

The historical analysis of Part I demonstrates that ever since international organisations established international peacekeeping operations, the participating forces have been subject to the exclusive criminal jurisdiction of their sending States and are exempted from the host States' exercise of criminal jurisdiction. There are hardly any exceptions to this widespread practice and the principle was not even called into question after the investigations into the alleged misconduct of UN-peacekeepers. On several occasions the UN has referred to absolute immunity as an international customary rule without States having disputed this position. Exclusive criminal jurisdiction that sending States exercise over participating forces and the resulting forces' criminal immunity can today be regarded as a rule of international customary law.

This rule applies vis-à-vis the host States on whose territory operations take place. Members of the international forces who travel to other States, for instance, to spend their leave, are not automatically entitled to criminal immunity because of their position as members of the peacekeeping force. Neither will crisis management activities taking place in third States automatically imply full immunity of the forces. Similar to the framework of consensual stationing during armed conflict, activities that are not taking place within the area of operations, or not in direct support of the crisis management operation, do not directly give rise to the operational necessity for sending States to exercise their jurisdiction. Moreover, as the operation does not take place on the territory of the host States themselves, local interest in the operation may be less strong. Another element that may come into play is that in those circumstances it will often be individual sending States that negotiate the SOFAs, instead of an international organisation or a State on behalf of a coalition. As the international importance of supporting operations is perhaps less clear, the sending States' national interests may carry less weight in the negotiations.

14.2.4.3 International Military Cooperation

Within the framework of peacetime international military cooperation the status of armed forces during their extraterritorial presence is different from the other two frameworks discussed above. Only in exceptional cases are the forces then subject to the exclusive criminal jurisdiction of the sending States and do they enjoy full immunity. Generally, visiting armed forces are entitled to immunity from host State exercise of criminal jurisdiction for offences committed on duty. Be that as it may, many SOFAs provide for more extensive rights of jurisdiction. Often, *NATO-SOFA*'s well-balanced approach to criminal jurisdiction is taken as a reference. Only rarely do sending States allow the threshold of functional immunity to be lowered.

International military cooperation takes place under normal peacetime conditions. In order to keep up a sufficient level of training and operational readiness, military commanders must be able to directly exercise control over their units. However, in peacetime conditions the host States' exercise of jurisdiction will generally not be in conflict with the visiting units' duties to the extent that it does not seriously affect training level and operational readiness. So, functional immunity, in conformity with international law, suffices in the framework of military cooperation. Viewed from a military operational law perspective, a wider range of immunities can even run counter to the sending States' interests, if they then would exercise their criminal jurisdiction in a way the local population perceives as unjust, although other instruments, such as a flexible and expedient approach to settle claims, may mitigate the possibly negative impact.

Nevertheless, armed forces generally enjoy a wide range of immunities, which can be explained in part by the changing nature of their foreign presence. Since World War II international military cooperation has increased significantly. As a consequence, forces stay more frequently and for longer periods of time within the territory of other States. Furthermore, military personnel may be accompanied by their families, whereas their stay is often not restricted to one single garrison or military site and they can move freely inside the territory of host States and maintain contacts with the local population.

On the one hand, these circumstances increase the chances that military personnel commit offences violating host State law, affecting the local population's interests, which increases the interests of host States in exercising their criminal jurisdiction over the visiting forces. Moreover, many offences may be committed off-duty, which makes sending States' exercise of jurisdiction not a matter of course. On the other hand, however, prosecution of the perpetrators of these offences by the host States may be a disproportional burden on local criminal justice systems. Thus, a well-balanced allocation of jurisdiction is in the interests of all States involved. How the allocation will work out in specific situations cannot be established in advance and depends, inter alia, on aspects such as mutual trust and dependence of the States involved.

In general, the interests of States involved in international military cooperation are most likely better balanced than during armed conflict or in crisis management operations. The balance can be described as a type of *quid pro quo* commitment, in which host States grant sending States the right to be present on their territory, accepting a certain degree of restriction of their sovereign rights, while, in return, sending States provide military assistance, economic benefits, or security. These interests will hardly ever be in perfect balance. States can be in a dependent position and, influenced by this unbalance of power, grant sending States' forces more generous immunities.

Although functional immunity is generally the point of departure in determining the status of visiting forces within the framework of international military cooperation, ultimately the issue will be decided in negotiations between the parties involved. The results of the negotiations are reflected in formal arrangements, mostly taking the form of international agreements. Contemporary SOFAs show many similarities in respect of criminal jurisdiction. Be that as it may, international practice varies to the extent that no international customary rule can be accepted that provides a level of immunity beyond functional immunity. So, the status of forces in the framework of international military cooperation is primarily treaty-based.

14.3 Proposal for a Status-of-Forces Compendium

Based on the theory of criminal jurisdiction over military personnel stationed abroad as described above, this section builds on the theory and proposes the development of a practical tool for drafting and using SOFAs. After briefly addressing the future of SOFAs, it will be proposed to develop a Status-of-Forces Compendium based on international experiences.

14.3.1 Future Foreign Presence of Forces

In many States defence budgets are under pressure, forcing states to step up international military cooperation to efficaciously put the available scarce military means to use. As cooperation is not just a matter of choice, but a mere necessity,[1] stationing of forces abroad will continue to take place in the next couple of years. As a result, existing partnerships will be strengthened and expanded. This process, however, will not require many adjustments in respect of current SOFAs.

More dynamics are to be expected in the field of multinational crisis management operations. Future operations are likely to take place in areas of tension in Africa and Asia and to be complex in nature, forcing States to combine

[1] *Dutch Parliamentary Papers II* 2011/12, 33 279 nr. 3 (Memorandum on international military cooperation), p. 3.

their resources to prepare and execute these missions. Recent missions underscore the importance of international military cooperation, as operations take place in remote areas and cannot solely rely on support from the territory of the sending States. Operational and logistic hubs are essential for the transit of personnel, equipment and supplies to the area of operation and for the execution of the mission.

Today foreign presence of armed forces may be more limited and occur less frequent than was the case in the Cold War era. This practice reduces the impact on host States as economic and social pressure will remain limited, in particular on the local communities where the forces are based. Furthermore, the visiting forces will depend on host State support, for example, for the provision of services, which puts more emphasis on the cooperative nature of the relation between the armed forces of host States and sending States. Visiting forces will thus be regarded more like temporary guests than, for example, colonial rulers or occupying forces, as sometimes happened in the past.

In these circumstances the presence of foreign armed forces will not necessarily be experienced as a serious infringement of host State sovereignty. Functional immunity of the visiting forces is, with a view to the nature of the forces' presence, in conformity with international legal standards and does not call for specific arrangements. Nevertheless, most sending States will want to conclude SOFAs in order to secure additional immunities and rights for their armed forces and, in the light of the general desire to guarantee the best protection possible for their military personnel, may further elaborate on the provisions on criminal jurisdiction.

14.3.2 Reducing the Burden

Practice has shown that negotiating SOFAs can be a lengthy and cumbersome process that requires a considerable amount of time and commitment from the States involved, without them being completely certain that this investment will lead to timely and desired results. Efforts can be reduced when sending States focus on a specific group of States or regions for international military cooperation. This practice prevents that again and again SOFAs must be negotiated with new partner-States.

The choice of particular States and regions is above all a political or policy consideration, but the military must inform the political leadership if military cooperation with specific States can be mutually beneficial. The latter aspect is of importance. When the interests of the sending States and the host States are in balance it is likely that a balanced SOFA can be concluded that meets the common interest. In addition, it may be considered to give the agreement a reciprocal character, emphasising the equality of the partnership.

Another option is to make use of less formal instruments than treaties. Most States opt to conclude SOFAs by legally binding international agreements in view of the perceived legal certainty for their personnel. However, if national law does not specifically require a treaty to deal with status of forces issues, non-legally binding instruments, like a Memorandum of Understanding (MOU), can be a viable alternative. MOUs bind the participants in political and moral sense and provide an informal and flexible procedure for reaching an international arrangement.

SOFAs are not always strictly necessary for short-lasting and infrequent activities like port visits of warships and training courses, involving just a limited number of unarmed servicemen. It must be estimated how likely it is that military personnel become involved in criminal offences and in what manner host State criminal justice authorities could react. Also, sending States must take into consideration if possible risks could be reduced by taking preventive measures, such as restrictions of the freedom of movement of visiting personnel.

In any event, it is vital that host State consent with the foreign forces' presence on its territory is clearly expressed. In addition, in their communication with the host States sending States must voice that it is their understanding that the status of visiting military personnel will be respected in accordance with international law. If host States do not contradict this position, their tacit acceptance together with the consent given provides a sufficient basis for assuming functional immunity of the visiting forces.

14.3.3 Status-of-Forces Compendium

For other activities SOFAs will continue to be necessary. In order to reduce the burden and to save time for all parties involved in negotiating SOFAs, a universal and widely accepted SOFA would be extremely useful. It is, however, highly unlikely that such an agreement will be concluded within a reasonable timeframe, as the nature of cooperation and the specific wishes of States are too diverse. Therefore, as an alternative, it would be advisable to develop a Status-of-Forces Compendium based on years of practice of a wide range of States and international organisations, which contains the best practices in the field of status of forces as building blocks for future SOFAs, thus expediting the now often cumbersome process of negotiating specific SOFAs. The following subsections indicate how this Compendium could be developed and used.

14.3.3.1 General Explanatory Note

The Status-of-Forces Compendium should start with an explanatory note on the legal principles of status of forces in general. In the note the position of SOFAs within the context of the law of visiting forces should be emphasised by clarifying the underlying legal bases for foreign military presence. These bases can be further addressed in the Compendium itself by suggesting that a reference to underlying treaties and other relevant legal bases should be included in the preamble of new SOFAs.

Furthermore, the explanatory note must emphasise the leading role of international law and the relevance of host State law which, on the one hand, reflects that the foreign military presence is without prejudice to host State sovereignty and, on the other, that local law remains applicable to the visiting forces. In separate sections of the explanatory note specific themes can be addressed, such as respect for local law, the question whether an offence has been committed in the performance of duty, the relevant arrangements on the use of force, and the right of self-defence.

14.3.3.2 Topics

The explanatory note can be followed by sections, each of which identifying the various topics that could be included in a SOFA. Each section can provide a choice of possible SOFA provisions on that particular topic, which can be used as building blocks for new SOFAs (see Sect. 14.3.3.3). The possible SOFA-provisions must take into account both host State and sending State interests, expressing per topic how the balance moves on a sliding scale from the interest of one State to that of another. For every topic an explanation must be added clarifying under which conditions specific options are to be preferred, possibly referring to existing SOFA-provisions.

Being the core element of SOFAs, the exercise of criminal jurisdiction over foreign military personnel obviously constitutes one of the key topics of the Compendium. The first possible provision may, in accordance with international law, express functional immunity of military personnel. The last option, favouring the sending States' interests, would then deal with the sending States' exclusive criminal jurisdiction over their forces. Other provisions can express in detail all intermediate possibilities, for instance by extending functional immunity to apply to certain offences, locations, situations, etc.

In this context the Status-of-Forces Compendium can also refer to related topics in a SOFA. With respect to the exercise of criminal jurisdiction, for instance, the authority to conduct criminal investigations could be addressed. When sending States' forces enjoy a wide range of immunities, it is essential that they also have sufficient authority to bring national criminal proceedings to a satisfactory conclusion. To that end they must, for instance, have certain investigative powers to collect evidence and hear witnesses. Preferably, these powers should be exercised in close coordination and cooperation with the host States. This cooperation may benefit both States, if they agree to share insights and training on the methods and techniques used.

The section on the exercise of criminal jurisdiction can also refer to fundamental rights military personnel stationed abroad are entitled to in criminal proceeding under national law. If a SOFA does not provide full immunity, sending States may want to lay down in the SOFA that these rights are respected when host States exercise criminal jurisdiction. In exceptional situations States may even agree to further restrict functional immunity of visiting forces. This may result in the absence of any immunity with regard to specific acts, even if performed on duty. In my opinion, sending States should only accept such a restriction if the visiting forces' fundamental rights are respected during the criminal procedures in the host States.

14.3.3.3 Using the Compendium

Subsequently, States may borrow building blocks from the Compendium to construct a well-balanced SOFA that does justice to their cooperation and individual interests. It is an option to give SOFAs a more flexible character than they usually have, for instance, by adopting a provision stipulating that under clearly defined circumstances, or at a specific point in time, different or additional rules will apply. This provision ensures that when the legal basis of the foreign military presence changes, the SOFA will take these conditions into account. It goes without saying that modification of the legal basis must be fully clear to the host State and has received its consent.

For example, States can make arrangements on military cooperation that include the possibility for foreign forces to conduct training or to participate in exercises in the host State. If sending States would then decide to support, or participate in, a crisis management operation in another State and want to operate from the host State's territory with its consent, it is conceivable from a military operational law perspective that sending States want to have far-reaching immunities and rights for their forces. In case the SOFA already sees to such arrangements, they could be put into effect immediately and, as soon as the activities have ended, be terminated without the need for a revision of the treaty.

14.3.3.4 Provision of Information

SOFA provisions affecting the rights and obligations of individual servicemen can deviate from the rules they are familiar with. It is essential that host State law is explained to them and that they are informed about obligations flowing from the SOFA. Conversely, SOFAs will also have an impact on local authorities and chances are that they are not fully aware of all relevant provisions. Therefore, the commander of the visiting forces must stay in close contact with local authorities and, when incidents take place, ensure prompt consultation.

In addition, military personnel based in the host State can be provided with a so-called status-chit: a pocket-sized status card. This status-chit should give an instant overview of the most important rights and obligations of both visiting forces and local authorities. Preferably, the status-chit should be printed in two languages to facilitate use by both visiting military personnel and the local officials. Furthermore, the Status-of-Forces Compendium may contain a specimen with an explanatory note indicating which topics should be included in a status-chit.

14.3.3.5 Accountability

When drafting the Status-of-Forces Compendium experiences of as many States and international organisations as possible from different regions must be included. Also, practices of States with an extensive experience in foreign deployment of their armed forces, as well as States that have regularly received foreign troops on their territory, must be taken into account. This approach gives the Compendium a broad basis, making it an acceptable tool for a wide range of States and international organisations.

The Compendium is not intended to be a legally binding document, like a treaty, but simply serves as a tool for negotiating and using SOFAs. This characteristic may lower the threshold for States to make use of the document in practice. Furthermore, its non-legally binding nature simplifies amendment, if practical developments so require.

The Status-of-Forces Compendium makes the preparatory phase of SOFAs more transparent, because it clearly expresses the principles on which SOFAs are based. Furthermore, the negotiations can, at least partly, be conducted based on existing provisions that have proven their value in practice. Likewise, the Compendium can facilitate the practical application of SOFAs, if the drafters of SOFAs include explanatory notes that are either based on the Compendium or refer to it. These notes may assist the commander of forces stationed abroad when applying the provisions of the SOFA in the planning and execution of his activities. Furthermore, host State authorities can use the notes to align cooperation with, and support of, the visiting forces.

Admittedly, the drafting of a Status-of-Forces Compendium is not to be underestimated. Current practice shows that a topic, such as the exercise of criminal jurisdiction over visiting forces, can constitute a controversial issue evoking many emotions. Therefore, the drafting will require time and frequent consultation between the parties involved. Both the drafting process and the final document can contribute to a better understanding of SOFAs and the principles on which they are based. This may possibly encourage States to consider concluding SOFAs using more flexible instruments, like MOUs.

14.4 Conclusion

Especially from World War II onwards the practice of international organisations and States shows a patchwork of SOFAs with diverging provisions on the exercise of criminal jurisdiction over armed forces stationed abroad. This practice has been summarised in Part I, the historical analysis of this book. The myriad of SOFAs may have obscured the impact of international law and military operational law on the status of forces, leading some authors to assume that the legal status of military personnel stationed abroad is purely treaty-based. That assumption could lead to the erroneous conclusion that in the absence of a SOFA the status of military personnel stationed abroad is not different from that of foreign tourists.[2] The use of treaties in the field of law of visiting forces is remarkable indeed: a practice that can be explained by the desire of the States involved to adopt specific arrangements on the status of forces, in particular regarding the exercise of criminal jurisdiction. However, this practice may divert attention from the solid international customary legal basis of the status of armed forces stationed abroad.

As a corollary of State immunity, State officials enjoy immunity from the foreign courts' exercise of criminal jurisdiction during the performance of their official duties. In this respect, international law does not distinguish between the different categories of State officials and does not exclude military personnel. Therefore, military personnel, who with host State consent are present on foreign territory, enjoy criminal immunity while on duty.

However, functional criminal immunity of the forces does not meet operational requirements during military operations, such as allied support during armed conflict or participation in crisis management operations. Under these conditions armed forces must be subject to the exclusive criminal jurisdiction of the sending States, which entails full immunity from the foreign courts' exercise of criminal jurisdiction. This practice can be justified from a military operational law point of view, as the specific military tasks require the commander's full command and control over the forces. Today, this practice is widely applied and accepted to the extent that the exclusive criminal jurisdiction of sending States over their armed forces and the resulting full immunity of these forces participating in crisis management operations or directly involved in supporting allied States in armed conflict, can be considered to be international customary law.

In the framework of international military cooperation, functional immunity generally suffices for armed forces to carry out peacetime tasks effectively. However, sending States tend to protect military personnel abroad as much as possible against unknown and sometimes incomprehensible or even failing foreign legal systems. Negotiations with the host State on the status of forces may lead to arrangements that grant military personnel broad, or sometimes even full immunity.

Many partnerships follow the *NATO-SOFA* approach on the subject of criminal jurisdiction. This approach, which ensures a well-balanced exercise of criminal jurisdiction over foreign military personnel by courts of the sending States, on the one hand, and host States, on the other, is sometimes followed closely, but is in many cases applied in a somewhat modified way. In addition, in the framework of military cooperation a wide variety of other arrangements has been agreed upon, ranging from SOFAs that deny sending States the right to exercise jurisdiction over their forces, to SOFAs granting them the exclusive right to exercise their jurisdiction. Based on this very mixed practice it cannot be said that the *NATO-SOFA*-approach reflects a rule of international customary rule.

---

[2] For example, Conderman 2013, para 1(2). Albeit a heavily armed tourist; Smith 2003, p. 14.

In the framework of international military cooperation the content of SOFAs remains highly dependent on the results of negotiations between the parties involved and is influenced by elements, such as the power balance between States involved, their interests in the presence of forces, and the specific circumstances of the situation at hand. Considering that international cooperation remains necessary in the future and that the conclusion of SOFAs requires considerable time and effort from all parties involved, this book proposes a Status-of-Forces Compendium. The Compendium should compile the best practices of sending States and host States and explain both the international law and the military operational law perspectives of SOFAs. It may serve as a tool to reach a well-balanced choice of treaty provisions and function as a point of reference when drafting and using specific SOFAs.

References

Conderman PJ (2013) Status of armed forces on foreign territory agreements (SOFA). Max Planck encyclopedia of public international law. http://www.mpepil.com. Accessed Nov 2014

Smith C (2003) Lawyers at war. Am Bar Assoc J 89(2):14–16

Index

© T.M.C. ASSER PRESS and the author 2015
J. Voetelink, *Status of Forces: Criminal Jurisdiction over Military Personnel Abroad*,
DOI 10.1007/978-94-6265-057-2

MIX
Papier aus verantwortungsvollen Quellen
Paper from responsible sources
FSC® C105338

If you have any concerns about our products,
you can contact us on
ProductSafety@springernature.com

In case Publisher is established outside the EU,
the EU authorized representative is:
Springer Nature Customer Service Center GmbH
Europaplatz 3, 69115 Heidelberg, Germany

Printed by Libri Plureos GmbH
in Hamburg, Germany